FRE

Vocabulary

Second Edition

by

Christopher Kendris

B.S., M.S., M.A., Ph.D.
Diplômé, Faculté des Lettres, Université de Paris et
Institut de Phonétique, Paris (en Sorbonne)
Former Chairman
Department of Foreign Languages
Farmingdale High School
Farmingdale, New York

and

Theodore N. Kendris

B.A., Union College
M.A., Northwestern University
Ph.D., Université Laval

BARRON'S

BARRON'S EDUCATIONAL SERIES, INC.

With love to

Yolanda, Alex, Tina, Fran, Bryan, Daniel, Matthew, Andrew,
Athena, Tom, Donna, Amanda, Laura, Thomas,
Mary Ann, Hilda, Arthur, Karen, George, Christopher, Matthew, Joe, Sue, Justin

All inquiries should be addressed to:
Barron's Educational Series, Inc.
250 Wireless Boulevard
Hauppauge, New York 11788
http://www.barronseduc.com

International Standard Book No. 0-7641-1999-0

Library of Congress Catalog Card No. 2002018506

Library of Congress Cataloging-in-Publication Data

Kendris, Christopher.
    French vocabulary : a dictionary of basic words, phrases, and expressions, with
  English equivalents arranged by topics, with an easy guide to pronunciation /
  by Christopher Kendris and Theodore Kendris.—2nd ed.
      p. cm.
    ISBN 0-7641-1999-0
    1. French language—Glossaries, vocabularies, etc. 2. French language—
  Conversation and phrase books—English I. Kendris, Theodore. II. Title.
  PC2680 .K46 2002
  448.2′421—dc21   2002018506

PRINTED IN CHINA
9 8 7 6 5

CONTENTS

CONTENTS

ABOUT THE AUTHORS

Dr. Christopher Kendris has worked as interpreter and translator of French for the U.S. State Department at the American Embassy in Paris. He earned his B.S. and M.S. degrees at Columbia University in the City of New York, where he held a New York State Scholarship, and his M.A. and Ph.D. degrees at Northwestern University in Evanston, Illinois, where he held a Teaching Assistantship and Tutorial Fellowship during four years. He also earned two diplomas with *Mention très Honorable* at the Université de Paris (en Sorbonne), Faculté des Lettres, École Supérieure de Préparation et de Perfectionnement des Professeurs de Français à l'Étranger, and at the Institut de Phonétique, Paris. In 1986 he was one of ninety-five teachers in the United States who was awarded a Rockefeller Foundation Fellowship for Teachers of Foreign Languages in American High Schools. He has taught French at the College of The University of Chicago as visiting summer lecturer, at Colby College, Duke University, Rutgers—The State University of New Jersey, and the State University of New York at Albany. He was Chairman of the Department of Foreign Languages and Supervisor of sixteen foreign language teachers on the secondary level at Farmingdale High School, Farmingdale, New York, where he was also a teacher of all levels of French and Spanish. Dr. Kendris is the author of twenty-two school and college books, workbooks, and other language guides of French and Spanish. He is listed in *Contemporary Authors* and *Directory of American Scholars*.

Dr. Theodore N. Kendris earned his B.A. degree in Modern Languages at Union College, Schenectady, New York, where he received the Thomas J. Judson Memorial Book Prize for modern language study. He went on to earn his M.A. degree in French Language and Literature at Northwestern University, Evanston, Illinois, where he held a Teaching Assistantship. He earned his Ph.D. degree in French Literature at Université Laval in Quebec City, where he studied the Middle Ages and Renaissance. While at Université Laval he taught French writing skills as a *chargé de cours* in the French as a Second Language program and, in 1997, he was awarded a doctoral scholarship by the *Fondation de l'Université Laval*. He is currently teaching in the Department of English and Foreign Languages at the University of St. Francis in Joliet, Illinois.

HOW TO USE THIS BOOK

This book is one of a popular series of handy vocabulary reference guides. It is designed for students, business people, and others who want to "brush up" their knowledge of French vocabulary in any given subject area. This is not a book of French grammar with exercises and it is not a book of French civilization or culture. It is a book that will help you build, improve, and expand your French vocabulary on many different topics, as you can see in the table of contents. Previous knowledge of French vocabulary has not been taken for granted in these pages. As for French grammar explained simply with many examples in French and English, please consult the Barron's book, *Master the Basics: French*, by Christopher Kendris.

OVERALL DESIGN

The French vocabulary in this pocket reference book is arranged by topics. Subtopics contain several themes related in thought to the main topic. Under a subtopic you can find many commonly used basic words, phrases, and expressions useful in everyday situations. These are valuable not only for students and teachers but also for the general public; for example, travelers in France and other French-speaking countries and regions, persons in the world of business, banking, science and technology, politics, the fine arts, telecommunications, mathematics, the natural sciences, and many others.

The first thing to do is browse through the table of contents. You will find topics of special interest to you because of the wide range of topics. For example, the second chapter is of interest to everyone because it is about people: members of a family, relatives, friends, descriptions of people, personalities, social traits, moods, general human characteristics, basic personal information, parts of the human body, bodily processes and movements, sensory perception, and looking after one's health. If any given topic is of particular interest to you, turn to the page where it begins. We are certain that the section you select will provide you with many interesting and useful basic words, phrases, and expressions.

FEATURES

English words are listed on the left side of the page. French equivalents appear in the middle of the page. Next to the French, you will find abbreviations that indicate gender or part of speech. On the right side of the page you are given sound transcriptions to help you pronounce the French words effectively for communication. The pronunciation guide in the beginning pages of the book introduces you to a simple system of sound transcriptions that we devised.

We sincerely hope that this book will be of some help to you in expanding your knowledge and power of French vocabulary.

Theodore N. Kendris   Christopher Kendris
B.A., M.A., Ph.D.   B.S., M.S., M.A., Ph.D.

FRENCH PRONUNCIATION GUIDE

The purpose of this guide is to help you pronounce French words as correctly as possible so you can communicate effectively. It is not intended to perfect your pronunciation of French; that is accomplished by imitating correct spoken French.

In French there are several spellings for the same sound; for example, the following spellings are all pronounced *ay*, as in the English word *say*.

et   (j')**ai**   (parl)**é**   (av)**ez**   (all)**er**   (l)**es**

The system of transcription of French sounds used here is English letters in italics. As soon as you catch on to this system, you will find it *ee-zee*. At first, you will have to refer to the list repeatedly until it is fixed in your mind. The sounds are arranged alphabetically in a list in transcription form. This is the easiest way for you to find the transcription quickly as you read the English letters next to the French words.

Consonant sounds are approximately the same in French and English. Any variations in the pronunciation of some French consonants are found in the sound transcriptions. When speaking French, stress is evenly distributed on the vowels but you must raise your voice slightly on the last transcription sound when more than one is in a group; for example, in pronouncing **s'il vous plaît** (please), raise your voice slightly on *pleh* in *seel-voo-pleh*.

There are only four nasal vowel sounds in French. They are expressed in the following catchy phrase, which means a good white wine.

un   **bon**   **vin**   **blanc**
UH   *bOH*   *vEH*   *blAH*

A nasal vowel is indicated by two italicized capital letters. How do you nasalize a vowel in French? Instead of letting your breath (air) out of your mouth, you must push it up your nose so that it does not come out of your mouth.

Remember that the two italicized capital letters are nasal vowels. They do not indicate any stress or raising of your voice in pronunciation.

The hyphens in the transcription sounds do not indicate a division of words into syllables. They indicate a separation of the different sounds so you can find them easily in the alphabetical list of italicized transcription letters. Whenever the final consonant of a French word is pronounced and linked, as in a liaison, with the first vowel or silent **h** of the word that follows, this is indicated in the sound transcriptions; for example, normally, **vous** is pronounced *voo*, but in **vous avez** it is pronounced *voo-zavay*.

Transcription letters	Pronounced approximately as in the English word	French word	Sound transcription
a	**a**t	**la**	*la*
ah	**ah**!	p**a**s	*pah*
ay	s**ay**	**ai**	*ay*
e	th**e**	l**e**	*le*
ee	s**ee**	**i**c**i**	*ee-see*
eh	**e**gg	m**è**re	*mehr*
ew	f**ew**	l**u**	*lew*
ew-ee	**you** **ea**t	h**ui**t	*ew-eet*
ny	ca**ny**on	monta**gne**	*mOH-ta-ny*
o	**a**lso	h**ô**tel	*o-tehl*
oh	**oh**!	ch**o**se	*sh-oh-z*
oo	t**oo**	**ou**	*oo*
or	**or**	p**or**te	*port*
sh	**sh**ip	**ch**ose	*sh-oh-z*
ss	ki**ss**	**c**esse	*seh-ss*
u	b**u**n	b**o**nne	*bun*
uh	p**u**dding	p**eu**x	*puh*
ur	p**ur**r	h**eu**re	*ur*
y	**y**es	jo**y**eux	*zh-wah-yuh*
yay	**yea**	pa**yer**	*pay-yay*
z	**z**ero	**z**éro	*zay-roh*
zh	mea**s**ure	**j**e	*zhe*

NASAL VOWELS

UH	s**u**ng	**un**	*UH*
OH	s**o**ng	b**on**	*bOH*
EH	s**a**ng	v**in**	*vEH*
AH	**yo**nder	bl**anc**	*blAH*

ABBREVIATIONS

adj	adjective		*n*	noun
adv	adverb		*pl*	plural
conj	conjunction		*pol*	polite form
f	feminine		*prep*	preposition
fam	familiar form		*pron*	pronoun
indef	indefinite		*s*	singular
m	masculine		*v*	verb

BASIC INFORMATION

1. ARITHMETIC

a. CARDINAL NUMBERS

zero	zéro	*zay-ro*
one	un	*UH*
	une	*ewn*
two	deux	*duh*
three	trois	*trwah*
four	quatre	*katr*
five	cinq	*sEHk*
six	six	*seess*
seven	sept	*seht*
eight	huit	*ew-eet*
nine	neuf	*nuf*
ten	dix	*dees*
eleven	onze	*OH-z*
twelve	douze	*dooz*
thirteen	treize	*trehz*
fourteen	quatorze	*ka-torz*
fifteen	quinze	*kEHz*
sixteen	seize	*sehz*
seventeen	dix-sept	*dee-seht*
eighteen	dix-huit	*dee-zew-eet*
nineteen	dix-neuf	*deez-nuf*
twenty	vingt	*vEH*
twenty-one	vingt et un	*vEH tay UH*
twenty-two	vingt-deux	*vEH-duh*
twenty-three	vingt-trois	*vEH-trwah*
twenty-four	vingt-quatre	*vEH-katr*
twenty-five	vingt-cinq	*vEH-sEHk*
twenty-six	vingt-six	*vEH-seess*
twenty-seven	vingt-sept	*vEH-seht*
twenty-eight	vingt-huit	*vEH-tew-eet*
twenty-nine	vingt-neuf	*vEH-nuf*
thirty	trente	*trAHt*
thirty-one	trente et un	*trAHt-ay-UH*
thirty-two	trente-deux	*trAHt-duh*
thirty-three	trente-trois	*trAHt-trwah*
...		
forty	quarante	*ka-rAHt*
forty-one	quarante et un	*ka-rAHt-ay-UH*
forty-two	quarante-deux	*ka-rAHt-dUH*
forty-three	quarante-trois	*ka-rAHt-trwah*

. . .

fifty	cinquante	*sEH-k'AHt*
fifty-one	cinquante et un	*sEH-kAHt-ay-UH*
fifty-two	cinquante-deux	*sEH-kAHt-duh*
fifty-three	cinquante-trois	*sEH-kAHt-trwah*

. . .

sixty	soixante	*swa-sAHt*
sixty-one	soixante et un	*swa-sAHt-ay-UH*

. . .

seventy	soixante-dix	*swa-sAHt-dees*
seventy-one	soixante-et-onze	*swa-sAHt-ay-OH-z*

. . .

eighty	quatre-vingts	*katr-vEH*
eighty-one	quatre-vingt-un	*katr-vEH-UH*

. . .

ninety	quatre-vingt-dix	*katr-vEH-dees*
ninety-one	quatre-vingt-onze	*katr-vEH-OH-z*

. . .

one hundred	cent	*sAH*
one hundred and one	cent un	*sAH-UH*
one hundred and two	cent deux	*sAH-duh*

. . .

two hundred	deux cents	*duh-sAH*
two hundred and one	deux cent un	*duh-sAH-UH*

. . .

three hundred	trois cents	*trwah-sAH*

. . .

one thousand	mille	*meel*
one thousand and one	mille un	*meel-UH*

. . .

two thousand	deux mille	*duh meel*
two thousand and one	deux mille un	*duh meel UH*

. . .

three thousand	trois mille	*trwah meel*

. . .

four thousand	quatre mille	*katr meel*

. . .

one hundred thousand	cent mille	*sAH meel*

. . .

two hundred thousand	deux cent mille	*duh sAH meel*

. . .

one million	un million	*UH meel-yOH*
one million and one	un million un	*UH meel-yOH UH*
one million and two	un million deux	*UH meel-yOH duh*

...

| two million | deux millions | *duh meel-yOH* |

...

| three million | trois millions | *trwah meel-yOH* |

...

| one hundred million | cent millions | *sAH meel-yOH* |

...

| one billion | un milliard | *UH meel-yar* |

...

| two billion | deux milliards | *duh meel-yar* |

b. ORDINAL NUMBERS

first	premier (*adj/m*)	*prem-yay*
	première (*adj/f*)	*prem-yehr*
second	second	*se-gOH*
	seconde	*se-gOH-d (if the 2nd of 2)*
	deuxième	*duhz-yehm (if the 2nd of more than 2)*
third	troisième	*trwahz-yehm*
fourth	quatrième	*katr-yehm*
fifth	cinquième	*sEHk-yehm*
sixth	sixième	*seez-yehm*
seventh	septième	*seht-yehm*
eighth	huitième	*ew-eet-yehm*
ninth	neuvième	*nuhv-yehm*
tenth	dixième	*deez-yehm*
eleventh	onzième	*OHz-yehm*
twelfth	douzième	*dooz-yehm*
thirteenth	treizième	*trehz-yehm*

...

twenty-third	vingt-troisième	*vEH-trwahz-yehm*
thirty-third	trente-troisième	*trAHt-trwahz-yehm*
forty-third	quarante-troisième	*ka-rAHt-trwahz-yehm*

...

| **hundredth** | centième | *sAHt-yehm* |

...

| **thousandth** | millième | *meel-yehm* |

...

| **millionth** | millionième | *meel-yun-yehm* |

...

| **billionth** | milliardième | *meel-yard-yehm* |

c. FRACTIONS

a (one) half	un demi	*UH dmee*
a (one) third	un tiers	*UH tyehr*
a (one) fourth	un quart	*UH kar*
a (one) fifth	un cinquième	*UH sEHk-yehm*

APPROXIMATE AMOUNTS

about ten	une dizaine	*ewn dee-zehn*
about fifteen	une quinzaine	*ewn kEH-zehn*
about twenty	une vingtaine	*ewn vEH-tehn*
about thirty	une trentaine	*ewn trAH-tehn*
about forty	une quarantaine	*ewn karAH-tehn*
about fifty	une cinquantaine	*ewn sEH-kAH-tehn*
about sixty	une soixantaine	*ewn swa-sAH-tehn*
about a hundred	une centaine	*ewn sAH-tehn*
about a thousand	un millier	*UH meel-yay*

d. TYPES OF NUMBERS

number	nombre (*m*)	*nOH-bre*
	numéro (*m*)	*new-may-ro*
• **number**	numéroter (*v*)	*new-may-rut-ay*
• **numeral**	numéral (*m*)	*new-may-ral*
• **numerical**	numérique (*adj*)	*new-may-reek*
Arabic	arabe (*adj*)	*arab*
binary	binaire (*adj*)	*bee-nehr*
cardinal	cardinal (*adj*)	*kar-dee-nal*
complex	complexe (*adj*)	*kOH-plehks*
digit	chiffre (*m*)	*sheefre*
even	pair (*adj*)	*pehr*
fraction	fraction (*f*)	*fraks-yOH*
• **fractional**	fractionnel (*adj*)	*fraks-yun-ehl*
imaginary	imaginaire (*adj*)	*ee-ma-zh-ee-nehr*
integer	nombre entier (*m*)	*nOH-bre AHt-yay*
irrational	irrationnel (*adj*)	*ee-ras-yun-ehl*
natural	naturel (*adj*)	*na-tewr-ehl*
negative	négatif (*adj*)	*nay-ga-teef*
odd	impair (*adj*)	*EH-pehr*
ordinal	ordinal (*adj*)	*or-dee-nal*
positive	positif (*adj*)	*pu-see-teef*
prime number	nombre premier (*m*)	*nOH-bre prem-yay*
rational	rationnel (*adj*)	*ras-yun-ehl*

real	réel (*adj*)	*ray-ehl*
reciprocal	réciproque (*adj*)	*ray-see-pruk*
Roman	romain (*adj*)	*rum-EH*

e. BASIC OPERATIONS

arithmetical operations	opérations fondamentales (*f, pl*)	*up-ay-ras-yOH fOH-da-mAH-tal*
add (on)	ajouter (*v*)	*azh-oo-tay*
• **addition**	addition (*f*)	*a-dee-sy-OH*
• **plus**	plus	*plewss*
	et	*ay*
• **two plus two equals four**	deux et deux font quatre	*duh ay duh fOH katr*
subtract	soustraire (*v*)	*soos-trehr*
• **subtraction**	soustraction (*f*)	*soos-trak-sy-OH*
• **minus**	moins	*mwEH*
• **three minus two equals one**	trois moins deux font un	*trwah mwEH duh fOH UH*
multiply	multiplier (*v*)	*mewl-tee-ply-ay*
• **multiplication**	multiplication (*f*)	*mewl-tee-plee-kas-yOH*
• **multiplication table**	table de multiplication (*f*)	*tabl de mewl-tee-plee-kas-yOH*
• **multiplied by**	multiplié par	*mewl-tee-ply-ay-par*
• **three times two equals six**	trois fois deux font six	*trwah fwa duh fOH seess*
divide	diviser (*v*)	*dee-vee-zay*
• **divided by**	divisé par	*dee-vee-zay par*
• **division**	division (*f*)	*dee-vee-zyOH*
• **six divided by three equals two**	six divisés par trois font deux	*seess dee-vee-zay par trwah fOH duh*
raise to a power	élever (*v*) à une puissance	*ayl-vay a ewn pew-ee-sAH-ss*
• **to the power of**	à la puissance de	*a la pew-ee-sAH-ss de*
• **squared**	au carré	*oh ka ray*
• **cubed**	au cube	*oh kewb*
• **to the fourth power**	à la quatrième puissance	*a la katr-yehm pew-ee-sAH-ss*
• **to the nth power**	à la puissance n	*a la pew-ee-sAH-ss ehn*
• **two squared equals four**	deux au carré égalent quatre	*duh oh ka-ray ay-gal katr*
extract a root	extraire (*v*) la racine	*eks-trehr la ra-seen*
• **square root**	racine au carré	*ra-seen oh ka-ray*
• **cube root**	racine cubique	*ra-seen kew-beek*
• **nth root**	à la racine n	*a la ra-seen ehn*
• **(the) square root of nine is three**	la racine au carré de neuf est trois	*la ra-seen oh ka-ray de nuf eh trwah*

ratio   proportion (*f*)   *pru-por-syOH*
• **twelve is to four**   douze est à quatre   *dooz eh ta katr kum nuf*
  as nine is to   comme neuf est à   *eh ta trwah*
  three   trois

FOCUS: Arithmetical Operations

Addition—Addition
$2 + 3 = 5$ two plus three equals five   deux et trois font cinq

Subtraction—Soustraction
$9 - 3 = 6$ nine minus three equals six   neuf moins trois font six

Multiplication—Multiplication
$4 \times 2 = 8$ four times two equals eight   quatre fois deux font huit
$4 \cdot 2 = 8$ four multiplied by two   quatre multipliés par
                     equals eight   deux égalent huit

Division—Division
$10 \div 2 = 5$ ten divided by two equals   dix divisés par deux
                     five   font cinq

Raising to a power—Elévation à une puissance
$3^2 = 9$ three squared (or to the   trois au carré égalent
                     second power) equals nine   neuf
$2^3 = 8$ two cubed (or to the third   deux au cube égalent
                     power) equals eight   huit
$2^4 = 16$ two to the fourth power   deux à la quatrième
                     equals sixteen   égalent seize
x^n x to the nth power   x à la puissance n

Extraction of root—Extraction d'une racine
$\sqrt[2]{4} = 2$ the square root of four is   la racine carrée de
                     two   quatre est deux
$\sqrt[3]{27} = 3$ the cube root of twenty-   la racine cubique de
                     seven is three   vingt-sept est trois
$\sqrt[n]{x}$ the nth root of x   la racine n de x

Ratio—Proportion
$12 : 4 = 9 : 3$ twelve is to four as nine is   douze est à quatre
                     to three   comme neuf est à trois

---

f. ADDITIONAL MATHEMATICAL CONCEPTS

algebra   algèbre (*f*)   *al-zh-ehbr*
• **algebraic**   algébrique (*adj*)   *al-zh-ay-breek*

arithmetic	arithmétique (f)	a-reet-may-teek
• arithmetical	arithmétique (adj)	a-reet-may-teek
average	moyenne (f)	mwa-yehn
calculate	calculer (v)	kal-kew-lay
• calculation	calcul (m)	kal-kewl
constant	constante (f)	kOH-stAHt
count	compter (v)	kOH-tay
• countable	comptable (adj)	kOH-tabl
decimal	décimal (adj)	day-see-mal
difference	différence (f)	dee-fay-rAH-ss
equality	égalité (f)	ay-ga-lee-tay
• equals	est égal à	eh tay-gal a
• does not equal	n'est pas égal à	neh pa-zay-gal a
• is equivalent to	est équivalent à	eh tay-kee-val-AH a
• is greater than	est supérieur à	eh sew-pay-ry-ur a
• is less than	est inférieur à	eh tEH-fay-ry-ur a
• is similar to	est pareil à	eh pa-ray a
equation	équation (f)	ay-kwas-yOH
factor	facteur (m)	fak-tur
• factor	mettre en facteurs (v)	meht-re AH fak-tur
• factorization	factorielle (f)	fak-tu-ry-ehl
function	fonction (f)	fOH-ks-yOH
logarithm	logarithme (m)	lug-a-reet-me
logarithmic	logarithmique (adj)	lug-a-reet-meek
multiple	multiple (m)	mewl-teepl
percent	pour cent	poor sAH
• percentage	pourcentage (m)	poor-sAH-tazh
problem	problème (m)	prub-lehm
• problem to solve	problème à résoudre	prub-lehm a ray-zoo-dr
product	produit (m)	prud-ew-ee
quotient	quotient (m)	kuss-yAH
set	ensemble (m)	AH-sAH-bl
solution	solution (f)	sul-ew-syOH
• solve	résoudre (v)	ray-zoo-dr
statistics	statistique (f)	sta-tees-teek
• statistical	statistique (adj)	sta-tees-teek
sum	somme (f)	sum
• sum up	sommer (v)	sum-ay
symbol	symbole (m)	sEH-bul
variable	variable (f)	var-ya-bl

2. GEOMETRY

a. FIGURES

plane figures	figures planes (f)	feeg-ewr plan
triangle	triangle (m)	tree-yAH-gl
• acute-angled	acutangle (adj)	akew-tAH-gl

• **equilateral**	équilatéral (*adj*)	*ay-kew-ee-la-tay-ral*
• **isosceles**	isocèle (*adj*)	*ee-zu-sehl*
• **obtuse-angled**	obtusangle (*adj*)	*up-tew-zAH-gl*
• **right-angled**	rectangle (*adj*)	*rehk-tAH-gl*
• **scalene**	scalène (*adj*)	*ska-lehn*
four-sided figures	figures à quatre côtés	*feeg-ewr a katr ko-tay*
• **parallelogram**	parallélogramme (*m*)	*para-lay-lu-gram*
• **rectangle**	rectangle (*m*)	*rehk-tAH-gl*
• **rhombus**	rhombe (*m*)	*rOH-b*
• **square**	carré (*m*)	*ka-ray*
• **trapezoid**	trapèze (*m*)	*tra-pehz*
n-sided figures	figures à côtés n	*fee-gewr a ko-tay ehn*
• **pentagon**	pentagone (*m*)	*pAH-ta-gun*
• **hexagon**	hexagone (*m*)	*ehg-za-gun*
• **heptagon**	heptagone (*m*)	*eph-ta-gun*
• **octagon**	octogone (*m*)	*uk-tug-un*
• **decagon**	décagone (*m*)	*day-ka-gun*
circle	cercle (*m*)	*sehr-kl*
• **center**	centre (*m*)	*sAH-tr*
• **circumference**	circonférence (*f*)	*seer-kOH-fay-rAH-ss*
• **diameter**	diamètre (*m*)	*dya-meh-tr*
• **radius**	rayon (*m*)	*reh-yOH*
• **tangent**	tangente (*f*)	*tAH-zh-AHt*
solid figures	figures solides (*f, pl*)	*feeg-ewr sul-eed*
prism	prisme (*m*)	*preesm*
• **right prism**	prisme droit	*preesm drwa*
cube	cube (*m*)	*kewb*
pyramid	pyramide (*f*)	*pee-ra-meed*
polyhedron	polyèdre (*m*)	*pul-yehdr*
• **tetrahedron**	tétraèdre (*m*)	*tay-tra-ehdr*
• **octahedron**	octaèdre (*m*)	*uk-ta-ehdr*
• **dodecahedron**	dodécaèdre (*m*)	*doh-day-ka-ehdr*
• **icosahedron**	icosaèdre (*m*)	*ee-koh-sa-ehdr*
cylinder	cylindre (*m*)	*see-lEH-dr*
cone	cône (*m*)	*kOHn*
sphere	sphère (*f*)	*sfehr*

FOCUS: Geometrical Figures

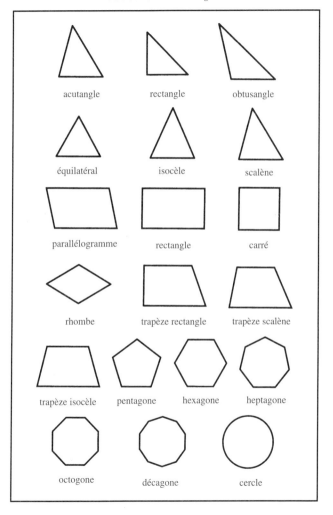

acutangle   rectangle   obtusangle

équilatéral   isocèle   scalène

parallélogramme   rectangle   carré

rhombe   trapèze rectangle   trapèze scalène

trapèze isocèle   pentagone   hexagone   heptagone

octogone   décagone   cercle

FOCUS: Geometrical Solids

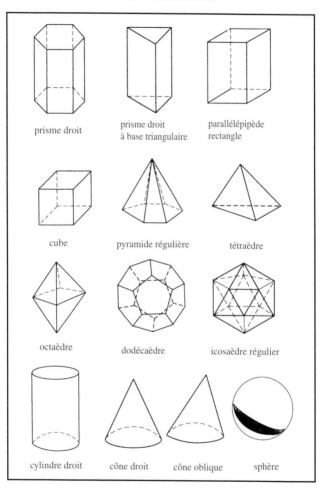

prisme droit

prisme droit
à base triangulaire

parallélépipède
rectangle

cube

pyramide régulière

tétraèdre

octaèdre

dodécaèdre

icosaèdre régulier

cylindre droit

cône droit

cône oblique

sphère

FOCUS: Angles

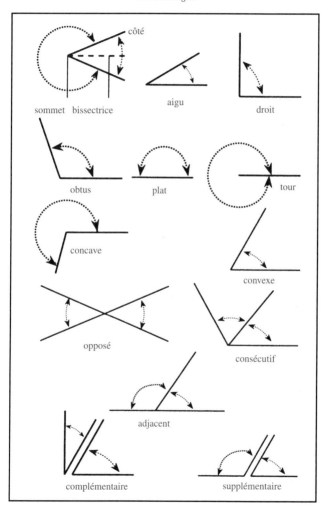

b. CONCEPTS

angle	angle (*m*)	*AH-gl*
• **acute**	aigu (*adj*)	*ay-gew*
• **adjacent**	adjacent (*adj*)	*ad-zha-sAH*
• **bisector**	bissectrice (*f*)	*bee-sehk-treess*
• **complementary**	complémentaire (*adj*)	*kOH-play-mAH-tehr*
• **concave**	concave (*adj*)	*kOH-kav*
• **consecutive**	consécutif (*adj*)	*kOH-say-kew-teef*
• **convex**	convexe (*adj*)	*kOH-vehks*
• **obtuse**	obtus (*adj*)	*up-tew*
• **one turn (360°)**	tour (*m*)	*toor*
• **opposite**	opposé (*adj*)	*up-oh-zay*
• **right**	droit (*adj*)	*drwa*
• **side**	côté (*adj*)	*koh-tay*
• **straight**	droit (*adj*)	*drwa*
• **supplementary**	supplémentaire (*adj*)	*sew-play-mAH-tehr*
• **vertex**	sommet (*m*)	*sum-eh*

FOCUS: Lines

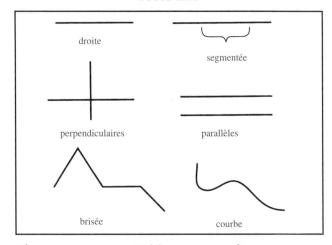

axis	axe (*m*)	*aks*
coordinate	coordonnée (*f*)	*ku-or-dun-ay*
degree	degré (*m*)	*de-gray*
draw	dessiner (*v*)	*day-see-nay*

drawing instruments	instruments de dessin	*EH-strew-mAH de day-sEH*
• compass	compas (*m*)	*kOH-pa*
• eraser	gomme (*f*)	*gum*
• pen	stylo (*m*)	*steel-o*
• pencil	crayon (*m*)	*kreh-yOH*
• protractor	goniomètre (*m*)	*gun-yu-mehtr*
• ruler	règle (*f*)	*rehgl*
• template	gabarit (*m*)	*ga-ba-ree*
geometry	géométrie (*f*)	*zhay-u-may-tree*
• geometrical	géométrique (*adj*)	*zhay-u-may-treek*
line	ligne (*f*)	*lee-ny*
• broken	brisée (*adj*)	*bree-zay*
• curved	courbe (*adj*)	*koorb*
• parallel	parallèle (*adj*)	*pa-ra-lehl*
• perpendicular	perpendiculaire (*adj*)	*pehr-pAH-dee-kew-lehr*
• segment	segmentée (*adj*)	*sehg-mAH-tay*
• straight	droite (*adj*)	*drwat*
point	point (*m*)	*pwEH*
space	espace (*m*)	*ehs-pas*
trigonometry	trigonométrie (*f*)	*tree-gun-u-may-tree*
• trigonometric	trigonométrique (*adj*)	*tree-gun-u-may-treek*
• cosecant	cosécante (*f*)	*kus-ay-kAHt*
• cosine	cosinus (*m*)	*kus-ee-newss*
• cotangent	cotangente (*f*)	*kut-AH-zhAHt*
• secant	sécante (*f*)	*say-kAHt*
• sine	sinus (*m*)	*see-news*
• tangent	tangente (*f*)	*tAH-zhAHt*
vector	vecteur (*m*)	*vehk-tur*

3. QUANTITY AND SPACE

a. **WEIGHTS AND MEASURES**

area	surface (*f*)	*sewr-fas*
	superficie (*f*)	*sew-pehr-fee-see*
• hectare	hectare (*m*)	*ehk-tar*
• square centimeter	centimètre carré	*sAH-tee-mehtr ka-ray*
• square kilometer	kilomètre carré	*kee-lu-mehtr ka-ray*
• square meter	mètre carré	*mehtr ka-ray*
• square millimeter	millimètre carré	*meel-ee-mehtr ka-ray*
length	longueur (*f*)	*lOH-gur*
• centimeter	centimètre (*m*)	*sAH-tee-mehtr*
• kilometer	kilomètre (*m*)	*keel-u-mehtr*
• meter	mètre (*m*)	*mehtr*
• millimeter	millimètre (m)	*meel-ee-mehtr*

speed	vitesse (*f*)	*vee-tess*
• **per hour**	à l'heure	*a-lur*
• **per minute**	à la minute	*a-la-meen-ewt*
• **per second**	à la seconde	*a-la-se-gOHd*
velocity	vélocité (*f*)	*vay-luss-ee-tay*
volume	volume (*m*)	*vul-ewm*
• **cubic centimeter**	centimètre cubique	*sAH-tee-mehtr kew-beek*
• **cubic kilometer**	kilomètre cubique	*keel-u-mehtr kew-beek*
• **cubic meter**	mètre cubique	*mehtr kew-beek*
• **cubic millimeter**	millimètre cubique	*meel-ee-mehtr kew-beek*
• **liter**	litre (*m*)	*leetr*
• **quart**	quart de gallon	*kar de gal-OH*
weight	poids (*m*)	*pwah*
• **gram**	gramme (*m*)	*gram*
• **hectogram**	hectogramme (*m*)	*ehk-tu-gram*
• **kilogram**	kilogramme (*m*)	*keel-u-gram*
weight (due to gravity)	pesanteur (*f*)	*pe-zAH-tur*

b. WEIGHING AND MEASURING

dense	dense (*adj*)	*dAH-s*
• **density**	densité (*f*)	*dAH-see-tay*
dimension	dimension (*f*)	*dee-mAH-sy-OH*
extension	extension (*f*)	*ehks-tAH-sy-OH*
heavy	lourd (*adj, m*)	*loor*
	lourde (*f*)	*loord*
light	léger (*adj, m*)	*lay-zhay*
	légère (*f*)	*lay-zh-ehr*
long	long (*adj, m*)	*lOH*
	longue (*f*)	*lOH-g*
mass	masse (*f*)	*mas*
maximum	maximum (*m*)	*maks-ee-mum*
measure	mesurer (*v*)	*me-zewr-ay*
measuring tape	mètre à ruban	*mehtr a rew-bAH*
medium	moyenne (*f*)	*mwa-y-ehn*
	moyen (*adj, m*)	*mwa-yEH*
minimum	minimum (*m*)	*mee-nee-mum*
narrow	étroit (*adj, m*)	*ay-trwa*
	étroite (*f*)	*ay-trwat*
short (thing)	court (*adj, m*)	*koor*
	courte (*f*)	*koort*
size	mesure (*f*)	*me-zewr*
	taille (*f*)	*ta-y*
tall	haut (*adj, m*)	*oh*
	haute (*f*)	*oh-t*
	grand (*m*)	*grAH*
	grande (*f*)	*grAH-d*

thick	épais *(adj, m)*	*ay-peh*
	épaisse *(f)*	*ay-pehs*
thin	maigre *(adj)*	*meh-gr*
	mince *(adj)*	*mEHss*
weigh	peser *(v)*	*pe-zay*
wide	large *(adj)*	*larzh*
• width	largeur *(f)*	*lar-zh-ur*

c. CONCEPTS OF QUANTITY

a lot, much	beaucoup *(adv)*	*bo-koo*
	une grande quantité	*ewn grAH-d kAH-tee-tay*
all, everything	tout *(adj)*	*too*
	toute chose	*toot sh-oh-z*
• everyone	tout le monde	*tool mOH-d*
almost, nearly	presque *(adv)*	*prehs-ke*
approximately	à peu près *(adv)*	*a puh preh*
	environ	*AH-vee-rOH*
as much as	tant que	*tAH ke*
	autant que	*oh-tAH ke*
big, large	grand *(adj, m)*	*grAH*
	grande *(f)*	*grAH-d*
	gros *(adj, m)*	*gro*
	grosse *(f)*	*gros*
• become big	grandir *(v)*	*grAH-deer*
	agrandir *(v)*	*a-grAH-deer*
	grossir *(v)*	*gro-seer*
both	les deux	*lay duh*
	tous *(m)* les deux	*too lay duh*
	toutes *(f)* les deux	*toot lay duh*
capacity	capacité *(f)*	*ka-pa-see-tay*
decrease	diminution *(f)*	*dee-mee-newss-yOH*
• decrease	diminuer *(v)*	*dee-mee-new-ay*
double	double *(adj)*	*doobl*
empty	vide *(adj)*	*veed*
• empty	vider *(v)*	*vee-day*
enough	assez *(adv)*	*a-say*
	suffisant *(adj)*	*sew-fee-zAH*
• be enough	suffire *(v)*	*sew-feer*
	être assez *(v)*	*eh-tre a-say*
entire	entier *(adj)*	*AH-ty-ay*
	entière	*AH-ty-ehr*
every, each	chaque *(adj)*	*shak*
fill	remplir *(v)*	*rAH-pleer*
• full	plein *(adj)*	*plEH*
	pleine	*plehn*
grow	croître *(v)*	*krwa-tr*
• growth	croissance *(f)*	*krwa-sAH-s*

half	demi (*m*)	*de-mee*
	demie (*f*)	*de-mee*
how much (many)	combien (*adv*)	*kOH-byEH*
increase	augmentation (*f*)	*ug-mAH-ta-syOH*
• **increase**	augmenter (*v*)	*ug-mAH-tay*
less	moins (*adv*)	*mwEH*
little (size)	petit (*adj, m*)	*ptee*
	petite (*f*)	*pteet*
• **a little**	peu (*adv*), un peu	*puh, UH-puh*
more	plus (*adv*)	*plew, plewss*
no one	personne (*pro*)	*pehr-sun*
nothing	rien (*adv/pro*)	*ryEH*
	nul (*adj/pro, m*)	*newl*
	nulle (*f*)	*newl*
pair	paire (*f*)	*pehr*
part	part (*f*)	*par*
	partie (*f*)	*par-tee*
piece	pièce (*f*)	*pyehs*
portion	morceau (*m*)	*mor-so*
	portion (*f*)	*porsyOH*
quantity	quantité (*f*)	*kAH-tee-tay*
several	plusieurs (*adj/adv*)	*plew-zy-ur*
small	petit (*adj, m*)	*ptee*
	petite (*f*)	*pteet*
• **become small**	rendre plus petit	*rAH-dr plew ptee*
	rapetisser (*v*)	*rap-tee-say*
some	quelque(s) (*adj*)	*kehl-ke*
• **some of it, them**	en (*pro*)	*AH*
• **I have some of it/them.**	J'en ai.	*Zh-AH nay*
suffice	suffire (*v*)	*sew-feer*
• **sufficient**	suffisant (*adj*)	*sew-fee-zAH*
too much	trop (*adv*)	*troh*
triple	triple (*adj*)	*tree-pl*

d. CONCEPTS OF LOCATION

above	au-dessus (*adv*)	*ohd-sew*
	en haut	*AH oh*
across	à travers (*prep*)	*a-tra-vehr*
ahead, forward	avant (*adv*)	*a-vAH*
among	parmi (*prep*)	*parmee (among more than two)*
around	autour de	*oh-toor-de*
away	au loin (*adv*)	*oh-lwEH*
back, backward	en arrière (*adv*)	*AH-na-ree-ehr*
beside, next to	à côté (de) (*prep*)	*a-ko-tay (de)*
between	entre (*prep*)	*AH-tre (between only two)*

beyond	au-delà (de) *(adv/prep)*	*ohd-la (de)*
bottom	fond *(m)*	*fOH*
• **at the bottom**	au fond	*oh-fOH*
	en bas	*AH-bah*
compass	boussole *(f)*	*boo-sul*
direction	direction *(f)*	*dee-rehk-syOH*
distance	distance *(f)*	*dee-stAH-s*
down	bas *(adv)*	*bah*
	en bas	*AH-bah*
east	est *(m)*	*ehst*
• **eastern**	oriental *(adj)*	*or-yAH-tal*
• **to the east**	à l'est	*a-lehst*
edge	bord *(m)*	*bor*
• **at the edge of**	au bord de	*oh-bor-de*
far	loin *(adv)*	*lwEH*
	lointain *(adj)*	*lwEH-tEH*
fast	vite *(adj/adv)*	*veet*
	rapide	*ra-peed*
from	de *(prep)*	*de*
here	ici *(adv)*	*ee-see*
horizontal	horizontal *(adj)*	*or-ee-zOH-tal*
in	dans *(prep)*	*dAH*
• **inside**	dedans *(adv)*	*de-dAH*
in front of	devant *(adv/prep)*	*dvAH*
in the middle	au centre	*oh-sAHtr*
	au milieu	*oh-meel-yuh*
left	gauche *(adj)*	*gohsh*
• **to the left**	à gauche	*a-gohsh*
level	niveau *(m)*	*nee-voh*
near	près (de) *(adv)*	*preh (de)*
north	nord *(m)*	*nor*
• **northern**	septentrional *(adj)*	*sehp-tAH-tree-yun-al*
• **to the north**	au nord	*oh-nor*
nowhere	nulle part *(adv)*	*newl-par*
on	sur *(prep)*	*sewr*
outside	dehors *(adv)*	*de-or*
place	endroit *(m)*	*AH-drwa*
	lieu *(m)*	*lyuh*
position	position *(f)*	*pu-zee-syOH*
right	droit *(adj, m)*	*drwa*
	droite *(f)*	*drwat*
• **to the right**	à droite	*a-drwat*
somewhere	quelque part	*kehl-ke par*
south	sud *(m)*	*sewd*
• **southern**	méridional *(adj)*	*may-ree-dy-un-al*
• **to the south**	au sud	*oh-sewd*
there	là *(adv)*	*la*

through	par (*prep*)	*par*
	à travers	*a-tra-vehr*
to, at	à (*prep*)	*a*
• **to, at someone's place**	chez (*prep*)	*shay*
top	sommet (*m*)	*sum-eh*
• **at the top**	au sommet	*oh-sum-eh*
	en haut	*AH-oh*
toward	vers (*prep*)	*vehr*
under	sous (*prep*)	*soo*
up	haut (*adv*)	*oh*
	en haut	*AH-oh*
vertical	vertical (*adj*)	*vehr-tee-kal*
west	ouest (*m*)	*west*
• **western**	occidental (*adj*)	*uk-see-dAH-tal*
• **to the west**	à l'ouest	*al-west*
where	où (*adv*)	*oo*

FOCUS: Compass Points

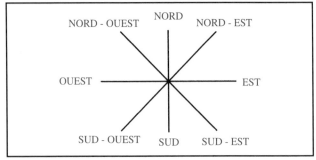

e. MOVEMENT

arrive	arriver (*v*)	*a-ree-vay*
come	venir (*v*)	*vneer*
drive	conduire (*v*)	*kOH-dew-eer*
enter	entrer (*v*)	*AH-tray*
fall	tomber (*v*)	*tOH-bay*
follow	suivre (*v*)	*sew-eevr*
get up, rise	se lever (*v*)	*se-levay*
go	aller (*v*)	*alay*
• **go away**	s'en aller (*v*)	*sAH-nalay*
• **go down, descend**	descendre (*v*)	*day-sAH-dr*

• **go on foot**	aller à pied (*v*)	*alay a pyay*
• **go out, exit**	sortir (*v*)	*sor-teer*
• **go up, climb**	monter (*v*)	*mOH-tay*
leave, depart	partir (*v*)	*par-teer*
	quitter (*v*)	*kee-tay*
lie down	se coucher (*v*)	*se-koo-shay*
lift	lever (*v*)	*le-vay*
motion	motion (*f*)	*mo-syOH*
move	bouger (*v*)	*boo-zhay*
	remuer (*v*)	*re-mew-ay*
• **move oneself**	se déplacer (*v*)	*se-day-pla-say*
	bouger (*v*)	*boo-zhay*
• **movement**	mouvement (*m*)	*moov-mAH*
pass by	passer (*v*)	*pa-say*
pull	tirer (*v*)	*tee-ray*
put	mettre (*v*)	*meht-re*
	placer (*v*)	*pla-say*
• **put down**	poser (*v*)	*po-zay*
quickly	vite (*adv*)	*veet*
return	retourner (*v*)	*re-toor-nay*
run	courir (*v*)	*koo-reer*
send	envoyer (*v*)	*AH-vwa-yay*
sit down	s'asseoir (*v*)	*sa-swar*
slow	lent (*adj, m*)	*lAH*
	lente (*f*)	*lAHt*
• **slowly**	lentement (*adv*)	*lAHt-mAH*
stop	arrêter (*v*)	*a-reht-ay*
• **stop oneself**	s'arrêter (*v*)	*sa-reht-ay*
turn	tourner (*v*)	*toor-nay*
walk	marcher (*v*)	*marsh-ay*
	aller (*v*) à pied	*alay a pyay*
• **walk**	promenade (*f*)	*prum-nad*
• **take a walk**	faire (*v*) une promenade	*fehr ewn prum-nad*

4. TIME

a. GENERAL EXPRESSIONS OF TIME

afternoon	après-midi (*m*)	*apreh-mee-dee*
• **in the afternoon**	dans l'après-midi	*dAH lap-reh mee-dee*
	de l'après-midi	*de lap-reh-mee-dee*
• **this afternoon**	cet après-midi	*seht-apreh-mee-dee*
• **tomorrow afternoon**	demain après-midi	*de-mEH apreh-mee-dee*
dawn	aube (*f*)	*ohb*
day	jour (*m*)	*zh-oor*
• **all day**	toute la journée	*toot la zh-oor-nay*

evening	soir (*m*)	*swar*
• **in the evening**	dans le soir	*dAHl-swar*
	du soir	*dew swar*
• **this evening**	ce soir	*se-swar*
• **tomorrow evening**	demain soir	*de-mEH swar*
midnight	minuit (*m*)	*mee-new-ee*
• **at midnight**	à minuit	*a-mee-new-ee*
morning	matin (*m*)	*ma-tEH*
• **in the morning**	dans le matin	*dAHl-ma-tEH*
	du matin	*dew-ma-tEH*
• **this morning**	ce matin	*se-ma-tEH*
• **tomorrow morning**	demain matin	*de-mEH ma-tEH*
night	nuit (*f*)	*new-ee*
• **at night**	de nuit	*de-new-ee*
	dans la nuit	*dAH-la-new-ee*
• **last night**	cette nuit	*seht-new-ee (actual night)*
	hier soir	*yehr swar (actual evening)*
• **this night**	cette nuit	*seht new-ee*
• **tomorrow night**	demain pendant la nuit	*de-mEH pAH-dAH la new-ee (actual night)*
	demain soir	*de-mEH swar (actual evening)*
noon	midi (*m*)	*mee-dee*
• **at noon**	à midi	*a-mee-dee*
sunrise	lever (*m*) du soleil	*le-vay dew sul-ay*
sunset	coucher (*m*) du soleil	*koo-shay dew sul-ay*
time (*in general*)	temps (*m*)	*tAH*
• **time (hour)**	heure (*f*)	*ur*
• **time (as in *every time*)**	fois (*f*)	*fwa*

> **Time flies!** = Le temps fuit! *le tAH few-ee*
> **at the present time** = à l'heure actuelle *a-lur ak-tew ehl*
> **Once upon a time . . .** = Il était une fois *eel ay-teh tewn fwa*
> **to be on time** = être à l'heure *eh-tre a-lur*

today	aujourd'hui (*adv*)	*oh-zhoor-dew-ee*
tomorrow	demain (*adv*)	*de-mEH*
• **day after tomorrow**	lendemain (*adv*)	*lAHd-mEH*
• **the day after tomorrow**	lendemain (*m*)	*lAHd-mEH*

tonight	cette nuit	*seht new-ee (actual night)*
	ce soir	*se swar (evening)*
yesterday	hier *(adv)*	*yehr*
• day before yesterday	avant-hier *(adv)*	*avAH-tyehr*
• yesterday afternoon	hier après-midi	*yehr apreh-mee-dee*
• yesterday morning	hier matin	*yehr ma-tEH*

b. TELLING TIME

What time is it?	Quelle heure est-il?	*kehl ur eh-teel*
• It's 1:00.	Il est une heure.	*eel eh-tewn ur*
• It's 2:00.	Il est deux heures.	*eel eh duh-zur*
• It's 3:00.	Il est trois heures.	*eel eh trwa-zur*
• It's exactly 3:00.	Il est trois heures précises.	*eel eh trwa-zur pray-seez*
• It's 3:00 on the dot.	Il est trois heures juste.	*eel eh trwa-zur zh-ewst*
	Il est trois heures pile.	*eel eh trwa-zur peel*
• It's 1:10.	Il est une heure dix.	*eel eh tewn ur dees*
• It's 4:25.	Il est quatre heures vingt-cinq.	*eel eh katr ur vEH-sEHk*
• It's 3:15.	Il est trois heures et quart.	*eel eh trwa-zur ay kar*
• It's 3:30.	Il est trois heures et demie.	*eel eh trwa-zur ayd-mee*
• It's 2:45.	Il est trois heures moins le quart.	*eel eh trwa-zur mwEH-le kar*
	Il est deux heures quarante-cinq.	*eel eh duh-zur ka-rAHt sEHk*
• It's 5:50.	Il est six heures moins dix.	*eel eh see-zur mwEH dees*

> The 24-hour clock is used throughout France.

Another way to tell time is the official time used by the French government on radio and TV, in railroad and bus stations, and at airports.

- It is the twenty-four-hour system.
- In this system, *quart*, *demi*, *demie*, *moins*, and *et* are not used.
- When you hear or see the stated time, subtract twelve from the number you hear or see. If the number is less than twelve, it is A.M. time, except for *24 heures*, which is midnight; *zéro heure* is also midnight.

EXAMPLES

> *Il est treize heures.* / It is 1:00 P.M.
> *Il est quinze heures.* / It is 3:00 P.M.
> *Il est vingt heures trente.* / It is 8:30 P.M.
> *Il est minuit.* / It is midnight.
> *Il est seize heures trente.* / It is 4:30 P.M.
> *Il est dix-huit heures quinze.* / It is 6:15 P.M.
> *Il est vingt heures quarante-cinq.* / It is 8:45 P.M.
> *Il est vingt-deux heures cinquante.* / It is 10:50 P.M.

The abbreviation for *heure* or *heures* is *h.*

EXAMPLES

> *Il est 20 h. 20.* / It is 8:20 P.M.
> *Il est 15 h. 50.* / It is 3:50 P.M.
> *Il est 23 h. 30.* / It is 11:30 P.M.

• It's 5:00 A.M.	Il est cinq heures.	*eel eh sEH-kur*
• It's 5:00 P.M.	Il est dix-sept heures.	*eel eh dee-seht ur*
• It's 10:00 A.M.	Il est dix heures.	*eel eh dee-zur*
• It's 10:00 P.M.	Il est vingt-deux heures.	*eel eh vEH-duh zur*

At what time?	À quelle heure?	*a kehl ur*
• At 1:00.	À une heure.	*a ewn ur*
• At 2:00.	À deux heures.	*a duh-zur*
• At 3:00.	À trois heures.	*a trwa-zur*

c. UNITS OF TIME

century	siècle (*m*)	*see-ehkl*
day	jour (*m*)	*zhoor*
• daily	quotidien (*adj*)	*kut-ee-dy-EH*
	quotidiennement (*adv*)	*kut-ee-dy-ehn-mAH*
decade	décennie (*f*)	*day-sehn-ee*
hour	heure (*f*)	*ur*
• hourly	à l'heure	*a-lur*

instant	instant (*m*)	*EH-stAH*
millennium	millénaire (*m*)	*meel-ay-nehr*
minute	minute (*f*)	*meen-ewt*
moment	moment (*m*)	*mum-AH*
month	mois (*m*)	*mwa*
• monthly	mensuellement (*adv*)	*mAH-sew-ehl-mAH*
	mensuel (*adj*)	*mAH-sew-ehl*
second	seconde (*f*)	*se-gOHd*
week	semaine (*f*)	*smehn*
• weekly	hebdomadaire (*adj*)	*ehb-dum-ad-ehr*
	hebdomadairement (*adv*)	*ehb-dum-ad-ehr-mAH*
year	an (*m*)	*AH*
	année (*f*)	*a-nay*
• yearly, annually	annuel, annuelle (*adj*)	*a-new-ehl*
	annuellement (*adv*)	*a-new-ehl-mAH*
year two thousand	an (*m*) deux mille	*AH-duh-meel*

d. TIMEPIECES

alarm clock	réveille-matin (*m*)	*ray-veh-y mat-EH*
	réveil (*m*)	*ray-veh-y*
clock	horloge (*f*)	*or-lu-zh*
dial	cadran (*m*)	*ka-drAH*
grandfather clock	horloge à pendule (*f*)	*or-lu-zh a pAH-dewl*
	horloge normande (*f*)	*or-lu-zh nor-mAHd*
hand (of a clock)	aiguille (*f*)	*ayg-ew-ee-y*
watch	montre (*f*)	*mOH-tre*
• The watch is fast.	La montre avance.	*la mOH-tre avAH-s*
• The watch is slow.	La montre retarde.	*la mOH-tre re-tard*
watchband	bracelet (*m*) d'une montre	*bras-leh dewn mOH-tre*
watch battery	pile d'une montre	*peel dewn mOH-tre*
wind	remonter (*v*)	*re-mOH-tay*
wristwatch	bracelet-montre (*m*)	*bras-leh mOH-tre*

e. CONCEPTS OF TIME

after	après (*adv*)	*apreh*
again	encore une fois (*adv*)	*AH-kor ewn fwa*
	de nouveau (*adv*)	*de-noo-voh*
ago	il y a (*adv*)	*eel-yah*
almost never	presque jamais (*adv*)	*prehs-ke zh-a-meh*
already	déjà (*adv*)	*day-zh-a*
always	toujours (*adv*)	*too-zh-oor*

anterior	antérieur(e) (*adj*)	*AH-tay-ree-ur*
as soon as	dès que (*conj*)	*deh-ke*
	aussitôt que (*conj*)	*o-see-toh-ke*
at the same time	en même temps	*AH-mehm-tAH*
	à la fois	*a-la-fwa*
be about to, be on	être sur le point de	*eh-tre sewr le pwEH de*
the point/verge of		
be on time	être à l'heure	*eh-tre a-lur*
become	devenir (*v*)	*devneer*
before	avant (*adv*)	*avAH*
	auparavant (*adv*)	*o-par-avAH*
begin	commencer (*v*)	*kum-AH-say*
• beginning	commencement (*m*)	*kum-AH-smAH*
	début (*m*)	*day-bew*
brief	bref, brève (*adj, m, f*)	*brehf, brehv*
• briefly	en bref	*AH brehf*
	brièvement (*adv*)	*bree-ehv-mAH*
change	changer (*v*)	*shAH-zh-ay*
continue	continuer (*v*)	*kOH-teen-ew-ay*
• continually	continuellement (*adv*)	*kOH-teen-ew-ehl-mAH*
during	pendant (*prep*)	*pAH-dAH*
early	tôt (*adv*)	*toh*
	de bonne heure (*adv*)	*de-bun-ur*
• be early	être tôt (*v*)	*eh-tre-toh*
	être de bonne heure (*v*)	*eh-tre de-bun-ur*
end, finish	finir (*v*)	*fee-neer*
• end	fin (*f*)	*fEH*
frequent	fréquent(e) (*adj, m, f*)	*fray-kAH(t)*
• frequently	fréquemment (*adv*)	*fray-kam-AH*
future	futur (*m*)	*few-tewr*
	avenir (*m*)	*avneer*
happen, occur	se produire (*v*)	*se-pro-dew-eer*
	arriver (*v*)	*a-ree-vay*
in an hour's time	dans une heure	*dAH-zewn-ur*
• in two minutes'	dans deux minutes	*dAH duh meen-ewt*
time		
in the meantime	entre-temps (*adv*)	*AH-tre-tAH*
in time	à temps	*a-tAH*
just now	à l'instant	*a-lEH-stAH*
last	durer (*v*)	*dewr-ay*
• last a long time	durer longtemps (*v*)	*dew-rayl-OH-t-AH*
• last a short time	durer peu de temps (*v*)	*dewr-ay puh de tAH*

last	dernier (*adj, m*)	*dehrn-yay*
	dernière (*f*)	*dehrn-yehr*
	passé(e) (*adj*)	*pah-say*
• **last month**	le mois dernier	*le mwa dehrn-yay*
	(passé)	*(pah-say)*
• **last year**	l'an dernier (*m*)	*lAH dehrn-yay*
	l'année dernière (*f*)	*la-nay dehrn-yehr*
late	tard	*tar*
	en retard (*adv*)	*AH re-tar*
• **be late**	être tard (en retard)	*eh-tre tar (AH-re-tar)*

> **Better late than never!** Mieux vaut tard que jamais!
> *myuh voh tar ke zh-a-meh*

long-term	à long terme	*a-lOH-tehrm*
look forward to	s'attendre à (*v*)	*sat-AH-dre-a*
never	jamais (*adv*)	*zh-a-meh*
• **almost never**	presque jamais (*adv*)	*prehs-ke zh-a-meh*
now	maintenant (*adv*)	*mEHt-nAH*
	à présent (*adv*)	*a pray-zAH*
• **for now**	pour le moment	*poorl-mum-AH*
• **from now on**	dès maintenant	*deh mEHt-nAH*
	désormais (*adv*)	*day-zor-meh*
nowadays	de nos jours	*de noh zh-oor*
occasionally	de temps en temps	*de-tAH-zAH-tAH*
	(*adv*)	
often	souvent (*adv*)	*soovAH*
once	une fois	*ewn fwa*
• **once in a while**	de temps à autre	*de tAH za oh-tre*
• **once upon a time**	il était une fois	*eel ay-teh tewn fwa*
only	seulement (*adv*)	*sulmAH*
past	passé (*m*)	*pah-say*
posterior	postérieur(e) (*adj*)	*pus-tay-ree-ur*
present	présent (*m*)	*prayz-AH*
	présent(e) (*adj, m, f*)	*prayz-AH(t)*
	actuel(le) (*adj, m, f*)	*ak-tew-ehl*
• **presently**	actuellement (*adv*)	*ak-tew-ehlm-AH*
previous	précédent(e) (*adj, m, f*)	*pray-sayd-AH(t)*
	auparavant (*adv*)	*oh-par-avAH*
• **previously**	précédemment (*adv*)	*pray-say-dam-AH*
rare	rare (*adj*)	*rahr*
• **rarely**	rarement (*adv*)	*rahrm-AH*

recent	récent(e) (*adj, m, f*)	*rayss-AH(t)*
• **recently**	récemment (*adv*)	*ray-sam-AH*
regular	régulier (*adj, m*)	*ray-gewl-yay*
	régulière (*f*)	*ray-gewl-yehr*
• **regularly**	régulièrement (*adv*)	*ray-gewl-yehrm-AH*
right away	tout de suite (*adv*)	*tood-sweet*
short-term	à court terme	*a-koor-tehrm*
simultaneous	simultané(e) (*adj, m, f*)	*seem-ewl-ta-nay*
• **simultaneously**	simultanément (*adv*)	*seem-ewl-ta-naym-AH*
since, for	depuis (*prep*)	*de-pew-ee*
• **since Monday**	depuis lundi	*de-pew-ee-lUH-dee*
• **since yesterday**	depuis hier	*de-pew-ee-yehr*
• **for three days**	depuis trois jours	*de-pew-ee trwa zhoor*
slow	lent(e) (*adj, m, f*)	*l-AH-(t)*
• **slowly**	lentement (*adv*)	*l-AH-tem-AH*
soon	bientôt (*adv*)	*by-EH toh*
• **as soon as**	dès que (*conj*)	*deh-ke*
	aussitôt que	*o-see-toh-ke*
• **sooner or later**	tôt ou tard (*adv*)	*toh oo tar*
spend (*time*)	passer (*v*)	*pah-say*
spend (*money*)	dépenser (*v*)	*daypAH-say*
sporadic	sporadique (*adj*)	*spu-ra-deek*
• **sporadically**	sporadiquement (*adv*)	*spu-ra-deek-m-AH*
still	encore (*adv*)	*AH-kor*
	toujours	*too-zhoor*
take place	avoir lieu	*avwar lee-yuh*
temporary	temporaire (*adj*)	*tAH-pu-rehr*
• **temporarily**	temporairement (*adv*)	*tAH-pu-rehrm-AH*
then	lors	*lor*
	ensuite (*adv*)	*AH-sweet*
	alors (*adv*)	*a-lor*
timetable, schedule	horaire (*m*)	*u-rehr*
to this day	jusqu'à ce jour (*adv*)	*zh-ews-ka-se-zhoor*
until	jusque(s) (*prep*)	*zh-ews-ke*
usually	d'habitude (*adv*)	*da-bee-tewd*
wait (for)	attendre (*v*)	*at-AH-dre*
when	quand (*adv*)	*k-AH*
while	pendant que (*conj*)	*p-AH-d-AH-ke*
within (*a certain time*)	en (*prep*)	*AH*
yet	encore (*adv*)	*AH-kor*

5. DAYS, MONTHS, AND SEASONS

a. DAYS OF THE WEEK

day of the week	jour (*m*) de la semaine	*zhoord-la-smehn*
• **Monday**	lundi (*m*)	*lUH-dee*
• **Tuesday**	mardi (*m*)	*mar-dee*
• **Wednesday**	mercredi (*m*)	*mehr-kre-dee*
• **Thursday**	jeudi (*m*)	*zhuh-dee*
• **Friday**	vendredi (*m*)	*vAH-dre-dee*
• **Saturday**	samedi (*m*)	*sam-dee*
• **Sunday**	dimanche (*m*)	*dee-mAH-sh*
• **on Mondays**	le lundi	*le-l-UH-dee*
• **on Saturdays**	le samedi	*le-sam-dee*
• **on Sundays**	le dimanche	*le-dee-mAH-sh*
holiday	un jour férié	*UH zhoor fay-ree-ay*
weekend	la fin de semaine	*laf-EH-de-smehn*
	le week-end	*le-wee-kehn*
What day is it?	Quel jour est-ce?	*kehl zhoor eh-ss*
• **It's Monday.**	C'est lundi.	*say-lUH-dee*
workday	un jour de travail	*UH zhoor-de-tra-va-y*

b. MONTHS OF THE YEAR

month of the year	mois (*m*) de l'année	*mwad-la-nay*
• **January**	janvier (*m*)	*zh-AH-vee-ay*
• **February**	février (*m*)	*fay-vree-ay*
• **March**	mars (*m*)	*marss*
• **April**	avril (*m*)	*avreel*
• **May**	mai (*m*)	*meh*
• **June**	juin (*m*)	*zh-ew-EH*
• **July**	juillet (*m*)	*zh-ew-ee-yay*
• **August**	août (*m*)	*oo (oot)*
• **September**	septembre (*m*)	*sehpt-AH-bre*
• **October**	octobre (*m*)	*uktubre*
• **November**	novembre (*m*)	*nuv-AH-bre*
• **December**	décembre (*m*)	*dayss-AH-bre*
calendar	calendrier (*m*)	*kal-AH-dree-yay*
leap year	une année bissextile	*ewn anay bee-sehks-teel*
monthly	mensuellement (*adv*)	*m-AH-sew-ehlm-AH*
school year	année scolaire	*anay skul-ehr*
What month are we in?	Quel mois sommes-nous?	*kehl mwa sum noo*
What month is it?	Quel mois est-ce?	*kehl mwa eh-ss*

c. SEASONS

season	saison (*f*)	*sehz-OH*
• **spring**	printemps (*m*)	*preEH-tAH*
• **summer**	été (*m*)	*ay-tay*
• **fall**	automne (*m*)	*oh-tun*
• **winter**	hiver (*m*)	*eev-ehr*
equinox	équinoxe (*m*)	*ay-kee-nuks*
moon	lune (*f*)	*lewn*
solstice	solstice (*m*)	*sulsteess*
sun	soleil (*m*)	*sul-ay*

FOCUS: The Seasons

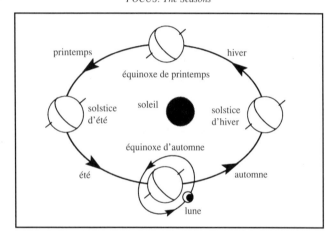

d. THE ZODIAC

horoscope	horoscope (*m*)	*u-rus-kup*
zodiac	zodiaque (*m*)	*zud-yak*
• **signs of the zodiac**	signes du zodiaque	*see-ny dew zud-yak*
Aries	Bélier (*m*) (*21 mars–20 avril*)	*bayl-yay*
Taurus	Taureau (*m*) (*21 avril–21 mai*)	*toro*
Gemini	Gémeaux (*m, pl*) (*22 mai–21 juin*)	*zhay-mo*

Cancer	Cancer (*m*)	*kAH-sehr*
	(*22 juin–22 juillet*)	
Leo	Lion (*m*)	*ly-OH*
	(*23 juillet–23 août*)	
Virgo	Vierge (*f*)	*vy-ehrzh*
	(*24 août–23 septembre*)	
Libra	Balance (*f*)	*bal-AH-ss*
	(*24 septembre–23 octobre*)	
Scorpio	Scorpion (*m*)	*skor-pyOH*
	(*24 octobre–22 novembre*)	
Sagittarius	Sagittaire (*m*)	*sa-zh-ee-tehr*
	(*23 novembre–21 décembre*)	
Capricorn	Capricorne (*m*)	*kap-ree-korn*
	(*22 décembre–20 janvier*)	
Aquarius	Verseau (*m*)	*vehr-so*
	(*21 janvier–18 février*)	
Pisces	Poissons (*m, pl*)	*pwas-OH*
	(*19 février–20 mars*)	

e. EXPRESSING THE DATE

| **What's today's date?** | Quelle est la date aujourd'hui? | *kehl eh la dat oh-zhoor-dew-ee* |

Use the ordinal *premier* (also written as *1er or 1er*) for the first of each month, and cardinal numbers for the other days.

• **It's October first.**	C'est le premier octobre.	*seh le prem-yay uktubre*
• **It's January second.**	C'est le deux janvier.	*seh le duh zh-Ah-vee-ay*
• **It's May third.**	C'est le trois mai.	*seh le trwa meh*
What year is it?	Quelle année est-ce?	*kehl anay eh-ss*
• **It's 2002.**	C'est 2002.	*seh 2002*
When were you born?	Quand êtes-vous né? (*m, pol*)	*kAH eht-voo nay*
	Quand êtes-vous née? (*f, pol*)	*kAH eht-voo nay*

	Quand es-tu né (m, fam)	kAH eh-tew nay
	Quand es-tu née (f, fam)	kAH eh-tew nay
• **I was born in** ...	Je suis né (m)/née (f) en ...	zhe sew-ee nay AH

f. IMPORTANT DATES

the New Year	le Nouvel An	le noo-vehl AH
New Year's Day	le Jour de l'An	le zhoor del AH
New Year's Eve	la Nuit de la Saint-Sylvestre	la-new-eed-la-sEH-seel-vestr
Assumption (August 15, National French holiday)	Assomption (f)	as-OH-psy-OH
Easter	Pâques (f, pl)	pahk
Christmas	Noël (m)	nuh-ehl
Passover	la Pâque	la-pahk
Ramadan	le ramadan	le-ra-ma-dAH

6. TALKING ABOUT THE WEATHER

a. GENERAL WEATHER VOCABULARY

air	air (m)	ehr
atmosphere	atmosphère (f)	at-muss-fehr
• **atmospheric conditions**	conditions atmosphériques (f, pl)	kOH-dee-sy-OH at-muss-fay-reek
awful	mauvais (adj)	muv-eh
• **be awful (weather)**	faire (v) un temps mauvais	fehr UH tAH muv-eh
beautiful	beau (adj)	bo
• **be beautiful (weather)**	faire (v) beau temps	fehr bo tAH
clear	clair (adj)	klehr
• **The sky is clear.**	Le ciel est clair.	le syehl eh klehr
climate	climat (m)	klee-ma
• **continental**	continental(e) (adj)	kOH-teen-AH-tal
• **dry**	sec (adj, m)	sehk
	sèche (f)	seh-sh
• **humid**	humide (adj)	ew-meed
	lourd (adj)	loor
	lourde (f)	loord
• **Mediterranean**	méditerranéen (adj, m)	may-dee-tehr-anay-EH
	méditerranéenne (f)	may-dee-tehr-anay-ehn

• **tropical**	tropical(e) *(adj, m, f)*	*trup-ee-kal*
cloud	nuage *(m)*	*new-azh*
• **cloudy**	nuageux *(adj, m)*	*new-azh-uh*
	nuageuse *(f)*	*new-azh-uhz*
	couvert *(adj, m)*	*koo-vehr*

> **to be in the clouds (to have one's head in the clouds)** = être dans les nuages *eh-tre dAH lay new-azh*

cold	froid *(m, adj)*	*frwa*
• **be cold** (weather)	faire froid	*fehr frwa*
cool	frais *(adj)*	*freh*
• **be cool** (weather)	faire frais	*fehr freh*
dark	sombre *(adj)*	*sOH-bre*
• **It's dark today.**	Il fait sombre aujourd'hui.	*eel feh sOH-bre oh-zhoor-dew-ee*
drop (e.g., of rain)	goutte *(f)*	*goot*
fog	brouillard *(m)*	*broo-yar*
• **foggy**	brumeux *(adj)*	*brewm-uh*
freeze	geler *(v)*	*zhe-lay*
• **frozen**	gelé(e) *(adj, m, f)*	*zhe-lay*
hail	grêle *(f)*	*grehl*
• **hail**	grêler *(v)*	*gray-lay*
How's the weather?	Quel temps fait-il?	*kehl tAH feh-teel*
• **Its a bit hot.**	Il fait un peu chaud.	*eel feh UH puh sho*
It's a bit cold.	Il fait un peu froid.	*eel feh UH puh frwa*
• **It's awful.**	Il fait un temps affreux.	*eel feh UH tAH af-ruh*
• **It's beautiful.**	Il fait beau temps.	*eel feh bo tAH*
• **It's cloudy.**	Il fait un temps couvert.	*eel feh UH tAH koo-vehr*
• **It's cold.**	Il fait froid.	*eel feh frwa*
• **It's cool.**	Il fait frais.	*eel feh freh*
• **It's foul** (weather).	Il fait un temps pourri.	*eel feh UH tAH poo-ree*
• **It's hot.**	Il fait chaud.	*eel feh sho*
• **It's humid.**	Il fait humide.	*eel feh ew-meed*
• **It's mild.**	Il fait doux.	*eel feh doo*
• **It's muggy.**	Il fait un temps lourd.	*eel feh UH tAH loor*
• **It's pleasant.**	Il fait un temps agréable.	*eel feh UH tAH a-gray-ahble*
• **It's raining.**	Il pleut.	*eel pluh*

It's raining buckets. = Il pleut à seaux. *eel pluh a so*		

• **It's snowing.**	Il neige.	*eel neh-zh*
• **It's sunny.**	Il fait (du) soleil.	*eel feh (dew) sul-ay*
• **It's thundering.**	Il tonne.	*eel tun*
• **It's very cold.**	Il fait très froid.	*eel feh treh frwa*
• **It's very hot.**	Il fait très chaud.	*eel feh treh sho*
• **It's windy.**	Il fait du vent.	*eel feh dew vAH*
• **There's lightning.**	Il fait des éclairs.	*eel feh day zay-klehr*
humid, damp	humide (*adj*)	*ew-meed*
• **be humid**	faire humide	*fehr ew-meed*
• **humidity**	humidité (*f*)	*ew-mee-dee-tay*
hurricane	ouragan (*m*)	*oor-ag-AH*
ice	glace (*f*)	*glass*
light	lumière (*f*)	*lew-myehr*
lightning	éclair (*m*)	*ay-klehr*
• **flash/bolt of lightning**	faire (*v*) des éclairs	*fehr day zay-klehr*
	un coup d'éclair	*UH koo day-klehr*
mild	doux (*adj, m*)	*doo*
	douce (*f*)	*doos*
• **be mild**	faire doux	*fehr doo*
moon	lune (*f*)	*lewn*
mugginess	lourdeur (*f*)	*loord-ur*
• **muggy**	lourd (*adj, m*)	*loor*
	lourde (*f*)	*loord*
• **be muggy**	faire un temps lourd	*fehr UH tAH loor*
rain	pluie (*f*)	*plew-ee*
• **rain**	pleuvoir (*v*)	*pluh-vwar*
• **It's rainy.**	Il fait un temps pluvieux.	*eel feh UH tAH plewv-yuh*
sea	mer (*f*)	*mehr*
shadow, shade	ombre (*f*)	*OH-bre*
sky	ciel (*m*)	*syehl*
snow	neige (*f*)	*neh-zh*
• **snow**	neiger (*v*)	*nay-zh-ay*
star	étoile (*f*)	*ay-twal*
storm	tempête (*f*)	*tAH-peht*
sun	soleil (*m*)	*sul-ay*
thunder, clap of thunder	tonnerre (*m*)	*tun-ehr*
	coup de tonnerre (*m*)	*kood-tun-ehr*
• **thunder**	faire un bruit de tonnerre	*fehr UH brew-ee de tun-ehr*
	tonner	*tun-ay*
tornado	tornade (*f*)	*tor-nad*

weather	temps (*m*)	*tAH*
• The weather is beautiful.	Il fait beau temps.	*eel feh bo tAH*

The weather is rotten. = Il fait un temps pourri. *eel feh UH tAH poo-ree*

---

wind	vent (*m*)	*vAH*
• be windy	faire (*v*) du vent	*fehr dew vAH*

b. REACTING TO THE WEATHER

be cold	avoir (*v*) froid	*avwar frwa*
• I am cold.	J'ai froid.	*zh-ay frwa*
be hot	avoir (*v*) chaud	*avwar sho*
• I am hot.	J'ai chaud.	*zh-ay sho*
have chills	être (*v*) frileux (frileuse)	*eh-tre free-luh (free-luhz)*
I can't stand the cold.	Je ne supporte pas le froid.	*zhen sew-port pahl frwa*
I can't stand the heat.	Je ne supporte pas la chaleur.	*zhen sew-port pah la sha-lur*
I love the cold.	J'aime le froid.	*zh-ehm le frwa*
I love the heat.	J'aime la chaleur.	*zh-ehm la sha-lur*
perspire	transpirer (*v*)	*trAH-spee-ray*
warm up	se chauffer (*v*)	*se-sho-fay*

c. WEATHER-MEASURING INSTRUMENTS AND ACTIVITIES

barometer	baromètre (*m*)	*ba-rum-eht-re*
• barometric pressure	pression (*f*) barométrique	*prehs-yOH ba-rum-ay-treek*
Celsius	Celsius	*sehl-see-ews*
Centigrade	centigrade (*adj*)	*sAH-tee-grad*
degree	degré (*m*)	*de-gray*
Fahrenheit	Fahrenheit	*fa-rehn-a-eet*
mercury	mercure (*m*)	*mehr-kewr*
minus	moins (*adv*)	*mwEH*
plus	plus (*adv*)	*plew(s)*
temperature	température (*f*)	*tAH-pay-ra-tewr*
• high	élevée (*adj*)	*ayl-vay*
• low	basse (*adj*)	*bahs*
• maximum	maximum (*adj*)	*mak-see-mum*
• minimum	minimum (*adj*)	*mee-nee-mum*
thermometer	thermomètre (*m*)	*tehrm-u-meht-re*
• boiling point	point (*m*) d'ébullition	*pwEH day-bewl-ee-syOH*
• melting point	point (*m*) de fusion	*pwEH de few-zyOH*

thermostat	thermostat (*m*)	*tehr-mus-ta*
weather forecast	prévision (*f*) scientifique du temps	*pray-veez-yOH syAH-tee-feek dew tAH*
	météo (*f*)	*may-tay-oh*
weather report, bulletin	bulletin (*m*) météorologique	*bewltEH may-tay-u-ru-lu-zh-eek*
zero	zéro (*m*)	*zay-ro*
• **above zero**	dessus zéro	*de-sew zay-ro*
• **below zero**	dessous zéro	*de-soo zay-ro*

7. COLORS

a. BASIC COLORS

What color is it?	De quelle couleur est-ce?	*de kehl koo-lur eh-ss*
It's . . .	C'est . . .	*seh*
• **black**	noir	*nwar*
• **blue**	bleu	*bluh*
• **dark blue**	bleu foncé	*bluh fOH-say*
• **light blue**	bleu clair	*bluh klehr*
• **brown**	brun, marron	*brUH, marOH*
• **gold**	or de couleur	*or-de-koo-lur*
	doré	*du-ray*
• **gray**	gris	*gree*
• **green**	vert	*vehr*
• **orange**	orangé	*or-AH-zh-ay*
• **pink**	rose	*rohz*
• **purple**	pourpre	*poor-pre*
	violet	*vyuh-leh*
• **red**	rouge	*roozh*
• **silver**	argenté	*ar-zh-AH-tay*
• **white**	blanc (*m*)	*blAH*
	blanche (*f*)	*blAH-sh*
• **yellow**	jaune	*zh-ohn*

---

to see life through rose-colored glasses = voir la vie en rose *vwar la vee AH rohz*
to be white with fear = être vert de peur *eh-tre vehr de pur* (literally, green with fear)
to become red with anger = devenir rouge de colère *devneer roozh de kul-ehr*
to force an uneasy smile = sourire jaune *soo-reer zh-ohn*

b. DESCRIBING COLORS

bright	éclatant	*ay-klat-AH*
dark	sombre	*sOH-bre*
	foncé	*fOH-say*
dull	terne	*tehrn*
light	clair	*klehr*
lively	vif	*veef*
opaque	opaque	*↓p-ak*
pale	pâle	*pahl*
pure	pur	*pewr*
transparent	transparent	*tr-AH-spar-AH*
vibrant	vibrant	*veebr-AH*

c. ADDITIONAL VOCABULARY: COLORS

color	couleur (*f*)	*koo-lur*
• **color**	colorer (*v*)	*kul-u-ray*
• **colored**	coloré(e) (*adj, m, f*)	*kul-u-ray*
• **coloring**	colorant (*m*)	*kul-ur-AH*
• **food coloring**	colorant alimentaire	*kul-ur-AH aleem-AH-tehr*
crayon	crayon (*m*) de couleur	*kreh-y-OH de koo-lur*
felt-tip pen	stylo-feutre (*m*)	*stee-loh fuh-tre*
paint	peindre (*v*)	*pEH-dre*
painter	peintre (*m*)	*pEH-tre*
	femme peintre (*f*)	*fam pEH-tre*
pen	stylo (*m*)	*stee-lo*
• **ballpoint**	pointe à bille	*pwEHt-a-bee*
tint	teinte (*f*)	*tEHt*
• **tint**	teindre (*v*)	*tEH-dre*

8. BASIC GRAMMAR

a. GRAMMATICAL TERMS

> For French grammar explained simply with many examples in French and English, please consult the Barron's book, *Master the Basics: French*, by Kendris.

adjective	adjectif (*m*)	*ad-zh-ehk-teef*
• **demonstrative**	démonstratif (*adj*)	*daym-OH-stra-teef*
• **descriptive**	descriptif (*adj*)	*dehs-kreep-teef*
• **indefinite**	indéfini (*adj*)	*EH-day-fee-nee*
• **interrogative**	interrogatif (*adj*)	*EH-teh-rug-a-teef*
• **possessive**	possessif (*adj*)	*puss-ay-seef*
• **predicate**	attribut (*m*)	*a-tree-bew*

adverb	adverbe (*m*)	ad-vehrb
alphabet	alphabet (*m*)	al-fa-beh
• accent	accent (*m*)	aks-AH
• consonant	consonne (*f*)	kOH-sun
• letter	lettre (*f*)	leht-re
• phonetics	phonétique (*f*)	fun-ay-teek
• pronunciation	prononciation (*f*)	prun-OH-syah-sy-OH
• vowel	voyelle (*f*)	vwa-yehl
article	article (*m*)	ar-teekle
• definite	défini (*adj*)	day-fee-nee
• indefinite	indéfini (*adj*)	EH-day-fee-nee
clause	proposition (*f*)	pru-poh-zee-syOH
• main	principale (*adj*)	prEH-see-pal
• relative	relative (*adj*)	re-la-teev
• subordinate	subordonnée (*adj*)	sew-bor-dun-ay
comparison	comparaison (*f*)	kOH-par-ayz-OH
conjunction	conjonction (*f*)	kOH-zh-OH-ksyOH
discourse	discours (*m*)	dees-koor
• direct	direct (*adj*)	deer-ehkt
• indirect	indirect (*adj*)	EH-deer-ehkt
gender	genre (*m*)	zh-AH-re
• masculine	masculin (*m*)	mas-kewl-EH
• feminine	féminin (*m*)	fay-meen-EH
grammar	grammaire (*f*)	gram-ehr
interrogative	interrogatif (*m*)	EH-teh-rug-a-teef
mood	mode (*m*)	mud
• conditional	conditionnel (*adj*)	kOH-dee-sy-un-ehl
• imperative	impératif (*adj*)	EH-pay-ra-teef
• indicative	indicatif (*adj*)	EH-dee-ka-teef
• subjunctive	subjonctif (*adj*)	sewb-zh-OH-kteef
noun	nom (*m*)	nOH
number	nombre (*m*)	nOH-bre
• plural	pluriel (*adj*)	plew-ry-ehl
• singular	singulier (*adj*)	sEH-gewl-yay
object	complément d'objet (*m*)	kOH-playm-AH dub-zh-eh
• direct	direct (*adj*)	deer-ehkt
• indirect	indirect (*adj*)	EH-deer-ehkt
participle	participe (*m*)	par-tee-seep
• past	passé (*adj*)	pah-say
• present	présent (*adj*)	prayz-AH
partitive	partitif (*m*)	par-tee-teef
person	personne (*f*)	pehr-sun
• first	première (*adj*)	prem-yehr
• second	deuxième (*adj*)	duhz-yehm
• third	troisième (*adj*)	trwahz-yehm
predicate	prédicat (*m*)	pray-dee-ka
preposition	préposition (*f*)	pray-poh-zee-sy-OH

pronoun	pronom (*m*)	*pro-nOH*
• demonstrative	démonstratif (*adj*)	*daym-OH-stra-teef*
• interrogative	interrogatif (*adj*)	*EH-teh-rug-a-teef*
• object	complément d'objet (*m*)	*kOH-playm-AH dub-zh-eh*
• personal	personnel (*adj*)	*pehr-sun-ehl*
• possessive	possessif (*adj*)	*puss-ay-seef*
• reflexive	personnel réfléchi (*adj*)	*pehr-sun-ehl ray-flay-shee*
• relative	relatif (*adj*)	*re-la-teef*
• subject	sujet (*m*)	*sew-zh-eh*
sentence	phrase (*f*)	*frahz*
• declarative	déclarative (*adj*)	*day-klar-a-teev*
• interrogative	interrogative (*adj*)	*EH-teh-rug-a-teev*
subject	sujet (*m*)	*sew-zh-eh*
tense	temps (*m*)	*tAH*
• future	futur (*m*)	*few-tewr*
• imperfect	imparfait (*m*)	*EH-par-feh*
• past	passé composé (*m*)	*pah-say kOH-poh-zay*
• past definite	passé simple (*m*)	*pah-say sEH-ple*
• perfect	parfait (*m*)	*par-feh*
• pluperfect	plus-que-parfait (*m*)	*plews-ke-par-feh*
• present	présent (*m*)	*prayz-AH*
verb	verbe (*m*)	*vehrb*
• active	actif (*adj*)	*ak-teef*
• conjugation	conjugaison (*f*)	*kOH-zh-ew-gehz-OH*
• gerund	gérondif (*m*)	*zh-ayr-OH-deef*
• infinitive	infinitif (*m*)	*EH-fee-nee-teef*
• intransitive	intransitif (*adj*)	*EH-tr-AH-see-teef*
• irregular	irrégulier (*adj*)	*eer-ray-gewl-yay*
• modal	modal (*adj*)	*mud-al*
• passive	passif (*adj*)	*pah-seef*
• reflexive	pronominal (*adj*)	*pru-num-ee-nal*
• regular	régulier (*adj*)	*ray-gewl-yay*
• transitive	transitif (*adj*)	*tr-AH-see-teef*

b. DEFINITE ARTICLES

the	le (*m, s*)	*le*
	la (*f, s*)	*la*
	l' (*m/f, s*)	*l*
	les (*m/f, pl*)	*lay*

FOCUS: The Definite Article System

SINGULAR		PLURAL
With Feminine Nouns		
la	*(before any consonant)* ——————→	les
l'	*(before any vowel or silent h)* ——→	
With Masculine Nouns		
le	*(before any consonant)* ——————→	les
l'	*(before any vowel or silent h)* ——→	

c. INDEFINITE ARTICLES

a, an   un *(m, s)*   *UH*
                            une *(f, s)*   *ewn*

FOCUS: The Indefinite Article System

WITH FEMININE NOUNS		WITH MASCULINE NOUNS	
une	*(before any consonant)*	un	*(before any consonant)*
une	*(before any vowel or silent h)*	un	*(before any vowel or silent h)*

d. THE PARTITIVE

some (any)   du *(m, s)*   *dew*
                            de l' *(m, s)*   *del*
                            de la *(f, s)*   *de la*
                            de l' *(f, s)*   *del*
                            des *(m/f, pl)*   *day*

FOCUS: The Partitive System

Simple Affirmative

J'ai **du** *café.* / I have some coffee.
J'ai **de la** *viande.* / I have some meat.
J'ai **de l'***eau.* / I have some water.
J'ai **des** *bonbons.* / I have some candy.

Simple Negative

Je **n'***ai* **pas de** *café.* / I don't have any coffee.
Je **n'***ai* **pas de** *viande.* / I don't have any meat.
Je **n'***ai* **pas d'***eau.* / I don't have any water.
Je **n'***ai* **pas de** *bonbons.* / I don't have any candy.

With an Adjective

J'ai **de jolis** *chapeaux.* / I have some pretty hats.
J'ai **de jolies** *robes.* / I have some pretty dresses.

Tip: French speakers don't always use the partitive when ordering something to eat or drink. For example, in France you will hear a customer ask for *un café, un thé,* rather than *du café, du thé* in a restaurant or coffee shop. Why? Because the pronunciation of *du* may be mistaken for *deux* and you may be served two cups of coffee instead of one.

---

e. DEMONSTRATIVE ADJECTIVES

this, that	ce (*m, s*)	*se*
	cet (*m, s*)	*seht*
	cette (*f, s*)	*seht*
these, those	ces (*m/f, pl*)	*say*

FOCUS: The Demonstrative Adjective System

Ce garçon est beau. / This boy is handsome.
Cet arbre est beau. / This tree is beautiful.
Cette femme est belle. / This woman is beautiful.
Ces hommes sont beaux. / These men are handsome.
Ces livres sont beaux. / These books are beautiful.
Ces dames sont belles. / These ladies are beautiful.

If you wish to make a contrast between "this" and "that" or "these" and "those," add *-ci* (this, these) or *-là* (that, those) to the noun with a hyphen.

Ce garçon-ci est plus fort que ce garçon-là. / This boy is stronger than that boy.

The form *cet* is used in front of a masculine singular noun or adjective beginning with a vowel or silent *h: cet arbre, cet homme*.
If there is more than one noun, a demonstrative adjective must be used in front of each noun: *cette dame et ce monsieur*.

For French grammar explained simply with many examples in French and English, please consult the Barron's book, *Master the Basics: French*, by Kendris.

---

f. POSSESSIVE ADJECTIVES

my	mon (*m, s*)	*mOH*
	ma (*f, s*)	*ma*
	mes (*m/f, pl*)	*may*
your (*pol*)	votre (*m/f, s*)	*vutr*
	vos (*m/f, pl*)	*vo*
your (*fam*)	ton (*m, s*)	*tOH*
	ta (*f, s*)	*ta*
	tes (*m,/f , pl*)	*tay*
his, her	son (*m, s*)	*sOH*
	sa (*f, s*)	*sa*
	ses (*m/f, pl*)	*say*
our	notre (*m/f, s*)	*nutr*
	nos (*m/f, pl*)	*no*
their	leur (*m/f, s*)	*lur*
	leurs (*m/f, pl*)	*lur*

FOCUS: The Possessive Adjective System

MASCULINE	
Singular	**Plural**
mon livre/my book	*mes livres*/my books
ton stylo/your pen	*tes stylos*/your pens
son ballon/his (her, its) balloon	*ses ballons*/his (her, its) balloons
notre parapluie/our umbrella	*nos parapluies*/our umbrellas
votre sandwich/your sandwich	*vos sandwiches*/your sandwiches
leur gâteau/their cake	*leurs gâteaux*/their cakes

FEMININE	
Singular	**Plural**
ma robe/my dress	*mes robes*/my dresses
ta jaquette/your jacket	*tes jaquettes*/your jackets
sa balle/his (her, its) ball	*ses balles*/his (her, its) balls
notre maison/our house	*nos maisons*/our houses
votre voiture/your car	*vos voitures*/your cars
leur sœur/their sister	*leurs sœurs*/their sisters

g. PREPOSITIONS

among	parmi	*par-mee*
at	à	*a*
between	entre	*AH-tre*
for	pour	*poor*
from	de	*de*
in	dans	*dAH*
of	de	*de*
on	sur	*sewr*
to	à	*a*
with	avec	*av-ehk*

FOCUS: Prepositional Contractions

Preposition	Article			Contraction
à *a*	+	le *le*	=	au *oh*
	+	les *lay*	=	aux *oh*
de *de*	+	le *le*	=	du *dew*
	+	les *lay*	=	des *day*

h. SUBJECT PRONOUNS

I	je	*zhe*
you	tu (*s, fam*)	*tew*
you	vous (*s, pol*)	*voo*
he, it	il	*eel*
she, it	elle	*ehl*
one	on (*indef*)	*OH*
we	nous	*noo*
you	vous (*pl*)	*voo*
they	ils (*m*)	*eel*
	elles (*f*)	*ehl*

i. DIRECT OBJECT PRONOUNS

me	me	*me*
you	te (*s, fam*)	*te*
you	vous (*s, pol*)	*voo*
him	le	*le*
her	la	*la*
it	le (*m*)	*le*
	la (*f*)	*la*
us	nous	*noo*
you	vous (*pl*)	*voo*
them	les	*lay*

FOCUS: Direct Object Pronouns

Person	Singular	Plural
1st	*me* (*m'*)/me	*nous*/us
2d	*te* (*t'*)/you (familiar)	*vous*/you (singular polite or plural)
3d	*le*(*l'*)/him, it	*les*/them (persons or things)
	la (*l'*)/her, it (person or thing)	

j. INDIRECT OBJECT PRONOUNS

to me	me	*me*
to you	te (*s, fam*)	*te*
	vous (*s, pol*)	*voo*
to him/to her	lui	*lew-ee*
to us	nous	*noo*
to you	vous (*pl*)	*voo*
to them	leur	*lur*

Note: For an explanation of French grammar and rules, please consult Barron's *French Now!* third edition by Kendris or any of the Barron's French grammar books. This book contains basic French vocabulary arranged by topics of general interest to build your word power.

FOCUS: Indirect Object Pronouns

Person	Singular	Plural
1st	*me* (*m'*) to me	*nous* to us
2d	*te* (*t'*) to you (familiar)	*vous* to you (singular polite or plural)
3d	*lui* to him, to her	*leur* to them

k. REFLEXIVE PRONOUNS (ALL BEFORE VERBS)

myself	me	*me*
yourself	te (*s, fam*)	*te*
yourself	vous (*s, pol*)	*voo*
himself/herself/ oneself	se	*se*
ourselves	nous	*noo*
yourselves	vous	*voo*
themselves	se	*se*

FOCUS: Reflexive Pronouns

Person	Singular	Plural
1st 2d	*je me lave* *tu te laves*	*nous nous lavons* *vous vous lavez*
3rd	{ *il se lave* { *elle se lave* { *on se lave*	{ *ils se lavent* { *elles se lavent*

l. DISJUNCTIVE PRONOUNS

FOCUS: Disjunctive Pronouns (as objects of prepositions)

Person	Singular		Plural	
1st 2nd	*moi* *toi*	me, I you (familiar)	*nous* *vous*	us, we you (formal singular or plural)
3rd	{ *soi* { *lui* { *elle*	oneself him, he her, she	{ *eux* { *elles*	them, they (m.) them, they (f.)

For French grammar explained simply with many examples in French and English, please consult the Barron's book, *Master the Basics: French*, by Kendris.

m. DEMONSTRATIVE PRONOUNS

FOCUS: Demonstrative Pronouns

	Singular	Plural
Masculine	*celui*/the one	*ceux*/the ones
Feminine	*celle*/the one	*celles*/the ones

n. POSSESSIVE PRONOUNS

FOCUS: Possessive Pronouns

MASCULINE

	Singular		Plural
le mien	mine	*les miens*	mine
le tien	yours (familiar)	*les tiens*	yours (familiar)
le sien	his, hers, its	*les siens*	his, hers, its
le nôtre	ours	*les nôtres*	ours
le vôtre	yours	*les vôtres*	yours
le leur	theirs	*les leurs*	theirs

FEMININE

	Singular		Plural
la mienne	mine	*les miennes*	mine
la tienne	yours (familiar)	*les tiennes*	yours (familiar)
la sienne	his, hers, its	*les siennes*	his, hers, its
la nôtre	ours	*les nôtres*	ours
la vôtre	yours	*les vôtres*	yours
la leur	theirs	*les leurs*	theirs

FOCUS: Word Order of Pronouns in Four Types of Sentences

Declarative Sentence with a Verb in a Simple Tense (e.g., present)

$$\text{SUBJECT} \rightarrow \textbf{ne (n')} + \begin{Bmatrix} me\ (m') \\ te\ (t') \\ se\ (s') \\ nous \\ vous \end{Bmatrix} \text{OR} \begin{Bmatrix} le \\ la \\ l' \\ les \end{Bmatrix} \text{AND/OR} \begin{Bmatrix} lui \\ leur \end{Bmatrix}$$

OR *y* + *en* + **VERB** → *pas*

TIP: Follow the words in the model sentences below with the basic word order given above.

Affirmative	Negative
1. **Je le leur dis.** I am telling it to them.	1. **Je ne le leur dis pas.** I am not telling it to them.
2. **Robert m'en donne un peu.** Robert is giving me a little of it.	2. **Robert ne m'en donne pas un peu.** Robert is not giving me a little of it.
3. **Elle nous les montre.** She is showing them to us.	3. **Elle ne nous les montre pas.** She is not showing them to us.
4. **Il y a des mouches dans le lait.** There are flies in the milk.	4. **Il n'y en a pas dans le lait.** There aren't any (of them) in the milk.

Declarative Sentence with a Verb in a Compound Tense
(e.g., passé composé)

$$\textbf{SUBJECT} \to \textit{ne (n')} + \begin{Bmatrix} me\ (m') \\ te\ (t') \\ se\ (s') \\ nous \\ vous \end{Bmatrix} \text{OR} \begin{Bmatrix} le \\ la \\ l' \\ les \end{Bmatrix} \text{AND/OR} \begin{Bmatrix} lui \\ leur \end{Bmatrix}$$

OR *y + en* + **VERB** → *pas* + past participle
(auxiliary verb
avoir or *être* in
a simple tense)

TIP: Follow the words in the model sentences below with the basic word order given above.

Affirmative

1. **Louis m'a donné les pommes.**
   Louis gave me the apples.

2. **Louis me les a données.**
   Louis gave them to me.

3. **Les cerises? Je les leur ai offertes.**
   The cherries? I have offered them to them.

Negative

1. **Louis ne m'a pas donné les pommes.**
   Louis has not given me the apples.

2. **Louis ne me les a pas données.**
   Louis has not given them to me.

3. **Les cerises? Je ne les leur ai pas offertes.**
   The cherries? I did not offer them to them.

Affirmative Imperative Sentence

$$\textbf{VERB} + \begin{Bmatrix} le \\ la \\ l' \\ les \end{Bmatrix} \text{OR} \begin{Bmatrix} moi\ (m') \\ toi\ (t') \\ nous \\ vous \end{Bmatrix} \text{AND/OR} \begin{Bmatrix} lui \\ leur \end{Bmatrix} \text{OR } y + en$$

TIP: Follow the words in the model sentences below with the basic word order given above. Then, compare these affirmative imperatives with those in the negative models that follow.

1. **Écrivez la lettre à Julie.**
   Write the letter to Julie.

2. **Écrivez-la.**
   Write it.

3. **Écrivez-la-lui**
   Write it to her.

4. **Répondez à la question.**
   Reply to the question.

5. **Répondez-y.**
   Reply to it.

6. **Donnez m'en.**
   Give me some (of it).

Negative Imperative Sentence

$$\text{Ne (N')} + \begin{Bmatrix} me\ (m') \\ te\ (t') \\ nous \\ vous \end{Bmatrix} \text{OR} \begin{Bmatrix} le \\ la \\ l' \\ les \end{Bmatrix} \text{OR} \begin{Bmatrix} lui \\ leur \end{Bmatrix} \text{OR}\ y$$

$$+\ en + \textbf{VERB} \rightarrow pas$$

TIP: Follow the words in the model sentences below with the basic word order given above. Then, compare these negative imperatives with those in the affirmative models on p. 47.

1. **N'écrivez pas la lettre à Julie.**
   Don't write the letter to Julie.
2. **Ne l'écrivez pas.**
   Don't write it.
3. **Ne la lui écrivez pas.**
   Don't write it to her.
4. **Ne répondez pas à la question.**
   Don't reply to the question.
5. **N'y répondez pas.**
   Don't reply to it.
6. **Ne m'en donnez pas.**
   Don't give me any (of it).

---

o. **OTHER PRONOUNS**

everyone	tout le monde (*m*)	*tool mOHd*
everything	tout (*m*)	*too*
	toute (*f*)	*toot*
no one	personne (*indef*)	*pehr-sun*
one (*in general*)	on (*indef*)	*OH*
others	autrui (*indef*)	*oh-trew-ee*
	les autres	*lay-zoh-tre*
some, of it, of them	en (*before or after a verb*)	*AH*
some (*people*)	des gens	*day zh-AH*
someone	quelqu'un (*m*)	*kehlk-UH*
	quelqu'une (*f*)	*kehlk-ewn*
something	quelque chose	*kehlke sh-oh-z*

p. **CONJUNCTIONS**

although	bien que	*byEH-ke*
	quoique	*kwa-ke*
and	et	*ay*
as (*since*)	comme	*kum*
as if	comme si	*kum-see*
as soon as	dès que	*deh-ke*
	aussitôt que	*oh-see-toh-ke*
because	parce que	*pars-ke*
but	mais	*meh*
even though	même si	*mehm-see*

however	pourtant	*poor-tAH*
if	si	*see*
in order that, so	afin que	*afEH-ke*
** that**	pour que	*poor-ke*
nevertheless	néanmoins	*nay-AH-mwEH*
or	ou	*oo*
provided that	pourvu que	*poor-vew-ke*
since	depuis que	*de-pew-ee-ke*
therefore, consequently	donc	*dOHk*
unless	à moins que	*a-mwEH-ke*
until	jusqu'à ce que	*zn-ews-kas-ke*
when	quand	*kAH*
while, whereas	tandis que	*tAH-dee-ke*

9. REQUESTING INFORMATION

answer	réponse (*f*)	*rayp-OH-s*
• answer	répondre (*v*)	*rayp-OH-dre*
ask (for)	demander (*v*)	*dem-AH-day*
• make a request	faire une demande	*fehr ewn dem-AH-de*
Can you tell	Pourriez-vous me	*poor-ee-ay voom deer*
** me . . . ?**	dire . . . ? (*pol*)	
	Peux-tu me dire	*puh-tewm deer*
	. . . ? (*fam*)	
How?	Comment?	*kum-AH*
How come?	Mais comment?	*meh*
		kum-AH
How much?	Combien?	*kOH-byEH*
I don't understand.	Je ne comprends	*zhen kOH-pr-AH pah*
	pas.	
So?	Et alors?	*ay al-or*
What?	Comment?	*kum-AH*
	Pardon?	*pard-OH*
	Quoi?	*kwah*
What do you call this	Comment appelle-t-	*kum-AH a-pehl-tOH se-*
** (that) in French?**	on ceci (cela) en	*see (sla) AH frAH-seh*
	français?	
What does it mean?	Que veut dire cela?	*ke-vuh-deer-sla*
	Que signifie cela?	*ke-see-ny-ee-fee-sla*
When?	Quand?	*kAH*
Where?	Où?	*oo*
Which (one)?	Lequel? (*m*)	*le-kehl*
	Laquelle? (*f*)	*la-kehl*
Which (ones)?	Lesquels? (*m*)	*lay-kehl*
	Lesquelles? (*f*)	*lay-kehl*
Who?	Qui?	*kee*
Why?	Pourquoi?	*poor-kwa*

PEOPLE

10. FAMILY AND FRIENDS

a. FAMILY MEMBERS

aunt	tante (*f*)	*tAHt*
brother	frère (*m*)	*frehr*
• **brother-in-law**	beau-frère (*m*)	*boh-frehr*
cousin	cousin (*m*)	*koo-zEH*
	cousine (*f*)	*koo-zeen*
dad	papa (*m*)	*pa-pa*
daughter	fille (*f*)	*fee-y*
• **daughter-in-law**	belle-fille (*f*)	*behl-fee-y*
	bru (*f*)	*brew*
family	famille (*f*)	*fa-mee-y*
• **family relationship**	parenté (*f*)	*pa-rAH-tay*
father	père (*m*)	*pehr*
• **father-in-law**	beau-père (*m*)	*boh-pehr*
grandchildren	petits-enfants (*m, f, pl*)	*ptee-zAH-fAH*
grandfather	grand-père (*m*)	*grAH-pehr*
grandmother	grand-mère (*f*)	*grAH-mehr*
husband	mari (*m*)	*ma-ree*
mom	maman (*f*)	*ma-mAH*
mother	mère (*f*)	*mehr*
• **mother-in-law**	belle-mère (*f*)	*behl-mehr*
nephew	neveu (*m*)	*ne-vuh*
niece	nièce (*f*)	*nee-ehss*
parents	parents (*m, pl*)	*pa-rAH*
relatives	proches parents (*m, pl*)	*prush parAH*
sister	sœur (*f*)	*sur*
• **sister-in-law**	belle-sœur (*f*)	*behl-sur*
son	fils (*m*)	*fee-ss*
• **son-in-law**	gendre (*m*)	*zh-AH-dre*
twin	jumeau (*m*)	*zh-ew-moh*
	jumelle (*f*)	*zh-ew-mehl*
uncle	oncle (*m*)	*OH-kle*
wife	femme (*f*)	*fam*
	épouse (*f*)	*ay-pooz*

b. FRIENDS

acquaintance	connaissance (*f*)	*kun-eh-sAH-ss*
boyfriend	ami (*m*)	*a-mee*
	petit ami (*m*)	*ptee-a-mee*
chum	copain (*m*)	*kup-EH*
	copine (*f*)	*kup-een*
colleague, work **associate**	collègue (*m, f*)	*kul-ehg*
enemy	ennemi(e) (*m, f*)	*ehn-mee*
fiancé	fiancé (*m*)	*fee-AH-say*
fiancée	fiancée (*f*)	*fee-AH-say*
friend	ami(e) (*m, f*)	*a-mee*
• **become friends**	devenir (*v*) amis	*de-vneer-a-mee*
	faire (*v*) l'amitié	*fehr la-mee-tee-ay*
• **between friends**	entre amis	*AH-tre a-mee*
• **break off a** **friendship**	rompre (*v*) une amitié	*rOHm-pre ewn a-mee-* *tee-ay*
• **close friend**	ami(e) intime (*m, f*)	*a-mee EH-teem*
• **dear friend**	cher (chère) ami(e) (*m, f*)	*sh-ehr a-mee*
• **family friend**	ami(e) (*m, f*) de famille	*a-meed fa-mee-y*
• **friendship**	amitié (*f*)	*a-mee-tee-ay*
girlfriend	amie (*f*)	*a-mee*
	petite amie (*f*)	*ptee-ta-mee*
lover	amant (*m*)	*a-mAH*
	amante (*f*)	*a-mAH-t*
• **love affair**	affaire (*f*) d'amour	*a-fehr da-moor*
	une liaison	*ew-n-lee-yay-zOH*

11. DESCRIBING PEOPLE

a. GENDER AND APPEARANCE

attractive	attrayant, beau, bel (*adj, m*)	*a-treh-yAH, boh,* *behl*
	attrayante, belle (*f*)	*a-treh-yAHt, behl*
beautiful, handsome	beau (*adj, m*)	*both*
	bel (*adj, m*)	*behl*
	belle (*f*)	*behl*
• **beauty**	beauté (*f*)	*boh-tay*
big	grand (*adj, m*)	*grAH*
	grande (*f*)	*grAHd*
• **bigness**	grandeur (*f*)	*grAH-dur*
• **become big**	grandir (*v*)	*grAH-deer*
blond	blond (*m*)	*blOH*
• **blonde**	blonde (*f*)	*blOHd*

body	corps (*m*)	*kor*
boy	garçon (*m*)	*gar-sOH*
clean	propre (*adj*)	*pru-pre*
curly-haired	cheveux bouclés	*shvuh boo-klay*
	cheveux frisés	*shvuh free-zay*
dark-haired	cheveux bruns	*shvuh brUH*
dirty	sale (*adj*)	*sal*
elegance	élégance (*f*)	*ay-lay-gAH-ss*
• **elegant**	élégant (*adj, m*)	*ay-lay-gAH*
	élégante (*f*)	*ay-lay-gAH-t*
• **elegantly**	élégamment (*adv*)	*ay-lay-ga-mAH*
• **inelegant**	inélégant (*adj, m*)	*ee-nay-lay-gAH*
	inélégante (*f*)	*ee-nay-lay-gAH-t*
fat	gros (*adj, m*)	*groh*
	grosse (*f*)	*groh-ss*
• **become fat**	grossir (*v*)	*groh-seer*
• **obesity**	obésité (*f*)	*u-bay-zee-tay*
female	femelle (*f*)	*fe-mehl*
• **feminine**	féminin (*adj, m*)	*fay-mee-nEH*
	féminine (*f*)	*fay-mee-neen*
gentleman	monsieur (*m*)	*me-sy-uh*
girl	jeune fille (*f*)	*zh-uhn fee-y*
health	santé (*f*)	*sAH-tay*
• **healthy**	sain (*adj, m*)	*sEH*
	saine (*f*)	*sehn*
	en bonne santé	*AH bun sAH-tay*
height	taille (*f*)	*tah-y*
	stature (*f*)	*sta-tewr*
• **How tall are you?**	Quelle taille avez-vous?	*kehl tah-y avay-voo*
• **I am . . . tall.**	J'ai la taille . . .	*zh-ay la tah-y*
• **medium (average) height**	la taille moyenne	*la tah-y mwa-y-ehn*
• **short**	petit (*adj, m*)	*ptee*
	petite (*f*)	*pteet*
• **tall**	grand (*adj, m*)	*grAH*
	grande (*f*)	*grAHd*
lady	dame	*dahm*
• **young lady**	demoiselle	*de-mwah-zehl*
large	grand (*adj, m*)	*grAH*
	grande (*f*)	*grAHd*
male	mâle	*mahl*
• **masculine**	masculin	*mas-kew-lEH*
man	homme	*um*
• **young man**	jeune homme	*zh-un um*
physique (appearance)	aspect physique	*as-peh fee-zeek*

red-haired	roux *(adj, m)*	*roo*
	rousse *(f)*	*roos*
sex	sexe *(m)*	*sehks*
sick	malade *(adj)*	*ma-lahd*
• sickness	maladie *(f)*	*ma-lah-dee*
• become sick	tomber *(v)* malade	*tOH-bay ma-lahd*
small, little	petit *(adj, m/f)*	*ptee*
	petite *(f)*	*pteet*
strength	force *(f)*	*forss*
• strong	fort *(adj, m)*	*for*
	forte *(f)*	*fort*
ugly	laid *(adj, m)*	*leh*
	laide *(f)*	*lehd*
• ugliness	laideur *(f)*	*lehd-ur*
virile	viril(e) *(m, f)*	*vee-reel*
weak	faible *(adj)*	*feh-ble*
• weakness	faiblesse *(f)*	*feh-bless*
• become weak	s'affaiblir *(v)*	*sa-feh-bleer*
weight	poids *(m)*	*pwah*
• heavy	lourd *(adj, m)*	*loor*
	lourde *(f)*	*loord*
• How much do you weigh?	Combien pesez-vous?	*kOH-byEH pe-zay voo*
• I weigh . . .	Je pèse . . .	*zhe pehz*
• light	léger *(adj, m)*	*lay-zh-ay*
	légère *(f)*	*lay-zh-ehr*
• skinny, thin	maigre *(adj)*	*meh-gr*
• slim, slender	mince	*mEH-ss*
	svelte	*svehlt*
• weigh oneself	se peser *(refl v)*	*se pe-zay*
• become thin	maigrir *(v)*	*meh-greer*
• gain weight	prendre *(v)* du poids	*prAH-dre dew pwah*
• lose weight	perdre *(v)* du poids	*pehr-dre dew pwah*
woman	femme	*fam*

b. CONCEPTS OF AGE

adolescence	adolescence *(f)*	*a-du-leh-sAH-ss*
• adolescent, teenager	adolescent *(m)*	*a-du-leh-sAH*
	adolescente *(f)*	*a-du-leh-sAH-t*
adult	adulte *(m, f)*	*a-dewlt*
age	âge *(m)*	*ah-zh*
baby, child	bébé *(m)*	*bay-bay*
	enfant *(m, f)*	*AH-fAH*
• children	enfants	*AH-fAH*
boy	garçon	*gar-sOH*

elderly person	une personne âgée	*ewn pehr-sun ah-zh-ay*
• have white hair	avoir les cheveux blancs	*a-vwahr lay shvuh blAH*
girl	(jeune) fille	*(zh-un) fee-y*
grow up	grandir (v)	*grAH-deer*
old	vieux (m)	*vyuh*
	vieil (m)	*vy-eh-y*
	vieille (f)	*vy-eh-y*
• old age	vieillesse (f)	*vyeh-yehss*
• older	plus vieux	*plew vyuh*
• older brother	frère aîné	*frehr eh-nay*
• older sister	sœur aînée	*sur eh-nay*
• How old are you?	Quel âge avez-vous (pol)?	*kehl ah-zh a-vay voo*
	Quel âge as-tu (fam)?	*kehl ah-zh a tew*
• I am . . . old.	J'ai . . . ans.	*zh-ay AH*
• two-year-old	de deux ans	*de duh zAH*
• three-year-old	de trois ans	*de trwah zAH*
• become old	vieillir (v)	*vyeh-yeer*
young	jeune (adj)	*zh-un*
• younger	plus jeune	*plew zh-un*
• younger brother	frère cadet	*frehr ka-deh*
• younger sister	sœur cadette	*sur ka-deht*
• youth	jeunesse (f)	*zh-un-ehss*
• youthful	juvénile (adj)	*zh-ew-vay-neel*
	jeune (adj)	*zh-un*

c. MARRIAGE AND THE HUMAN LIFE CYCLE

anniversary	anniversaire (m)	*a-nee-vehr-sehr*
• diamond anniversary	noces (f, pl) de diamant	*nuss de dya-mAH*
• golden anniversary	noces d'or	*nuss dor*
• silver anniversary	noces d'argent	*nuss dar-zh-AH*
bachelor, unmarried	célibataire	*say-lee-ba-tehr*
birth	naissance (f)	*neh-sAH-ss*
• birthday	anniversaire (m)	*a-nee-vehr-sehr*
• celebrate one's birthday	fêter (v) l'anniversaire	*feh-tay la-nee-vehr-sehr*
• Happy birthday!	Bon anniversaire!	*bun-a-nee-vehr-sehr*
• be born	naître (v)	*neh-tre*
• I was born on . . .	Je suis né(e) le . . .	*zhe sew-ee nay le*
bride	mariée (f)	*ma-ree-ay*
death	mort (f)	*mor*
• die	mourir (v)	*moo-reer*

divorce	divorce (m)	*dee-vorss*
• divorce	divorcer (v)	*dee-vor-say*
• divorced	divorcé (m, adj)	*dee-vor-say*
	divorcée (f)	*dee-vor-say*
engagement	fiançailles (f, pl)	*fee-AH-sa-y*
• become engaged	se fiancer (refl v)	*se fee-AH-say*
• engaged	fiancé (adj)	*fee-AH-say*
fiancé	fiancé	*fee-AH-say*
fiancée	fiancée	*fee-AH-say*
get used to	s'habituer (v)	*sa-bee-tew-ay*
gift	cadeau (m)	*ka-doh*
• give a gift	donner (v) un cadeau	*dun-ay UH ka-doh*
go to school	aller (v) à l'école	*alay a lay-kul*
groom (bridegroom)	marié (m)	*ma-ree-ay*
heredity	hérédité (f)	*ay-ray-dee-tay*
• inherit	hériter (v)	*ay-ree-tay*
honeymoon	lune (f) de miel	*lewn de mee-ehl*
husband	époux	*ay-poo*
	mari	*ma-ree*
kiss	baiser (m)	*beh-zay*
• kiss	embrasser (v)	*AH-bra-say*
life	vie (f)	*vee*
• live	vivre (v)	*vee-vre*
love	amour (m)	*a-moor*
• love	aimer (v)	*ay-may*
• fall in love	tomber (v) amoureux	*tOH-bay a-moo-ruh*
• in love	amoureux (adj)	*a-moo-ruh*
marital status	état civil	*ay-ta see-veel*
marriage, matrimony	mariage (m)	*ma-ree-ah-zh*
• married	marié(e) (n, adj, m, f)	*ma-ree-ay*
• marry (someone)	épouser (v)	*ay-poo-zay*
	se marier (v) avec	*se-ma-ree-ay avehk*
• unmarried	célibataire	*say-lee-ba-tehr*
• newlyweds	nouveaux-mariés (n, m, pl)	*noo-voh ma-ree-ay*
pregnancy	grossesse (f)	*groh-seh-ss*
• be pregnant	être (v) enceinte	*eh-tre AH-sEHt*
• give birth	accoucher (v)	*a-koo-shay*
• have a baby	avoir (v) un enfant	*avwar UH nAH-fAH*
raise (someone)	élever (v)	*ayl-vay*
reception	réception (f)	*ray-sehp-syOH*
separation	séparation (f)	*say-pa-ra-syOH*
• separate	se séparer (v)	*se say-pa-ray*
• separated	séparé (adj)	*say-pa-ray*
spouse	époux (m)	*ay-poo*
	épouse (f)	*ay-pooz*

wedding	mariage (*m*)	*ma-ree-ah-zh*
	noce (*f*)	*nuss*
• **wedding invitation**	faire-part de mariage (*m*)	*fehr par de ma-ree-ah-zh*
• **wedding ring**	anneau (*m*) d'alliance	*a-noh da-lee-AH-ss*
	alliance (*f*)	*a-lee-AH-ss*
	anneau (*m*) de mariage	*a-nohd-ma-ree-ah-zh*
widow	veuve	*vuv*
widower	veuf	*vuf*
wife	femme	*fam*
	épouse	*ay-pooz*

d. RELIGION AND RACE

> For nationalities see Section 30.

agnostic	agnostique (*adj/m, f*)	*ag-nus-teek*
archbishop	archevêque	*arsh-vehk*
atheism	athéisme (*m*)	*a-tay-ee-sm*
• **atheist**	athée (*m, f*)	*a-tay*
baptism	baptême (*m*)	*ba-tehm*
belief	crédence (*f*)	*kray-dAH-ss*
	croyance (*f*)	*krwah-yAH-ss*
• **believe**	croire (*v*)	*krwar*
• **believe in**	croire (*v*) en	*krwahr AH*
• **believer**	croyant (*m*)	*krwa-yAH*
	croyante (*f*)	*krwa-yAHt*
bishop	évêque	*ay-vehk*
Buddhism	Bouddhisme (*m*)	*boo-dees-me*
• **Buddhist**	Bouddhiste (*m, f*)	*boo-deest*
catechism	catéchisme (*m*)	*ka-tay-shee-sme*
Catholic	Catholique (*adj*)	*ka-tul-eek*
• **Catholicism**	Catholicisme (*m*)	*ka-tul-ee-sees-me*
Christian	Chrétien (*m*)	*kray-tee-yEH*
	Chrétienne (*f*)	*kray-tee-yehn*
• **Christianity**	Christianisme (*m*)	*krees-tee-a-nee-sme*
church	église (*f*)	*ay-gleez*
confirmation	confirmation (*f*)	*kOH-feer-ma-syOH*
faith	foi (*f*)	*fwa*
• **faithful**	fidèle (*adj*)	*fee-dehl*
God	Dieu	*dyuh*
Hebrew, Jewish	Hébreu	*ay-bruh*
	juif (*m*)	*zh-ew-eef*
	juive (*f*)	*zh-ew-eev*
human	humain (*m*)	*ew-mEH*
	humaine (*f*)	*ew-mehn*

• **human being**	être humain (*m*)	*eh-tre ew-mEH*
• **humanity**	humanité (*f*)	*ew-ma-nee-tay*
Hindu	Hindou (*n/adj, m*)	*EH-doo*
	Hindoue (*n/adj, f*)	*EH-doo*
Islamic	Islamique (*adj*)	*ee-sla-meek*
layperson	laïc, laïque (*adj, m, f*)	*la-eek*
• **laity, secularism**	laïcité (*f*)	*la-ee-see-tay*
Mass	Messe (*f*)	*mehss*
minister	ministre (*m*)	*mee-nee-stre*
monk	moine	*mwahn*
mosque	mosquée (*f*)	*mus-kay*
Muslim	Musulman (*m*)	*mew-zewl-mAH*
	Musulmane (*f*)	*mew-zewl-mahn*
myth	mythe (*m*)	*meet*
nun	religieuse	*re-lee-zh-yuhz*
oriental	oriental(e) (*m, f*)	*or-yAH-tal*
Orthodox	Orthodoxe	*or-tud-uks*
pagan	païen (*n/adj, m*)	*pa-yEH*
	païenne (*n, adj, f*)	*pa-yehn*
people	gens (*m & f, pl*)	*zh-AH*
person	personne (*f*)	*pehr-sun*
pray	prier (*v*)	*pree-yay*
• **prayer**	prière (*f*)	*pree-yehr*
priest	prêtre (*m*)	*preh-tre*
Protestant	Protestant (*m*)	*pru-tehs-tAH*
	Protestante (*f*)	*pru-tehs-tAHt*
• **Protestantism**	Protestantisme (*m*)	*pru-tehs-tAH-tees-me*
rabbi	rabbin	*ra-bEH*
race	race (*f*)	*rass*
religion	religion (*f*)	*re-lee-zh-yOH*
• **religious**	pieux (*adj, m*)	*pyuh*
	pieuse (*f*)	*pyuhz*
rite	rite (*m*)	*reet*
soul	âme (*f*)	*ahm*
spirit	esprit (*m*)	*ehs-pree*
• **spiritual**	spirituel(le) (*adj, m, f*)	*spee-ree-tew-ehl*
synagogue	synagogue (*f*)	*see-na-gug*
temple	temple (*m*)	*tAH-ple*
western	occidental(e) (*adj, m, f*)	*uks-ee-dAH-tal*

e. CHARACTERISTICS AND SOCIAL TRAITS

active	actif (*adj, m*)	*ak-teef*
	active (*f*)	*ak-teev*
• **activity**	activité (*f*)	*ak-tee-vee-tay*

adapt	adapter (*v*)	*a-dap-tay*
• **adaptable**	adaptable (*adj*)	*a-dap-ta-bl*
affection	affection (*f*)	*a-fehk-syOH*
• **affectionate**	affectueux (*adj, m*)	*a-fehk-tew-uh*
	affectueuse (*f*)	*a-fehk-tew-uhz*
aggressive	agressif (*adj, m*)	*a-greh-seef*
	agressive (*f*)	*a-greh-seev*
• **aggressiveness**	agressivité (*f*)	*a-greh-see-vee-tay*
altruism	altruisme (*m*)	*al-trew-ee-sm*
• **altruistic,**	altruiste (*m/f*)	*al-trew-eest*
altruist		
ambition	ambition (*f*)	*AH-bee-syOH*
• **ambitious**	ambitieux (*adj, m*)	*AH-bee-syuh*
	ambitieuse (*f*)	*AH-bee-syuhz*
anger	colère (*f*)	*kul-ehr*
• **angry**	en colère	*AH kul-ehr*
	fâché(e) (*adj*)	*fah-shay*
• **become angry**	se fâcher (*v*)	*se fah-shay*
anxious	anxieux (*adj, m*)	*AH-ksyuh*
	anxieuse (*f*)	*AH-ksyuhz*
• **anxiousness**	anxiété (*f*)	*AH-ksee-ay-tay*
arrogant	arrogant (*adj, m*)	*a-rug-AH*
	arrogante (*f*)	*a-rug-AHt*
art	art (*m*)	*ar*
artistic, talented	artistique (*adj*)	*ar-tees-teek*
astute	astucieux (*adj, m*)	*a-stew-syuh*
	astucieuse (*f*)	*a-stew-syuhz*
• **astuteness**	astuce (*f*)	*a-stewss*
attractive	attrayant, beau, bel (*adj, m*)	*a-treh-yAH, boh, behl*
	attrayante, belle (*f*)	*a-treh-yAHt, behl*
avarice, greed	avarice (*f*)	*a-va-rees*
• **avaricious,**	avare (*adj, n*)	*a-var*
greedy		
bad, mean	méchant (*adj, m*)	*may-shAH*
	méchante (*f*)	*may-shAHt*
• **meanness**	méchanceté (*f*)	*may-shAH-stay*
brash, bold	effronté(e) (*adj*)	*ay-frOH-tay*
brilliant	brillant(e) (*adj*)	*bree-yAH(t)*
calm	calme (*adj*)	*kalm*
• **calmness**	calme (*m*)	*kalm*
character	caractère (*m*)	*ka-rak-tehr*
• **characteristic**	caractéristique (*adj, n, f*)	*ka-rak-tay-rees-teek*
• **characterize**	caractériser (*v*)	*ka-rak-tay-ree-zay*
conformist	conformiste (*m, f*)	*kOH-form-eest*
• **nonconformist**	non-conformiste (*m, f*)	*nOH-kOH-form-eest*

conscience	conscience *(f)*	*kOH-syAH-ss*
• conscientious	consciencieux *(adj, m)*	*kOH-syAH-syuh*
	consciencieuse *(f)*	*kOH-syAH-syuhz*
conservative	conservateur *(adj, m)*	*kOH-sehr-va-tur*
	conservatrice *(f)*	*kOH-sehr-va-treess*
courage	courage *(m)*	*koo-ra-zh*
• courageous	courageux *(adj, m)*	*koo-ra-zh-uh*
	courageuse *(f)*	*koo-ra-zh-uhz*
courteous	courtois *(adj, m)*	*koor-twa*
	courtoise *(f)*	*koor-twaz*
• courtesy	courtoisie *(f)*	*koor-twa-zee*
• discourteous	discourtois *(adj, m)*	*dees-koor-twa*
	discourtoise *(f)*	*dees-koor-twaz*
crazy, mad	fou *(adj, m)*	*foo*
	fol *(adj, m)*	*ful*
	folle *(f)*	*ful*
• madness	folie *(f)*	*ful-ee*
creative	créatif *(adj, m)*	*kray-a-teef*
	créative *(f)*	*kray-a-teev*
critical	critique *(adj)*	*kree-teek*
cry	pleurer *(v)*	*plur-ay*
• crying	en larmes	*AH larm*
cultured	cultivé(e) *(adj, m, f)*	*kewl-tee-vay*
curiosity	curiosité *(f)*	*kew-ryo-zee-tay*
• curious	curieux *(adj, m)*	*kew-ry-uh*
	curieuse *(f)*	*kew-ry-uhz*
delicate	délicat(e) *(adj, m, f)*	*day-lee-ka(t)*
diligence	diligence *(f)*	*dee-lee-zh-AH-s*
• diligent, hard-working	diligent(e) *(adj, m, f)*	*dee-lee-zh-AH(t)*
diplomatic	diplomatique *(adj)*	*dee-plu-ma-teek*
dishonest	malhonnête *(adj)*	*mal-un-eht*
• dishonesty	malhonnêteté *(f)*	*mal-un-eht-tay*
dynamic	dynamique *(adj)*	*dee-na-meek*
eccentric	excentrique *(adj)*	*ehk-sAH-treek*
egoism	égoïsme *(m)*	*ay-gu-ees-me*
• egoist, egoistic	égoïste *(adj)*	*ay-gu-eest*
eloquence	éloquence *(f)*	*ay-luk-AH-s*
• eloquent	éloquent(e) *(adj, m, f)*	*ay-luk-AH(t)*
energetic	énergique *(adj)*	*ay-nehr-zh-eek*
• energy	énergie *(f)*	*ay-nehr-zh-ee*
envious	envieux *(adj, m)*	*AH-vyuh*
	envieuse *(f)*	*AH-vyuhz*
• envy	envie *(f)*	*AH-vee*
faithful	fidèle *(adj)*	*fee-dehl*
fascinate	fasciner *(v)*	*fa-see-nay*
• fascinating	fascinant(e) *(adj, m, f)*	*fa-see nAH(t)*

• **fascination, attractiveness**	fascination (*f*)	*fa-see-nah-syOH*
fool, clown	bouffon (*m*)	*boo-fOH*
	clown (*m*)	*kloon*
• **foolish, silly**	bête (*adj*)	*beht*
	sot (*adj, m*)	*soh*
	sotte (*f*)	*sut*
friendly	amical(e) (*adj, m, f*)	*a-mee-kal*
funny	drôle (*adj*)	*drohl*
	comique (*adj*)	*kum-eek*
	marrant(e) (*adj, m, f*)	*marAH(t)*
fussy	méticuleux (*adj, m*)	*may-tee-kew-luh*
	méticuleuse (*f*)	*may-tee-kew-luhz*
generosity	générosité (*f*)	*zh-ay-nay-roh-zee-tay*
• **generous**	généreux (*adj, m*)	*zh-ay-nay-ruh*
	généreuse (*f*)	*zh-ay-nay-ruhz*
gentle	doux (*adj, m*)	*doo*
	douce (*f*)	*doos*
good, kind	bon (*adj, m*)	*bOH*
	bonne (*f*)	*bun*
• **goodness, kindness**	bonté (*f*)	*bOH-tay*
good (*at something*)	habile (*adj*)	*a-beel*
graceful	gracieux (*adj, m*)	*gra-syuh*
	gracieuse (*f*)	*gra-syuhz*
habit	habitude (*f*)	*a-bee-tewd*
happiness	bonheur (*m*)	*bun-ur*
	contentement (*m*)	*kOH-tAHt-mAH*
	félicité (*f*)	*fay-lee-see-tay*
• **happy**	heureux (*adj, m*)	*ur-uh*
	heureuse (*f*)	*ur-uhz*
	content(e) (*adj, m, f*)	*kOH-tAH(t)*
	fortuné(e) (*adj, m, f*)	*for-tew-nay*
hate	haine (*f*)	*ehn*
• **hate**	haïr (*v*)	*a-eer*
• **hateful**	détestable (*adj*)	*day-tehs-tabl*
honest	honnête (*adj*)	*un-eht*
• **honesty**	honnêteté (*f*)	*un-eht-tay*
humanitarian	humanitaire (*adj*)	*ew-ma-nee-tehr*
humble	humble (*adj*)	*UH-bl*
• **humility**	humilité (*f*)	*ew-mee-lee-tay*
humor	humour (*m*)	*ew-moor*
• **sense of humor**	sens (*m*) de l'humour	*sAHs de lew-moor*
idealism	idéalisme (*m*)	*ee-day-a-leesm*
• **idealist, idealistic**	idéaliste (*m*)	*ee-day-a-leest*

imagination	imagination (*f*)	ee-ma-zh-ee-na-syOH
• **imaginative**	imaginatif (*adj, m*)	ee-ma-zh-ee-na-teef
	imaginative (*f*)	ee-ma-zh-ee-na-teev
impudence	impudence (*f*)	EH-pew-dAH-ss
• **impudent**	impudent(e) (*adj, m, f*)	EH-pew-dAH(t)
impulse	impulsion (*f*)	EH-pewl-syOH
• **impulsive**	impulsif (*adj, m*)	EH-pewl-seef
	impulsive (*f*)	EH-pewl-seev
indecisive	indécis(e) (*adj, m, f*)	EH-day-see(z)
independent	indépendant(e) (*adj, m, f*)	EH-day-pAH-dAH(t)
individualist	individualiste (*adj*)	EH-dee-vee-dew-al-eest
ingenious, clever	ingénieux (*adj, m*)	EH-zhay-nyuh
	ingénieuse (*f*)	EH-zhay-nyuhz
• **ingenuity, cleverness**	ingénuité (*f*)	EH-zhay-new-ee-tay
ingenuous, naive	ingénu(e) (*adj, m, f*)	EH-zhay-new
	naïf (*adj, m*)	na-eef
	naïve (*f*)	na-eev
innocence	innocence (*f*)	ee-nu-sAH-ss
• **innocent**	innocent(e) (*adj, m, f*)	ee-nu-sAH(t)
insolence	insolence (*f*)	EH-sul-AH-ss
• **insolent**	insolent(e) (*adj, m, f*)	EH-sul-AH(t)
intelligence	intelligence (*f*)	EH-tay-lee-zh-AH-s
• **intelligent**	intelligent(e) (*adj, m, f*)	EH-tay-lee-zh-AH(t)
irascible	irascible (*adj*)	ee-ra-see-bl
irony	ironie (*f*)	ee-run-ee
• **ironic**	ironique (*adj*)	ee-run-eek
irritable	irritable (*adj*)	ee-ree-tabl
jealous	jaloux (*adj, m*)	zh-a-loo
	jalouse (*f*)	zh-a-looz
kind	gentil(le) (*adj, m, f*)	zhAH-tee(y)
laugh	rire (*v*)	reer
• **laughter**	rire (*m*)	reer
laziness	paresse (*f*)	pa-reh-s
• **lazy**	paresseux (*adj, m*)	pa-reh-suh
	paresseuse (*f*)	pa-reh-suhz
liberal	libéral(e) (*adj, m, f*)	lee-bay-ral
lively	vif (*adj, m*)	veef
	vive (*f*)	veev
	vivace (*adj*)	vee-vas
love	amour (*m*)	a-moor
• **love**	aimer (*v*)	ay-may
• **lovable**	adorable (*adj*)	a-du-ra-bl

malicious	malicieux *(adj, m)*	*ma-lee-syuh*
	malicieuse *(f)*	*ma-lee-syuhz*
mischievous	capricieux *(adj, m)*	*ka-pree-syuh*
	capricieuse *(f)*	*ka-pree-syuhz*
miser	avare *(adj, m/f)*	*a-vahr*
mood	humeur *(f)*	*ew-mur*
• **be in a bad mood**	être de mauvaise humeur	*eh-tre de mu-vehz ew-mur*
• **be in a good mood**	être de bonne humeur	*eh-tre de bun ew-mur*
neat	ordonné(e) *(adj, m, f)*	*or-dun-nay*
nice	sympathique *(adj)*	*sEH-pa-teek*
not nice, odious	antipathique *(adj)*	*AH-tee-pa-teek*
obstinate	obstiné(e) *(adj, m, f)*	*up-stee-nay*
optimism	optimisme *(m)*	*up-tee-mee-sm*
• **optimist, optimistic**	optimiste *(m/f)*	*up-tee-meest*
original	original(e) *(adj, m, f)*	*o-ree-zh-ee-nal*
patience	patience *(f)*	*pa-sy-AH-s*
• **patient**	patient(e) *(adj, m, f)*	*pa-sy-AH(t)*
• **impatient**	impatient(e) *(adj, m, f)*	*EH-pa-sy-AH(t)*
perfection	perfection *(f)*	*pehr-fehk-syOH*
• **perfectionist**	perfectionniste *(m/f)*	*pehr-fehk-sy-un-eest*
personality	personnalité *(f)*	*pehr-sun-a-lee-tay*
pessimism	pessimisme *(m)*	*pay-see-mee-sm*
• **pessimist, pessimistic**	pessimiste *(m/f)*	*pay-see-meest*
picky	tatillon *(adj, m)*	*ta-tee-yOH*
	tatillonne *(f)*	*ta-tee-yun*
	difficile *(adj)*	*dee-fee-seel*
pleasant, likeable	aimable *(adj)*	*ay-ma-ble*
	sympathique *(adj)*	*sEH-pa-teek*
• **like**	aimer *(v)* bien	*ay-may byEH*
poor	pauvre *(adj)*	*poh-vr*
possessive	possessif *(adj, m)*	*pus-ay-seef*
	possessive *(f)*	*pus-ay-seev*
presumptuous	présomptueux *(adj, m)*	*pray-zOH-ptew-uh*
	présomptueuse *(f)*	*pray-zOH-ptew-uhz*
pretentious	prétentieux *(adj, m)*	*pray-tAH-syuh*
	prétentieuse *(f)*	*pray-tAH-syuhz*
proud	fier, fière *(adj, m, f)*	*fyehr*
prudent	prudent *(adj, m)*	*prew-dAH*
	prudente *(f)*	*prew-dAHt*
rebellious	rebelle *(adj, m, f)*	*re-behl*
refined	raffiné(e) *(adj, m, f)*	*ra-fee-nay*
reserved	réservé(e) *(adj, m, f)*	*ray-zehr-vay*
restless	agité(e) *(adj, m, f)*	*a-zh-ee-tay*

rich	riche (*adj/m/f*)	*reesh*
romantic	romantique (*adj*)	*rum-AH-teek*
rough	brut, brute (*adj, m, f*)	*brewt*
rude	rude (*adj*)	*rewd*
	grossier (*adj, m*)	*groh-sy-ay*
	grossière (*f*)	*groh-sy-ehr*
sad	triste (*adj*)	*treest*
• **sadness**	tristesse (*f*)	*tree-stehs*
sarcasm	sarcasme (*m*)	*sar-kasm*
• **sarcastic**	sarcastique (*adj*)	*sar-kas-teek*
seduction	séduction (*f*)	*say-dewk-syOH*
• **seductive**	séduisant(e) (*adj, m, f*)	*say-dew-ee-zAH(t)*
self-sufficient	indépendant(e) (*adj, m, f*)	*EH-day-pAH-dAH(t)*
sensitive	sensible (*adj*)	*sAH-seebl*
sentimental	sentimental(e) (*adj, m, f*)	*sAH-tee-mAH-tal*
serious	sérieux (*adj, m*)	*say-ryuh*
	sérieuse (*f*)	*say-ryuhz*
shrewd	rusé(e) (*adj, m, f*)	*rew-zay*
• **shrewdness**	ruse (*f*)	*rewz*
shy	timide (*adj*)	*tee-meed*
simple	simple (*adj*)	*sEH-pl*
sincere	sincère (*adj*)	*sEH-sehr*
• **sincerity**	sincérité (*f*)	*sEH-say-ree-tay*
sloppy, disorganized	désorganisé(e) (*adj, m, f*)	*day-zor-ga-nee-zay*
smart	intelligent(e) (*adj, m, f*)	*EH-tay-lee-zh-AH(t)*
smile	sourire (*m*)	*soo-reer*
• **smile**	sourire (*v*)	*soo-reer*
snobbish	hautain (*adj, m*)	*oh-tEH*
	hautaine (*f*)	*oh-tehn*
	snob (*adj*)	*snub*
stingy	radin (*m*)	*rad-EH*
	radine (*f*)	*rad-een*
strong	fort (*adj, m*)	*for*
	forte (*f*)	*fort*
stubborn	entêté (*adj, m*)	*AH-teht-ay*
	entêtée (*adj, f*)	*AH-teht-ay*
	têtu(e) (*adj*)	*teht-ew*
stupid	stupide (*adj*)	*stew-peed*
	bête (*adj*)	*beht*
superstitious	superstitieux (*adj, m*)	*sew-pehr-stee-syuh*
	superstitieuse (*f*)	*sew-pehr-stee-syuhz*
sweet	doux (*adj, m*)	*doo*
	douce (*f*)	*dooss*

traditional	traditionnel(le) *(adj, m, f)*	*tra-dee-sy-un-ehl*
troublemaker	provocateur *(m)*	*pru-vuk-a-tur*
	provocatrice *(f)*	*pru-vuk-a-treess*
vain	vaniteux *(adj, m)*	*va-nee-tuh*
	vaniteuse *(f)*	*va-nee-tuhz*
versatile	versatile *(adj)*	*vehr-sa-teel*
vulnerable	vulnérable *(adj)*	*vewl-nay-rabl*
weak	faible *(adj)*	*fehbl*
well-mannered	bien élevé(e) *(adj, m, f)*	*byEH ayl-vay*
willingly	volontiers *(adv)*	*vul-OH-tyay*
wisdom	sagesse *(f)*	*sa-zh-ess*
• **wise**	sage *(adj)*	*sa-zh*

f. BASIC PERSONAL INFORMATION

> For jobs and professions see Section 38.

address	adresse *(f)*	*a-drehss*
• **avenue**	avenue *(f)*	*av-new*
• **street**	rue *(f)*	*rew*
• **square**	place *(f)*	*plass*
• **live somewhere**	demeurer *(v)*	*de-mur-ay*
• **Where do you live?**	Où demeurez-vous *(pol)*?	*oo de-mur-ay voo*
	Où demeures-tu *(fam)*?	*oo de-mur tew*
• **I live on . . . Street.**	Je demeure rue . . .	*zhe de-mur rew*
• **house number**	numéro de la maison	*new-may-roh de la may-zOH*
be from	être de	*eh-tre de*
• **city, town**	ville *(f)*	*veel*
• **country**	pays *(m)*	*pay-ee*
• **state**	état *(m)*	*ay-ta*
• **village**	village *(m)*	*vee-lazh*
career	carrière *(f)*	*ka-ryehr*
date of birth	date *(f)* de naissance	*dat de neh-sAH-ss*
education	éducation *(f)*	*ay-dew-ka-syOH*
• **go to school**	aller *(v)* à l'école	*a-lay a lay-kul*
• **finish school**	finir *(v)* l'école	*fee-neer lay-kul*
• **university**	licence *(f)*	*lee-sAH-ss*
degree	doctorat *(m)*	*duk-tu-ra*

• **diploma**	diplôme (m)	*deep-lohm*
• **graduate**	obtenir un diplôme	*up-te-neer UH deep-lohm*
• **graduate** (*from university*)	obtenir sa licence	*up-te-neer sa lee-sAH-ss*
	obtenir son doctorat	*up-te-neer sOH duk-tu-ra*
employment	emploi (m)	*AH-plwa*
• **employer**	employeur (m)	*AH-plwa-yur*
	employeuse (f)	*AH-plwa-yuhz*
• **employee**	employé(e) (m, f)	*AH-plwa-yay*
identification	identification (f)	*ee-dAH-tee-fee-ka-syOH*
job	travail (m)	*tra-va-y*
name	nom (m)	*nOH*
• **first name**	prénom (m)	*pray-nOH*
• **family name, surname**	nom (m) de famille	*nOH de fa-meey*
• **be called**	s'appeler (v)	*sap-lay*
• **How do you spell your name?**	Comment s'écrit ton nom (*fam*)?	*kum-AH say-kree tOH nOH*
	Comment s'écrit votre nom (*pol*)?	*kum-AH say-kree vutre nOH*
• **Print your name.**	Ecrire (v) en caractères d'imprimerie	*ay-kreer AH ka-rak-tehr dEH-preem-ree*
• **What's your name?**	Quel est ton nom (*fam*)?	*kehl eh tOH nOH*
	Quel est votre nom (*pol*)?	*kehl eh vutre nOH*
• **My name is . . .**	Mon nom est . . .	*mOH nOH eh*
• **sign**	signer (v)	*see-ny-ay*
• **signature**	signature (f)	*see-ny-a-tewr*
nationality	nationalité (f)	*na-syun-a-lee-tay*
place of birth	lieu (m) de naissance	*lyuh de neh-sAH-ss*
place of employment	lieu d'emploi	*lyuh dAH-plwa*
profession	profession (f)	*pruf-ehs-yOH*
• **professional**	professionnel (m)	*pru-fehs-yun-ehl*
	professionnelle (f)	*pru-fehs-yun-ehl*
residence	domicile (m)	*dum-ee-seel*
telephone number	numéro (m) de téléphone	*new-may-ro de tay-lay-fun*
title	titre (m)	*teetr*
• **Dr.**	docteur (m)	*duktur*
• **Miss, Ms.**	mademoiselle	*mad-mwa-zehl*
• **Mr.**	monsieur	*me-sy-uh*
• **Mrs., Ms.**	madame	*ma-dam*
• **Prof.**	professeur (m)	*pruf-ehs-ur*

work

	travail (*m*)	*tra-va-y*
• **work**	travailler (*v*)	*tra-va-yay*
• **line of work**	genre de travail	*zh-AH-r de tra-va-y*

12. THE BODY

FOCUS: Parts of the Body

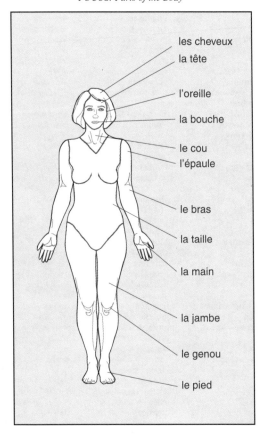

les cheveux
la tête
l'oreille
la bouche
le cou
l'épaule
le bras
la taille
la main
la jambe
le genou
le pied

a. PARTS OF THE BODY

> See also Section 40.

ankle	cheville (*f*)	*sh-e-vee-y*
arm	bras (*m*)	*bra*
beard	barbe (*f*)	*barb*
blood	sang (*m*)	*sAH*
body	corps (*m*)	*kor*
bone	os (*m*)	*us*
	les os (*pl*)	*lay zoh*
brain	cerveau (*m*)	*sehr-vo*
breast	sein (*m*)	*sEH*
cheek	joue (*f*)	*zh-oo*
chest	poitrine (*f*)	*pwa-treen*
chin	menton (*m*)	*mAH-tOH*
ear	oreille (*f*)	*u-reh-y*
elbow	coude (*m*)	*kood*
eye	œil (*m*)	*u-y*
	les yeux (*pl*)	*lay zyuh*
eyebrow	sourcil (*m*)	*soor-see*
eyelash	cil (*m*)	*seel*
eyelid	paupière (*f*)	*po-py-ehr*
face	visage (*m*)	*vee-za-zh*
	figure (*f*)	*fee-gewr*
finger	doigt (*m*)	*dwa*
fingernail	ongle (*m*)	*OH-gl*
foot	pied (*m*)	*pyay*
forehead	front (*m*)	*frOH*
hair	cheveux (*m, pl*)	*shvuh*
hand	main (*f*)	*mEH*
head	tête (*f*)	*teht*
heart	cœur (*m*)	*kur*
heel	talon (*m*)	*talOH*
hip	hanche (*f*)	*AH-sh*
index finger	index (*m*)	*EH-dehks*
jaw	mâchoire (*f*)	*mah-sh-war*
knee	genou (*m*)	*zh-noo*
knuckles	les jointures (*f*) des doigts	*lay zh-wEH-tewr day dwa*
leg	jambe (*f*)	*zh-AH-b*
lip	lèvre (*f*)	*leh-vr*
little finger	petit doigt (*m*)	*ptee dwa*
lung	poumon (*m*)	*poo-mOH*
middle finger	médius (*m*)	*may-dy-ewss*
moustache	moustache (*f*)	*moos-tash*

mouth	bouche (*f*)	*boosh*
muscle	muscle (*m*)	*mews-kl*
neck	cou (*m*)	*koo*
nose	nez (*m*)	*nay*
nostril	narine (*f*)	*na-reen*
penis	pénis (*m*)	*pay-nees*
ring finger	annulaire (*m*)	*a-new-lehr*
shoulder	épaule (*f*)	*ay-pohl*
sideburns	pattes (*f, pl*)	*paht*
skin	peau (*f*)	*poh*
stomach	estomac (*m*)	*ehs-tum-a*
thigh	cuisse (*f*)	*kew-ees*
throat	gorge (*f*)	*gor-zh*
thumb	pouce (*m*)	*poos*
toe	orteil (*m*)	*or-teh-y*
tongue	langue (*f*)	*lAH-g*
tooth	dent (*f*)	*dAH*
vagina	vagin (*m*)	*va-zh-EH*
waist	taille (*f*)	*tah-y*
wrist	poignet (*m*)	*pwa-ny-eh*

---

to be at the tip of one's tongue = être sur le bout de la langue *eh-tre sewr le boo de la lAH-g*
to pay through the nose; to pay an arm and a leg = payer un œil *pay-yay UH nu-y*
He (She) is a pain in the neck! = C'est un casse-pieds! *seh tUH kahs-pyay*
Knucklehead! = Tête de nœud! *teht de nuh*

---

b. PHYSICAL STATES AND ACTIVITIES

be cold	avoir (*v*) froid	*avwar frwa*
be hot	avoir (*v*) chaud	*avwar sho*
be tired	être (*v*) fatigué(e)	*eh-tre fa-tee-gay*
breathe	respirer (*v*)	*rehs-pee-ray*
drink	boire (*v*)	*bwar*
eat	manger (*v*)	*mAH-zh-ay*
fall asleep	s'endormir (*v*)	*sAH-dor-meer*
feel bad	se sentir (*v*) mal	*se sAH-teer mal*
	avoir (*v*) mal	*avwar mal*
feel well	se sentir (*v*) bien	*se sAH-teer byEH*
	aller (*v*) bien	*a-lay byEH*
get up	se lever (*v*)	*se le-vay*
go to bed	se coucher (*v*)	*se koo-shay*
hunger	faim (*f*)	*fEH*
• **be hungry**	avoir (*v*) faim	*avwar fEH*
relax	se relaxer (*v*)	*se re-laks-ay*

rest	se reposer (v)	se re-po-zay
run	courir (v)	koo-reer
sleep	dormir (v)	dorm-eer
• be sleepy	avoir (v) sommeil	avwar sum-ay
thirst	soif (f)	swaf
• be thirsty	avoir (v) soif	avwar swaf
wake up	se réveiller (v)	se ray-vay-yay
walk	marcher (v)	marshay
	aller (v) à pied	alay a pyay

c. SENSORY PERCEPTION

blind person	aveugle (m/f)	a-vuh-gl
• blindness	cécité (f)	say-see-tay
deaf person	sourd (m)	soor
	sourde (f)	soord
• deafness	surdité (f)	sewr-dee-tay
flavor	saveur (f)	sa-vur
• taste	goûter (v)	goo-tay
hear	entendre (v)	AH-tAH-dr
• hearing	ouïe (f)	wee
listen (to)	écouter (v)	ay-koo-tay
look	regarder (v)	re-gar-day
mute person	muet (m)	mew-eh
	muette (f)	mew-eht
noise	bruit (m)	brew-ee
• noisy	bruyant(e) (adj, m, f)	brew-yAH(t)
perceive	percevoir (v)	pehr-se-vwar
	apercevoir (v)	a-pehr-se-vwar
• perception	perception (f)	pehr-sehp-syOH
see	voir (v)	vwar
• sight	vision (f)	vee-zyOH
	vue (f)	vew
sense	sens (m)	sAH-s
• sense, feel	sentir (v)	sAH-teer
smell	odeur (f)	ud-ur
	senteur (f)	sAHt-ur
• smell	sentir (v)	sAH-teer
sound	son (m)	sOH
touch	toucher (m)	too-shay
• touch	toucher (v)	too-shay

d. PERSONAL CARE

| barber | coiffeur (m) | kwa-fur |
| • barber shop | salon (m) de coiffure pour hommes | salOH de kwa-fewr poor um |

beautician	esthéticien (*m*)	*ehs-tay-tee-syEH*
	esthéticienne (*f*)	*ehs-tay-tee-syehn*
brush	brosse (*f*)	*bruss*
• brush	se brosser (*v*)	*se bruss-ay*
clean	propre (*adj*)	*prup-re*
• clean oneself	se débarbouiller (*v*)	*se day-bar-boo-yay*
comb	peigne (*m*)	*peh-ny*
• comb	se peigner (*v*)	*se peh-ny-ay*
curls	boucles (*f*) de cheveux	*book-le de shvuh*
	cheveux (*m, pl*) frisés	*shvuh free-zay*
• curler	bigoudi (*m*)	*bee-goo-dee*
cut one's hair	se faire couper (*v*) les cheveux	*se fehr koo-pay lay sh-vuh*
dirty	sale (*adj*)	*sal*
dry oneself	se sécher (*v*)	*se say-shay*
grooming	toilette (*f*)	*twa-leht*
hair spray	laque (*f*) pour les cheveux	*lak poor lay shvuh*
	spray (*m*) pour les cheveux	*spreh poor lay shvuh*
hairdresser	coiffeur (*m*)	*kwa-fur*
	coiffeuse (*f*)	*kwa-fuhz*
hygiene	hygiène (*f*)	*ee-zh-y-ehn*
• hygienic	hygiénique (*adj*)	*ee-zh-y-ay-neek*
makeup	fard (*m*)	*far*
	maquillage (*m*)	*mak-ee-y-ah-zh*
• put on makeup	se farder (*v*)	*se far-day*
	se maquiller (*v*)	*se mak-ee-yay*
manicure	soins (*m, pl*) esthétiques des mains	*swEH ehs-tay-teek day mEH*
mascara	mascara (*m*)	*mas-ka-ra*
massage	massage (*m*)	*ma-sazh*
nail polish	vernis (*m*) à ongles	*vehr-nee a OH-gl*
perfume	parfum (*m*)	*par-fUH*
• put on perfume	se parfumer (*v*)	*se par-few-may*
permanent (wave)	permanente (*f*)	*pehr-ma-nAH-t*
razor	rasoir (*m*)	*rahz-war*
• electric razor	rasoir électrique (*m*)	*rahz-war ay-lehk-treek*
• razor blade	lame (*f*)	*lam*
scissors	ciseaux (*m*)	*see-zoh*
shampoo	shampooing (*m*)	*sh-AH-pwEH*
shave (*oneself*)	(se) raser (*v*)	*(se) rah-zay*
soap	savon (*m*)	*sa-vOH*
toothbrush	brosse (*f*) à dents	*bruss a dAH*
toothpaste	pâte dentifrice (*f*)	*paht dAH-tee-frees*

towel, handcloth	serviette de toilette (*f*)	*sehr-vee-y-eht de twa-leht*
wash oneself	se laver (*v*)	*se la-vay*
• **wash one's hair**	se laver les cheveux	*se la-vay lay shvuh*
washcloth	gant (*m*) de bain	*gAHd-bEH*
	gant (*m*) de toilette	*gAHd-twa-leht*

THE PHYSICAL, PLANT, AND ANIMAL WORLDS

13. THE PHYSICAL WORLD

> For signs of the Zodiac, see Section 5.

a. THE UNIVERSE

asteroid	astéroïde (*m*)	*astay-ro-eed*
astronomy	astronomie (*f*)	*as-trun-um-ee*
comet	comète (*f*)	*kum-eht*
cosmos	cosmos (*m*)	*kus-mohs*
eclipse	éclipse (*f*)	*ay-kleeps*
• **lunar eclipse**	éclipse lunaire	*ay-kleeps lew-nehr*
• **solar eclipse**	éclipse solaire	*ay-kleeps sul-ehr*
galaxy	galaxie (*f*)	*ga-lak-see*
gravitation	gravitation (*f*)	*gra-vee-tahs-yOH*
• **gravity**	gravité (*f*)	*gra-vee-tay*
light	lumière (*f*)	*lewm-yehr*
• **infrared light**	lumière infrarouge	*lewm-yehr EH-fra-roozh*
• **ultraviolet light**	lumière ultraviolette	*lewm-yehr ewl-tra-vy-uh-leht*
light year	année (*f*) lumière	*a-nay lewm-yehr*

> **to come to light** = mettre en lumière *meht-re AH lewm-yehr*
> **to shed light on** = tirer quelque chose au clair *tee-ray kehlke sh-oh-z oh klehr*

meteor	météore (*m*)	*may-tay-or*
meteorite	météorite (*f*)	*may-tay-or-eet*
moon	lune (*f*)	*lewn*
• **full moon**	pleine lune	*plehn lewn*
• **moonbeam, ray**	rayon (*m*) de lune	*ray-yOHd lewn*
• **new moon**	nouvelle lune	*noo-vehl lewn*

> **honeymoon** = une lune de miel *ewn lewn de mee-ehl*
> **to be absent-minded** = être dans la lune *eh-tre dAH la lewn*

orbit	orbite (f)	or-beet
• orbit	mettre (v) en orbite	mehtr AH nor-beet
	placer (v) sur orbite	pla-say sewr or-beet
	être (v) en orbite	eh-tre AH nor-beet
planet	planète (f)	plan-eht
• Earth	Terre (f)	tehr
• Jupiter	Jupiter (m)	zh-ew-pee-tehr
• Mars	Mars (m)	mars
• Mercury	Mercure (m)	mehr-kewr
• Neptune	Neptune (m)	nehp-tewn
• Pluto	Pluton (m)	plewt-OH
• Saturn	Saturne (m)	sa-tewrn
• Uranus	Uranus (m)	ewr-an-ewss
• Venus	Vénus (f)	vay-newss
satellite	satellite (m)	sa-tehl-eet
space	espace (m)	ehs-pas
• three-dimensional space	espace tridimensionnel	ehs-pas tree-deem-AH-sy-un-ehl
star	étoile (f)	ay-twal
sun	soleil (m)	sul-ay
• sunlight	lumière solaire	lewm-yehr sul-ehr
• sunray	rayon (m) de soleil	ray-yOHd sul-ay
• solar system	système (m) solaire	sees-tehm sul-ehr
universe	univers (m)	ew-nee-vehr
world	monde (m)	mOHd

b. THE ENVIRONMENT

> See also Section 44.

archipelago	archipel (m)	arsh-ee-pehl
atmosphere	atmosphère (f)	at-muss-fehr
• atmospheric	atmosphérique (adj)	at-muss-fay-reek
basin	bassin (m)	bas-EH
bay	baie (f)	beh
beach	plage (f)	pla-zh
channel	canal (m)	ka-nal
cloud	nuage (m)	new-azh
	nuée (f)	new-ay
coast	côte (f)	koht
desert	désert (m)	dayz-ehr
earthquake	tremblement (m) de terre	trAH-ble-mAH de tehr
environment	environnement (m)	AH-veer-un-mAH
farmland	terrain (m) agricole	tehr-EH a-gree-kul

field	champ (*m*)	*shAH*
forest	forêt (*f*)	*for-eh*
grass	herbe (*f*)	*ehrb*
gulf	golfe (*m*)	*gulf*
hill	colline (*f*)	*kul-een*
	coteau (*m*)	*kut-o*
ice	glace (*f*)	*glas*
island	île (*f*)	*eel*
lake	lac (*m*)	*lak*
land	terre (*f*)	*tehr*
	terrain (*m*)	*tehr-EH*
landscape	paysage (*m*)	*pay-eez-azh*
lawn	pelouse (*f*)	*pe-looz*
layer	couche (*f*)	*koosh*
mountain	montagne (*f*)	*mOH-ta-ny*
• **mountain chain**	chaîne (*f*) de montagnes	*sh-ehn de mOH-ta-ny*
• **mountainous**	montagneux (*adj, m*)	*mOH-ta-ny-uh*
	montagneuse (*f*)	*mOH-ta-ny-uhz*
• **peak**	sommet (*m*)	*sum-eh*
nature	nature (*f*)	*na-tewr*
• **natural**	nature(le) (*adj, m, f*)	*na-tewr-ehl*
ocean	océan (*m*)	*us-ay-AH*
• **Antarctic**	Antarctique (*adj*)	*AH-tark-teek*
• **Arctic**	Arctique (*adj*)	*ark-teek*
• **Atlantic**	Atlantique (*adj*)	*atl-AH-teek*
• **Pacific**	Pacifique (*adj*)	*pa-see-feek*
peninsula	péninsule (*f*)	*payn-EH-sewl*
	presqu'île (*f*)	*prehs-keel*
plain	plaine (*f*)	*plehn*
rainforest	forêt (*f*) pluviale	*for-eh plew-vyal*
river (large)	fleuve (*m*)	*fl-uhv*
• **flow**	couler (*v*)	*koo-lay*
• **small river**	rivière (*f*)	*reev-yehr*
rock	roche (*f*)	*rush*
	rocher (*m*)	*rush-ay*
sand	sable (*m*)	*sah-bl*
sea	mer (*f*)	*mehr*
sky	ciel (*m*)	*see-ehl*
stone	pierre (*f*)	*py-ehr*
tide	marée (*f*)	*mar-ay*
• **high tide**	marée haute	*mar-ay oht*
• **low tide**	marée basse	*mar-ay bahss*
valley	vallée (*f*)	*val-ay*
	val (*m*)	*val*
vegetation	végétation (*f*)	*vay-zh-ay-tas-yOH*

volcano	volcan (*m*)	*vulk-AH*
• **eruption**	éruption (*f*)	*ay-rewps-yOH*
• **lava**	lave (*f*)	*lav*
wave	onde (*f*)	*OHd*
	vague (*f*)	*vag*
	flot (*m*)	*floh*
woods	bois (*m, s/pl*)	*bwah*

c. MATTER AND THE ENVIRONMENT

See also Section 42.

acid	acide (*m*)	*a-seed*
air	air (*m*)	*ehr*
ammonia	ammoniaque (*f*)	*am-un-yak*
atom	atome (*m*)	*a-tohm*
• **charge**	charge (*f*)	*shar-zhe*
• **electron**	électron (*m*)	*ay-lehk-tr-OH*
• **neutron**	neutron (*m*)	*nuh-tr-OH*
• **nucleus**	noyau (*m*)	*nwa-yoh*
• **proton**	proton (*m*)	*prut-OH*
bronze	bronze (*m*)	*br-OH-z*
carbon (*element*)	carbone (*m*)	*kar-bun*
chemical	chimique (*adj*)	*shee-meek*
• **chemistry**	chimie (*f*)	*shee-mee*
chemical formula	formule (*f*) chimique	*for-mewl-shee-meek*
chlorine	chlore (*m*)	*klor*
coal	charbon (*m*)	*sharb-OH*
• **coal mine**	mine (*f*) de houille	*meen de oo-y*
• **coal mining**	houille (*f*)	*oo-y*
compound	composé (*m*)	*kOH-po-zay*
copper	cuivre (*m*)	*kew-eevr*
cotton	coton (*m*)	*kut-OH*
diesel	gazole (*m*)	*ga-zul*
electrical	électrique (*adj*)	*ay-lehk-treek*
• **electricity**	électricité (*f*)	*ay-lehk-tree-see-tay*
element	élément (*m*)	*ay-laym-AH*
energy	énergie (*f*)	*ay-nehr-zh-ee*
• **fossil**	fossile (*m*)	*fus-eel*
• **nuclear energy**	énergie nucléaire	*ay-nehr-zh-ee new-klay-ehr*
• **radioactive waste**	déchets (*m, pl*) radioactifs	*day-sh-eh rad-yu-ak-teef*
• **solar energy**	énergie solaire	*ay-nehr-zh-ee sul-ehr*
fiber	fibre (*f*)	*fee-br*
fire	feu (*m*)	*fuh*

fuel	carburant (*m*)	*kar-bewr-AH*
	combustible (*m*)	*kOH-bews-teebl*
• **fossil fuel**	combustibles (*m, pl*) fossiles	*kOH-bews-teebl fu-seel*
gas	gaz (*m*)	*gahz*
• **car gas, gasoline, automobile fuel**	essence (*f*)	*ays-AH-s*
• **natural gas**	gaz naturel	*gahz na-tewr-ehl*
gold	or (*m*)	*or*
heat	chaleur (*f*)	*sha-lur*
hydrogen	hydrogène (*m*)	*eed-ru-zh-ehn*
industrial	industriel(le) (*adj, m, f*)	*EH-dews-tree-ehl*
• **industry**	industrie (*f*)	*EH-dews-tree*
iodine	iode (*m*)	*yud*
iron	fer (*m*)	*fehr*
laboratory	laboratoire (*m*)	*la-bor-a-twar*
lead	plomb (*m*)	*plOH*
leather	cuir (*m*)	*kew-eer*
liquid	liquide (*m*)	*lee-keed*
material	matériel (*m*)	*ma-tayr-y-ehl*
matter	matière (*f*)	*mat-yehr*
mercury	mercure (*m*)	*mehr-kewr*
metal	métal (*m*)	*may-tal*
methane	méthane (*m*)	*may-tahn*
microscope	microscope (*m*)	*meek-ru-skup*
mineral	minéral (*m*)	*mee-nay-ral*
molecule	molécule (*f*)	*mul-ay-kewl*
• **model**	modèle (*m*)	*mud-ehl*
• **molecular formula**	formule (*f*) moléculaire	*for-mewl mul-ay-kew-lehr*
• **structure**	structure (*f*)	*strewk-tewr*
natural resources	ressources (*f, pl*) naturelles	*re-soorss na-tewr-ehl*
nitrogen	azote (*m*)	*a-zut*
	nitrogène (*m*)	*neet-ru-zh-ehn*
oil	huile (*f*)	*ew-eel*
organic	organique (*adj*)	*or-gan-eek*
• **inorganic**	inorganique (*adj*)	*een-or-gan-eek*
oxygen	oxygène (*m*)	*uks-ee-zh-ehn*
particle	particule (*f*)	*par-tee-kewl*
petroleum	pétrole (*m*)	*pay-trul*
physical	physique (*adj*)	*fee-zeek*
• **physics**	physique (*f*)	*fee-zeek*
plastic	plastique (*m*)	*plas-teek*
platinum	platine (*m*)	*pla-teen*
pollution	pollution (*f*)	*pul-ews-yOH*
salt	sel (*m*)	*sehl*

silk	soie (*f*)	*swa*
silver	argent (*m*)	*ar-zh-AH*
smoke	fumée (*f*)	*fewm-ay*
sodium	sodium (*m*)	*sud-yum*
solid	solide (*m*)	*sul-eed*
steel	acier (*m*)	*as-yay*
• stainless steel	acier inoxydable	*as-yay een-uks-eed-abl*
stuff	étoffe (*f*)	*ay-tuf*
	tissu (*m*)	*tees-ew*
substance	substance (*f*)	*sewp-st-AH-s*
sulphur	soufre (*m*)	*soof-re*
	sulfure (*m*)	*sewl-fewr*
• sulphuric acid	acide (*m*) sulfurique	*a-seed sewl-fewr-eek*
textile	textile (*m*)	*tehk-steel*
vapor	vapeur (*f*)	*va-pur*
water	eau (*f*)	*oh*
wool	laine (*f*)	*lehn*

d. CHARACTERISTICS OF MATTER

artificial	artificiel (*adj*)	*ar-tee-fee-sy-ehl*
authentic	authentique (*adj*)	*ut-AH-teek*
density	densité (*f*)	*dAH-see-tay*
elastic	élastique (*adj*)	*ay-las-teek*
fake	faux (*adj*)	*foh*
hard	dur (*adj*)	*dewr*
heavy	lourd (*adj*)	*loor*
light	léger (*adj*)	*lay-zh-ay*
malleable	malléable (*adj*)	*mal-ay-abl*
opaque	opaque (*adj*)	*up-ak*
pure	pur (*adj*)	*pewr*
resistant	résistant (*adj*)	*ray-zeest-AH*
robust	robuste (*adj*)	*rub-ewst*
rough	rude (*adj*)	*rewd*
smooth	lisse (*adj*)	*lees*
soft	mou (*adj*)	*moo*
	doux (*adj*)	*doo*
	mœlleux (*adj*)	*mwal-uh*
soluble	soluble (*adj*)	*sul-ew-bl*
stable	stable (*adj*)	*sta-bl*
strong	fort (*adj*)	*for*
synthetic	synthétique (*adj*)	*sEH-tay-teek*
transparent	transparent (*adj*)	*tr-AH-spar-AH*
weak	faible (*adj*)	*feh-bl*

e. GEOGRAPHY

> For names of countries, cities, etc. see Section 30.

Antarctic Circle	Cercle (*m*) antarctique	*sehr-kle AH-tark-teek*
Arctic Circle	Cercle (*m*) arctique	*sehr-kle ark-teek*
area	superficie (*f*)	*sewp-ehr-fee-see*
	surface (*f*)	*sewr-fas*
border	frontière (*f*)	*frOH-ty-ehr*
• border	borner (*v*)	*bor-nay*
	toucher (*v*)	*too-shay*
city	ville (*f*)	*veel*
• capital	capitale (*f*)	*ka-pee-tal*
continent	continent (*m*)	*kOH-teen-AH*
• continental	continental(e) (*adj*, *m*, *f*)	*kOH-teen-AH-tal*
country	pays (*m*)	*pay-ee*

> **From what country are you?** = De quel pays êtes-vous? *de kehl pay-ee eht-voo*

equator	équateur (*m*)	*ay-kwa-tur*
geographical	géographique (*adj*)	*zh-ay-u-gra-feek*
• geography	géographie (*f*)	*zh-ay-u-gra-fee*
globe	globe (*m*)	*glub*
hemisphere	hémisphère (*m*)	*ay-mees-fehr*
• hemispheric	hémisphérique (*adj*)	*ay-mees-fay-reek*
latitude	latitude (*f*)	*la-tee-tewd*
longitude	longitude (*f*)	*lOH-zh-ee-tewd*
locate	localiser (*v*)	*luk-al-ee-zay*
	situer (*v*)	*see-tew-ay*
• location	localité (*f*)	*luk-al-ee-tay*
• be located	se trouver (*v*)	*se-troo-vay*
map	carte (*f*)	*kart*
meridian	méridien (*m*)	*may-reed-y-EH*
• prime meridian	méridien origine	*may-reed-y-EH or-ee-zh-een*
nation	nation (*f*)	*nahs-y-OH*
• national	national(e) (*adj*, *m*, *f*)	*nahs-yun-al*
pole	pôle (*m*)	*pohl*
• North Pole	Pôle Nord	*pohl nor*
• South Pole	Pôle Sud	*pohl sewd*
province	province (*f*)	*pruv-EH-s*

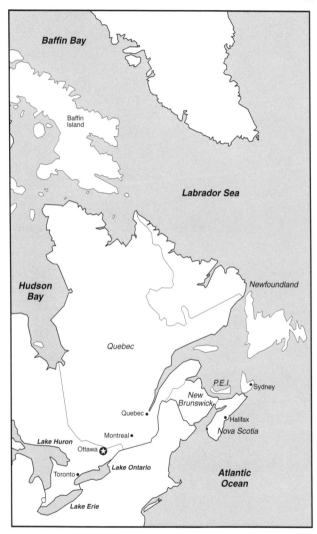

region	région (*f*)	*ray-zh-y-OH*
state	état (*m*)	*ay-ta*
territory	territoire (*m*)	*tehr-eet-war*
tropic	tropique (*m*)	*trup-eek*
• **Tropic of Cancer**	Tropique du Cancer	*trup-eek dew kAH-sehr*
• **Tropic of Capricorn**	Tropique du Capricorne	*trup-eek dew ka-pree-korn*
• **tropical**	tropique (*adj*)	*trup-eek*
zenith	zénith (*m*)	*zay-neet*
zone	zone (*f*)	*zohn*

14. PLANTS

a. GENERAL VOCABULARY

agriculture	agriculture (*f*)	*a-gree-kewl-tewr*
bloom	fleurir (*v*)	*flur-eer*
botanical	botanique (*adj*)	*but-a-neek*
• **botany**	botanique (*f*)	*but-a-neek*
branch	branche (*f*)	*brAHsh*
bud	bourgeon (*m*)	*boor-zh-OH*
• **bud**	bourgeonner (*v*)	*boor-zh-un-ay*
bulb	bulbe (*m*)	*bewlb*
cell	cellule (*f*)	*sehl-ewl*
• **membrane**	membrane (*f*)	*mAH-bran*
• **nucleus**	noyau (*m*)	*nwah-yo*
chlorophyll	chlorophylle (*f*)	*klu-ru-feel*
cultivate	cultiver (*v*)	*kewl-tee-vay*
• **cultivation**	culture (*f*)	*kewl-tewr*
dig	creuser (*v*)	*kruh-zay*
flower	fleurir (*v*)	*flur-eer*
foliage	feuillage (*m*)	*fuh-ya-zh*
gather, reap	récolter (*v*)	*ray-kul-tay*
	cueillir (*v*)	*kuh-yeer*
grain, wheat	froment (*m*)	*frum-AH*
	blé (*m*)	*blay*
greenhouse	serre (*f*)	*sehr*
hedge	haie (*f*)	*eh*
horticulture	horticulture (*f*)	*or-tee-kewl-tewr*
leaf	feuille (*f*)	*fuh-y*
organism	organisme (*m*)	*or-gan-ee-sm*
photosynthesis	photosynthèse (*f*)	*fu-tus-EH-tehz*
plant	plante (*f*)	*pl-AH-t*
• **plant**	planter (*v*)	*pl-AH-tay*
pollen	pollen (*m*)	*pul-AH*
reproduce	reproduire (*v*)	*re-prud-ew-eer*
• **reproduction**	reproduction (*f*)	*re-prud-ewks-y-OH*

ripe	mûr(e) (*adj, m, f*)	*mewr*
root	racine (*f*)	*ra-seen*
rotten	pourri(e) (*adj, m, f*)	*poor-ee*
sap	sève (*f*)	*seh-v*
seed	semence (*f*)	*sem-AH-s*
• **seed**	semer (*v*)	*se-may*
species	espèce (*f*)	*ehs-pehs*
stem	tige (*f*)	*tee-zh*
transplant	transplantation (*f*)	*tr-AH-spl-AH-tahs-y-OH*
• **transplant**	transplanter (*v*)	*tr-AH-spl-AH-tay*
trunk	tronc (*m*)	*tr-OH*
water	arroser (*v*)	*a-ro-zay*

b. FLOWERS

carnation	œillet (*m*)	*uh-yeh*
cyclamen	cyclamen (*m*)	*seek-la-men*
dahlia	dahlia (*m*)	*dal-ya*
daisy	marguerite (*f*)	*mar-ge-reet*
flower	fleur (*f*)	*flur*
• **bouquet of flowers**	botte (*f*) de fleurs	*but de flur*
• **flower bed**	parterre (*m*) de fleurs	*par-tehr de flur*
• **wildflower**	fleur sauvage	*flur so-va-zh*
• **wilted flower**	fleur (*f*) fanée	*flur fan-ay*
geranium	géranium (*m*)	*zh-ay-ra-ny-um*
gladiolus	glaïeul (*m*)	*gla-yul*
lily	lis/lys (*m*)	*lees*
orchid	orchidée (*f*)	*or-kee-day*
petal	pétale (*m*)	*pay-tal*
petunia	pétunia (*m*)	*pay-tewn-ya*
pick flowers	cueillir (*v*) des fleurs	*kuh-yeer day flur*
poppy	pavot (*m*)	*pa-vo*
	coquelicot (*m*)	*kuk-lee-ko*
rose	rose (*f*)	*rohz*
thorn	épine (*f*)	*ay-peen*
tulip	tulipe (*f*)	*tew-leep*
violet	violette (*f*)	*vyu-leht*

c. TREES

beech tree	hêtre (*m*)	*eh-tr*
chestnut tree	châtaignier (*m*)	*sha-tay-ny-ay*
cypress tree	cyprès (*m*)	*see-preh*
fir tree	sapin (*m*)	*sap-EH*

fruit tree	fruitier (*m*)	*frew-eet-yay*
• **apple tree**	pommier (*m*)	*pum-yay*
• **cherry tree**	cerisier (*m*)	*se-reez-yay*
• **fig tree**	figuier (*m*)	*feeg-yay*
• **lemon tree**	citronnier (*m*)	*see-trun-yay*
• **olive tree**	olivier (*m*)	*ul-eev-yay*
• **orange tree**	oranger (*m*)	*or-AH-zh-ay*
• **peach tree**	pêcher (*m*)	*pay-shay*
• **pear tree**	poirier (*m*)	*pwa-ree-yay*
• **walnut tree**	noyer (*m*)	*nwa-yay*
maple tree	érable (*m*)	*ay-ra-ble*
oak tree	chêne (*m*)	*sh-ehn*
palm tree	palmier (*m*)	*palm-yay*
pine tree	pin (*m*)	*pEH*
poplar tree	peuplier (*m*)	*puh-plee-yay*
tree	arbre (*m*)	*ar-br*

d. FRUITS

apple	pomme (*f*)	*pum*
apricot	abricot (*m*)	*a-bree-ko*
banana	banane (*f*)	*ba-nan*
cherry	cerise (*f*)	*sreez*
chestnut	marron (*m*)	*mar-OH*
	châtaigne (*f*)	*sha-teh-ny*
citrus	agrumes (*m, pl*)	*ag-rewm*
• **citric**	citrique (*adj*)	*see-treek*
date	datte (*f*)	*dat*
fig	figure (*f*)	*feeg*
fruit	fruit (*m*)	*frew-ee*
grapefruit	pamplemousse (*m/f*)	*pAH-ple-mooss*
grape	raisin (*m*)	*rehz-EH*
lemon	citron (*m*)	*seetr-OH*
mandarin orange	mandarine (*f*)	*mAH-da-reen*
melon	melon (*m*)	*mel-OH*
olive	olive (*f*)	*ul-eev*
orange	orange (*f*)	*or-AH-zh*
peach	pêche (*f*)	*peh-sh*
pear	poire (*f*)	*pwar*
pineapple	ananas (*m*)	*a-na-nas*
plum	prune (*f*)	*prewn*
prune	pruneau (*m*)	*prew-no*
raisin	raisin (*m*) sec	*rehz-EH sehk*
raspberry	framboise (*f*)	*fr-AH-bwaz*
strawberry	fraise (*f*)	*frehz*
tomato	tomate (*f*)	*tum-at*
walnut	noix (*f*)	*nawh*
watermelon	pastèque (*f*)	*pas-tehk*

e. VEGETABLES AND HERBS

artichoke	artichaut (*m*)	*ar-tee-sh-o*
asparagus	asperge (*f*)	*as-pehr-zh*
basil	basilic (*m*)	*ba-zee-leek*
bean	haricot (*m*)	*aree-ko*
	fèves (*f*) de haricot	*fehv de aree-ko*
beet	betterave (*f*)	*beht-rav*
broccoli	brocoli (*m*)	*bruk-u-lee*
cabbage	chou (*m*)	*shoo*
carrot	carotte (*f*)	*ka-rut*
cauliflower	chou-fleur (*m*) (*pl*, choux-fleurs)	*shoo-flur*
celery	céleri (*m*)	*sehl-ree*
corn	maïs (*m*)	*ma-ees*
cucumber	concombre (*m*)	*kOH-kOH-br*
eggplant	aubergine (*f*)	*o-behr-zh-een*
fennel	fenouil (*m*)	*fe-noo-y*
garden	jardin (*m*)	*zh-ard-EH*
• vegetable garden	potager (*m*)	*pu-ta-zh-ay*
garlic	ail (*m*)	*ah-y*
grass	herbe (*f*)	*ehrb*
green bean	haricot (*m*) vert	*aree-ko veh-r*
green pepper	poivron (*m*) vert	*pwa-vrOH veh-r*
lentil	lentille (*f*)	*l-AH-tee-y*
lettuce	laitue (*f*)	*lay-tew*
lima bean	fève (*f*)	*fehv*
mint	menthe (*f*)	*m-AH-t*
mushroom	champignon (*m*)	*sh-AH-pee-ny-OH*
onion	oignon (*m*)	*u-ny-OH*
parsley	persil (*m*)	*pehr-see*
pea	(petits) pois (*m*)	*(ptee) pwa*
potato	pomme (*f*) de terre	*pum de tehr*
pumpkin	citrouille (*f*)	*see-troo-y*
radish	radis (*m*)	*ra-dee*
rosemary	romarin (*m*)	*rum-ar-EH*
spinach	épinards (*m, pl*)	*ay-pee-nar*
string bean	haricot vert (*m*)	*aree-ko vehr*
vegetable	légume (*m*)	*layg-ewm*
zucchini	courgette (*f*)	*koor-zh-eht*

15. THE ANIMAL WORLD

a. ANIMALS

animal	animal (*m*)	*a-nee-mal*
bat	chauve-souris (*f*)	*sh-ohv-soo-ree*
	pipistrelle (*f*)	*pee-pee-strehl*

bear	ours (*m*)	*oors*
beast	bête (*f*)	*beht*
buffalo	buffle (*m*)	*bew-fl*
bull	taureau (*m*)	*tor-o*
camel	chameau (*m*)	*sha-mo*
cat	chat (*m*)	*sha*
	chatte (*f*)	*shat*
• **meow**	miauler (*v*)	*mee-yo-lay*
cow	vache (*f*)	*vash*
deer	cerf (*m*)	*sehr*
dog	chien (*m*)	*sh-y-EH*
	chienne (*f*)	*sh-y-ehn*
• **bark**	aboyer (*v*)	*a-bwa-yay*
donkey	âne (*m*)	*ahn*
elephant	éléphant (*m*)	*ay-layf-AH*
farm	ferme (*f*)	*fehrm*
• **barn**	grange (*f*)	*gr-AH-zh*
• **farmer**	fermier (*m*)	*fehrm-yay*
	fermière (*f*)	*fehrm-yehr*
• **fence**	clôture (*f*)	*klo-tewr*
	barrière (*f*)	*bar-yehr*
fox	renard (*m*)	*re-nar*
giraffe	girafe (*f*)	*zh-ee-raf*
goat	chèvre (*f*)	*sh-ehvre*
hare	lièvre (*m*)	*lee-ehvre*
hippopotamus	hippopotame (*m*)	*ee-pu-pu-tam*
horse	cheval (*m*)	*shval*
• **neigh**	hennir (*v*)	*ehn-eer*
human	humain (*adj, m*)	*ew-mEH*
	humaine (*adj, f*)	*ew-mehn*
human being	être (*m*)	*eh-tr*
	être (*m*) humain	*eh-tr ew-mEH*
hunter	chasseur (*m*)	*sha-sur*
	chasseuse (*f*)	*sha-suhz*
• **hunting**	chasse (*f*)	*shass*
hyena	hyène (*f*)	*yehn*
lamb	agneau (*m*)	*a-ny-o*
leopard	léopard (*m*)	*lay-up-ar*
lion	lion (*m*)	*lee-y-OH*
• **roar**	rugir (*v*)	*rew-zh-eer*
mammal	mammifère (*m*)	*ma-mee-fehr*
mole	taupe (*f*)	*tohp*
monkey	singe (*m*)	*sEH-zh*
mouse	souris (*f*)	*soo-ree*
mule	mulet (*m*)	*mew-leh*
ox	bœuf (*m*)	*buhf*
	bœufs (*pl*)	*buh*
paw	patte (*f*)	*pat*

pet	animal favori (domestiqué) (*m*)	*a-nee-mal fa-vor-ee (dum-ehs-tee-kay)*
pig	cochon (*m*)	*ku-sh-OH*
pony	poney (*m*)	*pun-eh*
primate	primate (*m*)	*pree-mat*
rabbit	lapin (*m*)	*lap-EH*
rat	rat (*m*)	*ra*
rhinoceros	rhinocéros (*m*)	*reen-u-say-rus*
sheep	mouton (*m*)	*moot-OH*
• **bleat**	bêler (*v*)	*bay-lay*

---

to stand in line, to line up, queue up = faire la queue *fehr la kuh*

---

tail	queue (*f*)	*kuh*
tiger	tigre (*m*)	*teeg-re*
vertebrate	vertébré(e) (*adj, m, f*)	*vehr-tay-bray*
• **invertebrate**	invertébré(e) (*adj, m, f*)	*EH-vehr-tay-bray*
wild animal	animal sauvage (*m*)	*a-nee-mal so-va-zh*
wolf	loup (*m*)	*loo*
• **howl**	hurler (*v*)	*ewr-lay*
zebra	zèbre (*m*)	*zeh-bre*
zoo	zoo (*m*)	*zoh-oh*
	jardin zoologique (*m*)	*zh-ard-EH zu-ul-uzh-eek*
• **zoological**	zoologique (*adj*)	*zu-ul-uzh-eek*
• **zoology**	zoologie (*f*)	*zu-ul-uzh-ee*

FOCUS: Some Common Animals

le chat   la vache   le poney   le chien

le tigre   le lion   le cerf   le cheval

le loup   le cochon   l'éléphant   l'ours

b. BIRDS AND FOWL

albatross	albatros *(m)*	*al-ba-tros*
beak	bec *(m)*	*behk*
bird	oiseau *(m)*	*wa-zoh*
blackbird	merle *(m)*	*mehrl*
chick	poussin *(m)*	*poos-EH*
chicken	poule *(f)*	*pool*
	poulet *(m)*	*pool-eh*
crow	corbeau *(m)*	*kor-bo*
dove	colombe *(f)*	*kul-OH-b*
duck	canard *(m)*	*kan-ar*
eagle	aigle *(m)*	*ehg-l*
falcon	faucon *(m)*	*fo-kOH*
feather	plume *(f)*	*plewm*
goose	oie *(f)*	*wa*
hen	poule *(f)*	*pool*

nightingale	rossignol *(m)*	*rus-ee-ny-ul*
ostrich	autruche *(f)*	*oh-trew-sh*
owl	hibou *(m)*	*ee-boo*
	chouette *(f)*	*sh-wet*
parakeet	perruche *(f)*	*pay-rew-sh*
parrot	perroquet *(m)*	*pehr-uk-eh*
pelican	pélican *(m)*	*pay-leek-AH*
penguin	pingouin *(m)*	*pEH-gwEH*
pigeon	pigeon *(m)*	*pee-zh-OH*

---

to be the fool in an affair = être le pigeon dans une affaire *eh-tr le pee-zh-OH d-AH zewn a-fehr*

---

robin	rouge-gorge *(m)*	*roo-zhe gor-zhe*
rooster	coq *(m)*	*kuk*
seagull	mouette *(f)*	*mweht*
sparrow	moineau *(m)*	*mwa-no*
	piaf *(m)*	*pyaf*
stork	cigogne *(f)*	*see-gu-ny*
swallow	hirondelle *(f)*	*eer-OH-dehl*
swan	cygne *(m)*	*see-ny*
turkey	dinde *(f)*	*dEH-d*
wing	aile *(f)*	*ehl*

c. FISH, REPTILES, AMPHIBIANS, AND MARINE ANIMALS

catfish	poisson-chat *(m)*	*pwas-OH-sha*
codfish	morue *(f)*	*mor-ew*
crocodile	crocodile *(m)*	*kru-ku-deel*
dolphin	dauphin *(m)*	*dof-EH*
eel	anguille *(f)*	*AH-gee-y*
fish	poisson *(m)*	*pwas-OH*
• **fin**	nageoire *(f)*	*na-zh-war*
• **fish**	pêcher *(v)*	*pay-shay*
	aller *(v)* à la pêche	*a-lay a la peh-sh*
• **fishbone**	arête *(f)*	*ar-eht*
• **fisherman**	pêcheur *(m)*	*peh-sh-ur*
	pêcheuse *(f)*	*peh-sh-uhz*
• **fishing**	pêche *(f)*	*peh-sh*
• **fishing rod**	canne *(f)* à pêche	*kan a peh-sh*
• **hook**	hameçon *(m)*	*ams-OH*
frog	grenouille *(f)*	*gre-noo-y*
goldfish	poisson rouge *(m)*	*pwas-OH roo-zh*
octopus	pieuvre *(f)*	*pee-yuv-re*
	poulpe *(m)*	*poolp*
reptile	reptile *(m)*	*rehp-teel*

salamander	salamandre (*f*)	*sa-la-mAH-dr*
sardine	sardine (*f*)	*sar-deen*
seal	phoque (*m*)	*fuk*
snake	serpent (*m*)	*sehrp-AH*
sole fish	sole (*f*)	*sul*
swordfish	espadon (*m*)	*ehs-pad-OH*
toad	crapaud (*m*)	*kra-po*
trout	truite (*f*)	*trew-eet*
tuna	thon (*m*)	*tOH*
turtle	tortue (*f*)	*tor-tew*
whale	baleine (*f*)	*bal-ehn*

d. INSECTS AND OTHER INVERTEBRATES

ant	fourmi (*f*)	*foor-mee*
bed bug	punaise (*f*)	*pew-nehz*
bee	abeille (*f*)	*a-beh-y*
butterfly	papillon (*m*)	*pa-pee-y-OH*
caterpillar	chenille (*f*)	*she-nee-y*
cockroach	blatte (*f*)	*blat*
	cafard (*m*)	*ka-far*
flea	puce (*f*)	*pewss*
fly	mouche (*f*)	*moosh*
insect	insecte (*m*)	*EH-sehkt*
louse	pou (*m*) (*pl*, poux)	*poo*
maggot	asticot (*m*)	*as-tee-ko*
metamorphosis	métamorphose (*f*)	*may-ta-mor-foz*
mosquito	moustique (*m*)	*moos-teek*
moth	phalène (*f*)	*fal-ehn*
organism	organisme (*m*)	*organ-ees-me*
scorpion	scorpion (*m*)	*shor-py-OH*
silkworm	ver (*m*) à soie	*vehr a swa*
spider	araignée (*f*)	*ar-ay-ny-ay*
termite	termite (*m*)	*tehr-meet*
tick	tique (*f*)	*teek*
wasp	guêpe (*f*)	*gehp*
worm	ver (*m*)	*vehr*

COMMUNICATING, FEELING, AND THINKING

16. BASIC SOCIAL EXPRESSIONS

a. GREETINGS AND FAREWELLS

Farewell!	Adieu!	*ad-yuh*
Good afternoon!	Bonjour!	*bOH-zhoor*
Good evening!	Bonsoir!	*bOH-swar*
Good morning!	Bonjour!	*bOH-zhoor*
Good night!	Bonsoir!	*bOH-swar*
	Bonne nuit! (*when going to bed*)	*bun new-ee*
Good-bye!	Au revoir!	*or-vwar*
greet	saluer (*v*)	*sal-ew-ay*
• greeting	salut (*m*)	*sal-ew*
	salutation (*f*)	*sal-ew-tas-y-OH*
Hello!	Bonjour! (*during daytime*)	*bOH-zhoor*
	Bonsoir! (*during evening hours*)	*bOH-swar*
Hi!	Salut!	*sal-ew*
How are you?	Comment allez-vous? (*pol*)	*kum-AH tal-ay voo*
	Comment vas-tu? (*fam*)	*kum-AH va-tew*
How's it going?	Comment ça va?	*kum-AH sa-va*
	Ça va?	*sa-va*
• Bad(ly)!	Mal!	*mal*
• Fine!	Bien!	*byEH*
• Not bad!	Pas mal!	*pah mal*
• Quite well!	Très bien!	*treh byEH*
• So, so!	Comme-ci, comme-ça!	*kum-see kum-sa*
• Very well!	Très bien!	*treh byEH*
Please give my regards/greetings to . . .	Mon bon souvenir à . . .	*mOH bOH soov-neer a*
See you!	Salut!	*sal-ew*
• See you later!	À tout à l'heure!	*a-too-ta-lur*
• See you soon!	À bientôt!	*a-byEH-toh*
• See you Sunday!	À dimanche!	*a-deem-AH-sh*
shake hands	serrer (*v*) la main à quelqu'un	*sehr-ay lam-EH a kehlk-UH*
	donner (*v*) la main à quelqu'un	*dun-ay lam-EH a kehlk-UH*
• handshake	poignée de main (*f*)	*pwa-ny-ayd-mEH*

b. FORMS OF ADDRESS AND INTRODUCTIONS

A pleasure!	C'est un plaisir!	*seht-UH-play-zeer*
• The pleasure is mine!	C'est mon plaisir!	*sehm-OH play-zeer*
acquaintance	connaissance (*f*)	*kun-eh-SAH-s*
Allow me to introduce myself.	Permettez-moi de me présenter.	*pehrm-eht-ay-mwa dem prayz-AH-tay*
Allow me to introduce you to . . .	Permettez-moi de vous présenter à . . .	*pehrm-eht-ay-mwa de voo-prayz-AH-tay a*
be seated	s'asseoir (*v*)	*sas-war*
• Be seated, please.	Asseyez-vous, s'il vous plaît. (*pol*)	*ass-ay-yay-voo seel-voo-pleh*
	Assieds-toi, s'il te plaît. (*fam*)	*ass-yay-twa seel-te-pleh*
be on a first-name basis	tutoyer (*v*)	*tew-twa-yay*
be on a formal basis	vouvoyer (*v*)	*voo-vwa-yay*
calling card	carte (*f*) de visite	*kart de vee-zeet*
Come in!	Entrez! (*pol*)	*AH-tray*
	Entre! (*fam*)	*AH-tre*
• enter (into)	entrer (*v*) (dans)	*AH-tray (dAH)*
Delighted!	Heureux! (*m*)	*ur-uh*
	Heureuse! (*f*)	*ur-uhz*
Happy to make your acquaintance!	Heureux(-euse) de faire votre connaissance! (*pol*)	*ur-uh(-uhz) de fehr vut-re kun-eh-sAH-s*
	Heureux(-euse) de faire ta connaissance! (*fam*)	*ur-uh(-uhz) de fehr ta kun-eh-sAH-s*
introduce someone	présenter (*v*) quelqu'un	*prayz-AH-tay kehl-kUH*
• introduction	présentation (*f*)	*prayz-AH-tas-y-OH*
know someone	connaître quelqu'un	*kun-eht-re kehl-kUH*
Let me introduce you to . . .	Je vous présente à . . . (*pol*)	*zhe-voo-prayz-AH-t a*
	Je te présente à . . . (*fam*)	*zh-te-prayz-AH-t a*
meet, run into someone	rencontrer (*v*)	*rAH-kOH-tray*
	pour la première fois (*for the first time*)	*poor la prem-yehr fwa*
title	titre (*m*)	*tee-tre*
• Dr. (*M.D. degree*)	docteur (*m*)	*duk-tur*
	docteur femme (*f*)	*duk-tur fahm*

• **Dr.** (*Ph.D. degree*)	docteur (*m*)	*duk-tur*
	doctoresse (*f*)	*duk-tur-ehs*
• **Miss, Ms.**	mademoiselle	*mad-mwa-zehl*
• **Mr.**	monsieur	*me-sy-uh*
• **Mrs.**	madame	*ma-dahm*
What's your name?	Comment vous appelez-vous? (*pol*)	*kum-AH voo-zap-lay-voo*
	Comment t'appelles-tu? (*fam*)	*kum-AH tap-ehl-tew*
• **My name is . . .**	Je m'appelle . . .	*zhem-ap-ehl*
• **I'm . . .**	Je suis . . .	*zhe-swee*

c. COURTESY

Best wishes!	Meilleurs vœux!	*meh-y-ur vuh*
Bless you! (*after a sneeze*)	Dieu vous (te) bénisse!	*dyuh voo (te) bay-neess*
	À vos souhaits! (*pol*)	*a-vo-sw-eh*
	À tes souhaits! (*fam*)	*a-tay-sw-eh*
Cheers!	À votre santé!	*a vut-re sAH-tay*
	À la vôtre!	*a-la-voh-tre*
Congratulations!	Félicitations!	*fay-lee-see-tas-y-OH*
Don't mention it!	De rien!	*der-yEH*
	Il n'y a pas de quoi!	*eel-ny-a-pahd-kwa*
Enjoy your meal!	Bon appétit!	*bun-apay-tee*
Excuse me!	Excusez-moi! (*pol*)	*ehks-kew-zay-mwa*
	Excuse-moi! (*fam*)	*ehks-kewz-mwa*
	Pardonnez-moi! (*pol*)	*par-dun-ay-mwa*
	Pardonne-moi! (*fam*)	*par-dun-mwa*
Good luck!	Bonne chance!	*bun-sh-AH-s*
Happy New Year!	Bonne et heureuse année!	*bun ay ur-uhz a-nay*
Have a good holiday!	Bonnes vacances!	*bun vak-AH-s*
Have a good time!	Amusez-vous bien! (*pol*)	*a-mew-zay-voo byEH*
	Amuse-toi bien! (*fam*)	*a-mewz-twa byEH*
Have a good trip!	Bon voyage!	*bOH vwa-ya-zh*
Have a happy birthday!	Bon anniversaire!	*bun a-nee-vehr-sehr*
Many thanks!	Merci mille fois!	*mehr-see meel fwa*
	Merci infiniment!	*mehr-see EH-fee-neem-AH*
May I come in?	Puis-je entrer?	*pew-ee-zh AH-tray*
May I help you?	Vous désirez?	*voo day-zee-ray*
	Puis-je vous aider?	*pew-ee-zh voo-zay-day*
Merry Christmas!	Joyeux Noël!	*zh-wa-yuh nu-ehl*
No!	Non!	*nOH*

OK!	D'accord!	*dak-or*
	Entendu!	*AH-t-AH-dew*
Please!	S'il vous plaît! (*pol*)	*seel-voo-pleh*
	S'il te plait! (*fam*)	*seel-te-pleh*
Season's Greetings	Meilleurs voeux	*meh-y-ur vuh*
Thank you!	Merci!	*mehr-see*
Yes!	Oui!	*wee*
You're welcome!	Je vous en prie! (*pol*)	*zhe-vooz-AH-pree*
	Je t'en prie! (*fam*)	*zh-tAH-pree*
	De rien!	*dur-yEH*
	Il n'y a pas de quoi!	*eel-nya-pad-kwa*

17. SPEAKING AND TALKING

a. SPEECH ACTIVITIES AND TYPES

advice	conseil (*m*)	*k-OH-say*
• advise	conseiller (*v*)	*k-OH-say-yay*
allude	faire (*v*) allusion	*fehr al-ewz-y-OH*
analogy	analogie (*f*)	*a-na-luzh-ee*
announce	annoncer (*v*)	*an-OH-say*
• announcement	annonce (*f*)	*an-OH-s*
answer	réponse (*f*)	*rayp-OH-s*
• answer	répondre (*v*)	*rayp-OH-dre*
argue	disputer (*v*)	*dees-pew-tay*
• argument	dispute (*f*)	*dees-pewt*
	argument (*m*)	*ar-gewn-AH*
articulate	articuler (*v*)	*ar-tee-kew-lay*
ask	demander (*v*)	*dem-AH-day*
beg to do	prier (*v*) de faire	*pree-yayd fehr kehlke*
(*something*)	quelque chose	*sh-oh-z*
call	appeler (*v*)	*aplay*
change subject	changer (*v*) de sujet	*sh-AH-zh-ayd sew-*
		zh-eh
chat	causer (*v*)	*ko-zay*
communicate	communiquer (*v*)	*kum-ewn-ee-kay*
• communication	communication (*f*)	*kum-ewn-ee-kas-y-OH*
compare	comparer (*v*)	*k-OH-pa-ray*
• comparison	comparaison (*f*)	*k-OH-par-ehz-OH*
conclude	conclure (*v*)	*k-OH-klewr*
• conclusion	conclusion (*f*)	*k-OH-klewz-y-OH*
congratulate	féliciter (*v*)	*fay-lee-see-tay*
conversation	conversation (*f*)	*k-OH-vehr-sas-y-OH*
debate	débat (*m*)	*day-ba*
• debate	débattre (*v*)	*day-bat-re*
declare	déclarer (*v*)	*day-klar-ay*
deny	nier (*v*)	*nee-yay*
describe	décrire (*v*)	*day-kreer*
• description	description (*f*)	*dehs-kreeps-y-OH*

dictate	dicter (v)	deek-tay
digress	faire (v) une digression	fehr ewn deeg-rays-y-OH
discuss	discuter (v)	dees-kew-tay
• discussion	discussion (f)	dees-kews-y-OH
emphasis	emphase (f)	AH-fahz
• emphasize	accentuer (v)	aks-AH-tew-ay
excuse	excuse (f)	ehks-kewz
• excuse oneself	s'excuser (v)	sehks-kew-zay
explain	expliquer (v)	ehks-plee-kay
• explanation	explication (f)	ehks-plee-kahs-y-OH
express	exprimer (v)	ehks-pree-may
• express oneself	s'exprimer (v)	sehks-pree-may
• expression	expression (f)	ehks-prehs-y-OH
figure of speech	figure (f) de rhétorique	feeg-ewr de ray-tor-eek
• allegory	allégorie (f)	al-ay-gor-ee
• literal	litéral(e) (adj, m, f)	lee-tay-ral
• metaphor	métaphore (f)	may-ta-for
• symbol	symbole (m)	s-EH-bul
gossip	potin (m)	put-EH
• gossip	potiner (v)	put-een-ay
hesitation	hésitation (f)	ay-zee-tahs-y-OH
• hesitate	hésiter (v)	ay-zee-tay
identify	identifier (v)	eed-AH-teef-yay
indicate, point out	indiquer (v)	EH-dee-kay
• indication	indication (f)	EH-dee-kahs-y-OH
inform	informer (v)	EH-form-ay
	faire savoir (v)	fehr savwar
interrupt	interrompre (v)	EH-tayr-OH-pre
• interruption	interruption (f)	EH-tayr-ewps-y-OH
invite	inviter (v)	EH-vee-tay
jest	plaisanter (v)	plehz-AH-tay
joke	plaisanterie (f)	plehz-AH-tree
	blague (f)	blag
• tell a joke	raconter (v) une plaisanterie	rak-OH-tay ewn plehz-AH-tree
keep quiet	se taire (v)	se-tehr
lecture	conférence (f)	kOH-fayr-AH-s
• lecture	donner (v) une conférence	dun-ay ewn kOH-fayr-AH-s
lie	mensonge (m)	m-AH-s-OH-zh
• lie	mentir (v)	m-AH-teer
• liar	menteur (m)	m-AH-tur
	menteuse (f)	mAH-tuhz
listen to	écouter (v)	ay-koo-tay
malign, speak badly	diffamer (v)	deef-a-may

mean	signifier (v)	*see-ny-eef-yay*
	vouloir dire (v)	*vool-war deer*
• meaning	signification (f)	*see-ny-ee-fee-kas-y-OH*
	sens (m)	*sAHs*
mention	mentionner (v)	*mAH-sy-un-ay*
mumble	grommeler (v)	*grum-lay*
murmur	murmurer (v)	*mewr-mew-ray*
nag	grogner (v)	*gru-ny-ay*
offend	offenser (v)	*uf-AH-say*
oral	oral(e) (adj, m, f)	*or-al*
• orally	oralement (adv)	*or-alm-AH*
order	ordre (m)	*or-dre*
• order	ordonner (v)	*or-dun-ay*
• order (food)	commander (v)	*kum-AH-day*
outspokenly	franchement (adv)	*frAH-sh-mAH*
	carrément (adv)	*kar-ay-mAH*
praise	louer (v)	*lway*
pray	prier (v)	*pree-yay*
• prayer	prière (f)	*pree-yehr*
preach	prêcher (v)	*pray-shay*
• sermon	sermon (m)	*sehrm-OH*
promise	promesse (f)	*prum-ehs*
• promise	promettre (v)	*prum-eh-tre*
pronounce	prononcer (v)	*prun-OH-say*
• pronunciation	prononciation (f)	*prun-OH-see-yas-yOH*
propose	proposer (v)	*prup-OH-zay*
recommend	recommander (v)	*re-kum-AH-day*
relate	raconter (v)	*rak-OH-tay*
repeat	répéter (v)	*ray-pay-tay*
• repetition	répétition (f)	*ray-pay-tees-y-OH*
report	compte rendu (m)	*kOHt-rAH-dew*
• report	faire (v) un compte rendu	*fehr UH kOHt-rAH-dew*
	faire (v) un rapport sur	*fehr UH ra-por sewr*
reproach	reprocher (v)	*re-prush-ay*
request	demande (f)	*dem-AH-d*
• request	demander (v)	*dem-AH-day*
rhetoric	rhétorique (f)	*ray-tor-eek*
• rhetorical	rhétorique (adj)	*ray-tor-eek*
• rhetorical question	question (f) rhétorique	*kehst-yOH ray-tor-eek*
rumor	bruit (m)	*brew-ee*
• Rumor has it that . . .	Le bruit court que . . .	*le brew-ee koor ke*
say, tell	dire (v)	*deer*
shout, yell	cri (m)	*kree*
• shout, yell	crier (v)	*kree-yay*

Shut up!	Ferme-la!	*ferm-la*
silence	silence (*m*)	*seel-AHs*
• **silent**	silencieux(-euse) (*adj, m, f*)	*seel-AHs-yuh(-yuhz)*
speak, talk	parler (*v*)	*par-lay*
• **speech, talk**	discours (*m*)	*dees-koor*
state	affirmer (*v*)	*a-feerm-ay*
• **statement**	affirmation (*f*)	*a-feerm-as-y-OH*
story	conte (*m*)	*kOHt*
	histoire (*f*)	*ees-twar*
• **tell** (*a story*)	conter (*v*)	*kOH-tay*
	raconter (*v*) une histoire	*rakOH-tay ewn ees-twar*
suggest	suggérer (*v*)	*sewg-zh-ay-ray*
summarize	résumer (*v*)	*ray-zewm-ay*
• **summary**	sommaire (*m*)	*sum-ehr*
	résumé (*m*)	*ray-zewm-ay*
swear (*e.g., in court*)	jurer (*v*)	*zh-ew-ray*
• (*e.g., profanity*)	dire (*v*) des jurons	*deer day zh-ewr-OH*
thank	remercier (*v*)	*re-mehr-see-yay*
threat	menace (*f*)	*me-nas*
• **threaten**	menacer (*v*)	*me-nas-ay*
toast	toast (*m*)	*tost*
• **toast**	porter (*v*) un toast	*por-tay UH tost*
translate	traduire (*v*)	*trad-ew-eer*
• **translation**	traduction (*f*)	*trad-ewks-yOH*
vocabulary	vocabulaire (*m*)	*vu-ka-bew-lehr*
warn	avertir (*v*)	*a-vehr-teer*
	prévenir (*v*)	*pray-vneer*
• **warning**	avis (*m*)	*a-vee*
	prévenance (*f*)	*pray-vn-AH-s*
whisper	chuchoter (*v*)	*shew-shut-ay*
word	mot (*m*) (*written*)	*mOH*
	parole (*f*) (*spoken*)	*pa-rul*
yawn	bâillement (*m*)	*bah-y-mAH*
• **yawn**	bâiller (*v*)	*bah-yay*

b. USEFUL EXPRESSIONS

Actually	Effectivement (*adv*)	*ay-fehk-teev-mAH*
As a matter of fact	En fait	*AH-feht*
Briefly	En bref	*AH-brehf*
By the way	À propos	*a-pro-po*
Go ahead!	Allez-y! (*pol*)	*a-lay-zee*
	Vas-y! (*fam*)	*va-zee*
How do you say . . . in French?	Comment dit-on . . . en français?	*kum-AH deet-OH . . . AH frAH-seh*

I don't understand!	Je ne comprends pas!	*zhen-kOH-prAH-pah*
I'm sure that	Je suis sûr(e) (*m, f*) que	*zhe swee sewr ke*
Isn't it so?	N'est-ce pas?	*nehs-pah*
It seems that	Il semble que	*eel sAH-bl ke*
It's necessary that	Il faut que	*eel foh ke*
	Il est nécessaire que	*eel eh nay-say-sehr ke*
It's not true!	Ce n'est pas vrai!	*se-neh-pah vreh*
It's obvious that	Il est évident que	*eel eh tay-veed-AH ke*
It's true!	C'est vrai!	*seh vreh*
Listen	Écoutez (*pol*)	*ay-koo-tay*
	Écoute (*fam*)	*ay-koot*
Now	Maintenant	*mEHt-nAH*
To sum up	En somme	*AH sum*
What was I saying?	Qu'est-ce que je disais?	*kehs-ke zhe dee-zeh*
Who knows?	Qui sait?	*kee seh*

FOCUS: Some Common Gestures

> In common speech situations, French people gesticulate quite noticeably.
> They also tend to touch each other much more upon greeting each other.

| Are you crazy? | Êtes-vous (*pol*) fou (*m*)/folle (*f*)? | *eht-voo foo (ful)* |
| | Es-tu (*fam*) fou (*m*)/folle (*f*)? | *eh-tew foo (ful)* |

| Come here! | Venez (*pol*) ici! | *vnay-zee-see* |
| | Viens (*fam*) ici! | *vy-EH-zee-see* |

Hello (*pol*)!

Bonjour! (*during daytime*)	*bOH-zhoor*
Bonsoir! (*during evening hours*) (see also 16a)	*bOH-swar*

Hi (*fam*)!

Salut!   *sal-ew*

Let me introduce you to . . .

Je vous (*pol*) présente à . . .	*zhe voo prayz-AH-t a . . .*
Je te (*fam*) présente à . . .	*zh-te prayz-AH-t a . . .*

No way!

Pas de moyen!	*pahd-mwa-yEH*
Pas possible!	*pah pus-eebl*
Pas question!	*pah-kehst-yOH*

It's very good!

C'est très bon!   *seh treh bOH*

18. THE TELEPHONE

a. TELEPHONES AND ACCESSORIES

answering machine	répondeur (*m*) téléphonique	*rayp-OH-dur tay-lay-fun-eek*
	téléphone-répondeur (*m*)	*tay-lay-fun rayp-OH-dur*
cable	câble (*m*) téléphonique	*kah-bl tay-lay-fun-eek*
caller ID	afficheur (*m*)	*a-feesh-ur*
fax machine	télécopieur (*m*)	*tay-lay-kup-yur*

intercom	interphone (m)	EH-tehr-fun
optic fiber	fibre (f) optique	feebr-up-teek
pager	pager (m)	pa-zh-ur
receiver (*handset*)	combiné (m)	kOH-bee-nay
• earphone	écouteur (m)	ay-koot-ur
telecommunication	télécommunication (f)	tay-lay-kum-ew-nee-kas-yOH
• telecommunications satellite	satellite (m) de télécommunications	sat-eh-leet de tay-lay-kum-ew-nee-kas-yOH
telephone	téléphone (m)	tay-lay-fun
• cellular phone	téléphone (m) cellulaire	tay-lay-fun-sehl-yew-lehr
• cordless phone	téléphone (m) sans fil	tay-lay-fun-sAH-feel
• outlet (*phone*)	prise (f)	preez
• pay phone	téléphone (m) public	tay-lay-fun pew-bleek
• phone book	annuaire (m) du téléphone	a-new-ehr dew tay-lay-fun
	bottin (m)	but-EH
• phone booth	cabine (f) téléphonique	ka-been tay-lay-fun-eek
• plug	fiche (f) téléphonique	feesh tay-lay-fun-eek
• portable phone	téléphone (m) portatif	tay-lay-fun por-ta-teef
• telephone set	appareil (m) téléphonique	a-pa-ray tay-lay-fun-eek
• telephone	téléphoner (v)	tay-lay-fun-ay
telephone credit card	télécarte (f)	tay-lay-kart
token	jeton (m)	zh-tOH
• slot (*for tokens*)	fente (f)	fAHt
yellow pages	pages (f, pl) jaunes	pazh zh-ohn

b. USING THE TELEPHONE

answer	répondre (v)	rayp-OH-dre
• pick up (the phone)	décrocher (v)	day-krush-ay
area code	code (m) régional	kud ray-zh-un-al
collect call	téléphoner en P.C.V.	tay-lay-fun-ay AH pay-say-vay
dial	composer le numéro	kOH-poh-zayl new-may-roh
• direct dialing	téléphoner en direct	tay-lay-fun-ay AH dee-rehkt
fax	télécopie (f)	tay-lay-kup-ee
hang up	raccrocher (v)	rak-rush-ay
information	renseignement (m)	rAH-seh-ny-mAH

long-distance call	appel à l'extérieur	*ap-ehl al ehks-tay-ree-ur*
make a call	faire (*v*) un appel téléphonique	*fehr UH nap-ehl tay-lay-fun-eek*
• Hello!	Allô!	*a-loh*
• Is . . . in?	Est-ce que . . . est là?	*ehs-ke eh la*
• This is . . .	Ici . . .	*ee-see*
• Who's speaking?	Qui parle?	*kee parl*
• Wrong number!	Mauvais numéro!	*muv-eh new-may-roh*
message	message (*m*)	*may-sa-zh*
operator	téléphoniste (*m/f*)	*tay-lay-fun-eest*
• switchboard operator	standardiste (*m/f*)	*stAH-dard-eest*
phone	téléphoner (*v*)	*tay-lay-fun-ay*
phone bill	facture (*f*)	*fak-tewr*
phone call	appel (*m*) téléphonique	*ap-ehl tay-lay-fun-eek*
phone line	ligne (*f*) téléphonique	*lee-ny tay-lay-fun-eek*
• busy (line)	occupée (*adj*)	*uk-ew-pay*
• free (line)	libre (*adj*)	*lee-bre*
phone number	numéro (*m*) de téléphone	*new-may-rohd tay-lay-fun*
ring (*phone*)	sonner (*v*)	*sun-ay*
telex	télex (*m*)	*tay-lehks*

For information on computer terminology, see Section 42.

---

19. LETTER WRITING

a. FORMAL SALUTATIONS/CLOSINGS

Dear Sir	Monsieur	*me-sy-uh*
Dear Madam	Madame	*ma-dahm*
To whom it may concern	À qui de droit	*a-kee de drwa*
Yours truly	salutations distinguées	*sa-lew-tas-yOH deest-EH-gay*
With cordial greetings	Sentiments cordiaux	*sAH-teem-AH kord-y-oh*
Please accept	Veuillez accepter	*vuh-yay ak-sehp-tay*
	Veuillez agréer	*vuh-yay a-gray-ay*

b. FAMILIAR SALUTATIONS/CLOSINGS

Dear	Cher (*adj/m*); (*pl*, Chers)	*sh-ehr*
	Chère (*f*); (*pl*, Chères)	*sh-ehr*
Yours	Bien à toi	*byEH a twa*
Greetings	Sincères salutations	*sEH-sehr sa-lew-tas-yOH*
Affectionately	Affectueusement (*adv*)	*a-fehk-tew-uhz-mAH*
Give my regards to	Un bon souvenir à	*UH bOH soo-vneer a*
A kiss	baiser (*m*), bise (*f*)	*bay-zay, beez*
A hug	embrassement (*m*)	*AH-bras-mAH*
	étreinte (*f*)	*ay-trEHt*
• **give me a kiss**	donne-moi un bisou	*dun-mwa-UH-bee-zoo*
• **love and kisses**	grosses bises (*f*, *pl*)	*gros-beez*

c. PARTS OF A LETTER/PUNCTUATION

body	contenu (*m*)	*kOH-te-new*
	corps (*m*)	*kor*
closing	formule (*f*) finale	*for-mewl fee-nal*
	salutation (*f*) finale	*sa-lew-tas-yOH fee-nal*
date	date (*f*)	*dat*
heading	l'en-tête (*f*)	*lAH-teht*
	vedette (*f*)	*ve-deht*
place	lieu (*m*)	*ly-uh*
punctuation	ponctuation (*f*)	*pOHk-tew-as-yOH*
• **accent**	accent (*m*)	*aks-AH*
• **apostrophe**	apostrophe (*f*)	*a-pus-truf*
• **asterisk**	astérisque (*m*)	*as-tay-reesk*
• **bracket**	crochet (*m*)	*krush-eh*
• **capital letter**	lettre majuscule (*f*)	*leht-re ma-zh-ews-kewl*
• **colon**	deux points (*m*, *pl*)	*duh pwEH*
• **comma**	virgule (*f*)	*veerg-ewl*
• **exclamation point**	point (*m*) d'exclamation	*pwEH dehks-kla-mas-yOH*
• **hyphen**	tiret (*m*)	*teer-eh*
	trait (*m*) d'union	*trehd-ew-ny-OH*
• **italics**	en italique (*m*)	*AH nee-ta-leek*
• **parenthesis**	parenthèse (*f*)	*par-AH-tehz*
• **period**	point (*m*)	*pwEH*
• **question mark**	point (*m*) d'interrogation	*pwEH-dEH-tay-rug-as-yOH*
• **quotation mark**	guillemet (*m*)	*gee-y-meh*
• **semicolon**	point (*m*) virgule (*f*)	*pwEH veerg-ewl*
• **small letter**	lettre minuscule (*f*)	*leht-re meen-ews-kewl*

• **square bracket**	crochet (m)	krush-eh
• **underlining**	soulignement (m)	soo-lee-ny-mAH
salutation	formule (f) initiale	for-mew-lee-nees-yal
sentence	phrase (f)	frahz
signature	signature (f)	see-ny-a-tewr
• **sign**	signer (v)	see-ny-ay
spelling	orthographe (f)	or-tug-raf
text	texte (m)	tehkst
• **abbreviation**	abréviation (f)	ab-rayv-y-as-yOH
• **letter** (*of the alphabet*)	lettre (f)	leht-re
• **line**	ligne (f)	lee-ny
• **margin**	marge (f)	mar-zh
• **P. S.**	P. S.	pay-ehs
	post-scriptum (m)	pust-skreep-tum
• **paragraph**	paragraphe (m)	pa-ra-graf
• **phrase**	phrase (f)	frahz
word	mot (m)	moh

d. WRITING MATERIALS AND ACCESSORIES

adhesive tape	ruban (m) adhésif transparent	rewbAH ad-ay-zeef trAHs-par-AH
envelope	enveloppe (f)	AH-vlup
eraser	gomme (f)	gum
glue	colle (f)	kul
ink	encre (f)	AH-kre
letter	lettre (f)	leht-re
letterhead	papier (m) à en-tête	pap-yay a AH-teht
marker	marqueur (m)	mark-ur
	crayon-feutre (m)	kray-yOH fuh-tr
pad	bloc-notes (m)	bluk nut
page	page (f)	pazh
paper	papier (m)	pap-yay
paper clip	trombone (m)	trOH-bun
pen	stylo (m)	stee-loh
• **ballpoint pen**	stylo (m) à bille	stee-loh à bee-y
• **felt-tip pen**	stylo-feutre (m)	stee-loh fuh-tr
pencil	crayon (m)	kray-yOH
ruler	règle (f)	reh-gle
scissors	ciseaux (m, pl)	see-zoh

FOCUS: Letters

Formal	
Lieu et date	Paris, le premier (1er) juin 20 . . .
Destinataire	M. Charles DURAND, Directeur Institut de Beauté 2, Square Henri Delormel 75014 Paris
Formule (Salutation) initiale	Monsieur le Directeur,
le contenu (le corps)	Veuillez m'envoyer . . . .
Formule (Salutation) finale	Veuillez agréer, Monsieur, l'expression de mes sentiments distingués.
Signature	_____ Monique PAULY 29, rue des Jardins 75008 Paris

Familiar
Paris, le 2 juin 20 . . .
Chers amis, 　J'écris ces quelques mots pour . . . . 　　　　Grosses bises, 　　　　Dominique

staple	agrafe (f)	ag-raf
• **stapler**	agrafeuse (f)	ag-gra-fuhz
string	ficelle (f)	fee-sehl
typewriter	machine (f) à écrire	ma-sheen a ay-kreer
• **carriage**	chariot (m)	shar-ee-oh
• **keyboard**	clavier (m)	klav-yay
• **ribbon**	ruban (m)	rewb-AH
• **space bar**	barre (f) d'espacement	bar-dehs-pas-mAH
• **tab**	tabulateur (m)	ta-bew-la-tur
• **type**	taper (v) à la machine	ta-pay a la ma-sheen

e. AT THE POST OFFICE

abroad	à l'étranger	ul-ay-trAH-zh-ay
address	adresse (f)	ad-rehs
• **return address**	adresse (f) de l'expéditeur	ad-rehs de lehks-pay-dee-tur
addressee	destinataire (m)	day-steen-a-tehr
airmail	par avion	par av-yOH
business letter	lettre (f) commerciale	leht-re kum-ehrs-yal
clerk	commis (m)	kum-ee
	employé(e) (m, f)	AH-plwa-yay
clerk's window	guichet (m)	geesh-eh
correspondence	correspondance (f)	kor-ehs-pOH-dAH-ss
• **envelope**	enveloppe (f)	AH-vlup
general delivery	poste (f) restante	pust rehstAHt
invitation	invitation (f)	EH-veet-as-yOH
• **wedding/other**	faire-part (m)	fehr-par
letter carrier	facteur (m) (de lettres)	fak-tur (de leht-re)
mail	courrier (m)	koor-yay
	poste (f)	pust
• **mail**	mettre (v) une lettre à la poste	meht-re ewn leht-re a la pust
mail delivery	distribution (f) du courrier	dees-tree-bews-yOH dew koor-yay
mailbox (slot)	boîte (f) à lettres	bwat a leht-re
money order	mandat (m) de paiement	mAHda de pehmAH
note	billet (m)	beey-eh
package	colis (m)	kul-ee
	paquet (m)	pa-kay
post office	bureau (m) de poste	bew-rohd pust
post office box	boîte (f) postale	bwat pus-tal
	case (f) postale	kahz pus-tal

postage	affranchissement (m)	a-frAH-shees-mAH
• meter	vignette (f)	vee-ny-eht
postal code	code (m) postal	kud pus-tal
postal rate	tarif (m)	tar-eef
postcard	carte (f) postale	kart pus-tal
printed matter	imprimés (m, pl)	EH-pree-may
receive	recevoir (v)	res-vwar
registered letter	lettre (f) recommandée	leht-re re-kum-AH-day
reply	réponse (f)	raypOHs
• reply	répondre (v)	rayp-OH-dre
send	expédier (v)	ehks-payd-yay
	envoyer (v)	AH-vwa-yay
sender	expéditeur (m)	ehks-pay-dee-tur
special delivery	expédition (f) express	ehks-payd-ees-yOH ehks-press
stamp (postage)	timbre-poste (m)	tEH-bre pust
wait for	attendre (v)	at-AH-dre
write	écrire (v)	ay-kreer

20. THE MEDIA

a. PRINT MEDIA

advertising	publicité (f)	pew-blee-see-tay
appendix	appendice (m)	ap-AH-deess
atlas	atlas (m)	at-lahss
author	auteur (m)	oh-tur
	femme (f) auteur	fahm oh-tur
book	livre (m)	leev-re
comics	bande (f) dessinée	bAHd day-see-nay
cover	couverture (f)	koo-vehr-tewr
essay	essai (m)	ay-seh
fiction	ouvrage (m) de fiction	oov-ra-zh de feeks-yOH
• nonfiction	ouvrage (m) de réalité	oov-ra-zh de ray-al-ee-tay
• science fiction	science-fiction (f)	syAHs-feeks-yOH
index	index (m)	EH-dehks
magazine	magazine (m)	ma-ga-zeen
	revue (f)	re-vew
newspaper	journal (m)	zh-oor-nal
• article	article (m)	ar-teekl
• criticism	critique (f)	kree-teek
• daily newspaper	quotidien (m)	kut-eed-y-EH
• editor	rédacteur (m)	ray-dak-tur
	rédactrice (f)	ray-dak-treess
• editorial	éditorial (m)	ay-dee-tor-yal

• front page	la une (*f*)	la-ewn
	première page (*f*)	prem-yehr pazh
• heading	rubrique (*f*)	rew-breek
• headline	manchette (*f*)	mAH-sh-eht
• illustration	illustration (*f*)	eel-ew-stras-yOH
• interview	interview (*f*)	EH-tehr-vew
• journalist	journaliste (*m/f*)	zh-oor-nal-eest
• news	actualités (*f*)	ak-tew-a-leet-ay
• obituary	notice (*f*)	nut-eess
	nécrologique	nay-kru-lu-zheek
	nécrologie (*f*)	nay-kru-lu-zhee
• photo	photo(graphie) (*f*)	fu-tu(graf-ee)
• reader	lecteur (*m*)	lehk-tur
	lectrice (*f*)	lehk-treess
• reporter	reporter (*m/f*)	re-port-ehr
• review	critique (*f*)	kree-teek
• weekly periodical	hebdomadaire (*adj/n, m, f*)	ehb-dum-a-dehr
note	note (*f*)	nut
• footnote	note (*f*) en bas de page	nut-AH-bahd-pazh
novel	roman (*m*)	rum-AH
• adventure	d'aventure	dav-AH-tewr
• best-seller	best-seller (*m*)	behst-sehl-ur
• mystery	policier (*adj*)	pul-ees-yay
• plot	intrigue (*f*)	EH-treeg
• romance	d'amour	da-moor
page	page (*f*)	pazh
pamphlet, brochure	dépliant (*m*)	day-plee-yAH
	brochure (*f*)	brush-ewr
play	pièce (*f*) de théâtre	pee-ehss de tay-ah-tre
• comedy	comédie (*f*)	kum-ay-dee
• drama	drame (*m*)	drahm
• tragedy	tragédie (*f*)	tra-zh-ay-dee
pocket book/paperback	livre (*m*) de poche	leev-re de push
poem	poème (*m*)	pu-ehm
poetry	poésie (*f*)	pu-ay-zee
printing	imprimerie (*f*)	EH-preem-ree
• editor (correcting)	correcteur (*m*)	kur-ehk-tur
• editor (writing)	rédacteur (*m*)	ray-dak-tur
• print	imprimer (*v*)	EH-preem-ay
• printing, typography	typographie (*f*)	teep-ug-raf-ee
• printing edition (in publishing)	tirage (*m*)	tee-ra-zh
• proofreader	correcteur (*m*)	kur-ehk-tur
publish	publier (*v*)	pew-blee-yay
• publisher	éditeur (*m*)	ay-deet-ur

read	lire (v)	leer
reference book	ouvrage (m) de référence	oov-ra-zh de ray-fayr-AH-s
• definition	définition (f)	day-fee-nees-yOH
• dictionary	dictionnaire (m)	deek-see-yun-ehr
• encyclopedia	encyclopédie (f)	AH-see-klup-ay-dee
science fiction	science-fiction (f)	syAHs-feeks-yOH
short story	conte (m)	kOHt
	nouvelle (f)	noo-vehl
text	texte (m)	tehkst
title	titre (m)	teet-re
turn pages, leaf through	tourner (v) les pages feuilleter (v)	toor-nay lay pahzh fuh-y-tay
write	écrire (v)	ay-kreer

b. ELECTRONIC MEDIA

antenna	antenne (f)	AH-tehn
audio-visual equipment	appareils (m, pl) audio-visuels	a-pa-reh-y ohd-hyu vee-zew-ehl
• blank cassette	cassette vierge (f)	kas-eht vee-ehr-zh
• cassette	cassette (f)	kas-eht
• compact disc	disque compact (m)	deesk-kOH-pakt
• DVD	D.V.D. (m)	day-vay-day
• headphones	casque (m) à écouteurs	kask-a-ay-koo-tur
• loudspeaker	haut-parleur (m)	oh-par-lur
• microphone	microphone (m)	meek-ruf-un
• play a record	passer un disque	pah-say UH deesk
• receiver, tuner	dispositif (m) d'accord	dees-poh-zee-teef dak-or
• record	disque (m)	deesk
	enregistrer (v)	AH-re-zh-ees-tray
• record player	tourne-disque (m)	toorn-deesk
• speaker	caisse (f) acoustique	kehs-akoos-teek
	baffle (m)	bah-fle
• stereo	stéréo(phonique) (adj)	stay-ray-u-(fun-eek)
	chaîne-stéréo (f)	shen-stay-ray-o
• tape	bande (f) magnétique	bAHd ma-ny-ay-teek
• tape recorder	magnétophone (m)	ma-ny-ay-tu-fun
program	programme (m)	prug-ram
	émission (f)	ay-mees-yOH
projector	projecteur (m)	pruzh-ehk-tur
• slide projector	pour diapositives (f)	poor dee-a-poh-zee-teev
radio	radio (f)	rad-yo

• car radio	autoradio (m)	u-tu-rad-yo
• listen to	écouter (v)	ay-koo-tay
• news report	nouvelles (f, pl)	noo-vehl
• newscast	journal (m) parlé	zh-oor-nal par-lay
• portable radio	radio portative (f)	rad-yo port-a-teev
• station	station (f) de radio	stas-yOH-de-rad-yo
show	spectacle (m)	spehk-tak-le
television	télévision (f)	tay-lay-veez-yOH
• cable television	télévision (f) par câble	tay-lay-veez-yOH par kahbl
• channel	canal (m)	ka-nal
	chaîne (f)	sh-ehn
• closed circuit	circuit fermé (m)	seer-kew-ee fehrm-ay
• commercial	publicité (f)	pew-blee-see-tay
• documentary	documentaire (m)	duk-ewm-AH-tehr
• interview	interview (f)	EH-tehr-vew
• look at, watch	regarder (v)	re-gar-day
• network	réseau (m)	ray-zoh
• news report	actualités (f)	ak-tew-a-leet-ay
• newscast	journal (m) télévisé	zh-oor-nal tay-lay-vee-zay
• on the air	en émission	AH-nay-mees-yOH
• remote control	télécommande (f)	tay-lay-kum-AH-d
• satellite television	télévision (f) par satellite	tay-lay-veez-yOH par sa-tay-leet
• series	série (f) d'émissions	say-ree day-mees-yOH
• soap opera	mélo (m)	may-lo
• television set	téléviseur (m)	tay-lay-veez-ur
• transmission	émission (f)	ay-mees-yOH
• TV	télé (f)	tay-lay
• TV movie	téléfilm (m)	tay-lay feelm
• VCR	système (m) d'enregistrement (m) à vidéocassettes	sees-tehm dAH-re-zh-eestremAH a vee-day-o kas-eht
	magnétoscope (m)	man-yay-tus-kup
	VCR (m)	vay-say-ehr
• VHS/SECAM/TV	VHS/SECAM/TV (m)	vay-ash-ehs say-kahm tay-vay
	système (m) séquentiel à mémoire	sees-tehm say-kAH-syehl a may-mwar
• video game	jeu-vidéo (m)	zh-uh vee-day-o
• videocassette	vidéocassette (f)	vee-day-o kas-eht
• videorock	vidéorock (m)	vee-day-o ruk
• videotape	bande (f) magnétique	bAHd ma-ny-ay-teek
• volume control	réglage (m) de volume	ray-glazh de vul-ewm

turn off	éteindre (v)	*ayt-EH-dre*
turn on	allumer (v)	*al-ew-may*
walkie-talkie	talkie-walkie (m)	*tuk-ee-wuk-ee*

FOCUS: Colloquial Expressions

Here are a few idioms dealing with ways of expressing displeasure:

Come on!	Allons donc!	*al-OH dOH*
Cut it out!	Arrêtez!	*a-reht-ay*
Damn it!	Zut!	*zewt*
"dirty word"	"mot grossier (m)"	*moh gros-yay*
Get lost!	Allez-vous en!	*a-lay-vooz-AH*
No way!	Pas question!	*pah-kehst-yOH*
Shut up!	Ferme-la!	*ferm-la*
Yuch!	Berk! pouah!	*berk/pwa*

21. FEELINGS

a. MOODS/ATTITUDES/EMOTIONS

affection	affection (f)	*af-ehks-yOH*
agree	être (v) d'accord	*eh-tre dak-or*
anger	colère (f)	*kul-ehr*
• **angry**	fâché(e) (adj, m, f)	*fah-shay*
anxiety, anxiousness	anxiété (f)	*AHks-yay-tay*
• **anxious**	anxieux (adj, m)	*AHks-yuh*
	anxieuse (adj, f)	*AHks-yuhz*
assure	assurer (v)	*a-sewr-ay*
attitude	attitude (f)	*a-tee-tewd*
be able to	pouvoir (v)	*poo-vwar*
be down	avoir (v) le cafard	*avwar le ka-far*
be up	être (v) remonté(e)	*eh-tre rem-OH-tay*
bore	ennuyer (v)	*AH-new-ee-yay*
• **become bored**	s'ennuyer (v)	*sAH-new-ee-yay*
• **feel bored**	crever (v) d'ennui	*kre-vay dAH-new-ee*
• **boredom**	ennui (m)	*AH-new-ee*
complain	se plaindre (v)	*se-plEH-dre*
• **complaint**	plainte (f)	*plEHt*
cry (weep)	pleurer (v)	*plur-ay*
• **tears**	larmes (f)	*larm*

depressed	déprimé(e) *(adj, m, f)*	*day-preem-ay*
• **depression**	dépression *(f)*	*day-prays-yOH*
desperate	désespéré(e) *(adj, m, f)*	*dayz-ehs-pay-ray*
• **desperation**	désespoir *(m)*	*dayz-ehs-pwar*
disagree	être *(v)* en désaccord	*eh-tre AH day-za-kor*
• **disagreement**	désaccord *(m)*	*day-za-kor*
• **be against**	être *(v)* contre	*eh-tre kOHtre*
disappoint	décevoir *(v)*	*day-svwar*
• **disappointed**	déçu(e) *(adj/m, f)*	*dayss-ew*
disappointment	déception *(f)*	*day-sehp-syOH*
dissatisfaction	insatisfaction *(f)*	*EH-sa-tees-faks-yOH*
• **dissatisfied**	insatisfait(e) *(adj, m, f)*	*EH-sa-tees-feh(t)*
encourage	encourager *(v)*	*AH-koor-azh-ay*
• **encouragement**	encouragement *(m)*	*AH-koor-azh-mAH*
faith, trust	confiance *(f)*	*kOH-fy-AH-s*
• **trust**	avoir *(v)* confiance en	*avwar kOH-fy-AH-s AH*
fear	peur *(f)*	*pur*
• **be afraid**	avoir *(v)* peur	*avwar pur*
feel	sentir *(v)*	*sAH-teer*
• **feel like**	avoir *(v)* envie de	*avwar AH-vee-de*
flatter	flatter *(v)*	*flat-ay*
• **flattery**	flatterie *(f)*	*flat-ree*
fun, enjoyment	amusement *(m)*	*a-mewz-mAH*
• **have fun, enjoy oneself**	s'amuser *(v)*	*sa-mewz-ay*
happiness	bonheur *(m)*	*bun-ur*
• **happy**	heureux *(adj, m)*	*ur-uh*
	heureuse *(adj, f)*	*ur-huz*
	content(e) *(adj, m, f)*	*kOHt-AH(t)*
have reason to be worried	avoir de quoi s'inquiéter	*avward-kwa-sank-ee-ay-tay*
have to, must	devoir *(v)*	*de-vwar*
hope	espoir *(m)*	*ehs-pwar*
• **hope**	espérer *(v)*	*ehs-pay-ray*
indifference	indifférence *(f)*	*EH-dee-fay-rAH-s*
• **indifferent**	indifférent(e) *(adj, m, f)*	*EH-dee-fay-rAH(t)*
joy	joie *(f)*	*zh-wa*
laugh	rire *(v)*	*reer*
• **laughter**	rire *(m)*	*reer*

• to laugh halfheartedly, reluctantly	rire (*v*) jaune, rire (*v*) à contrecoeur	*reer-zh-ohn,* *reer-a-kOH-tre-kur*
matter	importer (*v*)	*EH-por-tay*
mood	humeur (*f*)	*ew-mur*
• bad mood	mauvaise humeur	*muv-ehz ew-mur*
• good mood	bonne humeur	*bun ew-mur*
need	besoin (*m*)	*be-zwEH*
• need	avoir (*v*) besoin de	*avwar be-zwEH de*
patience	patience (*f*)	*pas-yAHs*
• have patience	avoir (*v*) de la patience	*avwar-dla-pas-yAHs*
relief	soulagement (*m*)	*sool-azh-mAH*
• sigh of relief	soupir (*m*) de soulagement	*soo-peer de sool-azh-mAH*
sad	triste (*adj*)	*treest*
• sadness	tristesse (*f*)	*treest-ehs*
satisfaction	satisfaction (*f*)	*sa-tees-faks-yOH*
• satisfied	satisfait(e) (*adj, m, f*)	*sa-tees-feh(t)*
shame	honte (*f*)	*OHt*
• be ashamed	avoir (*v*) honte	*avwar OHt*
smile	sourire (*v & n, m*)	*soo-reer*
sorrow	chagrin (*m*)	*shag-rEH*
surprise	surprise (*f*)	*sewr-preez*
• surprise	surprendre (*v*)	*sewr-prAH-dre*
• surprised	surpris(e) (*adj, m, f*)	*sewr-pree(z)*
sympathy	compassion (*f*)	*kOH-pahs-yOH*
• sympathetic	compatissant(e) (*adj, m, f*)	*kOH-pa-tees AH(t)*
thankfulness	gratitude (*f*)	*gra-tee-tewd*
	reconnaissance (*f*)	*re-kun-ehs-AH-s*
• thankful	reconnaissant(e) (*adj, m, f*)	*re-kun-ehs-AH(t)*
• thank	remercier (*v*)	*re-mehr-see-yay*
tolerance	tolérance (*f*)	*tul-ay-rAH-s*
• tolerate	tolérer (*v*)	*tul-ay-ray*
want to	vouloir (*v*)	*vool-war*
	désirer (*v*)	*day-zee-ray*

b. LIKES AND DISLIKES

accept	accepter (*v*)	*aks-ehp-tay*
• acceptable	acceptable (*adj*)	*aks-ehp-ta-ble*
• unacceptable	inacceptable (*adj*)	*een-aks-ehp-ta-ble*

approval	approbation (*f*)	*ap-rub-ahs-yOH*
• **approve**	approuver (*v*)	*ap-roov-ay*
be fond of	avoir (*v*) une passion pour	*avwar ewn pahs-yOH poor*
detest	détester (*v*)	*day-tehst-ay*
disgust	dégoût (*m*)	*day-goo*
• **disgusted**	dégoûté(e) (*adj, m, f*)	*day-goo-tay*
hate	haïr (*v*)	*a-eer*
• **hatred**	haine (*f*)	*ehn*
I can't stand him (her)!	Je ne peux pas le (la) supporter!	*zhen puh pahl(la) sew-por-tay*
kiss	embrasser (*v*)	*AH-bra-say*
like	aimer (*v*) bien	*ay-may byEH*
• **liking** (*taste*)	penchant (*m*)	*pAH-shAH*
	goût (*m*)	*goo*
• **dislike** (*not to like*)	ne pas aimer (*v*)	*ne-pah-zay-may*
love	amour (*m*)	*a-moor*
• **love**	aimer (*v*)	*ay-may*
mediocre	médiocre (*adj*)	*mayd-y-uk-re*
pleasant	agréable (*adj*)	*a-gray-abl*
• **unpleasant**	désagréable (*adj*)	*dayz-a-gray-abl*
prefer	préférer (*v*)	*pray-fay-ray*
Too bad!	Dommage!	*dum-azh*

c. EXPRESSING EMOTIONS

Are you joking?	Vous plaisantez? (*pol*)	*voo-pleh-zAH-tay*
	Tu plaisantes? (*fam*)	*tew-pleh-zAHt*
Be careful!	Attention!	*atAHs-yOH*
Enough!	Assez!	*a-say*
Fortunately!	Heureusement! (*adv*)	*ur-uhz-mAH*
Good heavens!/Oh my!	Oh! là! là!	*oh-la-la*
I don't believe it!	Je ne le crois pas!	*zhen le krwah pah*
I don't feel like . . .	Je n'ai pas envie de . . .	*zhen ay pah AH-vee de . . .*
I wish! (If only . . . !)	Si seulement . . . !	*see sulmAH*
I'm serious!	Je suis sérieux (*m*) sérieuse (*f*)	*zhe swee say-ry-uh (say-ry-uhz)*
I'm sorry!	Je regrette!	*zher-greht*
Impossible!	Pas possible!	*pah-pus-eebl*
It doesn't matter!	Peu importe!	*puh EH-port*
My God!	Mon Dieu!	*mOH dy-uh*
Poor man!	Pauvre homme!	*poh-vr um*
Poor woman!	Pauvre femme!	*poh-vr fahm*
Quiet!	Silence!	*seel-AHs*
Really?	Vraiment?	*vrehm-AH*

Keep quiet!	Taisez-vous!	*teh-zay-voo*
	Tais-toi! (*fam*)	*teh-twa*
Thank goodness!	Grâce à Dieu!	*grahss a dy-uh*
Ugh!	Pouah!	*pwa*
Unbelievable!	Incroyable!	*EH-krwa-yabl*
Unfortunately!	Malheureusement!	*mal-ur-uhz-mAH*
What a bore!	Quel raseur! (*m*)	*kehl rahz-ur*
	Quelle raseuse! (*f*)	*kehl rahz-uhz*

22. THINKING

a. DESCRIBING THOUGHT

complicated	compliqué(e) (*adj*, *m*, *f*)	*kOH-plee-kay*
concept	concept (*m*)	*kOH-sehpt*
conscience	conscience (*f*)	*kOH-sy-AHs*
conscientious	consciencieux (*adj*, *m*)	*kOH-sy-AHs-yuh*
	consciencieuse (*f*)	*kOH-sy-AHs-yuhz*
difficult	difficile (*adj*)	*dee-fee-seel*
doubt	doute (*m*)	*doot*
easy	facile (*adj*)	*fa-seel*
existence	existence (*f*)	*ehg-zees-tAHs*
hypothesis	hypothèse (*f*)	*ee-pu-tehz*
idea	idée (*f*)	*ee-day*
ignorant	ignorant(e) (*adj*, *m*, *f*)	*ee-ny-or-AH(t)*
imagination	imagination (*f*)	*ee-ma-zh-ee-nas-yOH*
interesting	intéressant(e) (*adj*, *m*, *f*)	*EH-tay-rehs-AH(t)*
judgment	jugement (*m*)	*zh-ew-zh-mAH*
justice	justice (*f*)	*zh-ewss-teess*
knowledge	connaissance (*f*)	*kun-ehs-AHs*
knowledgeable	connaisseur (*adj*, *m*)	*kun-ehs-ur*
	connaisseuse (*f*)	*kun-ehs-uhz*
mind	esprit (*m*)	*ehs-pree*
opinion	opinion (*f*)	*up-ee-ny-OH*
• **in my opinion**	à mon avis (*m*)	*a-mOH-nah-vee*
problem	problème (*m*)	*prub-lehm*
• **No problem!**	Pas de problème!	*pahd-prub-lehm*
reason	raison (*f*)	*reh-zOH*
simple	simple (*adj*)	*sEH-pl*
thought	pensée (*f*)	*pAH-say*
wisdom	sagesse (*f*)	*sa-zh-ehs*

b. BASIC THOUGHT PROCESSES

agree	être (*v*) d'accord	*eh-tre dak-or*
be interested in	s'intéresser (*v*) à	*sEH-tay-ray-say a*

be right	avoir (*v*) raison	*avwar rehz-OH*
be wrong	avoir (*v*) tort	*avwar tor*
believe	croire (*v*)	*krwar*
convince	convaincre (*v*)	*kOH-vEH-kre*
demonstrate	démontrer (*v*)	*day-mOH-tray*
doubt	douter (*v*)	*doo-tay*
forget	oublier (*v*)	*oobl-yay*
imagine	imaginer (*v*)	*ee-ma-zh-een-ay*
know	savoir (*v*)	*sav-war*
	connaître (*v*)	*kun-eht-re*
learn	apprendre (*v*)	*ap-rAH-dre*
persuade	persuader (*v*)	*pehr-sew-a-day*
reason	raisonner (*v*)	*reh-zun-ay*
reflect	réfléchir (*v*)	*ray-flay-sheer*
remember	se rappeler (*v*)	*se-rap-lay*
	se souvenir de	*se-soov-neer de*
study	étudier (*v*)	*ay-tewd-yay*
think	penser (*v*)	*pAH-say*
understand	comprendre (*v*)	*kOH-prAH-dre*
• **What do you**	Qu'en pensez-vous?	*kAH-pAH-say-voo*
think?	(*pol*)	
	Qu'en penses-tu?	*kAH-pAH-s tew*
	(*fam*)	

DAILY LIFE

23. AT HOME

a. PARTS OF THE HOUSE

attic	grenier (*m*)	*gren-yay*
basement	sous-sol (*m*)	*soo-sul*
bathtub	baignoire (*f*)	*beh-ny-war*
ceiling	plafond (*m*)	*plafOH*
chimney	cheminée (*f*)	*shmeen-ay*
corridor	couloir (*m*)	*kool-war*
door	porte (*f*)	*port*
doorbell	sonnette (*f*)	*sun-eht*
entrance	entrée (*m*)	*AHtray*
faucet	robinet (*m*)	*rub-een-ay*
fireplace	cheminée (*f*)	*shmee-nay*
floor	plancher (*m*)	*plAH-shay*
	parquet (*m*)	*par-kay*
floor (*level*)	étage (*m*)	*ay-ta-zh*
garage	garage (*m*)	*gar-azh*
garden	jardin (*m*)	*zh-ard-EH*
ground floor	rez-de-chaussée (*m*)	*rayd-sh-oh-say*
house	maison (*f*)	*meh-zOH*
mailbox	boîte (*f*) à lettres	*bwat-a-leht-re*
porch	porche (*m*)	*porsh*
	véranda (*f*)	*vay-rAH-da*
roof	toit (*m*)	*twa*
shelf	étagère (*f*)	*ay-ta-zy-ehr*
shower	douche (*f*)	*doosh*
sink	évier (*m*)	*ayv-yay*
	lavabo (*m*) (*in a bathroom*)	*la-va-boh*
stairs	escalier (*m*)	*ehs-kal-yay*
switch	interrupteur (*m*)	*EH-tehr-ewp-tur*
terrace	terrasse (*f*)	*tehr-ahs*
wall	mur (*m*)	*mewr*
window	fenêtre (*f*)	*fneht-re*
window sill	rebord (*m*) de la fenêtre	*re-bor-dla-fneht-re*

b. ROOMS

bathroom	salle (*f*) de bains	*sal de bEH*
bedroom	chambre (*f*) à coucher	*shAH-br a koo-shay*

closet	armoire (f)	arm-war
	placard (m)	plak-ar
dining room	salle (f) à manger	sal a mAHzh-ay
kitchen	cuisine (f)	kew-ee-zeen
living room	salon (m)	salOH
	salle (f) de séjour	sal de say-zh-oor
room	pièce (f)	py-ehs
wine cellar	cave (f) à vin	kav a vEH

c. FURNITURE AND DECORATION

armchair	fauteuil (m)	foh-tuh-y
bed	lit (m)	lee
bedside table	table (f) de chevet	ta-bl de sh-veh
	table (f) de nuit	ta-bl-de-new-ee
bookcase	étagère (f) à livres	ay-ta-zh-er a leevr
carpet, rug	tapis (m)	ta-pee
chair	chaise (f)	sh-ehz
chest of drawers, dresser	commode (f)	kum-ud
curtains	rideaux (m)	reed-oh
decorating	décoration (f)	day-kor-as-yOH
drawer	tiroir (m)	teer-war
furniture	meuble (m)	muh-bl
lamp	lampe (f)	lAHp
mirror	miroir (m)	meer-war
painting	tableau (m)	tab-loh
sofa	canapé (m)	ka-na-pay
stool	tabouret (m)	tab-oor-eh
table	table (f)	tabl
wall-to-wall carpeting	moquette (f)	muk-eht
writing desk	secrétaire (m)	sek-ray-tehr

d. APPLIANCES AND COMMON HOUSEHOLD ITEMS

bag	sac (m)	sak
• shopping bag	sac à provisions	sak-a-pru-veez-yOH
basket	corbeille (f)	kor-bay
	panier (m)	pan-yay
bedspread	couvre-lit (m)	koo-vre-lee
blanket	couverture (f)	koov-ehr-tewr
bottle	bouteille (f)	boo-tay
box	boîte (f)	bwat
broom	balai (m)	bal-eh
case	douille (f)	doo-y
	bac (m)	bak
clothes hanger	cintre (m)	sEH-tre

coffee machine	cafetière (*f*) électrique	*kaf-tyehr ay-lehk-treek*
	percolateur (*m*)	*pehrk-u-la-tur*
coffee pot	cafetière (*f*)	*kaf-tyehr*
cup	tasse (*f*)	*tas*
dishwasher	lave-vaisselle (*m*)	*lav-veh-sehl*
dryer	sèche-linge (*m*)	*sesh-lEH-zh*
	sécheuse (*f*)	*say-sh-uhz*
fork	fourchette (*f*)	*foorsh-eht*
freezer	congélateur (*m*)	*kOHzh-ay-la-tur*
glass (*drinking*)	verre (*m*)	*vehr*
kettle	bouilloire (*f*)	*boo-y-war*
key	clef (*f*)	*klay*
knife	couteau (*m*)	*koo-toh*
• **blade**	lame (*f*)	*lahm*
• **handle**	manche (*m*)	*mAH-sh*
ladle	louche (*f*)	*loosh*
lid	couvercle (*m*)	*koov-ehr-kl*
microwave oven	four (*m*) à micro-ondes (*f, pl*)	*foor a meek-ro-OHd*
napkin	serviette (*f*)	*sehrv-yeht*
oven	four (*m*)	*foor*
pail	seau (*m*)	*soh*
pan	casserole (*f*)	*kas-rul*
	sauteuse (*f*)	*soh-tuhz*
pillow	oreiller (*m*)	*or-ay-yay*
pillowcase	taie (*f*) d'oreiller	*teh dor-ay-yay*
plate	assiette (*f*)	*as-yeht*
pot	faitout (*m*)	*feh-too*
	marmite (*f*)	*mar-meet*
radio	radio (*f*)	*rad-yo*
refrigerator	frigo (*m*)	*free-go*
	réfrigérateur (*m*)	*ray-free-zh-ay-ra-tur*
saucer	soucoupe (*f*)	*soo-koop*
sewing machine	machine (*f*) à coudre	*ma-sheen-a-kood-re*
sheet (*bed*)	drap (*m*)	*dra*
spoon	cuiller (*f*)	*kew-ee-yehr*
• **tablespoon**	cuiller (*f*) à soupe	*kew-ee-yehr-a-soop*
• **teaspoon**	cuiller (*f*) à café	*kew-ee-yehr-a-ka-fay*
stove	cuisinière (*f*)	*kew-ee-zeen-yehr*
• **electric**	électrique	*ay-lekh-treek*
• **gas**	à gaz	*a gaz*
tablecloth	nappe (*f*)	*nap*
tableware	ustensiles (*m, pl*) à table	*ewst-AH-seel-a-tabl*
teapot	théière (*f*)	*tay-yehr*
television set	téléviseur (*m*)	*tay-lay-veez-ur*
toaster	grille-pain (*m*)	*gree-y pEH*

tools	outils (*m, pl*)	*oo-tee*
tray	plateau (*m*) à servir	*pla-toh a sehr-veer*
vacuum cleaner	aspirateur (*m*)	*as-pee-ra-tur*
washing machine	lave-linge (*m*)	*lav-lEH-zh*
	machine (*f*) à laver	*ma-sheen a la-vay*

e. SERVICES

air conditioning	climatisation (*f*)	*klee-ma-tee-zass-yOH*
• air conditioner	climatiseur (*m*)	*klee-ma-tee-zuhr*
electricity	électricité (*f*)	*ay-lehk-tree-see-tay*
furnace	chaudière (*f*)	*sh-ohd-yehr*
gas	gaz (*m*)	*gaz*
heating	chauffage (*m*) central	*sh-oh-fazh sAH-tral*
light, power	éclairage (*m*)	*ay-klehr-azh*
telephone	téléphone (*m*)	*tay-lay-fun*
water	eau (*f*)	*oh*

f. ADDITIONAL HOUSEHOLD VOCABULARY

at home	à la maison	*a-la-mehz-OH*
	chez soi	*shay-swa*
build	construire (*v*)	*kOH-strew-eer*
buy	acheter (*v*)	*ash-tay*
clean	nettoyer (*v*)	*neht-wa-yay*
clear the table	desservir (*v*) la table	*day-sehr-veer la ta-bl*
live (in)	habiter (*v*)	*a-bee-tay*
make the bed	faire (*v*) le lit	*fehr le lee*
move (*out of a house*)	déménager (*v*)	*day-may-na-zh-ay*
paint	peindre (*v*)	*pEH-dr*
put a room in order	mettre (*v*) une pièce en ordre	*meh-tr ewn py-ehs AH-nor-dr*
restore	restaurer (*v*)	*re-sto-ray*
sell	vendre (*v*)	*vAH-dr*
set the table	mettre (*v*) le couvert	*meh-tr le koo-vehr*
wash	laver (*v*)	*la-vay*
• wash the clothes	laver (*v*) le linge	*la-vay-le-lEHzh*
• wash the dishes	faire (*v*) la vaisselle	*fehr la veh-sehl*

g. LIVING IN AN APARTMENT

apartment	appartement (*m*)	*a-par-tem-AH*
apartment building	immeuble (*m*)	*eem-uh-bl*
building	édifice (*m*)	*ay-dee-feess*
condominium	immeuble (*m*) en copropriété (*f*)	*eem-uh-bl AH ko-pro-pree-ay-tay*

elevator	ascenseur (*m*)	*ass-AH-sur*
ground floor	rez-de-chaussée (*m*)	*rayd-sh-oh-say*
landlord	propriétaire (*m/f*)	*prup-pree-yay-tehr*
rent	loyer (*m*)	*lwa-yay*
• rent	louer (*v*)	*lway*
superintendent (*of apartment building*)	concierge (*m/f*)	*kOH-see-ehr-zh*
tenant	locataire (*m/f*)	*luk-a-tehr*

24. EATING AND DRINKING

a. MEALS

breakfast	petit déjeuner (*m*)	*ptee day-zh-un-ay*
dinner	dîner (*m*)	*dee-nay*
food	nourriture (*f*)	*noo-ree-tewr*
lunch	déjeuner (*m*)	*day-zh-un-ay*
meal	repas (*m*)	*re-pah*
snack	casse-croûte (*m*)	*kass-kroot*
	goûter (*m*)	*goo-tay*

b. PREPARATION

broiled, grilled	grillé(e) (*adj, m, f*)	*gree-yay*
cooking, cuisine	cuisine (*f*)	*kew-ee-zeen*
marinated	mariné(e) (*adj, m, f*)	*ma-ree-nay*
medium	à point	*a-pwEH*
rare	saignant(e) (*adj, m, f*)	*seh-ny-AH(t)*
roast	rôti(e) (*adj, m, f*)	*roh-tee*
well-done	bien cuit(e) (*adj, m, f*)	*byEH kwee(t)*
with sauce (gravy)	au jus	*oh-zh-ew*

c. MEAT AND POULTRY

bacon	bacon (*m*)	*bay-kun*
beef	bœuf (*m*)	*buhf*
chicken	poulet (*m*)	*poo-leh*
cold cuts	charcuterie (*f*)	*shar-kew-tree*
duck	canard (*m*)	*kan-ar*
ham	jambon (*m*)	*zh-AH-bOH*
lamb	agneau (*m*)	*a-ny-oh*
liver	foie (*m*)	*fwa*
meat	viande (*f*)	*vee-y-AHd*
pork	porc (*m*)	*por*
poultry	volaille (*f*)	*vul-ah-yuh*

salami	salami (*m*)	*sa-la-mee*
sausage	saucisse (*f*)	*so-seess*
turkey	dinde (*f*)	*dEH-d*
veal	veau (*m*)	*voh*

d. FISH, SEAFOOD, AND SHELLFISH

anchovy	anchois (*m*)	*AH-sh-wa*
clam	palourde (*f*)	*pa-loord*
cod	morue (*f*)	*mu-rew*
dried cod	merluche (*f*)	*mehr-lewsh*
eel	anguille (*f*)	*AH-gee-y*
fish	poisson (*m*)	*pwassOH*
herring	hareng (*m*)	*ar-AH*
lobster	homard (*m*)	*um-ar*
	langouste (*f*)	*lAH-goost*
mussels	moules (*f, pl*)	*mool*
oyster	huître (*f*)	*ew-eet-re*
prawn	langoustine (*f*)	*lAH-goos-teen*
salmon	saumon (*m*)	*so-mOH*
sardine	sardine (*f*)	*sar-deen*
seafood	fruits de mer (*m, pl*)	*frew-eed-mehr*
shellfish	crustacés (*m, pl*)	*krew-sta-say*
shrimp	crevette (*f*)	*kre-veht*
sole	sole (*f*)	*sul*
squid	calmar (*m*)	*kal-mar*
trout	truite (*f*)	*trew-eet*
tuna	thon (*m*)	*tOH*

e. VEGETABLES

artichoke	artichaut (*m*)	*ar-tee-sh-oh*
asparagus	asperge (*f*)	*as-pehr-zh*
bean	fève (*f*)	*fehv*
	haricot (*m*)	*a-ree-koh*
beet	betterave (*f*)	*beht-rav*
broccoli	brocoli (*m*)	*bruk-ul-ee*
cabbage	chou (*m*)	*shoo*
carrot	carotte (*f*)	*kar-ut*
cauliflower	chou-fleur (*m*)	*shoo-flur*
celery	céleri (*m*)	*sehl-ree*
cucumber	concombre (*m*)	*kOH-kOH-br*
eggplant	aubergine (*f*)	*oh-behr-zh-een*
lettuce	laitue (*f*)	*leht-ew*
mushroom	champignon (*m*)	*shAH-pee-ny-OH*
olive	olive (*f*)	*ul-eev*
onion	oignon (*m*)	*u-ny-OH*

peas	pois (*m*); petits pois (*m, pl*)	*pwa; ptee pwa*
potato	pomme (*f*) de terre	*pum-de-tehr*
potato salad	salade (*f*) de pommes de terre	*sa-lad-de-pum-de-tehr*
spinach	épinards (*m, pl*)	*ay-pee-nar*
string bean	haricot vert (*m*)	*a-ree-koh-vehr*
vegetables	légumes (*m, pl*)	*lay-gewn*

f. FRUITS

apple	pomme (*f*)	*pum*
apricot	abricot (*m*)	*a-bree-ko*
banana	banane (*f*)	*ba-nan*
blueberry	myrtille (*f*)	*meer-tee-y*
cherry	cerise (*f*)	*sreez*
date	datte (*f*)	*daht*
fig	figue (*f*)	*feeg*
fruit	fruit (*m*)	*frew-ee*
grapefruit	pamplemousse (*m/f*)	*pAH-ple-mooss*
grapes	raisins (*m, pl*)	*reh-zEH*
lemon	citron (*m*)	*seet-rOH*
mandarin orange	mandarine (*f*)	*mAH-da-reen*
orange	orange (*f*)	*or-AH-zh*
peach	pêche (*f*)	*peh-sh*
peanut	arachide (*f*)	*a-rash-eed*
	cacahouète (*f*)	*ka-ka-weht*
pineapple	ananas (*m*)	*a-na-nass*
plum	prune (*f*)	*prewn*
prune	pruneau (*m*)	*prewn-oh*
raisin	raisin sec (*m*)	*reh-zEH sehk*
raspberry	framboise (*f*)	*frAH-bwahz*
strawberry	fraise (*f*)	*frehz*
tomato	tomate (*f*)	*tum-at*
walnut	noix (*f*)	*nwa*
watermelon	pastèque (*f*)	*pas-tehk*

g. MEAL AND MENU COMPONENTS

aperitif	apéritif (*m*)	*a-pay-ree-teef*
appetizer	hors-d'œuvre variés (*m, pl*)	*or-duh-vre va-ree-yay*
broth	bouillon (*m*)	*boo-yOH*
cake	gâteau (*m*)	*gah-toh*
cutlet	côtelette (*f*)	*koht-leht*
dessert	dessert (*m*)	*day-sehr*
dumpling	boulette (*f*)	*boo-leht*

filet	filet (*m*)	fee-leh
fish stew	bouillabaisse (*f*)	boo-ya-behss
French fries	frites (*f, pl*)	freet
fruit tartlet	tartelette (*f*) aux fruits	tart-leht oh frew-ee
garlic	ail (*m*)	a-y
menu	carte (*f*)	kart
	menu (*m*)	me-new
of the day	du jour	dew zh-oor
pancake	crêpe (*f*)	krehp
pasta	pâtes (*f, pl*)	paht
pie	tarte (*f*)	tart
• apple	aux pommes	oh pum
• cherry	aux cerises	oh sreez
• chocolate	au chocolat	oh sh-uk-ul-a
• peach	aux pêches	oh peh-sh
quiche	quiche (*f*)	keesh
• cheese	au fromage	oh frum-azh
• ham	au jambon	oh zh-AH-bOH
rice with vegetables	riz (*m*) aux légumes	ree oh layg-ewm
roast beef	rosbif (*m*)	rohs-beef
salad	salade (*f*)	sa-lad
sandwich	sandwich (*m*)	sAHd-weesh
• cheese	au fromage	oh frum-azh
• ham	au jambon	oh zh-AH-bOH
sherbet	sorbet (*m*)	sor-beh
snails	escargots (*m, pl*)	ehs-kar-go
soup	soupe (*f*)	soop
	potage (*m*)	pu-tazh
• fish	au poisson	oh pwass-OH
• onion	à l'oignon	al-u-ny-OH
• thick	purée	pew-ray
steak	bifteck (*m*)	beef-tehk

h. DAIRY PRODUCTS, EGGS, AND RELATED FOODS

butter	beurre (*m*)	bur
cheese	fromage (*m*)	frum-azh
• grated	râpé	rah-pay
• melted	fondu	fOHdew
• puffed	soufflé	soo-flay
cream	crème (*f*)	krehm
• whipped	crème Chantilly	krehm shAH-tee-yee
dairy product	produit (*m*) laitier	prud-ew-ee leht-yay
egg	œuf (*m*)	uhf
• two eggs	deux œufs	duh-zuh
• fried (sunny side up)	sur le plat	sewr le pla
• hard-boiled	dur	dewr

• **omelette**	omelette (*f*)	*um-leht*
• **cheese**	au fromage	*oh frum-azh*
• **ham**	au jambon	*oh zhAH-bOH*
• **whipped cream**	omelette mousseline	*um-leht moos-leen*
• **poached**	poché	*pu-shay*
• **soft-boiled**	à la coque	*a la kuk*
• **stuffed**	œuf dur farci	*uhf dewr far-see*
ice cream	glace (*f*)	*glass*
	crème (*f*) glacée	*krehm gla-say*
• **cone**	cornet (*m*)	*kor-neh*
• **chocolate**	au chocolat	*oh shuk-ul-a*
• **strawberry**	aux fraises	*oh frehz*
• **vanilla**	à la vanille	*a la van-ee-y*
milk	lait (*m*)	*leh*
• **buttermilk**	babeurre (*m*)	*ba-bur*
	lait de beurre	*lehd-bur*
• **skimmed**	écrémé	*ay-kray-may*
pudding	crème (*f*)	*krehm*
• **caramel**	au caramel	*oh ka-ra-mehl*
• **coffee**	au café	*oh ka-fay*
• **custard**	flan	*flAH*
• **rice**	de riz	*de ree*
• **tapioca**	tapioca au lait	*ta-pee-uk-a oh leh*
yogurt	yaourt (*m*)	*ya-oor*

FOCUS: A Few Popular French Cheeses

brie (*m*)	*bree*	gruyère (*m*)	*grew-yehr*
camembert (*m*)	*kamAH-behr*	port-salut (*m*)	*pohr-sa-lew*
cantal (*m*)	*kAH-tal*	reblochon (*m*)	*re-blu-shOH*
chèvre (*m*)	*sh-ehv-re*	roquefort (*m*)	*ruk-for*

i. GRAINS AND GRAIN PRODUCTS

barley	orge (*f*)	*or-zh*
bread	pain (*m*)	*pEH*
cookie	sablé (*m*)	*sa-blay*
	petit-beurre (*m*)	*ptee-bur*
	gâteau sec (*m*)	*gah-toh sehk*
corn	maïs (*m*)	*ma-eess*
crouton	croûton (*m*)	*kroot-OH*
crumb	miette (*f*)	*mee-yet*
crust	croûte (*f*)	*kroot*

flour	farine (*f*)	*fa-reen*
oat	avoine (*f*)	*av-wan*
pastry	pâtisserie (*f*)	*pah-tee-sree*
rice	riz (*m*)	*ree*
wheat	blé (*m*)	*blay*

FOCUS: French Breads

breads	les pains (*m*)	*lay pEH*
brioche	brioche (*f*)	*bree-yush*
croissant	croissant (*m*)	*krwasAH*
double roll	petit pain (*m*) double	*ptee pEH doobl*
gingerbread	pain (*m*) d'épices	*pEH day-peess*
long loaf of bread	pain (*m*) long	*pEH lOH*
long stick of bread	baguette (*f*)	*bag-eht*
	flûte (*f*)	*flewt*
pretzel	bretzel (*m*)	*bred-zehl*
pumpernickel	pain (*m*) noir	*pEH nwar*
roll	petit pain (*m*) chapelet	*ptee pEH shap-leh*
round bread	pain (*m*) rond	*pEH rOH*
rusk (Melba toast)	biscotte (*f*)	*beess-kut*
rye and wheat bread	pain (*m*) de campagne	*pEHd-kAH-pan-y*
rye bread	pain (*m*) au seigle	*pEH oh sehgl*
small round loaf of bread	petite boule (*f*)	*pteet bool*
whole wheat bread	pain (*m*) complet	*pEH kOH-pleh*

FOCUS: French Pastries

pastries	pâtisseries (*f*)	*pah-teess-ree*
cheesecake	gâteau (*m*) au fromage	*gah-toh oh frum-azh*
coconut macaroon	macaron (*m*)	*ma-karOH*
cream cake (pie)	gâteau (*m*) à la crème	*gah-toh a la krehm*
cream puff	chou (*m*) à la crème	*shoo a la krehm*
creamed horn	cornet (*m*) feuilleté à la crème	*korn-eh fu-y-tay a la krehm*
eclair	éclair (*m*)	*ay-klehr*
fruit flan	flan (*m*) aux fruits	*flAH oh frew-ee*
iced bun	gâteau (*m*) américain	*gah-toh amay-reek-EH*
icing, iced, glazed	glacé(e) (*adj*)	*gla-say*
jelly roll	roulé (*m*)	*roo-lay*
meringue	meringue (*f*)	*me-rEHg*
napoleon	millefeuille (*m*)	*meel-fu-y*
slice of cream cake	tranche (*f*) de gâteau à la crème	*trAHsh de gah-toh a la krehm*
tartlet	tartelette (*f*)	*tart-leht*
twist bun	tresse (*f*)	*trehss*
wafer	gaufrette (*f*)	*go-freht*
waffle	gaufre (*f*)	*go-fr*

j. CONDIMENTS AND SPICES

basil	basilic (*m*)	*ba-zee-leek*
garlic	ail (*m*)	*a-y*
herb	herbe (*f*)	*ehrb*
honey	miel (*m*)	*mee-yehl*
horseradish sauce	sauce (*f*) au raifort	*sohs-oh-reh-for*
jam (*preserves*)	confiture (*f*)	*kOH-fee-tewr*
jelly	gelée (*f*)	*zh-lay*
marmalade	confiture d'oranges	*kOH-fee-tewr dor-AH-zh*
mint	menthe (*f*)	*mAHt*
oil	huile (*f*)	*ew-eel*
parsley	persil (*m*)	*pehr-see*
pepper	poivre (*m*)	*pwa-vre*
rosemary	romarin (*m*)	*rum-ar-EH*
salt	sel (*m*)	*sehl*
spice	épice (*f*)	*ay-peess*
sugar	sucre (*m*)	*sew-kre*
vinegar	vinaigre (*m*)	*veen-ehg-re*

k. DRINKS

alcoholic beverage	boisson (f) alcoolique (adj)	bwass-OH al-ku-(u)-leek
beer	bière (f)	bee-yehr
camomile	camomille (f)	ka-mum-eel
coffee	café (m)	kafay
• **black**	noir	nwar
• **light (half-and-half)**	au lait	oh-leh
• **with cream**	café-crème	kafay-krehm
drink	boisson (f)	bwass-OH
juice	jus (m)	zh-ew
liqueur	liqueur (f)	lee-kur
mineral water	eau (f) minérale	oh mee-nay-ral
soft drink	gazeuse (f)	gaz-uhz
tea	thé (m)	tay
water	eau (f)	oh
wine	vin (m)	vEH

l. AT THE TABLE

bottle	bouteille (f)	boo-tay
bowl	bol (m)	bul
	assiette (f) creuse	ass-ee-yeht kruhz
cup	tasse (f)	tass
fork	fourchette (f)	foorsh-eht
glass (drinking)	verre (m)	vehr
knife	couteau (m)	koo-toh
napkin	serviette (f)	sehr-vee-yeht
plate	assiette (f)	ass-ee-yeht
saucer	soucoupe (f)	soo-koop
spoon	cuiller (f)	kew-ee-yehr
	cuillère (f)	kew-ee-yehr
table	table (f)	ta-bl
tablecloth	nappe (f)	nap
tableware	ustensiles (m, pl) de table	ewst-AH-seel de ta-bl
	couvert (m)	koo-vehr
teaspoon	cuiller (f) à café	kew-ee-yehr a kafay
toothpick	cure-dent (m)	kewr-dAH
tray (serving)	plateau (m) à servir	pla-toh a sehr-veer
wineglass	verre (m) à vin	vehr a vEH

Cheers!	À votre santé!	a-vutr-sAH-tay
Enjoy your meal!	Bon appétit!	bun-a-pay-tee

m. DINING OUT

bartender	barman (*m*)	*bar-man*
bill, check	addition (*f*)	*a-dee-syOH*
cafeteria	restaurant (*m*) self-service	*rehs-tor-AH sehlf-sehr-veess*
cover charge	couvert (*m*)	*koo-vehr*
fast food	fast-food (*m*)	*fahst-food*
fixed price	prix (*m*) fixe	*pree-feeks*
pizza parlor	pizzeria (*f*)	*peed-zayr-ya*
price	prix (*m*)	*pree*
reservation	réservation (*f*)	*ray-zehr-vas-yOH*
• **reserved**	réservé(e) (*adj, m, f*)	*ray-zehr-vay*
restaurant	restaurant (*m*)	*rehs-tor-AH*
• **informal restaurant**	bistro, bistrot (*m*)	*bee-stro*
service	service (*m*)	*sehr-veess*
snack bar	buffet (*m*)	*bew-feh*
take-out	à emporter (*v*)	*a-AH-por-tay*
tip	pourboire (*m*)	*poor-bwar*
• **tip**	donner (*v*) un pourboire	*dun-ay UH poor-bwar*
waiter	serveur (*m*)	*sehr-vur*
waitress	serveuse (*f*)	*sehr-vuhz*

n. BUYING FOOD AND DRINK

bakery	boulangerie (*f*)	*bool-AH-zh-ree*
butcher (shop)	boucherie (*f*)	*boosh-ree*
dairy	laiterie (*f*)	*leht-ree*
delicatessen	charcuterie (*f*)	*shar-kew-tree*
fish store	poissonnerie (*f*)	*pwa-sun-ree*
grocery store	épicerie (*f*)	*ay-peess-ree*
market	marché (*m*)	*marsh-ay*
pastry shop	pâtisserie (*f*)	*pah-tee-sree*
produce market	marché (*m*) aux légumes et fruits	*marsh-ay oh layg-ewm ay-frew-ee*
supermarket	supermarché (*m*)	*sew-pehr-marsh-ay*

o. FOOD AND DRINK: ACTIVITIES

add up the bill	faire (*v*) l'addition	*fehr la-dee-syOH*
be hungry	avoir (*v*) faim	*avwar fEH*
be thirsty	avoir (*v*) soif	*avwar swaf*
clear the table	desservir (*v*) la table	*day-sehr-veer la ta-ble*

cook	cuire (v)	kew-eer
	faire (v) la cuisine	fehr la kew-ee-zeen
	cuisiner (v)	kew-eez-ee-nay
cost	coûter (v)	koo-tay
cut	couper (v)	koo-pay
drink	boire (v)	bwar
eat	manger (v)	mAH-zh-ay
have a snack	prendre (v) un goûter	prAH-dre UH goo-tay
have dinner	dîner (v)	dee-nay
have lunch	déjeuner (v)	day-zh-un-ay
order	commander (v)	kumAH-day
peel	éplucher (v)	ay-plew-shay
pour	verser (v)	vehr-say
serve	servir (v)	sehr-veer
set the table	mettre (v) la table	meht-re la ta-ble
shop for food	acheter (v) des provisions	ash-tay day pru-veez-yOH
slice	trancher (v)	trAH-shay
take out (food to go)	emporter (v)	AH-por-tay
toast	griller (v)	gree-yay
weigh	peser (v)	pe-zay

p. DESCRIBING FOOD AND DRINK

appetizing	appétissant(e) (adj, m, f)	a-pay-tee-sAH(t)
bad	mauvais(e) (adj)	muv-eh(z)
baked	au four	oh-foor
bitter	amer, amère (adj, m, f)	a-mehr
cheap	à bon marché	a-bOH marsh-ay
	économe (adj)	ay-kun-um
cold	froid(e) (adj, m, f)	frwa(d)
expensive	cher, chère (adj, m, f)	sh-ehr
	coûteux(-euse) (adj, m, f)	koo-tuh(-tuhz)
fried	frit(e) (adj)	free(t)
good	bon (adj, m)	bOH
	bonne (f)	bun
hot	chaud(e) (adj, m, f)	sh-oh(d)
mild	tiède (adj)	tee-yehd
salty	salé(e) (adj, m, f)	sal-ay
sour	aigre (adj)	eh-gr
spicy	épicé(e) (adj, m, f)	ay-pee-say
sweet	doux (adj, m)	doo
	douce (f)	dooss

tasty	savoureux(-euse) *(adj, m, f)*	*sa-voor-uh(-uhz)*
with ice	avec glaçons *(m, pl)*	*a-vehk glasOH*

25. *SHOPPING AND ERRANDS*

a. GENERAL VOCABULARY

bag (*shopping*)	sac *(m)* à provisions	*sak a pru-veez-yOH*
become	devenir *(v)*	*de-vneer*
bill (*from cash register*)	fiche *(f)* de caisse *(f)*	*feesh de kehss*
• **bill** (invoice)	facture *(f)*	*fak-tewr*
bring	apporter *(v)*	*a-port-ay*
buy	acheter *(v)*	*ash-tay*
cash register	caisse *(f)*	*kehss*
• **cashier**	caissier *(m)*	*kehs-yay*
	caissière *(f)*	*kehs-yehr*
change (*money*)	monnaie *(f)*	*mun-eh*
	rendu *(m)*	*rAH-dew*
• **change**	changer *(v)*	*sh-AH-zh-ay*
cost	coût *(m)*	*koo*
	prix *(m)*	*pree*
• **cost**	coûter *(v)*	*koo-tay*
• **How much does it cost?**	Ça coûte combien?	*sa koot kOH-byEH*
• **How much does it come to?**	Ça fait combien?	*sa feh kOH-byEH*
• **How much is it?**	C'est combien?	*seh kOH-byEH*

It costs an arm and a leg! = Cela coûte les yeux de la tête (*lit.*, It costs both eyes from the head)! *sla koot lay-zyuhd la teht*

---

counter	comptoir *(m)*	*kOHtwar*
customer	client(e) *(m, f)*	*klee-yAH(t)*
department (*of a store*)	rayon *(m)*	*ray-yOH*
entrance	entrée *(f)*	*AHtray*
exchange	échanger *(v)*	*ay-shAHzh-ay*
exit	sortie *(f)*	*sor-tee*
gift	cadeau *(m)*	*ka-doh*
lack	manquer (à) *(v)*	*mAH-kay (a)*
look for something	chercher *(v)*	*sh-ehr-shay*
package	colis *(m)*	*kul-ee*
	paquet *(m)*	*pa-kay*
pay	payer *(v)*	*pay-yay*
• **cash**	en espèces	*AH-nehs-pehss*

• with a check	par chèque	*par sh-ehk*
• credit card	carte (*f*) de crédit	*kart de kray-dee*
price	prix (*m*)	*pree*
• discount	rabais (*m*)	*ra-beh*
	remise (*f*)	*re-meez*
• expensive	cher, chère (*adj, m, f*)	*sh-ehr*
	coûteux(-euse) (*adj, m, f*)	*koo-tuh(-tuhz)*
• fixed price	prix (*m*) fixe	*pree-feeks*
• inexpensive	à bon marché	*a-bOH marsh-ay*
	économe (*adj*)	*ay-kun-um*
• price tag, label	étiquette (*f*)	*ay-tee-keht*
• reduced price	prix (*m*) réduit	*pree ray-dew-ee*
purchase	achat (*m*)	*a-sha*
	acheter (*v*)	*ash-tay*
receipt	reçu (*m*)	*res-ew*
refund	rembourser (*v*)	*rAH-boor-say*
	rendre (*v*)	*rAH-dr*
sale	vente (*f*)	*vAHt*
• for sale	à vendre (*v*)	*a-vAH-dr*
• on sale	en vente (*f*)	*AH vAHt*
• sell	vendre (*v*)	*vAH-dre*
shop	boutique (*f*)	*boo-teek*
• shop	faire (*v*) des achats (*m, pl*)	*fehr day za-sha*
	faire (*v*) des emplettes (*f, pl*)	*fehr day zAH-pleht*
	faire (*v*) du shopping (*m*)	*fehr dew shup-een*
shopping mall	centre (*m*) commercial	*sAH-tre-kum-ehrs-yal*
	grande surface (*f*)	*grAHd-sewr-fahs*
spend (*money*)	dépenser (*v*)	*day-pAH-say*
store	magasin (*m*)	*ma-gaz-EH*
• closed	fermé (*adj*)	*fehr-may*
• deparment store	grand magasin (*m*)	*grAH ma-gaz-EH*
• open	ouvert (*adj*)	*oo-vehr*
• store clerk	employé(e) (*m, f*)	*AH-plwa-yay*
• store hours	heures (*f, pl*)	*ur*
• opening hours	heures d'ouverture (*f*)	*ur doov-ehr-tewr*
• closing hours	heures de fermeture (*f*)	*ur de fehrm-tewr*
• store/shop window	vitrine (*f*)	*vee-treen*
take	prendre (*v*)	*prAH-dr*
• take back (return an item)	rendre (*v*)	*rAH-dr*

b. HARDWARE

battery	pile (*f*)	*peel*
cable	câble (*m*)	*kah-ble*
clamp	étau (*m*)	*ay-toh*
drill	foreuse (*f*)	*for-uhz*
electrical	électrique (*adj*)	*ay-lehk-treek*
file	lime (*f*)	*leem*
flashlight	lampe (*f*) de poche	*lAHp de pu-sh*
fuse	fusible (*m*)	*few-zee-bl*
	plomb (*m*) fusible	*plOH few-zee-bl*
hammer	marteau (*m*)	*mar-toh*
hardware store	quincaillerie (*f*)	*kEH-kah-y-ree*
insulation	isolant (*m*)	*ee-zul-AH*
ladder	échelle (*f*)	*ay-shell*
lawnmower	tondeuse (*f*)	*tOH-duhz*
light bulb	ampoule (*f*)	*AH-pool*
• **fluorescent**	fluorescent(e) (*adj, m, f*)	*flew-or-ay-sAH(t)*
• **neon**	au néon	*oh-nay-OH*
masking tape	papier (*m*) cache	*pap-yay kash*
mechanical	mécanique (*adj*)	*may-kan-eek*
nail	clou (*m*)	*kloo*
outlet	prise (*f*)	*preez*
pick	pic (*m*)	*peek*
	pioche (*f*)	*pee-yush*
plane	rabot (*m*)	*ra-boh*
pliers	pinces (*f, pl*)	*pEHss*
	tenailles (*f, pl*)	*ten-ah-y*
plug	fiche (*f*) de prise (*f*) de courant	*feesh de preez de koor-AH*
plumbing	plomberie (*f*)	*plOHbree*
punch	poinçon (*m*)	*pwEH-sOH*
rake	râteau (*m*)	*rah-toh*
saw	scie (*f*)	*see*
screw	vis (*f*)	*veess*
screwdriver	tournevis (*m*)	*toorn-veess*
shovel	pelle (*f*)	*pehl*
tool	outil (*m*)	*oo-tee*
transformer	transformateur (*m*)	*trAHs-form-at-ur*
wire	fil (*m*) métallique	*feel may-ta-leek*
wrench	pince (*f*) universelle	*pEHss ew-nee-vehr-sehl*

c. STATIONERY

adhesive tape	ruban (*m*) adhésif	*rewbAH ad-ay-zeef*
ballpoint pen	stylo (*m*) à bille	*stee-lo a bee-y*

briefcase	serviette (*f*)	*sehr-vee-yeht*
envelope	enveloppe (*f*)	*AHvlup*
marker	marqueur (*m*)	*mark-ur*
paper	papier (*m*)	*pap-yay*
pen	stylo (*m*)	*stee-lo*
pencil	crayon (*m*)	*kreh-yOH*
sheet (*of paper*)	feuille (*f*) de papier (*m*)	*fuh-y de pap-yay*
staple	agrafe (*f*)	*ag-raf*
stapler	agrafeuse (*f*)	*ag-ra-fuhz*
stationery store	papeterie (*f*)	*pap-tree*
string	ficelle (*f*)	*fee-sehl*
writing/note pad	bloc-notes (*m*)	*bluk-nut*

d. PHOTO/CAMERA

camera	appareil (*m*) photo	*a-pa-reh-y foto*
• movie camera	caméra (*f*)	*ka-may-ra*
	appareil cinématographique	*a-pa-reh-y see-nay-ma-tu-gra-feek*
• video camera	caméra vidéo (*f*)	*ka-may-ra vee-day-o*
camera shop	magasin (*m*) de photo	*ma-gaz-EH de foto*
film	film (*m*)	*feelm*
• roll of film	rouleau (*m*) de film	*roo-lohd feelm*
	rouleau (*m*) de pellicule (*f*)	*roo-lohd pay-leek-ewl*
	pellicule (*f*)	*pay-leek-ewl*
flash	flash (*m*)	*flash*
lens	objectif (*m*)	*ub-zh-ek-teef*
light bulb	ampoule (*f*)	*AH-pool*
photo, picture	photo(graphie) (*f*)	*foto(gra-fee)*
• clear (picture)	photo (*f*) nette	*foto neht*
• out of focus	photo (*f*) floue	*foto floo*
• color (picture)	en couleur (*f*)	*AH koo-lur*
• focus	mettre (*v*) en mise au point	*meht-r AH meez oh pwEH*
• in black and white	en noir et blanc	*AH nwar ay blAH*
• take a picture	prendre (*v*) une photo	*prAH-dr ewn foto*
• The picture turned out badly.	La photo a mal réussi.	*la foto a mal ray-ew-see*
• The picture turned out well.	La photo a bien réussi.	*la foto a byEH ray-ew-see*
screen	écran (*m*)	*ay-krAH*

| slide | diapositive (*f*) | *dya-po-zee-teev* |
| zoom | zoom (*m*) | *zoom* |

e. TOBACCO

card	carte (*f*)	*kart*
cigar	cigare (*m*)	*see-gar*
cigarette	cigarette (*f*)	*see-gar-eht*
lighter	briquet (*m*)	*breek-eh*
matches	allumettes (*f*)	*a-lew-meht*
pipe	pipe (*f*)	*peep*
smoke shop	bureau (*m*) de tabac	*bew-rohd ta-ba*
tobacco	tabac (*m*)	*ta-ba*
tobacconist	buraliste (*m, f*)	*bewr-al-eest*

f. COSMETICS/TOILETRIES

bath oil	huile (*f*) de bain	*ew-eeld bEH*
blade	lame (*f*)	*lam*
brush	brosse (*f*)	*bruss*
cologne	eau (*f*) de cologne	*ohd ku-lu-ny*
comb	peigne (*m*)	*peh-ny*
cosmetics/perfume shop	parfumerie (*f*)	*par-fewm-ree*
cream	crème (*f*)	*krehm*
curler	bigoudi (*m*)	*bee-goo-dee*
deodorant	déodorant (*m*)	*day-ud-u-rAH*
electric razor	rasoir (*m*) électrique	*rahz-war ay-lehk-treek*
face powder	poudre (*f*)	*pood-re*
hair dryer	séchoir (*m*) à cheveux	*say-sh-war a sh-vuh*
lipstick	rouge (*m*) à lèvres	*roo-zh a leh-vre*
	fard (*m*) à lèvres	*far a leh-vre*
lotion	lotion (*f*)	*loh-syOH*
make-up	maquillage (*m*)	*ma-kee-ya-zh*
mascara	fard (*m*) pour les yeux	*far poor layz-yuh*
nail polish	vernis (*m*) à ongles	*vehr-nee a OHgle*
perfume	parfum (*m*)	*parfUH*
razor	rasoir (*m*)	*rahz-war*
shampoo	shampooing (*m*)	*sh-AH-pwEH*
shaving cream	crème (*f*) à raser	*krehm a rah-zay*
soap	savon (*m*)	*savOH*
talcum powder	talc (*m*)	*tal-k*

g. LAUNDRY

button	bouton (*m*)	*bootOH*
clean	propre (*adj*)	*prup-r*
clothes	vêtements (*m, pl*)	*veht-mAH*
• **clothes basket**	panier (*m*) à linge	*pan-yay a lEHzh*
• **clothespin**	pince (*f*) à linge	*pEHss a lEHzh*
dirty	sale (*adj*)	*sal*
dry cleaning	nettoyage (*m*) à sec	*neht-wa-ya-zh a sehk*
hole	trou (*m*)	*troo*
iron	fer (*m*) à repasser	*fehr a re-pah-say*
• **iron**	repasser (*v*)	*re-pah-say*
laundry	linge (*m*)	*lEHzh*
	lessive (*f*)	*leh-seev*
mend	raccommoder (*v*)	*ra-kum-ud-ay*
pocket	poche (*f*)	*pu-sh*
sew	coudre (*v*)	*koo-dr*
sleeve	manche (*f*)	*mAHsh*
soap powder	savon (*m*) en poudre	*savOH AH poo-dr*
spot, stain	tache (*f*)	*tash*
starch	amidon (*m*)	*a-meed-OH*
stitch	point (*m*)	*pwEH*
wash	laver (*v*)	*la-vay*
• **washable**	lavable (*adj*)	*la-va-bl*
zipper	fermeture (*f*) à glissière	*fehrm-tewr a gleess-yehr*
	fermeture (*f*) éclair	*fehrm-tewr ay-klehr*

h. PHARMACY/DRUGSTORE

adhesive strip	sparadrap (*m*)	*spa-ra-dra*
antibiotic	antibiotique (*m*)	*AH-tee-byu-teek*
antidepressant	antidépresseur (*m*)	*AH-tee-day-press-ur*
aspirin	aspirine (*f*)	*as-pee-reen*
bandage	pansement (*m*)	*pAHs-mAH*
cortisone	cortisone (*f*)	*kor-tee-zun*
drugstore/pharmacy	pharmacie (*f*)	*farma-see*
injection	injection (*f*)	*EH-zh-ehks-yOH*
	piqûre (*f*)	*peek-ewr*
insulin	insuline (*f*)	*EH-sewl-een*
medicine	médicament (*m*)	*may-deek-am-AH*
ointment	pommade (*f*)	*pum-ad*
penicillin	pénicilline (*f*)	*pay-nee-see-leen*
pharmaceutical drug	remède (*m*)	*re-mehd*
	médicament (*m*)	*may-deek-am-AH*
pharmacist	pharmacien (*m*)	*farm-ass-yEH*
	pharmacienne (*f*)	*farm-ass-yehn*

pill	pilule (*f*)	*peel-ewl*
powder	poudre (*f*)	*poo-dre*
prescription	ordonnance (*f*)	*or-dun-AH-ss*
sodium bicarbonate	bicarbonate (*m*) de soude (*f*)	*bee-kar-bun-at de sood*
sodium citrate	citrate (*m*) de soude (*f*)	*see-trat de sood*
syrup	sirop (*m*)	*see-roh*
tablet	comprimé (*m*)	*kOHpree-may*
thermometer	thermomètre (*m*)	*tehr-mum-eht-re*
tincture of iodine	teinture (*f*) d'iode (*m*)	*tEHtewr dy-ud*
tissue	mouchoir (*m*) de papier (*m*)	*moosh-war de pap-yay*
toothbrush	brosse (*f*) à dents	*bruss a dAH*
toothpaste	dentifrice (*m*)	*dAHtee-freess*
vitamin	vitamine (*f*)	*vee-ta-meen*

i. JEWELRY

artificial	artificiel(le) (*adj, m, f*)	*ar-tee-fee-sy-ehl*
bracelet	bracelet (*m*)	*bras-leh*
brooch	broche (*f*)	*brush*
carat	carat (*m*)	*ka-ra*
chain	chaîne (*f*)	*sh-ehn*
diamond	diamant (*m*)	*dy-am-AH*
earring	boucle (*f*) d'oreille (*f*)	*book-l dor-ay*
emerald	émeraude (*f*)	*ehm-rohd*
false	faux (*adj, m*)	*foh*
	fausse (*f*)	*foh-ss*
fix, repair	ajuster (*v*)	*a-zh-ew-stay*
	réparer (*v*)	*ray-pa-ray*
gold	or (*m*)	*or*
jewel	bijou (*m*)	*bee-zh-oo*
jewelry store	bijouterie (*f*)	*bee-zh-oo-tree*
	joaillerie (*f*)	*zh-u-ah-y-ree*
necklace	collier (*m*)	*kul-yay*
opal	opale (*f*)	*up-al*
pearl	perle (*f*)	*pehrl*
precious	précieux (*adj, m*)	*pray-sy-uh*
	précieuse (*f*)	*pray-sy-uhz*
ring	bague (*f*)	*bag*
	anneau (*m*)	*an-oh*
ruby	rubis (*m*)	*rew-bee*
sapphire	saphir (*m*)	*sa-feer*
silver	argent (*m*)	*ar-zh-ΛH*
topaz	topaze (*f*)	*tup-ahz*

watch	montre (*f*)	*mOH-tr*
• **alarm clock**	réveille-matin (*m*)	*ray-veh-y-matEH*
• **clock**	horloge (*f*)	*or-lu-zh*
• **dial**	cadran (*m*)	*kad-rAH*
• **hand**	aiguille (*f*)	*ehg-ew-ee-y*
• **spring**	ressort (*m*)	*re-sor*
• **watchband**	bracelet (*m*) d'une montre	*bra-sleh dewn mOHtr*
• **wind**	remonter (*v*)	*re-mOH-tay*
• **wristwatch**	bracelet-montre (*m*)	*bra-sleh-mOHtr*
	montre-bracelet (*f*)	*mOHtr bra-sleh*

j. MUSIC

cassette	cassette (*f*)	*kaseht*
classical music	musique (*f*) classique	*mew-zeek kla-seek*
compact disc	disque compact (*m*)	*deesk-kOH-pakt*
composer	compositeur (*m*)	*kOH-po-zeet-ur*
	compositrice (*f*)	*kOH-po-zeet-reess*
dance music	musique (*f*) de danse (*f*)	*mew-zeek de dAHs*
jazz	jazz (*m*)	*dzh-ahz*
music	musique (*f*)	*mew-zeek*
record	disque (*m*)	*deesk*
rock music	musique (*f*) rock	*mew-zeek ruk*
singer	chanteur (*m*)	*shAHtur*
	chanteuse (*f*)	*shAHtuhz*
song	chanson (*f*)	*shAH-sOH*
tape	bande (*f*)	*bAHd*

k. CLOTHING

bathing suit	maillot (*m*) de bain (*m*)	*ma-yod bEH*
belt	ceinture (*f*)	*sEH-tewr*
blouse	chemisier (*m*)	*sh-em-eez-yay*
bra	soutien-gorge (*m*)	*soot-y-EH gohr-zh*
cardigan	chandail (*m*)	*sh-AH-da-y*
clothing	habillement (*m*)	*ab-ee-y-mAH*
	vêtements (*m, pl*)	*veht-mAH*
coat (suit)	veste (*f*)	*vehst*
	veston (*m*)	*vehstOH*
dress	robe (*f*)	*rub*
dressing room	cabine (*f*)	*ka-been*
fashion	mode (*f*)	*mud*
fur coat	manteau (*m*) de fourrure	*mAH-toh de foor-ewr*
glove	gant (*m*)	*gAH*

handkerchief	mouchoir (*m*)	*moosh-war*
hat	chapeau (*m*)	*sha-poh*
jacket	veste (*f*)	*vehst*
	veston (*m*)	*vehstOH*
men's shop/clothing	magasin (*m*) d'habillement masculin	*ma-gaz-EH dab-ee-y-mAH mas-kewl-EH*
miniskirt	minijupe (*f*)	*mee-nee-zh-ewp*
pajamas	pyjama (*m*)	*pee-zha-ma*
pants	pantalon (*m*)	*pAH-tal-OH*
raincoat	imperméable (*m*)	*EH-pehr-may-abl*
scarf	écharpe (*f*)	*ay-sharp*
shirt	chemise (*f*)	*shmeez*
size, fit	taille (*f*)	*ta-y*
	mesure (*f*)	*me-zewr*
skirt	jupe (*f*)	*zh-ewp*
slip	jupon (*m*)	*zh-ewp-OH*
	fond (*m*) de robe	*fOH de rub*
	combinaison (*f*)	*kOH-been-ehzOH*
smock	blouse (*f*)	*blooz*
suit	costume (*m*)	*kus-tewm*
	complet (*m*)	*kOHpleh*
sweater	tricot (*m*)	*tree-koh*
	sweater (*m*)	*sweht-ehr*
	pull-over (*m*)	*pewl-uv-ehr*
tailored suit (*woman's*)	costume (*m*) tailleur	*kus-tewm ta-y-ur*
T-shirt	T-shirt (*m*)	*tee-sh-ehrt*
tie	cravate (*f*)	*kra-vat*
underwear	sous-vêtements (*m, pl*)	*soo-veht-mAH*
vest	gilet (*m*)	*zh-ee-leh*
windbreaker	blouson (*m*)	*blooz-OH*
women's shop/clothing	magasin (*m*) d'habillement féminin	*ma-gaz-EH dab-ee-y mAH fay-meen-EH*

1. DESCRIBING CLOTHING

> For colors, see Section 7.

beautiful	beau (*m*)	*boh*
	bel (*m, s*)	*behl*
	belle (*f, s, pl*)	*behl*
big	grand	*grAH*
	grande (*f*)	*grAHd*
cotton	coton (*m*)	*kutOH*

elegant	élégant(e)	*ay-lay-gAH(t)*
fabric	tissu (*m*)	*teess-ew*
in the latest	à la mode	*a-la-mud*
style/fashion	au dernier cri	*oh dehrn-yay kree*
leather	cuir (*m*)	*kew-eer*
loose	vague (*adj*)	*vag*
	non-ajusté(e) (*adj, m, f*)	*nOH a-zh-ew-stay*
	ample (*adj*)	*AHpl*
nylon	nylon (*m*)	*neelOH*
polyester	polyester (*m*)	*pu-lee-ehs-tehr*
silk	en soie (*f*)	*AHswa*
small	petit(e) (*adj, m, f*)	*ptee(t)*
striped	rayé(e) (*adj, m, f*)	*ray-yay*
This looks bad on me.	Ceci ne me va pas bien.	*se-see nem va pah byEH*
This looks nice on me.	Ceci me va bien.	*se-see me va byEH*
tight	serré(e) (*adj, m, f*)	*sehr-ay*
ugly	laid(e) (*adj, m, f*)	*leh(d)*
wool	en laine (*f*)	*AH lehn*

m. CLOTHING: ACTIVITIES

enlarge	faire (*v*) élargir (*v*)	*fehr ay-lar-zh-eer*
get dressed	s'habiller (*v*)	*sa-bee-yay*
lengthen	faire (*v*) allonger (*v*)	*fehr al-OH-zh-ay*
put on	(se) mettre (*v*)	*(se) meht-r*
shorten	raccourcir (*v*)	*ra-koor-seer*
shrink	rétrécir (*v*)	*ray-tray-seer*
take off	enlever (*v*)	*AH-lvay*
tighten	faire (*v*) serrer (*v*)	*fehr sehr-ay*
try on	essayer (*v*)	*ay-say-yay*
undress	se déshabiller (*v*)	*se day-za-bee-yay*
wear	porter (*v*)	*por-tay*

n. SHOES

boot	botte (*f*)	*but*
pair	paire (*f*)	*pehr*
shoe	chaussure (*f*)	*sh-oh-sewr*
shoe horn	chausse-pied (*m*)	*sh-ohss-pyay*
shoe repair store	cordonnerie (*f*)	*kor-dun-ree*
shoe store	magasin (*m*) de chaussures (*f*)	*ma-gaz-EH de sh-oh-sewr*
shoelace	lacet (*m*)	*la-seh*
size (*of shoe*)	pointure (*f*)	*pwEH-tewr*

slipper	pantoufle (*f*)	*pAH-too-fle*
	chausson (*m*)	*sh-oh-sOH*
sock	chaussette (*f*)	*sh-oh-seht*
stocking	bas (*m*)	*bah*

o. BOOKS

book	livre (*m*)	*lee-vr*
best-seller	best-seller (*m*)	*behst-sehl-ehr*
bookstore	librairie (*f*)	*lee-breh-ree*
book of adventure	livre (*m*) d'aventure (*f*)	*lee-vr dav-AH-tewr*
comics	bandes (*f, pl*) dessinées	*bAHd day-seen-ay*
cookbook	livre (*m*) de cuisine	*lee-vr de kew-ee-zeen*
dictionary	dictionnaire (*m*)	*deek-see-yun-ehr*
encyclopedia	encyclopédie (*f*)	*AH-see-klup-ay-dee*
guidebook	guide (*m*)	*geed*
magazine	magazine (*m*)	*ma-gaz-een*
	revue (*f*)	*re-vew*
mystery novel	roman (*m*) policier	*rumAH pul-eess-yay*
newspaper	journal (*m*)	*zh-oor-nal*
novel	roman (*m*)	*rumAH*
poetry	poésie (*f*)	*pu-ay-zee*
reference book	ouvrage (*m*) de référence (*f*)	*oov-ra-zh de ray-fayr-AH-s*
romance book	livre (*m*) d'amour	*lee-vr dahm-oor*
science-fiction book	livre (*m*) de science-fiction	*lee-vr de see-AH-s-feeks-yOH*
technical book	livre (*m*) de technologie (*f*)	*lee-vr de tehk-nu-lu-zh-ee*
textbook	livre (*m*) de classe (*f*)	*lee-vr de klahs*
	livre (*m*) d'étude (*f*)	*lee-vr day-tewd*

26. BANKING AND COMMERCE

> For numerical concepts, see Section 1.

account	compte (*m*)	*kOHt*
• **ATM**	guichet (*m*) automatique	*kee-sheh u-tum-a-teek*
• **close an account**	arrêter (*v*) un compte	*ar-eh-tay UH kOHt*
	clore (*v*) un compte	*klor UH kOHt*
• **debit card**	carte (*f*) de retrait	*kart de re-treh*

• open an account	ouvrir (v) un compte	oov-reer UH kOHt
bank	banque (f)	bAHk
• head office	siège (m) central	see-yeh-zh sAHtral
• work in a bank	travailler (v) dans une banque	tra-va-yay dAH zewn bAHk
bank book	carnet (m) de banque	kar-neh de bAHk
bank rate	taux (m) bancaire	toh bAH-kehr
• fixed	fixe (adj)	feeks
• variable	variable (adj)	va-ree-abl
bill, banknote	billet (m) de banque	bee-yeh de bAHk
• dollar	dollar (m)	dul-ar
• French franc	franc français	frAH frAH-seh
• large bill	gros billet (m)	groh bee-yeh
• small bill	petit billet (m)	ptee bee-yeh
bond	obligation (f)	ub-lee-gas-yOH
budget	budget (m)	bewd-zh-eh
cash	en espèces	AH-nehs-pehs
• cash a check	toucher (v) un chèque	too-shay UH sh-ehk
• cash register	caisse (f)	kehss
cashier, teller	caissier (m)	kehs-yay
	caissière (f)	kehs-yehr
check	chèque (m)	sh-ehk
• checkbook	carnet (m) de chèques	kar-neh de sh-ehk
cost of living	coût (m) de la vie	koo de la vee
credit	crédit (m)	kray-dee
• credit card	carte (f) de crédit	kart de kray-dee
currency	billets (m) de banque	bee-yeh de bAHk
	monnaie (f) fiduciaire	mun-eh fee-dew-see-yehr
current account	compte (m) courant	kOHt koor-AH
customer	client(e) (m, f)	klee-yAH(t)
debit	débit (m)	day-bee
debt	dette (f)	deht
deposit	versement (m)	vehrs-mAH
• deposit	verser (v) une somme au compte	vehr-say ewn sum oh kOHt
deposit slip	fiche (f) de versement	feesh de vehrs-mAH
	fiche (f) de dépôt bancaire	feesh de day-poh bAH-kehr
draft, promissory note	billet (m) à ordre	bee-yeh a or-dre
employee	employé(e) (m, f)	AH-plwa-yay
endorse	endosser (v)	AH-doh-say
• endorsement	endossement (m)	AH-dohs-mAH
	endos (m)	AH-doh

Eurocurrency	eurodevise (*f*)	*uh-rod-veez*
Eurodollar	eurodollar (*m*)	*uh-ro-du-lar*
exchange	change (*m*)	*shAH-zh*
• exchange	changer (*v*)	*shAH-zh-ay*
• exchange rates	cours (*m*) du change	*koor dew shAH-zh*
expiry (date)	échéance (*f*)	*ay-shay-AH-s*
income	revenu (*m*)	*rev-new*
insurance	assurance (*f*)	*as-ew-rAHs*
interest	intérêt (*m*)	*EH-tay-reh*
• interest rate	taux (*m*) d'intérêt	*toh dEH-tay-reh*
invest	investir (*v*)	*EH-vehs-teer*
• investment	investissement (*m*)	*EH-vehs-tees-mAH*
line	queue (*f*)	*kuh*
• line up	faire (*v*) la queue	*fehr la kuh*
loan	prêt (*m*)	*preh*
• get a loan	obtenir (*v*) un prêt	*up-te-neer UH preh*
loose change	monnaie (*f*)	*mun-eh*
manager	directeur(-trice) (*m, f*)	*dee-rehk-tur(-trice)*
money	argent (*m*)	*ar-zh-AH*
money order	mandat (*m*) de paiement (*m*)	*mAHda de peh-mAH*
mortgage	hypothèque (*f*)	*ee-pu-tehk*
pay	payer (*v*)	*pay-yay*
• pay off	acquitter (*v*)	*a-kee-tay*
• payment	paiement (*m*)	*peh-mAH*
postdate	postdater (*v*)	*pust-da-tay*
receipt	reçu (*m*)	*res-ew*
	acquit (*m*)	*a-kee*
	récépissé (*m*)	*ray-say-pee-say*
safe	coffre-fort (*m*)	*kuf-re-for*
• safety deposit box	coffre (*m*) de sécurité	*kuf-re de say-kew-ree-tay*
salary	salaire (*m*)	*sal-ehr*
save	économiser (*v*)	*ay-kun-um-ee-zay*
	épargner (*v*)	*ay-parn-yay*
• savings	épargne (*f*)	*ay-parn-y*
sign	signer (*v*)	*seen-yay*
• signature	signature (*f*)	*seen-ya-tewr*
stock, share	action (*f*)	*aks-yOH*
• stock market/exchange	Bourse (*f*)	*boorss*
teller's window	guichet (*m*)	*geesh-eh*
traveler's check	chèque (*m*) de voyage	*sh-ehk de vwa-ya-zh*
withdraw	prélever (*v*)	*prayl-vay*
• withdrawal	prélèvement (*m*)	*pray-lehv-mAH*

- **withdrawal slip**   fiche (*f*) de   *feesh de pray-lehv-*
                               prélèvement (*m*)   *mAH*

27. GAMES AND HOBBIES

a. GAMES AND HOBBIES

bingo	bingo (*m*)	*been-go*
• **bingo card**	fiche (*f*)	*feesh*
billiards, to play	jouer (*v*) au billard (*m*)	*zh-oo-ay oh bee-yar*
• **billiard ball**	bille (*f*)	*bee-y*
• **billiard table**	table (*f*) de billard (*m*)	*ta-bl de bee-yar*
• **cue**	queue (*f*) de billard (*m*)	*kuh de bee-yar*
• **cushion**	rebord (*m*) élastique	*re-bor ay-las-teek*
• **pocket**	trou (*m*)	*troo*
checkers (to play)	jouer (*v*) aux dames	*zh-oo-ay oh dahm*
• **checkerboard**	damier (*m*)	*dahm-yay*
• **checker piece**	pion (*m*)	*pee-yOH*
chess (to play)	jouer (*v*) aux échecs	*zh-oo-ay oh zay-sh-ehk*
• **bishop**	fou (*m*)	*foo*
• **chessboard**	échiquier (*m*)	*ay-sheek-yay*
• **king**	roi (*m*)	*rwa*
• **knight**	cavalier (*m*)	*ka-val-yay*
• **pawn**	pion (*m*)	*pee-yOH*
• **queen**	dame (*f*)	*dahm*
• **rook**	tour (*f*)	*toor*
coin	monnaie (*f*)	*mun-eh*
• **coin collecting**	numismatique (*f*)	*new-mees-ma-teek*
dice, to play	jouer (*v*) aux dés (*m, pl*)	*zh-oo-ay oh day*
game	jeu (*m*)	*zh-uh*
	partie (*f*)	*par-tee*
hobby	passe-temps (*m*)	*pahs-tAH*
play cards	jouer (*v*) aux cartes (*f, pl*)	*zh-oo-ay oh kart*
• **ace**	as (*m*)	*ahss*
• **ace of spades**	as (*m*) de pique (*f*)	*ahss de peek*
• **clubs**	trèfle (*m*)	*treh-fl*
• **diamonds**	carreau (*m*)	*kar-oh*
• **hearts**	cœur (*m*)	*kur*
• **joker**	joker (*m*)	*zh-uk-ur*
• **king**	roi (*m*)	*rwa*
• **queen**	reine (*f*)	*rehn*
	dame (*f*)	*dahm*
• **spades**	pique (*f*)	*peek*
• **tarot**	tarot (*m*)	*tar-oh*
stamp (postage)	timbre-poste (*m*)	*tEHbr-pust*

| • **stamp collecting** | collection (*f*) de timbres | *kul-ehks-yOH de tEHbr* |

b. SPORTS, PHYSICAL FITNESS, AND MARTIAL ARTS

aikido	aïkido (*m*)	*ah-y-keedoh*
amateur	amateur (*m*)	*a-ma-tur*
	dilettante (*m/f*)	*deel-ehtAHt*
athlete	athlète (*m/f*)	*at-leht*
ball	balle (*f*)	*bal*
• **catch**	attraper (*v*)	*a-trap-ay*
• **hit**	battre (*v*)	*bat-r*
• **kick**	donner (*v*) un coup de pied	*dun-ay UH kood pee-yay*
• **pass**	passer (*v*)	*pah-say*
• **throw**	lancer (*v*)	*lAH-say*
baseball	base-ball (*m*)	*behz-bol*
• **ball**	balle (*f*)	*bal*
• **base**	base (*f*)	*bahz*
• **bat**	batte (*f*)	*bat*
• **batter**	batteur (*m*)	*ba-tur*
• **catcher's mask**	masque (*m*) du receveur	*mask dew re-se-vur*
• **foul line**	ligne (*f*) de pénalité	*lee-ny de pay-na-lee-tay*
• **glove**	gant (*m*)	*gAH*
• **home base**	base (*f*) du batteur	*bahz dew ba-tur*
• **pitcher**	lanceur (*m*)	*lAH-sur*
basketball	basket(-ball) (*m*)	*bas-keht(-bol)*
• **ball**	ballon (*m*) de basket	*ba-lOH de bas-keht*
• **basket**	panier (*m*)	*pan-yay*
bicycle racing	courses (*f*) cyclistes	*koorss see-kleest*
body building	culturisme (*m*)	*kewl-tewr-ees-me*
• **weight lifting**	haltérophilie (*f*)	*al-tay-ru-feel-ee*
bowling	bowling (*m*)	*bul-een-y*
• **bowl**	jouer (*v*) au bowling (*m*)	*zh-oo-ay oh bul-een-y*
• **bowling alley**	piste (*f*)	*peest*
• **bowling ball**	boule (*f*)	*bool*
• **bowling pin**	quille (*f*)	*kee-y*
boxing	boxe (*f*)	*buks*
• **boxing glove**	gant (*m*) de boxe	*gAH de buks*
• **boxing ring**	ring (*m*)	*ree-ny*
• **ropes**	cordes (*f, pl*)	*kord*
car racing	courses (*f*) de voitures	*koorss de vwa-tewr*
coach	entraîneur (*m/f*)	*AH-trehn-ur*
competition	concours (*m*)	*kOHkoor*

fencing	escrime (f)	ehs-kreem
• **fence**	faire (v) de l'escrime	fehr de lehs-kreem
• **French foil**	fleuret (m) français	flur-eh frAHseh
• **mask**	masque (m)	mask
• **On guard!**	En garde! (f)	AH gard
• **saber (light)**	sabre (m) d'escrime (f)	sah-br dehs-kreem
• **Touché!**	Touché!	too-shay
field	champ (m)	shAH
football	football (m) américain	foot-bohl a-may-reek-EH
game, match	jeu (m)	zh-uh
	match (m)	mat-sh
	partie (f)	par-tee
goal	but (m)	bew(t)
• **goalie**	gardien(-ienne) (m, f) de but	gard-yEH(-yehn) de bew(t)
golf (to play)	jouer (v) au golf (m)	zh-oo-ay oh gulf
gymnasium	gymnase (m)	zh-eem-nahz
• **work out**	pratiquer (v) les exercices du corps	pra-tee-kay lay zehg-zehr-seess dew kor
gymnastics	gymnastique (f)	zh-eem-nas-teek
helmet	casque (m)	kask
hockey (ice)	hockey (m) sur glace	uk-eh sewr glahss
• **hockey player**	joueur(-euse) (m, f) de hockey	zh-oo-ur(-uhz) de uk-eh
• **hockey stick**	crosse (f)	kruss
	stick (m)	steek
• **puck**	palet (m)	pal-eh
	puck (m)	puk
• **skate**	patin (m) à glace	patEH a glahss
jog	faire (v) du jogging (m)	fehr dew dzh-ug-een
• **jogging**	jogging (m)	dzhug-een
judo	judo (m)	zh-ew-doh
karate	karaté (m)	ka-ra-tay
mountain climbing	alpinisme (m)	alp-een-ees-me
• **knapsack**	sac (m) à dos (m)	sak a doh
• **mountain boot**	chaussure (f) d'escalade (f)	sho-sewr dehs-ka-lad
• **rope**	corde (f) d'alpinisme (m)	kord dalp-een-ees-me
• **snow goggles**	lunettes (f, pl) de glacier (m)	lew-neht de glas-yay
net	but (m)	bew(t)
penalty	pénalité (f)	pay-nal-ee-tay
play	jeu (m)	zh-uh
• **player**	joueur (m)	zh-oo-ur
	joueuse (f)	zh-oo-uhz

point	marque (*f*)	*mark*
professional	professionel(-elle) (*m, f*)	*pruf-ehs-ee-yun-ehl*
race	course (*f*)	*koorss*
• horse racing	course (*f*) au galop	*koorss oh gal-oh*
	courses (*f*) de chevaux	*koorss de shvoh*
referee	arbitre (*m/f*)	*ar-beet-r*
run	courir (*v*)	*koo-reer*
score	marque (*f*)	*mark*
• draw, tie	match (*m*) nul	*mat-sh newl*
• draw	terminer (*v*) à match nul	*tehr-mee-nay a mat-sh newl*
	terminer (*v*) à égalité	*tehr-mee-nay a ay-gal-ee-tay*
• lose	perdre (*v*)	*pehr-dr*
• loss	perte (*f*)	*pehrt*
• win	gain (*m*)	*gEH*
	gagner (*v*)	*gan-yay*
skate	patiner (*v*)	*pa-teen-ay*
• to ice skate	patiner (*v*) sur glace	*pa-teen-ay sewr glahss*
• to roller skate	patiner (*v*) à roulettes	*pa-teen-ay a roo-leht*
ski	skier (*v*)	*skee-yay*
	faire (*v*) du ski	*fehr dew skee*
• cross-country skiing	ski (*m*) de fond	*skeed-fOH*
• downhill skiing	ski (*m*) alpin	*skee-alpEH*
• ski	ski (*m*)	*skee*
• skier	skieur (*m*)	*skee-ur*
	skieuse (*f*)	*skee-uhz*
• water skiing	ski (*m*) nautique	*skee noh-teek*
soccer	foot (*m*)	*foot*
• play soccer	jouer (*v*) au foot	*zh-oo-ay oh foot*
• soccer ball	ballon (*m*)	*balOH*
sport	sport (*m*)	*spor*
• practice a sport	faire (*v*) du sport (*m*)	*fehr dew spor*
• sports fan	fan (*m*)	*fahn*
	fanatique (*m/f*) du sport	*fan-a-teek dew spor*
	enthousiaste (*m/f*) du sport	*AH-too-zee-ast dew spor*
stadium	stade (*m*)	*stad*
swim	nager (*v*)	*na-zh-ay*
• swimming	natation (*f*)	*na-tas-yOH*
• swimming pool	piscine (*f*)	*pee-seen*
team	équipe (*f*)	*ay-keep*
tennis (*to play*)	jouer (*v*) au tennis	*zh-oo-ay oh tehn-eess*
• racket	raquette (*f*)	*ra-keht*

ticket	billet (*m*)	*bee-yeh*
	ticket (*m*)	*teek-eh*
track	piste (*f*)	*peest*
volleyball	volley-ball (*m*)	*vul-eh-bol*
water polo	water-polo (*m*)	*wa-tehr-pu-loh*
wrestling	lutte (*f*)	*lewt*

28. THE ARTS

a. CINEMA

actor	acteur (*m*)	*ak-tur*
actress	actrice (*f*)	*ak-treess*
aisle	allée (*f*)	*alay*
box office	guichet (*m*)	*geesh-eh*
cinema	cinéma (*m*)	*see-nay-ma*
	ciné (*m*)	*see-nay*
lobby	foyer (*m*)	*fwa-yay*
movie, film	film (*m*)	*feelm*
• **make a movie**	tourner (*v*) un film	*toor-nay UH feelm*
• **premiere showing**	première (*f*) représentation (*f*)	*prem-yehr re-prayz-AH-tas-yOH*
movie director	réalisateur (*m*)	*ray-al-eez-at-ur*
	metteur (*m*) en scène (*f*)	*meht-ur AH sehn*
movies	cinéma (*m*)	*see-nay-ma*
row	rang (*m*)	*rAH*
screen	écran (*m*)	*ay-krAH*
seat	place (*f*)	*plass*
	siège (*m*)	*see-yeh-zh*
soundtrack	bande (*f*) sonore	*bAHd sun-or*

FOCUS: Some Well-Known French Cinema Directors

Jean Cocteau (1889–1963)	*Orphée (Orpheus)* *La Belle et la Bête (Beauty and the Beast)* *Le Sang du poète (Blood of a Poet)*
Jean Renoir (1894–1979)	*La Grande illusion (Grand Illusion)*
François Truffaut (1932–1984)	*Les Quatre cents coups (400 Blows)* *Jules et Jim (Jules and Jim)*

Note: If you would like to know more names of famous French cinema directors and their productions, please consult a book on the subject of French cinematography.

b. ART/SCULPTURE/ARCHITECTURE

architecture	architecture (*f*)	arsh-ee-tehk-tewr
• **blueprint**	copie (*f*) cyanotype	kup-ee see-ano-teep
art	art (*m*)	ar
artist	artiste (*m/f*)	ar-teest
brush	pinceau (*m*)	pEHsoh
easel, tripod	chevalet (*m*)	sh-val-eh
exhibition	exposition (*f*)	ehks-poh-zees-yOH
fresco painting	fresque (*f*)	frehsk
masterpiece	chef (*m*) d'œuvre (*f*)	shay duv-re
paint	peindre (*v*)	pEH-dr
• **painter**	peintre (*m/f*)	pEH-tr
	artiste-peintre (*m/f*)	ar-teest pEH-tr
• **painting**	peinture (*f*)	pEH-tewr
	tableau (*m*)	tab-loh
palette	palette (*f*)	pal-eht
pastel	pastel (*m*)	pas-tehl
portrait	portrait (*m*)	port-reh
sculpt	sculpter (*v*)	skewl-tay
• **sculptor**	sculpteur (*m*)	skewl-tur
• **sculptress**	femme sculpteur (*f*)	fahm skewl-tur
• **sculpture**	sculpture (*f*)	skewl-tewr
watercolor	aquarelle (*f*)	ak-wa-rehl

FOCUS: Some Well-Known French Artists

Edgar Degas (1834–1917)	*Le Ballet (The Ballet)* *Danseuse (Dancer)* *Danseuse saluant (Dancer Taking a Bow)* *Scène de Ballet (Ballet Scene)*
Raoul Dufy (1877–1953)	*La Plage à Sainte-Adresse (The Beach at Sainte-Adresse)* *Baigneuses (Bathers)*
Jean-Honoré Fragonard (1732–1806)	*La Liseuse (Girl Reading a Book)*
Henri de Toulouse-Lautrec (1864–1901)	*Au Moulin de la Galette (At the Moulin de la Galette)*

Note: If you would like to know more names of famous French artists and their paintings, please consult a book on the subject of French artists and their art.

c. MUSIC/DANCE

accordion	accordéon (*m*)	*ak-or-day-OH*
ballet	ballet (*m*)	*bal-eh*
brass instruments	cuivres (*m, pl*)	*kew-eevre*
• **horn**	cor (*m*)	*kor*
• **trombone**	trombone (*m*)	*trOH-bun*
• **trumpet**	trompette (*f*)	*trOH-peht*
• **tuba**	tuba (*m*)	*tew-ba*
classical music	musique (*f*) classique	*mew-zeek kla-seek*
composer	compositeur (*m*)	*kOH-po-zee-tur*
	femme compositeur (*f*)	*fahm kOH-po-zee-tur*
• **composition**	composition (*f*)	*kOH-po-zees-yOH*
concert	concert (*m*)	*kOH-sehr*
dance	bal (*m*)	*bal*
• **dance**	danser (*v*)	*dAH-say*
• **dancer**	danseur (*m*)	*dAH-sur*
	danseuse (*f*)	*dAH-suhz*
folk music	musique (*f*) folklorique	*mew-zeek fulk-lur-eek*
guitar	guitare (*f*)	*geet-ar*
• **guitarist**	guitariste (*m, f*)	*geet-ar-eest*
harmony	harmonie (*f*)	*arm-un-ee*
harp	harpe (*f*)	*arp*

instrument	instrument (*m*)	*EH-strew-mAH*
• **play an instrument**	jouer (*v*) de (du, de l', de la)	*zh-oo-ay de (dew, del, de la)*
jazz	jazz (*m*)	*dzh-ahz*
keyboard instruments	instruments (*m/pl*) à clavier (*m*)	*EH-strew-mAH a klav-yay*
• **grand piano**	piano (*m*) à queue (*f*)	*pee-yan-oh a kuh*
• **harpsichord**	clavecin (*m*)	*klav-sEH*
• **organ**	orgue (*m*)	*org*
• **pianist**	pianiste (*m, f*)	*pee-yan-eest*
• **piano**	piano (*m*)	*pee-yan-oh*
• **synthesizer**	synthétiseur (*m*)	*sEH-tay-teez-ur*
• **upright piano**	piano (*m*) droit	*pee-yan-oh drwa*
light music	musique (*f*) légère	*mew-zeek lay-zh-ehr*
mandolin	mandoline (*f*)	*mAH-dul-een*
music	musique (*f*)	*mew-zeek*
• **musician**	musicien (*m*)	*mew-zees-yEH*
	musicienne (*f*)	*mew-zees-yehn*
note	note (*f*)	*nut*
opera	opéra (*m*)	*up-ay-ra*
orchestra	orchestre (*m*)	*or-kehs-tre*
orchestra conductor	chef (*m*) d'orchestre (*m*)	*sh-ehf dor-kehs-tre*
percussion instruments	instruments (*m, pl*) à percussion (*f*)	*EH-strew-mAH a pehr-kewss-yOH*
• **bass drum**	grosse caisse (*f*)	*groh-ss kehss*
• **cymbals**	cymbales (*f, pl*)	*sEH-bal*
• **drum**	tambour (*m*)	*tAH-boor*
• **set of drums**	batterie (*f*)	*bat-ree*
• **timpani**	timbale (*f*)	*tEH-bal*
player	joueur (*m*)	*zh-oo-ur*
	joueuse (*f*)	*zh-oo-uhz*
rap	rap (*m*)	*rap*
rhythm	rythme (*m*)	*reet-me*
show	spectacle (*m*)	*spehk-takl*
song	chanson (*f*)	*shAH-sOH*
• **sing**	chanter (*v*)	*shAH-tay*
• **singer**	chanteur (*m*)	*shAH-tur*
	chanteuse (*f*)	*shAH-tuhz*
stringed instruments	instruments (*m, pl*) à cordes (*f*)	*EH-strewm-AH a kord*
• **bow**	archet (*m*) de violon (*m*)	*arsh-eh de vee-yulOH*
• **cello**	violoncelle (*m*)	*vee-yulOH-sehl*
• **double bass**	contrebasse (*f*)	*kOH-tre-bahss*
• **string**	corde (*f*)	*kord*
• **viola**	viole (*f*)	*vee-yul*
• **violin**	violon (*m*)	*vee-yulOH*
• **violinist**	violoniste (*m, f*)	*vee-yul-un-eest*

symphony	symphonie (f)	sEH-fun-ee
wind instruments	instruments (m, pl) à vent (m)	EH-strew-mAH a vAH
• bagpipes	cornemuse (f)	korn-mewz
• bassoon	basson (m)	bahsOH
• clarinet	clarinette (f)	kla-reen-eht
• flute	flûte (f)	flewt
• oboe	hautbois (m)	oh-bwah
• saxophone	saxophone (m)	saks-uf-un

FOCUS: Some Well-Known French Composers

Georges Bizet (1838–1875)	*Carmen*
Gustave Charpentier (1860–1956)	*Louise*
Jules Massenet (1842–1912)	*Manon*

Note: If you would like to know more names of famous French composers and their works, please consult a book on the subject of French music and composers.

d. LITERATURE

appendix	appendice (m)	ap-EH-deess
autobiography	autobiographie (f)	ut-ub-yug-ra-fee
biography	biographie (f)	bee-yug-ra-fee
chapter	chapitre (m)	sh-ap-eet-re
character (in *a novel, play*)	personnage (m)	pehr-sun-azh
criticism	critique (f)	kree-teek
fable	fable (f)	fah-bl
fairy tale	conte (m) de fées (f)	kOHt de fay
fiction	livre (m) de fiction (f)	lee-vre de feeks-yOH
genre	genre (m)	zh-AH-re
literature	littérature (f)	lee-tay-ra-tewr
myth	mythe (m)	meet
mythology	mythologie (f)	meet-ul-u-zh-ee
novel	roman (m)	rumAH
plot	intrigue (f)	EH-treeg
poet	poète (m)	pu-eht
	femme (f) poète	fahm pu-eht
poetry	poésie (f)	pu-ay-zee

preface	préface (*f*)	*pray-fass*
rhetoric	rhétorique (*f*)	*ray-tu-reek*
short story	conte (*m*)	*kOHt*
	nouvelle (*f*)	*noo-vehl*
style	style (*m*)	*steel*
theme	thème (*m*)	*tehm*
work (*literary*)	ouvrage (*m*)	*oov-razh*
writer	écrivain (*m*)	*ay-kreev-EH*
	femme (*f*) écrivain	*fahm ay-kreev-EH*

FOCUS: Some Well-Known French Writers

Gustave Flaubert (1821–1880)	*Madame Bovary*
Michel de Montaigne (1533–1592)	*Les Essais (The Essays)*
Jean-Paul Sartre (1905–1980)	*Les Mots (The Words)*
Simone de Beauvoir (1908–1986)	*Les Mandarins (The Mandarins)*
Albert Camus (1913–1960)	*L'Étranger (The Stranger)*

Note: If you would like to know more names of famous French writers, please consult a book on the subject of French writers and their literary works.

e. THEATER

act	acte (*m*)	*akt*
• **act**	jouer (*v*) dans une pièce	*zh-oo-ay dAH zewn pee-yehs*
applause	applaudissement (*m*)	*ap-loh-dees-mAH*
• **applaud**	applaudir (*v*)	*ap-loh-deer*
audience	spectateurs (*m, pl*)	*spehk-ta-tur*
comedian	acteur(-trice) (*m, f*) comique	*ak-tur(-treess) kum-eek*
comedy	comédie (*f*)	*kum-ay-dee*
curtain	rideau (*m*) de scène (*f*)	*reed-oh de sehn*
drama	drame (*m*)	*drahm*
hero	héros (*m*)	*ay-roh*
heroine	héroïne (*f*)	*ay-ru-een*
intermission	entracte (*m*)	*AH-trakt*
mime	mime (*m, f*)	*meem*
pantomime	pantomime (*f*)	*pAH-tum-eem*
play	pièce (*f*) de théâtre (*m*)	*pee-yehs de tay-ah-tr*

playwright	dramaturge (*m, f*)	*dra-ma-tewr-zh*
	auteur (*m*) dramatique	*oh-tur dra-ma-teek*
	femme (*f*) auteur dramatique	*fahm oh-tur dra-ma-teek*
plot	intrigue (*f*)	*EH-treeg*
production	mise (*f*) en scène (*f*)	*meez-AH-sehn*
program	programme (*m*)	*prug-ram*
rehearsal	répétition (*f*)	*ray-pay-tee-syOH*
scene	scène (*f*)	*sehn*
scenery	décor (*m*)	*day-kor*
stage	scène (*f*)	*sehn*
theater	théâtre (*m*)	*tay-ah-tr*
tragedy	tragédie (*f*)	*tra-zh-ay-dee*

FOCUS: Some Well-Known French Playwrights

Paul Claudel (1868–1955)   *L'Annonce faite à Marie (Tidings Brought to Mary)*

Jean Giraudoux (1882–1949)   *La Folle de Chaillot (The Madwoman of Chaillot)*

Jean-Baptiste Poquelin Molière (1622–1673)   *L'Avare (The Miser)*
Le Malade imaginaire (The Imaginary Invalid)
Le Bourgeois gentilhomme (The Would-Be Gentleman)

Jean-Paul Sartre (1905–1980)   *Huis Clos (No Exit)*

Note: If you would like to know more names of famous French playwrights and their works, please consult a book on the subject of French theater.

---

29. HOLIDAYS AND GOING OUT

a. HOLIDAYS/SPECIAL OCCASIONS

anniversay	anniversaire (*m*)	*a-nee-vehr-sehr*
Bastille Day (July 14)	La Prise de la Bastille	*la preez dla bastee-y*
birthday	anniversaire (*m*) de naissance (*f*)	*a-nee-vehr-sehr de neh-sAHss*
Christmas	Noël (*m*)	*nu-ehl*
Easter	Pâques (*f, pl*)	*pahk*

engagement	fiançailles (*f, pl*)	*fee-yAH-sah-y*
Feast of the Assumption (Aug. 15)	Assomption (*f*)	*a-sOH-ps-yOH*
French National Holiday (July 14)	la Fête Nationale (le Quatorze Juillet)	*la feht nas-yun-al*
holiday (official)	jour (*m*) férié	*zh-oor fay-ree-yay*
holidays	jours (*m, pl*) de fête (*f*)	*zh-oor de feht*
name day	fête (*f*)	*feht*
New Year's Day	le Jour de l'An (*m*)	*le zh-oor de lAH*
New Year's Eve	la Nuit de la Saint-Sylvestre	*la-new-eed-la-sEH-seel-vestr*
Passover	Pâque (*f*)	*pahk*
picnic	pique-nique (*m*)	*peek-neek*
Ramadan	ramadan (*m*)	*ra-ma-dAH*
vacation	vacances (*f, pl*)	*va-kAH-ss*
wedding	mariage (*m*)	*mar-ee-yazh*
	noces (*f, pl*)	*nuss*

b. GOING OUT

dance	bal (*m*)	*bal*
• dance	danser (*v*)	*dAH-say*
disco	discothèque (*f*)	*dees-kut-ehk*
go out	sortir (*v*)	*sor-teer*
have fun	s'amuser (*v*)	*sam-ew-zay*
party	fête (*f*)	*feht*
remain	rester (*v*)	*rehs-tay*
return	retourner (*v*)	*re-toor-nay*
	revenir (*v*)	*rev-neer*
visit (*friends, relatives*)	rendre (*v*) visite à	*rAH-dr vee-zeet a*

c. SPECIAL GREETINGS

Best wishes!	Meilleurs vœux! (*m, pl*)	*meh-yur vuh*
Compliments!	Mes compliments! (*m, pl*)	*may kOH-pleem-AH*
Congratulations!	Félicitations! (*f, pl*)	*fay-lee-see-tas-yOH*
Happy Birthday!	Bon anniversaire! (*m*)	*bun-a-nee-vehr-sehr*
Happy Easter!	Bonnes Pâques! (*f, pl*) *or* Joyeuses Pâques!	*bun pahk* *zh-wah-yuh-z pahk*
Happy New Year!	Bonne année! (*f*)	*bun-a-nay*
	Heureuse année! (*f*)	*ur-uhz a-nay*
Have a good holiday!	Bonnes vacances! (*f, pl*)	*bun va-kAh-ss*

Have a nice day!	Bonne journée! (*f*)	*bun-zh-oor-nay*
Have fun!	Amusez-vous! (*pol*)	*a-mew-zay voo*
	Amuse-toi! (*fam*)	*a-mewz twa*
Merry Christmas!	Joyeux Noël (*m*)	*zh-wa-yuh nu-ehl*

TRAVEL

30. CHOOSING A DESTINATION

> For more related vocabulary, see Section 13.

a. AT THE TRAVEL AGENCY

abroad	à l'étranger	*al-ay-trAH-zh-ay*
brochure	brochure (*f*)	*brush-ewr*
charter flight	avion charter (*m*)	*av-yOH shar-tehr*
city	ville (*f*)	*veel*
• **capital city**	capitale (*f*)	*kap-ee-tal*
class	classe (*f*)	*klahss*
• **first class**	première classe (*f*)	*prem-yehr klahss*
• **economy class**	classe (*f*) touriste	*klahss tooreest*
continent	continent (*m*)	*kOH-teen-AH*
country	pays (*m*)	*peh-ee*
downtown	en ville	*AH veel*
	centre (*m*) de la ville	*sAH-tre de la veel*
excursion	excursion (*f*)	*ehks-kewrs-yOH*
insurance	assurance (*f*)	*ass-ewr-AHss*
nation	nation (*f*)	*nahss-yOH*
outskirts, suburbs	environs (*m, pl*)	*AH-veerOH*
	banlieue (*f*)	*bAHl-yuh*
see	voir (*v*)	*vwar*
ticket	billet (*m*)	*bee-yeh*
• **by boat**	en bateau (*m*)	*AH ba-toh*
• **by plane**	en avion (*m*)	*AH nav-yOH*
• **by train**	par le train	*parl trEH*
• **buy a ticket**	acheter (*v*) un billet	*ash-tay UH bee-yeh*
• **one-way ticket**	billet (*m*) simple	*bee-yeh sEHpl*
• **round-trip ticket**	billet (*m*) aller-retour	*bee-yeh alay retoor*
tour	voyage (*m*) organisé	*vwa-yazh organ-ee-zay*
tour bus	autocar (*m*) de tourisme	*u-toh-kar de toor-eesm*
	autocar (*m*) d'excursion	*u-toh-kar dehks-kewrs-yOH*
tour guide	guide (*m, f*)	*geed*
tourist	touriste (*m, f*)	*toor-eest*
travel	voyager (*v*)	*vwa-ya-zh-ay*
• **travel agency**	agence (*f*) de voyages	*azh-AH-ss de vwa-ya-zh*

trip, journey	voyage (m)	vwa-ya-zh
• **Have a nice trip!**	Bon voyage!	bOH vwa-ya-zh
• **take a trip**	faire (v) un voyage	fehr UH vwa-ya-zh
visit	visiter (v)	vee-zee-tay
world	monde (m)	mOHd

b. COUNTRIES AND CONTINENTS

Africa	Afrique (f)	af-reek
Algeria	Algérie (f)	al-zh-ay-ree
America	Amérique (f)	a-may-reek
• **Latin America**	Amérique (f) latine	a-may-reek la-teen
• **North America**	Amérique (f) du Nord	a-may-reek dew nor
• **South America**	Amérique (f) du Sud	a-may-reek dew sewd
Asia	Asie (f)	a-zee
Australia	Australie (f)	us-tra-lee
Austria	Autriche (f)	oh-treesh
Belgium	Belgique (f)	behl-zh-eek
Brazil	Brésil (m)	bray-zeel
Canada	Canada (m)	ka-na-da
Central America	Amérique (f) centrale	a-may-reek sAH-tral
China	Chine (f)	sheen
Denmark	Danemark (m)	dahn-mark
Egypt	Egypte (f)	ay-zh-eept
England	Angleterre (f)	AH-gle-tehr
Europe	Europe (f)	ur-up
France	France (f)	frAHs
Germany	Allemagne (f)	al-ma-ny
Greece	Grèce (f)	greh-ss
Haiti	Haïti (m)	ah-ee-tee
Holland	Hollande (f)	ul-AHd
India	Inde (f)	EHd
Ireland	Irlande (f)	eer-lAHd
Israel	Israël (m)	ees-ra-ehl
Italy	Italie (f)	ee-ta-lee
Japan	Japon (m)	zh-ap-OH
Luxembourg	Luxembourg (m)	lewx-AH-boor
Mexico	Mexique (m)	mehk-seek
New Zealand	Nouvelle-Zélande (f)	noo-vehl zayl-AHd
Norway	Norvège (f)	nor-veh-zh
Poland	Pologne (f)	pu-lu-ny
Portugal	Portugal (m)	por-tew-gal
Russia	Russie (f)	rew-see
Spain	Espagne (f)	ehs-pa-ny
Sweden	Suède (f)	sew-ed
Switzerland	Suisse (f)	sweess
Thailand	Thaïlande (f)	tah-y-lAHd

| United States of America | États-Unis (*m, pl*) d'Amérique | *ay-ta-zew-nee da-may-reek* |

c. A FEW CITIES

Algiers	Alger	*al-zh-ay*
Barcelona	Barcelone	*bar-se-lun*
Beijing/Peking	Béjing/Pékin	*bay-zheen/pay-keen*
Berlin	Berlin	*behrlEH*
Florence	Florence	*flu-rAH-ss*
Frankfurt	Francfort	*frAH-for*
London	Londres	*loH-dre*
Marseilles	Marseille	*mar-seh-y*
Milan	Milan	*meel-AH*
Montreal	Montréal	*mOH-ray-al*
Moscow	Moscou	*mus-koo*
Naples	Naples	*nap-le*
Paris	Paris	*pah-ree*
Rome	Rome	*rum*
Venice	Venise	*vneez*

to go to + country	aller (*v*) + prep. + country	
• to go to France	aller (*v*) en France	*a-lay AH frAHs*
to go to + city	aller (*v*) + à + city	
• to go to Paris	aller (*v*) à Paris	*a-lay a pah-ree*

d. NATIONALITIES AND LANGUAGES

Gender has not been provided for the names of languages, which are invariably masculine in French. Pronunciation has not been provided for the names of languages when it is the same as that of the masculine form of the nationality.

American	Américain (*m*)	*a-may-reekEH*
	Américaine (*f*)	*a-may-reek-ehn*
	(*languages:* **English**	
	anglais;	*AH-gleh;*
	American américain)	*a-may-reekEH*
Arab	Arabe (*m, f*)	*a-rab*
	(*language:* **Arabic**	
	arabe)	

Australian	Australien (*m*)	*us-tral-yEH*
	Australienne (*f*)	*us-tral-yehn*
	(*language:* **English** anglais)	
Austrian	Autrichien (*m*)	*oh-treesh-yEH*
	Autrichienne (*f*)	*oh-treesh-yehn*
	(*language:* **German** allemand)	*almAH*
Belgian	Belge (*m, f*)	*behl-zh*
	(*languages:* **French** français;	*frAH-seh*
	Flemish flamand)	*fla-mAH*
Brazilian	Brésilien (*m*)	*bray-zeel-yEH*
	Brésilienne (*f*)	*bray-zeel-yehn*
	(*language:* **Portuguese** portugais)	*por-tew-geh*
Canadian	Canadien (*m*)	*kan-ad-yEH*
	Canadienne (*f*)	*kan-ad-yehn*
	(*languages:* **English** anglais;	*AH-gleh*
	French français)	*frAH-seh*
Chinese	Chinois (*m*)	*sheen-wa*
	Chinoise (*f*)	*sheen-waz*
	(*language:* **Chinese** chinois)	
Danish	Danois (*m*)	*dan-wa*
	Danoise (*f*)	*dan-waz*
	(*language:* **Danish** danois)	
Dutch	Hollandais (*m*)	*ul-AH-deh*
	Hollandaise (*f*)	*ul-AH-dehz*
	(*language:* **Dutch** hollandais)	
English	Anglais (*m*)	*AH-gleh*
	Anglaise (*f*)	*AH-glehz*
	(*language:* **English** anglais)	
French	Français (*m*)	*frAH-seh*
	Française (*f*)	*frAH-sehz*
	(*language:* **French** français)	
German	Allemand (*m*)	*al-mAH*
	Allemande (*f*)	*al-mAHd*
	(*language:* **German** allemand)	

Greek	Grec (*m*)	*grehk*
	Grecque (*f*)	*grehk*
	(*language:* **Greek** grec)	
Irish	Irlandais (*m*)	*eer-lAH-deh*
	Irlandaise (*f*)	*eer-lAH-dehz*
	(*languages:* **English** anglais;	*AH-gleh*
	Gaelic gaélique)	*ga-ay-leek*
Israeli	Israélite (*m, f*)	*ees-ra-ay-leet*
	(*languages:* **Hebrew** hébreu;	*ay-bruh*
	Arabic arabe;	*a-rab*
	English anglais)	*AH-gleh*
Italian	Italien (*m*)	*ee-ta-lee-yEH*
	Italienne (*f*)	*ee-ta-lee-yehn*
	(*language:* **Italian** italien)	
Japanese	Japonais (*m*)	*zh-ap-un-eh*
	Japonaise (*f*)	*zh-ap-un-ehz*
	(*language:* **Japanese** japonais)	
Norwegian	Norvégien (*m*)	*nor-vay-zh-yEH*
	Norvégienne (*f*)	*nor-vay-zh-yehn*
	(*language:* **Norwegian** norvégien)	
Polish	Polonais (*m*)	*pul-un-eh*
	Polonaise (*f*)	*pul-un-ehz*
	(*language:* **Polish** polonais)	
Portuguese	Portugais (*m*)	*por-tew-geh*
	Portugaise (*f*)	*por-tew-gehz*
	(*language:* **Portuguese** portugais)	
Russian	Russe (*m, f*)	*rewss*
	(*language:* **Russian** russe)	
Spanish	Espagnol (*m*)	*ehs-pan-yul*
	Espagnole (*f*)	*ehs-pan-yul*
	(*language:* **Spanish** espagnol)	
Swede	Suédois (*m*)	*sew-ay-dwa*
	Suédoise (*f*)	*sew-ay-dwaz*
	(*language:* **Swedish** suédois)	

Swiss	Suisse (*m, f*)	*sweess*
	(*languages:* **French**	
	français;	*FrAH-seh*
	German allemand;	*al-MAH*
	Italian italien)	*ee-ta-lee-yEH*

31. PACKING AND GOING THROUGH CUSTOMS

baggage, luggage	bagages (*m, pl*)	*ba-ga-zh*
• **hand luggage**	bagages (*m, pl*) à main	*ba-ga-zh a mEH*
border	frontière (*f*)	*frOHt-yehr*
carry	porter (*v*)	*por-tay*
carry-on	sac (*m*) de voyage	*sak de vwa-ya-zh*
customs	douane (*f*)	*dwan*
• **customs officer**	douanier, (-ère) (*m, f*)	*dwan-yay*
declare	déclarer (*v*)	*day-kla-ray*
• **nothing to declare**	rien à déclarer	*ree-yEH a day-kla-ray*
• **something to declare**	quelque chose (*pron*) à déclarer	*kehl-ke sh-oh-z a day-kla-ray*
documents	documents (*m, pl*)	*duk-ewm-AH*
duty tax	tarif (*m*) douanier	*tar-eef dwan-yay*
• **pay customs/duty**	payer (*v*) les droits de douane	*pay-ay lay drwa de dwan*
foreign currency	monnaie (*f*) étrangère	*mun-eh ay-trAH-zh-ehr*
foreigner	étranger (*m*)	*ay-trAH-zh-ay*
	étrangère (*f*)	*ay-trAH-zh-ehr*
form (*to fill out*)	formule (*f*)	*form-ewl*
identification (*paper*)	carte (*f*) d'identité	*kart deed-AH-tee-tay*
import	importer (*v*)	*EH-por-tay*
knapsack	sac (*m*) à dos	*sak a doh*
pack (one's bags/luggage)	faire (*v*) les bagages	*fehr lay ba-ga-zh*
passport	passeport (*m*)	*pahs-por*
passport control	contrôle (*m*) de passeports	*kOH-trohl de pahs-por*
suitcase, piece of luggage	valise (*f*)	*val-eez*
tariff	tarif (*m*)	*tar-eef*
visa	visa (*m*)	*vee-za*
weight	poids (*m*)	*pwa*
• **heavy**	lourd(e) (*adj, m, f*)	*loor(d)*
• **light**	léger (*adj, m*)	*lay-zh-ay*
	légère (*f*)	*lay-zh-ehr*
• **maximum**	maximum (*m*)	*maks-ee-mum*

32. TRAVELING BY AIR

a. IN THE TERMINAL

airline	ligne (f) aérienne	*lee-ny a-ayr-yehn*
airport	aéroport (m)	*a-ay-rup-or*
arrival	arrivée (f)	*a-ree-vay*
baggage claim	délivrance (f) des bagages	*day-leev-rAH-s day ba-ga-zh*
connection	correspondance (f)	*kor-ehsp-OH-dAH-s*
departure	départ (m)	*day-par*
economy class	classe (f) touriste	*klahss toor-eest*
flight	vol (m)	*vul*
first class	première classe (f)	*prem-yehr klahss*
gate	porte (f)	*port*
go on board	monter (v) à bord	*mOHtay a bor*
• **boarding**	embarquement (m)	*AH-bark-mAH*
• **boarding pass**	carte (f) d'embarquement	*kart dAH-bark-mAH*
information desk	bureau (m) de renseignements	*bew-roh de rAH-seh-ny-mAH*
lost and found	objets (m, pl) perdus	*ub-zh-eh pehr-dew*
no smoking	défense de fumer	*dayf-AHs de few-may*
porter	porteur (m)	*por-tur*
reservation	réservation (f)	*ray-zehr-vas-yOH*
terminal	terminal (m)	*tehr-meen-al*
ticket	billet (m)	*bee-yeh*
ticket window	guichet (m)	*geesh-eh*
waiting room	salle (f) d'attente (f)	*sal dat-AHt*

b. FLIGHT INFORMATION

canceled flight	vol (m) annulé	*vul an-ew-lay*
early	tôt (adv)	*toh*
	en avance	*AH-nav-AH-s*
late	en retard	*AH re-tar*
on time	à l'heure	*al-ur*

c. ON THE PLANE

airplane	avion (m)	*av-yOH*
aisle	passage (m)	*pahs-azh*
	allée (f)	*alay*
cabin	cabine (f)	*kabeen*
co-pilot	copilote (m, f)	*kup-ee-lut*
crew	équipage (m)	*ay-keepa-zh*

emergency exit	sortie (*f*) de secours	*sorteed sekoor*
flight attendant	hôtesse (*f*) de l'air	*oh-tehss de lehr*
	steward (*m*)	*stew-ar*
headphones	casque (*m*) d'écoute	*kask-day-koot*
land	atterrir (*v*)	*a-tay-reer*
• **landing**	atterrissage (*m*)	*a-tay-rees-azh*
lifejacket	gilet (*m*) de sauvetage	*zh-ee-leh de sohv-tazh*
passenger	passager (*m*)	*pah-sa-zh-ay*
	passagère (*f*)	*pah-sa-zh-ehr*
runway	piste (*f*)	*peest*
seat	place (*f*)	*plahss*
• **aisle**	côté passage (*m*)	*koh-tay pahs-azh*
• **window**	côté (*m*) fenêtre	*koh-tay fneh-tre*
seat belt	ceinture (*f*) de sécurité	*sEH-tewr de say-kew-ree-tay*
• **buckle up, fasten**	boucler (*v*)	*boo-klay*
sit down	s'asseoir (*v*)	*sa-swar*
takeoff	décollage (*m*)	*day-kul-azh*
take off	décoller (*v*)	*day-kul-ay*
toilet	toilettes (*f, pl*)	*twa-leht*
tray	plateau (*m*)	*pla-toh*
turbulence	turbulence (*f*)	*tewr-bewlAHss*
wheel, landing gear	train (*m*) d'atterrissage	*trEH da-tay-rees-azh*
window	hublot (*m*)	*ew-bloh*
wing	aile (*f*)	*ehl*

33. ON THE ROAD

a. VEHICLES

ambulance	ambulance (*f*)	*AHbewlAHss*
automobile	automobile (*f*)	*oh-tum-u-beel*
	auto (*f*)	*oh-toh*
bicycle	bicyclette (*f*)	*bee-see-kleht*
• **bike**	vélo (*m*)	*vay-loh*
• **brake**	frein (*m*)	*frEH*
• **chain guard**	couvre-chaîne (*m*)	*koov-re sh-ehn*
• **handlebar**	guidon (*m*)	*geed-OH*
• **pedal**	pédale (*f*)	*pay-dal*
• **seat**	selle (*f*)	*sehl*
• **spoke**	rayon (*m*)	*reh-yOH*
• **tire**	pneu (*m*)	*pnuh*
bus	autobus (*m*)	*u-toh-bewss*
• **streetcar**	tram (*m*)	*tram*
	tramway (*m*)	*tram-weh*
• **trolley**	trolley (*m*)	*trul-eh*

car	auto (*f*)	*u-toh*
	voiture (*f*)	*vwa-tewr*
• rented car	auto (*f*) en location	*u-toh AH luk-as-yOH*
• sport utility vehicle	véhicule (*m*) sport utilitaire	*vay-ee-kewl-spor ew-teelee-tehr*
• sports car	voiture (*f*) de sport	*vwa-tewr de spor*
compact car	voiture (*f*) compacte	*vwa-tewr kOHpakt*
mini-van	fourgonnette (*f*)	*foor-gun-eht*
motorcycle	motocyclette (*f*)	*mu-tu-see-kleht*
	moto (*f*)	*mut-oh*
• driver	motocycliste (*m,f*)	*mu-tu-see-kleest*
• scooter	scooter (*m*)	*skoot-ehr*
station wagon	break (*m*)	*breh-k*
SUV	SUV (*m*)	*ehss-yew-vay*
	véhicule (*m*) sport utilitaire	*vay-ee-kewl sport ew-tee-lee-tehr*
taxi	taxi (*m*)	*tak-see*
trailer	remorque (*f*)	*re-mork*
truck	camion (*m*)	*kam-yOH*
• dump	à triple mouvement	*a-treeple-moov-mAH*
• fire	fourgon-pompe (*m*)	*foorgOH-pOHp*
• garbage	de collecte	*de-kul-ehkt*
• pickup	camionnette (*f*)	*kam-yun-eht*
• tanker	camion-citerne (*m*)	*kam-yOH-see-tehrn*
• tow	dépanneuse (*f*)	*day-pan-uhz*
• tractor	camion-tracteur (*m*)	*kam-yOH-trak-tur*
• transport	des marchandises	*day marsh-AH-deez*
van	fourgon (*m*)	*foorgOH*
• passenger van	fourgon (*m*) automobile	*foorgOH u-tum-u-beel*
vehicle	véhicule (*m*)	*vay-ee-kewl*

b. DRIVING: PEOPLE AND DOCUMENTS

driver (*of a car*)	chauffeur (*m*)	*shoh-fur*
	automobiliste (*m,f*)	*oh-tum-u-beel-eest*
• to drive	conduire (*v*)	*kOH-dew-eer*
driver's license	permis (*m*) de conduire	*pehr-mee de kOH-dew-eer*
insurance card	carte (*f*) d'assurance	*kart das-ewr-AH-s*
ownership papers	documents (*m*) de propriété	*duk-ewm-AH de prup-ree-yay-tay*
passenger	passager (*m*)	*pah-sa-zh-ay*
	passagère (*f*)	*pah-sa-zh-ehr*
pedestrian	piéton (*m*)	*pee-yay-tOH*
	piétonne (*f*)	*pee-yay-tun*

police	police (*f*)	*pul-eess*
• **highway police**	agent (*m*) de police routier	*azh-AHd pul-eess root-yay*
• **policeman**	agent (*m*) de police policier (*m*)	*azh-AHd pul-eess pul-ees-yay*
• **policewoman**	femme (*f*) policier	*fahm-pul-ees-yay*
• **traffice police**	agent (*m*) de patrouille	*azh-AHd pa-troo-y*
registration papers	carte (*f*) grise	*kart greez*
road map	carte (*f*) routière	*kart root-yehr*

c. DRIVING

accident	accident (*m*)	*ak-seed-AH*
back up	reculer (*v*)	*re-kew-lay*
brake	freiner (*v*)	*fray-nay*
break down	tomber (*v*) en panne	*tOH-bay AH-pahn*
breakdown	panne (*f*)	*pahn*
bridge	pont (*m*)	*pOH*
corner (street)	coin (*m*) de la rue	*kwEHd la rew*
curve	courbe (*f*)	*koorb*
distance	distance (*f*)	*deest-AH-s*
drive	conduire (*v*)	*kOH-dew-eer*
fine, ticket	contravention (*f*)	*kOH-trav-AH-syOH*
gas station	station-service (*f*)	*stas-yOH-sehr-veess*
• **check the oil**	vérifier (*v*) l'huile	*vay-reef-yay lew-eel*
• **fill up**	faire (*v*) le plein	*fehr le plEH*
• **fix**	réparer (*v*)	*ray-pa-ray*
• **gas**	essence (*f*)	*ay-sAH-ss*
• **leaded gas**	essence (*f*) plombée	*ay-sAH-ss plOH-bay*
• **mechanic**	mécanicien (*m*) mécanicienne (*f*)	*may-ka-nees-yEH may-ka-nees-yehn*
• **self-service**	self-service (*m*)	*sehlf-sehr-veess*
• **tools**	outils (*m, pl*)	*oo-tee*
• **unleaded gas**	essence (*f*) non-plombée	*ay-sAH-ss nOH-plOH-bay*
gears (*change*)	changer (*v*) de vitesse (*f*)	*sh-AH-zh-ay de veet-ehss*
go forward	avancer (*v*)	*av-AH-say*
highway	autoroute (*f*)	*u-toh-root*
intersection	carrefour (*m*) croisement (*m*)	*kar-foor krwaz-mAH*
lane (traffic)	piste (*f*)	*peest*
park	stationner (*v*)	*stas-yun-ay*
• **parking**	stationnement (*m*)	*stas-yun-mAH*
• **public parking**	stationnement (*m*) public	*stas-yun-mAH pew-bleek*
pass	dépasser (*v*)	*day-pah-say*

pedestrian crossing	passage (*m*) pour piétons	*pahs-azh poor pee-yay-tOH*
	passage (*m*) piétonnier	*pahs-azh pee-yay-tun-yay*
	passage (*m*) clouté	*pahs-azh kloo-tay*
ramp	rampe (*f*)	*rAHp*
road	chemin (*m*)	*sh-mEH*
rush hour	les heures (*f, pl*) d'affluence	*lay-zur daf-lew-AH-s*
	les heures (*f, pl*) de pointe	*lay-zur de pwEHt*
signal	signal (*m*)	*seen-yal*
speed	vitesse (*f*)	*veet-ehs*
• **slow down**	ralentir (*v*)	*ral-AH-teer*
• **speed up**	accélérer (*v*)	*aks-ay-lay-ray*
start (*car*)	mettre (*v*) en marche	*meht-re AH marsh*
	démarrer (*v*)	*day-ma-ray*
toll booth	poste (*m*) de péage	*pust de pay-azh*
traffic	circulation (*f*)	*seer-kew-las-yOH*
• **traffic jam**	embouteillage (*m*)	*AHboo-teh-yazh*
	encombrement (*m*)	*AH-kOH-bre-mAH*
traffic lights	les feux (*m, pl*)	*lay fuh*
tunnel	tunnel (*m*)	*tew-nehl*
turn	virer (*v*)	*vee-ray*
• **(to the) left**	à gauche	*a goh-sh*
• **(to the) right**	à droite	*a drwat*

d. ROAD SIGNS

Bicycle Path	Piste cycliste	*peest seek-leest*
Emergency Lane	Piste d'urgence	*peest dewr-zh-AH-s*
Intersection	Carrefour	*kar-foor*
Level Crossing	Passage à niveau	*pahs-azh a neev-oh*
Merge	Confluence	*kOH-flew-AH-s*
No Entry	Défense d'entrer	*dayf-AH-s dAH-tray*
	Entrée interdite	*AH-tray EH-tehr-deet*
No Left Turn	Virage à gauche interdit	*veer-azh a goh-sh EH-tehr-dee*
No Parking	Stationnement interdit	*stas-yun-mAH EH-tehr-dee*
No Passing	Interdiction de dépasser	*EH-tehr-deeks-yOH de day-pah-say*
No Right Turn	Virage à droite interdit	*veer-azh a drwat EH-tehr-dee*
No Stopping	Arrêt interdit	*a-reh EH-tehr-dee*
No Thoroughfare	Circulation interdite	*seer-kew-las-yOH EH-tehr-deet*

No U-turn

No passing

Border crossing

Traffic signal ahead

Speed limit

Traffic circle (roundabout) ahead

Minimum speed limit

All traffic turns left

End of no passing zone

One-way street

Danger ahead

Detour

Entrance to expressway

Expressway ends

Guarded railroad crossing

Yield

Stop

Right of way

Dangerous intersection
ahead

Gasoline (petrol) ahead

Parking

No vehicles

Dangerous curve

Pedestrian crossing

Oncoming traffic
has right of way

No bicycles

No parking

No entry

No left turn

No U-Turn	Demi-tour (*m*) interdit	*dmee-toor-EH-tehr-dee*
One Way	Sens unique	*sAHs ew-neek*
Passing Lane	Piste pour dépasser (doubler)	*peest poor day-pah-say (doo-blay)*
Slippery When Wet	Chaussée glissante	*sho-say glees-AHt*
Speed Limit	Vitesse maximum	*veet-ehs mak-see-mum*
Stop	Arrêt	*a-reh*
	Stop	*stup*
Toll	Péage	*pay-azh*
Tow-Away Zone	Zone de remorquage	*zohn de re-mork-azh*
Work in Progress	Travaux	*tra-voh*
Yield	Cédez	*say-day*

e. THE CAR

air bag	sac (*m*) gonflable	*sak gOH-flabl*
air conditioner	climatiseur (*m*)	*klee-ma-tee-zuhr*
battery	batterie (*f*)	*bat-ree*
	les accumulateurs (*m*, *pl*)	*lay-za-kew-mew-la-tur*
brake	frein (*m*)	*frEH*
bumper	pare-chocs (*m*)	*par-shuk*
car body	carrosserie (*f*)	*ka-russ-ree*
car window	vitre (*f*)	*veet-re*
carburetor	carburateur (*m*)	*kar-bew-ra-tur*
clutch (pedal)	pédale (*f*) d'embrayage	*pay-dal dAH-breh-ya-zh*
dashboard	tableau (*m*) de bord	*tab-loh de bor*
door	portière (*f*)	*port-yehr*
fender	pare-chocs intégré (*m*)	*par-sh-uk EH-tay-gray*
filter	filtre (*m*)	*feel-tre*
gas pedal	pédale (*f*) d'accélérateur	*pay-dal dak-say-lay-ra-tur*
gas tank	réservoir (*m*) d'essence	*ray-zehr-vwar day-sAH-ss*
gearshift	levier (*m*) de changement de vitesse	*lev-yay de sh-AH-zh-mAH de veet-ehss*
glove compartment	boîte (*f*) à gants	*bwat a gAH*
	vide-poches (*m*)	*veed-pu-sh*
handle	poignée (*f*)	*pwan-yay*
hazard flash	feux (*m*, *pl*) de détresse	*fuh de day-trehss*
heater	système (*m*) de chauffage	*sees-tehm de sh-oh-fazh*

hood	capot (*m*)	*ka-poh*
horn	klaxon (*m*)	*klak-sun*
	avertisseur (*m*) sonore	*a-vehr-tees-ur sun-or*
horsepower	cheval-vapeur (*m*)	*sh-val vap-ur*
license plate	plaque (*f*)	*plak*
lights	phares (*m, pl*)	*far*
	projecteurs (*m, pl*)	*pru-zh-ehkt-ur*
motor	moteur (*m*)	*mut-ur*
• fan	ventilateur (*m*) d'aération	*vAH-tee-lat-ur da-ay-ras-yOH*
• fuel pump	pompe (*f*) à essence	*pOHp-a-ay-sAH-ss*
• generator	génératrice (*f*)	*zh-ay-nay-rat-reess*
• piston	piston (*m*)	*peest-OH*
• shaft	arbre-moteur (*m*)	*ar-bre-mut-ur*
	arbre de couche	*ar-bre de koosh*
• spark plug	bougie (*f*)	*boo-zh-ee*
• valve	soupape (*f*)	*soo-pap*
	clapet (*m*)	*klap-eh*
muffler	pot (*m*) d'échappement	*poh day-shap-mAH*
oil	huile (*f*)	*ew-eel*
oil filter	filtre (*m*) à huile	*feel-tre-a-ew-eel*
power brake	servofrein (*m*)	*sehr-vu-frEH*
power steering	servodirection (*f*)	*sehr-vu-deer-ehks-yOH*
power window	vitre (*f*) à commande automatique	*veet-re-a-kum-AHd ut-um-at-eek*
radiator	radiateur (*m*)	*rad-yat-ur*
rear window	lunette (*f*) arrière	*lew-neht ar-yehr*
rearview mirror	rétroviseur (*m*) intérieur	*ray-truv-eez-ur EH-tayr-yuhr*
roof	toit (*m*)	*twa*
seat	siège (*m*)	*see-yeh-zh*
seat belt	ceinture (*f*) de sécurité	*sEH-tewr de say-kew-ree-tay*
side mirror	rétroviseur (*m*) extérieur	*ray-truv-eez-ur ehks-tayr-yuhr*
speedometer	compteur (*m*) de vitesse	*kOH-tur de veet-ehss*
steering wheel	volant (*m*)	*vul-AH*
tire	pneu(matique) (*m*)	*pnuh(ma-teek)*
trunk	coffre (*m*)	*kuf-re*
turn signal	clignotant (*m*)	*kleen-yut-AH*
vent	trou (*m*) d'aération (*f*)	*troo-da-ay-ras-yOH*
wheel	roue (*f*)	*roo*

windshield	pare-brise (m)	*par-breez*
• windshield wiper	essuie-glace (m)	*ehs-ew-ee-glahs*
	essuie-vitre (m)	*ehs-ew-ee-veet-re*

For pictures and words about a vehicle, see page 178.

34. TRAIN, BUS, AND SUBWAY

bus (*long-distance travel*)	autocar (m)	*ut-oh-kar*
	car (m) de voyage	*kar de vwa-ya-zh*
• driver	chauffeur (m)	*sh-oh-fur*
• station, depot	station (f)	*stas-yOH*
	gare (f)	*gahr*
coach	voiture (f)	*vwa-tewr*
	wagon (m)	*vag-OH*
compartment	compartiment (m)	*kOH-par-teem-AH*
• nonsmoking	non-fumeurs	*nOH fewm-ur*
• smoking	fumeurs	*fewm-ur*
conductor	conducteur (m)	*kOH-dewk-tur*
	conductrice (f)	*kOH-dewk-treess*
connection	correspondance (f)	*kor-ehs-pOHd-AH-s*
direct train	train (m) direct	*trEH deer-ehkt*
express bus	autocar (m) express	*ut-oh-kar ehks-prehss*
express train	train (m) express	*trEH ehks-prehss*
leave, depart	partir (v)	*par-teer*
local train	train (m) omnibus	*trEH um-nee-bewss*
miss (*the train, etc.*)	manquer (v)	*mAH-kay*
	rater (v)	*ra-tay*
newsstand	kiosque (m) à journaux	*kee-usk a zh-oor-noh*
porter	porteur (m)	*port-ur*
railroad	chemin (m) de fer	*shmEHd fehr*
• station	gare (f)	*gar*
schedule	horaire (m)	*or-ehr*
• early	tôt (*adv*)	*toh*
	en avance	*AH-nav-AH-s*
• late	en retard	*AH re-tar*
• on time	à l'heure	*al-ur*
seat	place (f)	*plahss*
• economy	en classe touriste	*AH klahss toor-eest*
• first class	en première classe	*AH prem-yehr klahss*
stop	arrêt (m)	*ar-eh*

subway	métro (m)	*may-troh*
• subway station	station (f)	*stas-yOH*
take/catch the train, *etc.*	prendre (v)	*prAH-dre*
ticket	billet (m)	*bee-yeh*
• buy a ticket	acheter (procurer) (v) un billet	*ash-tay (pruk-ew-ray) UH bee-yeh*
• ticket cancelling machine	composteur (m) de billets	*kOH-pust-ur de bee-yeh*
• ticket counter	délivrance (f) des billets (m, pl)	*day-leev-rAH-s day bee-yeh*
track	voie (f)	*vwa*
train	train (m)	*trEH*
• All aboard!	En voiture!	*AH vwa-tewr*
• coach	wagon (m)	*vagOH*
	voiture (f)	*vwa-tewr*
• train sation	gare (f)	*gahr*
wait for (the train, *etc.*)	attendre (v)	*atAH-dre*

35. HOTELS

a. LODGING

boarding house	pension (f)	*pAHs-yOH*
campground	terrain (m) de camping	*tehr-EHd kAH-pin*
chalet	chalet (m)	*shal-eh*
hotel	hôtel (m)	*oh-tehl*
• luxury hotel	hôtel (m) de luxe	*oh-tehl de lewks*
motel	motel (m)	*mut-ehl*
youth hostel	auberge (f) de la jeunesse	*oh-behr-zh de la zh-uh-nehs*

b. STAYING IN HOTELS

bill	compte (m)	*kOHt*
• ask for the bill	demander (v) le compte	*demAH-dayl kOHt*
• Charge it to my bill.	Mettez-le sur mon compte.	*meht-ay le sewr mOH kOHt*
bellhop	porteur (m)	*port-ur*
breakfast	petit déjeuner (m)	*ptee day-zh-un-ay*
• (breakfast) included	compris (adj)	*kOH-pree*
call for a taxi	appeler (v) un taxi	*a-play UH tak-see*
complain	se plaindre (v)	*se-plEH-dre*
• complaint	plainte (f)	*plEHt*

doorman	portier (*m*)	*port-yay*
elevator	ascenseur (*m*)	*ass-AH-sur*
entrance	entrée (*f*)	*AH-tray*
exit	sortie (*f*)	*sor-tee*
floor (*level*)	étage (*m*)	*ay-ta-zh*
garage	garage (*m*)	*gar-azh*
hotel clerk	employé (*m*)	*AH-plwa-yay*
	employée (*f*)	*AH-plwa-yay*
identification card	carte (*f*) d'identité	*kart deed-AH-tee-tay*
key	clef (*f*)	*klay*
• **give back the room key before leaving**	rendre (*v*) la clef de la chambre avant de partir	*rAH-dre la klayd la sh-AH-bre avAH de par-teer*
lobby	foyer (*m*)	*fwa-yay*
• **main door**	porte (*f*) principale	*port prEH-see-pal*
• **main floor**	rez-de-chaussée (*m*)	*rayd-sh-oh-say*
luggage	bagages (*m, pl*)	*ba-ga-zh*
maid	bonne (*f*)	*bun*
	domestique (*f*)	*dum-ehs-teek*
manager	gérant (*m*)	*zh-ayrAH*
	gérante (*f*)	*zh-ayrAHt*
	directeur (*m*)	*dee-rehkt-ur*
	directrice (*f*)	*dee-rehkt-reess*
message	message (*m*)	*mehs-azh*
passport	passeport (*m*)	*pahs-por*
pay	payer (*v*)	*pay-ay*
• **cash**	en espèces	*AH-nehs-pehs*
• **check**	chèque (*m*)	*sh-ehk*
• **credit card**	carte (*f*) de crédit	*kart de kray-dee*
• **traveler's check**	chèque (*m*) de voyage	*sh-ehk de vwa-ya-zh*
price, rate	tarif (*m*)	*ta-reef*
• **low season**	basse saison (*f*)	*bahss-sehz-OH*
• **peak season**	haute saison (*f*)	*oht-sehz-OH*
pool	piscine (*f*)	*pee-seen*
porter	porteur (*m*)	*port-ur*
• **give the porter a tip**	donner (*v*) un pourboire au porteur	*dun-ay UH poor-bwar oh port-ur*
receipt	reçu (*m*)	*res-ew*
reservation	réservation (*f*)	*ray-zehr-vas-yOH*
• **reserve**	réserver (*v*)	*ray-zehr-vay*
room	chambre (*f*)	*sh-AH-bre*
• **Do you have a vacant room?**	Avez-vous une chambre libre?	*avay-voo-ewn sh-AH-bre lee-bre*
• **double room**	chambre (*f*) double	*sh-AH-bre dooble*

• **have baggage taken to one's room**	faire (*v*) porter (*v*) les bagages dans la chambre	*fehr por-tay lay ba-ga-zh dAH la sh-AH-bre*
• **bridal suite**	chambre (*f*) matrimoniale	*sh-AH-bre ma-tree-mun-yal*
• **room with bath**	avec bain (*m*)	*a-vehk bEH*
• **room with two beds**	à deux lits (*m, pl*)	*a-duh lee*
• **single room**	à un lit (*m*)	*a UH lee*
services	services (*m, pl*)	*sehr-veess*
stairs	escalier (*m*)	*ehs-kal-yay*
view	vue (*f*)	*vew*
wake-up call	réveil (*m*) par téléphone	*ray-veh-y par tay-lay-fun*

c. THE HOTEL ROOM

> See also Section 23.

armchair	fauteuil (*m*)	*foh-tuh-y*
balcony	balcon (*m*)	*balk-OH*
• **sliding door**	porte (*f*) coulissante	*port kool-ee-sAHt*
bathroom	salle (*f*) de bains	*sal de bEH*
bathtub	baignoire (*f*)	*beh-ny-war*
bed	lit (*m*)	*lee*
• **double bed**	grand lit (*m*)	*grAH lee*
bedside table	table (*f*) de nuit (*f*)	*ta-ble de new-ee*
blanket	couverture (*f*)	*koo-vehr-tewr*
chest of drawers	commode (*f*)	*kum-ud*
closet	armoire (*f*)	*arm-war*
clothes hanger	cintre (*m*)	*sEH-tre*
curtains	rideaux (*m, pl*)	*ree-doh*
dresser	commode (*f*)	*kum-ud*
faucet	robinet (*m*)	*rub-ee-neh*
lamp	lampe (*f*)	*lAHp*
lights	lumières (*f, pl*)	*lewm-yehr*
• **current**	courant (*m*)	*koorAH*
• **switch**	interrupteur (*m*)	*EH-tehr-ewp-tur*
• **turn off**	éteindre (*v*)	*ay-tEH-dr*
• **turn on**	allumer (*v*)	*al-ew-may*
mirror	miroir (*m*)	*meer-war*
	glace (*f*)	*glahss*

pillow	oreiller (*m*)	*or-ay-yay*
radio	radio (*f*)	*rad-yo*
soap	savon (*m*)	*savOH*
shampoo	shampooing (*m*)	*sh-AH-pwEH*
sheets	draps (*m, pl*)	*dra*
shower	douche (*f*)	*doosh*
sink, wash basin	lavabo (*m*)	*la-va-boh*
• **cold water**	eau (*f*) froide	*oh frwad*
• **hot water**	eau (*f*) chaude	*oh sh-ohd*
table	table (*f*)	*ta-bl*
telephone	téléphone (*m*)	*tay-lay-fun*
television set	téléviseur (*m*)	*tay-lay-veez-ur*
thermostat	thermostat (*m*)	*tehrm-us-ta*
toilet	toilette (*f*)	*twa-leht*
	W. C. (*m, pl*)	*doo-ble-vay-say*
• **toilet paper**	papier (*m*) hygiénique	*pap-yay ee-zh-yay-neek*
towel	serviette (*f*) de bain	*sehrv-yeht de bEH*

36. ON VACATION

a. **SIGHTSEEING**

amphitheater	amphithéâtre (*m*)	*AH-feet-ay-ah-tre*
art gallery	galerie (*f*) d'art	*gal-ree dar*
avenue	avenue (*f*)	*av-new*
basilica	basilique (*f*)	*ba-zee-leek*
bell tower	campanile (*m*)	*kAH-pa-neel*
	clocher (*m*)	*klush-ay*
bridge	pont (*m*)	*pOH*
castle	château (*m*)	*sh-ah-toh*
cathedral	cathédrale (*f*)	*ka-tay-dral*
church	église (*f*)	*ay-gleez*
city	ville (*f*)	*veel*
city map	plan (*m*) de la ville	*plAHd la veel*
corner	coin (*m*)	*kwEH*
downtown	en ville	*AH veel*
	centre (*m*) de la ville	*sAH-tre de la veel*
garbage bin	poubelle (*f*)	*poo-behl*
guide	guide (*m, f*)	*geed*
intersection	croisement (*m*)	*krwaz-mAH*
	carrefour (*m*)	*kar-foor*
kiosk	kiosque (*m*) à journaux	*kee-usk a zh-oor-noh*

monument	monument (*m*)	*mun-ewm-AH*
museum	musée (*m*)	*mew-zay*
park	parc (*m*)	*park*
park bench	banc (*m*)	*bAH*
parking meter	parcmètre (*m*)	*park-meht-r*
pedestrian crosswalk	passage (*m*) pour piétons	*pahs-azh poor pee-yay-tOH*
public garden	jardin (*m*) public	*zh-ard-EH pew-bleek*
public notices	affiches (*f, pl*) publiques	*a-feesh pew-bleek*
public phone	téléphone (*m*) public	*tay-lay-fun pew-bleek*
public washroom	toilettes (*f, pl*) publiques	*twa-leht pew-bleek*
railway crossing	passage (*m*) à niveau	*pahs-azh a nee-voh*
sidewalk	trottoir (*m*)	*trut-war*
square	place (*f*)	*plahss*
street	rue (*f*)	*rew*
• **street sign**	plaque (*f*) de nom (*m*) de rue (*f*)	*plak de nOH de rew*
take an excursion	faire (*v*) une excursion	*fehr ewn eks-kewrs-yOH*
temple	temple (*m*)	*tAH-ple*
tower	tour (*f*)	*toor*
traffic lights	feux (*m, pl*)	*fuh*
water fountain	fontaine (*f*)	*fOH-tehn*

b. GETTING OUT OF THE CITY

beach	plage (*f*)	*plazh*
• **at the beach**	à la plage (*f*)	*a la plazh*
• **get a suntan**	se bronzer (*v*)	*se brOH-zay*
• **on vacation**	en vacances (*f, pl*)	*AH va-kAH-ss*
• **get some sun**	prendre (*v*) un peu de soleil	*prAHdr UH puhd sul-ay*
• **suntan lotion**	crème (*f*) solaire	*krehm sul-ehr*
• **take a holiday**	avoir (*v*) congé	*avwar kOH-zh-ay*
boat	bateau (*m*)	*ba-toh*
brook	ruisseau (*m*)	*rew-ee-soh*
camping area	camping (*m*)	*kAH-peen*
canoe	canoë (*m*)	*kan-u-ay*
cap	casquette (*f*)	*kas-keht*
cruise	croisière (*f*)	*krwaz-yehr*
fishing	pêche (*f*)	*peh-sh*
in the country	à la campagne	*a-la-kAH-pa-ny*
in the mountains	dans les montagnes (*f, pl*)	*dAH lay mOH-ta-ny*

knapsack	sac (m) à dos	sak a doh
lake	lac (m)	lak
mountain boots	chaussures (f, pl) de montagne	sh-oh-sewr de mOH-ta-ny
mountain climbing	alpinisme (m)	al-pee-nees-me
on vacation	en vacances (f, pl)	AH vak-AH-ss
river	fleuve (m)	fluhv
rope	corde (f)	kord
sea	mer (f)	mehr
skiing	ski (m)	skee
• ski resort	station (f) de ski	stas-yOH de skee
sleeping bag	sac (m) de couchage	sak de koosh-azh
tent	tente (f) de camping (m)	tAHt de kAH-peen
trip	voyage (m)	vwa-ya-zh
vacation	vacances (f, pl)	vak-AH-s

c. ASKING FOR DIRECTIONS

across	à travers (prep)	a-tra-vehr
ahead	avant (adv)	a-vAH
at the end of	au bout de	oh boo de
	à la fin de	a la fEH de
at the top of	au sommet de	oh sum-eh de
back	arrière (adv)	ar-yehr
behind	derrière (adv)	dehr-yehr
cross (over)	traverser (v)	trav-ehr-say
• cross the street	traverser (v) la rue	trav-ehr-say la rew
down	bas (adv)	bah
enter	entrer (v) (dans)	AH-tray (dAH)
everywhere	partout (adv)	par-too
exit, go out	sortir (v)	sor-teer
far (from)	loin (de) (adv)	lwEH de
follow	suivre (v)	sweev-re
go	aller (v)	al-ay
go down	descendre (v)	day-sAH-dre
go up	monter (v)	mOH-tay
here	ici (adv)	ee-see
in front of	devant (prep, adv)	de-vAH
inside	dedans (prep, adv)	de-dAH
near	près (de) (adv)	preh de
outside	dehors (adv)	de-or

straight ahead	tout droit (*adv*)	*too-drwa*
there	là (*adv*)	*lah*
through	par (*prep*)	*par*
to the east	à l'est	*al ehst*
to the left	à gauche	*a goh-sh*
to the north	au nord	*oh nor*
to the right	à droite	*a drwat*
to the south	au sud	*oh sewd*
to the west	à l'ouest	*al west*
toward	vers (*prep*)	*vehr*
turn	tourner (*v*)	*toor-nay*

Could you tell me where . . . ? Pourriez-vous me dire où . . . ? *poo-ree-yay voom deer oo*
How do you get to . . . ? Comment va-t-on à . . . ? *kumAH va-tOH a*
Where is . . . ? Où est . . . ? *oo eh*
Turn left . . . Tournez à gauche . . . *toor-nay a goh-sh*
Turn right . . . Tournez à droite . . . *toor-nay a drwat*
I am looking for . . . Je cherche . . . *zhe sh-ehrsh*
How far away . . . ? À quelle distance . . . ? *a kehl dee-stAH-s*

LA VOITURE
(L'AUTOMOBILE)
The Car

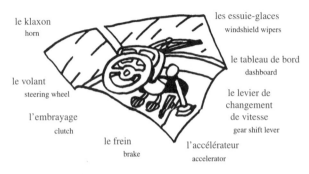

le klaxon
horn

les essuie-glaces
windshield wipers

le tableau de bord
dashboard

le volant
steering wheel

le levier de
changement
de vitesse
gear shift lever

l'embrayage
clutch

le frein
brake

l'accélérateur
accelerator

le pare-brise
windshield

le capot
hood

le moteur
motor

la batterie
battery

le radiateur
radiator

les phares
headlights

le phare de recul
backup light

le coffre
trunk

la lunette arrière
rear window

le clignotant
directional signal

le feu arrière
rear light

le stop
brakelight

la plaque
license plate

SCHOOL AND WORK

37. SCHOOL

a. TYPES OF SCHOOLS AND GRADES

coed school	école (*f*) mixte	*ay-kul meekst*
conservatory	conservatoire (*m*)	*kOH-sehr-va-twar*
day care	école (*f*) maternelle	*ay-kul ma-tehr-nehl*
elementary school	école (*f*) primaire élémentaire	*ay-kul pree-mehr ay-lay-mAH-tehr*
evening school	école (*f*) d'adultes	*ay-kul dad-ewlt*
	école du soir	*ay-kul dew swar*
grade	classe (*f*)	*klahss*
• **grade one**	première classe (*f*)	*prem-yehr klahss*
• **grade two**	deuxième classe (*f*)	*duhz-yehm klahss*
high school	école (*f*) d'enseignement secondaire	*ay-kul dAHseh-ny-mAH se-gOH-dehr*
	lycée (*m*)	*lee-say*
junior high school	école (*f*) d'enseignement de cours moyen	*ay-kul dAHseh-ny-mAH de koor mwa-y-EH*
kindergarten	jardin (*m*) d'enfants	*zh-ardEH dAH-fAH*
nursery school	école (*f*) maternelle	*ay-kul ma-tehr-nehl*
private school	école (*f*) privée	*ay-kul pree-vay*
technical/vocational school	institut (*m*) d'enseignement technique	*EHstee-tew dAHseh-ny-mAH tehk-neek*
university	université (*f*)	*ew-nee-vehr-see-tay*
year (*e.g., at university*)	année (*f*)	*a-nay*
• **first year**	première année (*f*)	*prem-yehr a-nay*
• **second year**	deuxième année (*f*)	*duhz-yehm a-nay*

b. THE CLASSROOM

assignment book	carnet (*m*)	*kar-neh*
	calepin (*m*)	*kalpEH*
atlas	atlas (*m*)	*at-lahs*
ballpoint pen	stylo (*m*) à bille	*stee-lo a bee-y*
blackboard	tableau (*m*)	*tab-loh*
blackboard eraser	éponge (*f*) mouillée	*aypOH-zh moo-yay*
	vieux chiffon (*m*)	*vy-uh sheef-OH*
book	livre (*m*)	*leev-r*

bookcase	étagère (f)	ay-ta-zh-ehr
	bibliothèque (f)	beeb-lee-yut-ehk
chalk	craie (f)	kreh
compass	compas (m)	kOH-pa
desk (pupil's)	pupitre (m)	pew-peet-re
• (teacher's)	bureau (m)	bew-roh
	chaire (f)	sh-ehr
dictionary	dictionnaire (m)	deek-see-yun-ehr
encyclopedia	encyclopédie (f)	AH-see-klup-ay-dee
eraser	gomme (f) à effacer	gum-a-ay-fa-say
eyeglasses	lunettes (f, pl)	lew-neht
film projector	projecteur (m) de film	pruzh-ehk-tur de feelm
ink	encre (f)	AH-kre
magazine	magazine (m)	ma-ga-zeen
	revue (f)	re-vew
map	carte (f) géographique	kart zh-ay-u-gra-feek
notebook	cahier (m)	ka-yay
overhead projector	rétroprojecteur (m)	ray-troh-pruzh-ehk-tur
paper	papier (m)	pap-yay
pen	stylo (m)	stee-lo
pencil	crayon (m)	kreh-yOH
ruler	règle (f)	reh-gle
school bag	sac (m) d'écolier	sak day-kul-yay
slide projector	projecteur (m) pour diapositives (f, pl)	pruzh-ehk-tur poor dee-ya-poh-zee-teev
tack	punaise (f)	pew-nehz
tape recorder	magnétophone (m)	man-yay-tu-fun
textbook	livre (m) de classe	leev-re de klahss
	livre (m) de cours	leev-re de koor
wall map	carte (f) murale	kart mew-ral

c. AREAS OF A SCHOOL

campus	campus (m)	kAH-pewss
classroom	salle (f) de classe	sal de klahss
gymnasium	gymnase (m)	zh-eem-nahz
	salle (f) de gymnastique	sal de zh-eem-nas-teek
hallway	couloir (m)	kool-war
laboratory	laboratoire (m)	la-bu-rat-war
language laboratory	laboratoire (m) de langues (f, pl)	la-bu-rat-war de lAHg
library	bibliothèque (f)	beeb-lee-yut-ehk
main office	direction (f)	deer-ehks-yOH
professor's office	cabinet (m) du professeur	ka-been-eh dew pruf-ehs-ur

school yard	cour (*f*)	*koor*
toilets	toilettes (*f, pl*)	*twa-leht*
	W. C. (*m, pl*)	*dooble-vay-say*

d. SCHOOL: PEOPLE

assistant	assistant(e) (*m, f*)	*ass-eest-AH(t)*
class (*of students*)	classe (*f*) d'élèves (d'étudiants)	*klahss day-lehv (day-tewd-yAH)*
janitor	nettoyeur (*m*)	*neht-wa-yur*
	nettoyeuse (*f*)	*neht-wa-yuhz*
librarian	bibliothécaire (*m, f*)	*beeb-lee-yut-ay-kehr*
president of a university	recteur (*m*)	*rehk-tur*
	femme (*f*) recteur	*fahm rehk-tur*
principal	directeur (*m*)	*dee-rehk-tur*
	directrice (*f*)	*dee-rehk-treess*
professor	professeur (*m*)	*pruf-ehs-ur*
	femme (*f*) professeur	*fahm pruf-ehs-ur*
pupil	élève (*m, f*)	*ay-lehv*
schoolmate	camarade (*m, f*) d'école	*ka-ma-rad day-kul*
secretary	secrétaire (*m, f*)	*se-kray-tehr*
student	étudiant (*m*)	*ay-tewd-yAH*
	étudiante (*f*)	*ay-tewd-yAHt*
teacher	enseignant(e) (*m, f*)	*AH-sehn-yAH(t)*
• **elementary school teacher**	maître (*m*)	*meht-re*
	maîtresse (*f*)	*meht-rehss*
• **high-school teacher/professor**	professeur (*m*)	*pruf-ehs-ur*
	femme (*f*) professeur	*fahm pruf-ehs-ur*
technician	technicien (*m*)	*tehk-nees-yEH*
	technicienne (*f*)	*tehk-nees-yehn*

e. SCHOOL: SUBJECTS

accounting	comptabilité (*f*)	*kOH-ta-bee-lee-tay*
anatomy	anatomie (*f*)	*a-na-tum-ee*
anthropology	anthropologie (*f*)	*AH-trup-ul-u-zh-ee*
archeology	archéologie (*f*)	*ar-kay-ul-u-zh-ee*
architecture	architecture (*f*)	*ar-shee-tehk-tewr*
art	art (*m*)	*ar*
arts, humanities	lettres (*f, pl*)	*leht-re*
astronomy	astronomie (*f*)	*as-trun-um-ee*
biology	biologie (*f*)	*bee-yul-u-zh-ee*
botany	botanique (*f*)	*but-an-eek*
calculus	calcul (*m*)	*kal-kewl*
chemistry	chimie (*f*)	*shee-mee*

commerce	commerce (*m*)	*kum-ehrs*
economics	économie (*f*)	*ay-kun-um-ee*
engineering	études (*f, pl*) polytechniques	*ay-tewd pul-ee-tehk-neek*
fine arts	beaux-arts (*m, pl*)	*boh-zar*
geography	géographie (*f*)	*zh-ay-ug-rafee*
geometry	géométrie (*f*)	*zh-ay-um-ay-tree*
history	histoire (*f*)	*eess-twar*
languages (foreign)	langues (*f, pl*) étrangères	*lAHg ay-trAH-zh-ehr*
law	études (*f, pl*) de droit	*ay-tewd de drwa*
literature	littérature (*f*)	*lee-tay-ra-tewr*
management	gestion (*f*)	*zh-est-yOH*
mathematics	mathématiques (*f, pl*)	*ma-tay-ma-teek*
medicine	médecine (*f*)	*mayd-seen*
music	musique (*f*)	*mew-zeek*
natural sciences	sciences (*f, pl*) naturelles	*syAHs na-tewr-ehl*
philosophy	philosophie (*f*)	*feel-uz-uf-ee*
physics	physique (*f*)	*fee-zeek*
physiology	physiologie (*f*)	*fee-zee-ul-uzh-ee*
political science	science (*f*) politique	*syAHs pul-ee-teek*
	science po	*syAHS-poh*
psychology	psychologie (*f*)	*psee-kul-uzh-ee*
sciences	sciences (*f, pl*)	*syAHs*
sociology	sociologie (*f*)	*suss-yul-uzh-ee*
statistics	statistique (*f*)	*sta-teess-teek*
subject	matière (*f*)	*mat-yehr*
trigonometry	trigonométrie (*f*)	*tree-gun-um-ay-tree*
zoology	zoologie (*f*)	*zu-ul-uzh-ee*

f. ADDITIONAL SCHOOL VOCABULARY

> For concepts of thought, see Section 22.

answer	réponse (*f*)	*rayp-OH-s*
• **answer**	répondre (*v*) (à)	*rayp-OH-dr (a)*
• **brief**	bref (*adj, m*)	*brehf*
	brève (*f*)	*brehv*
• **long**	long (*adj, m*)	*lOH*
	longue (*f*)	*lOHg*
• **right**	correct (*adj, m*)	*kor-ehkt*
	correcte (*f*)	*kor-ehkt*
• **short**	court (*adj, m*)	*koor*
	courte (*f*)	*koort*

• **wrong**	incorrect (*adj, m*)	*EHkor-ehkt*
	incorrecte (*f*)	*EHkor-ehkt*
assignments, **homework**	devoirs (*m, pl*)	*de-vwar*
attend school	assister (*v*) à l'école	*ass-ees-tay al ay-kul*
be absent	être (*v*) absent(e) (*adj, m, f*)	*eh-tre apsAH(t)*
be present	être (*v*) présent(e) (*adj, m, f*)	*eh-tre prayz-AH(t)*
be promoted	être (*v*) reçu(e) (*adj,* *m, f*)	*eh-tre res-ew*
class (*students*)	classe (*f*)	*klahss*
• (*process itself*)	leçon (*f*)	*le-sOH*
• **have a class**	avoir (*v*) une leçon	*avwar ewn le-sOH*
• **skip a class**	sécher (*v*) un cours	*say-shay UH koor*
• **skip school, play** **hooky**	faire (*v*) l'école buissonnière	*fehr lay-kul bew-ee-* *sun-yehr*
• **There is no class** **today.**	Il n'y a pas de classe aujourd'hui.	*eeln-ya-pahd klahss* *oh-zh-oor-dwee*
composition	thème (*m*)	*tehm*
copy	copie (*f*)	*kup-ee*
• **good, final copy**	bonne copie (*f*)	*bun kup-ee*
• **rough copy,** **draft**	copie (*f*) brute	*kup-ee brewt*
	copie (*f*) en état brut	*kup-ee AH-nay-ta* *brewt*
	brouillon (*m*)	*broo-yOH*
course	cours (*m*)	*koor*
• **take a** **course/subject**	suivre (*v*) un cours	*sweev-re UH koor*
degree (*university*)	diplôme (*m*) universitaire	*deep-lohm ew-nee-* *vehr-see-tehr*
• **Master**	licence (*f*)	*lee-sAHss*
• **Doctorate**	doctorat (*m*)	*duk-tor-a*
• **get a degree**	obtenir (*v*) un diplôme universitaire	*up-te-neer UH deep-* *lohm ew-nee-vehr-* *see-tehr*
dictation	dictée (*f*)	*deek-tay*
diploma	diplôme (*m*)	*deep-lohm*
• **high school**	baccalauréat (*m*)	*ba-ka-lor-ay-a*
• **get a diploma**	obtenir (*v*) un diplôme	*up-te-neer UH deep-* *lohm*
draw	dessiner (*v*)	*day-seen-ay*
• **drawing**	dessin (*m*)	*day-sEH*
education	éducation (*f*)	*ay-dew-kas-yOH*
• **get an education**	recevoir (*v*) une éducation	*res-vwar ewn ay-dew-* *kas-yOH*
	recevoir (*v*) une solide formation	*res-vwar ewn sul-eed* *formas-yOH*

error	erreur (f)	ehr-ur
	faute (f)	foht
exam	examen (m)	ehg-zam-EH
• entrance exam	examen (m) d'entrée	ehg-zam-EH dAH-tray
• oral exam	examen (m) oral	ehg-zam-EH or-al
• pass an exam	être (v) reçu(e) à un examen	eh-tre res-ew a UH nehg-zam-EH
• take an exam	passer (v) un examen	pah-say UH nehg-zam-EH
• written exam	examen (m) écrit	ehg-zam-EH ay-kree
exercise	exercice (m)	ehg-zehr-seess
explanation	explication (f)	ehks-plee-kas-yOH
• explain	expliquer (v)	ehks-plee-kay
fail an exam	échouer à un examen	ay-shway a UH nehg-zam-EH
	être (v) collé(e) à un examen	eh-tre kul-ay a UH nehg-zam-EH
field (of study)	matière (f) d'études	mat-yehr day-tewd
give/hand back	rendre (v)	rAH-dr
grade/mark	note (f)	nut
grammar	grammaire (f)	gram-ehr
learn	apprendre (v)	aprAH-dr
• learn by memory	apprendre (v) par cœur	aprAH-dr par kur
lecture	conférence (f)	kOHfay-rAHs
• lecture	faire (v) une conférence	fehr ewn kOHfay-rAHs
	donner (v) une conférence	dun-ay ewn kOHfay-rAHs
listen to	écouter (v)	ay-koo-tay
mistake	faute (f)	foht
• make mistakes	faire (v) des fautes	fehr day foht
note	note (f)	nut
• take notes	prendre (v) des notes	prAH-dr day nut
problem	problème (m)	prub-lehm
• solve a problem	résoudre (v) un problème	ray-zood-r UH prub-lehm
question	question (f)	kehst-yOH
• ask a question	poser (v) une question	poh-zay ewn kehst-yOH
read	lire (v)	leer
• reading (passage)	lecture (f)	lehk-tewr
registration	inscription (f)	EH-skreeps-yOH
• registration fee	droits (m, pl) d'inscription	drwa dEH-skreeps-yOH

repeat	répéter (v)	ray-pay-tay
review	révision (f)	ray-veez-yOH
• review	faire (v) une révision	fehr ewn ray-veez-yOH
school	école (f)	ay-kul
• finish school	finir (v) la dernière année d'école	fee-neer la dehrn-yehr a-nay day-kul
• go to school	assister (v) à l'école	a-seess-tay al ay-kul
study	étudier (v)	ay-tewd-yay
take attendance	faire (v) l'appel	fehr lap-ehl
teach	enseigner (v)	AH-sehn-yay
test	épreuve (f)	ay-pruhv
thesis	thèse (f)	tehz
type	taper (v) à la machine	tap-ay a la mash-een
typewriter	machine (f) à écrire	mash-een a ay-kreer
understand	comprendre (v)	kOH-prAH-dre
write	écrire (v)	ay-kreer

38. WORK

a. JOBS AND PROFESSIONS

accountant	comptable (m, f)	kOH-tabl
actor	acteur (m)	ak-tur
actress	actrice (f)	ak-treess
architect	architecte (m, f)	arsh-ee-tehkt
baker	boulanger (m)	bool-AH-zhay
	boulangère (f)	bool-AH-zh-ehr
barber	coiffeur (m)	kwaf-ur
bricklayer	maçon (m)	mass-OH
bus driver	chauffeur (m)	sh-oh-fur
	femme (f) chauffeur	fahm sh-oh-fur
businessman	homme (m) d'affaires	um daf-ehr
businesswoman	femme (f) d'affaires	fahm daf-ehr
butcher	boucher (m)	boosh-ay
	bouchère (f)	boosh-ehr
carpenter	menuisier (m)	me-new-eez-yay
cook	cuisinier (m)	kew-eez-een-yay
	cuisinière (f)	kew-eez-een-yehr
dentist	dentiste (m, f)	dAH-teest
doctor	médecin (m)	mayd-sEH
	femme (f) médecin	fahm mayd-sEH
	docteur (m)	duk-tur
	femme (f) docteur	fahm duk-tur
• eye doctor	ophtalmologiste (m, f)	uf-tal-mul-uzh-eest
	oculiste (m, f)	uk-ew-leest

editor	rédacteur (*m*)	*rayd-akt-ur*
	rédactrice (*f*)	*rayd-ak-treess*
electrician	électricien (*m*)	*ay-lehk-tree-syEH*
engineer	ingénieur (*m*)	*EH-zhayn-yur*
	femme (*f*) ingénieur	*fahm EH-zhayn-yur*
factory worker	ouvrier (*m*)	*oovr-yay*
	ouvrière (*f*)	*oovr-yehr*
farmer	fermier (*m*)	*fehrm-yay*
	fermière (*f*)	*fehrm-yehr*
fireman	pompier (*m*)	*pOHp-yay*
hairdresser	coiffeur (*m*)	*kwaf-ur*
	coiffeuse (*f*)	*kwaf-uhz*
job	métier (*m*)	*mayt-yay*
	occupation (*f*)	*uk-ewp-ass-yOH*
journalist	journaliste (*m, f*)	*zh-oor-nal-eest*
lawyer	avocat(e) (*m, f*)	*a-vu-ka(t)*
mechanic	mécanicien (*m*)	*may-ka-neess-yEH*
	mécanicienne (*f*)	*may-ka-neess-yehn*
movie director	réalisateur (*m*)	*ray-al-eez-at-ur*
	réalisatrice (*f*)	*ray-al-eez-at-reess*
	metteur (*m*) en scène	*met-ur AH sehn*
	femme (*f*) metteur en scène	*fahm met-ur AH sehn*
musician	musicien (*m*)	*mew-zee-syEH*
	musicienne (*f*)	*mew-zees-yehn*
nurse	infirmier (*m*)	*EH-feerm-yay*
	infirmière (*f*)	*EH-feerm-yehr*
occupation	occupation (*f*)	*uk-ewp-ass-yOH*
painter (*of buildings, rooms*)	peintre (*m*)	*pEH-tre*
	femme (*f*) peintre	*fahm pEH-tre*
• (artist)	artiste peintre (*m, f*)	*ar-teest pEH-tre*
pharmacist	pharmacien (*m*)	*farm-ass-yEH*
	pharmacienne (*f*)	*farm-ass-yehn*
pilot	pilote (*m, f*)	*pee-lut*
plumber	plombier (*m*)	*plOHb-yay*
policeman	agent (*m*) de police	*azh-AHd pul-eess*
	policier (*m*)	*pul-ees-yay*
policewoman	femme (*f*) policier	*fahm-pul-ees-yay*
professor	professeur (*m*)	*pruf-ehs-ur*
	femme (*f*) professeur	*fahm pruf-ehs-ur*
profession	profession (*f*)	*pruf-ehs-yOH*
professional	professionnel (*m*)	*pruf-ehs-yun-ehl*
	professionnelle (*f*)	*pruf-ehs-yun-ehl*

programmer	programmeur (*m*)	*prug-ram-ur*
	programmeuse (*f*)	*prug-ram-uhz*
psychiatrist	psychiatre (*m, f*)	*psee-kee-atr*
psychologist	psychologue (*m, f*)	*psee-kul-ug*
researcher	chercheur (*m*)	*sh-ehr-sh-ur,*
	chercheuse (*f*)	*sh-ehr-sh-uhz*
scientist	scientifique (*m, f*)	*sy-AH-tee-feek*
secretary	secrétaire (*m, f*)	*se-kray-tehr*
surgeon	chirurgien (*m*)	*sheer-ewr-zh-y-EH*
	femme (*f*)	*fahm sheer-ewr-zh-y-*
	chirurgien	*EH*
tailor	tailleur (*m*)	*tah-y-ur*
	couturière (*f*)	*koo-tewr-yehr*
teacher	professeur (*m*)	*pruf-ehs-ur*
	femme (*f*)	*fahm pruf-ehs-ur*
	professeur	
typist	dactylographe (*m, f*)	*dak-teel-ug-raf*
writer	écrivain (*m*)	*ay-kreev-EH*
	femme (*f*) écrivain	*fahm ay-kreev-EH*

b. INTERVIEWING FOR A JOB

> See also Section 11f—Basic Personal Information.

| **an interview** | une entrevue | *ewn AHtre-vew* |

<u>**Name**</u>	<u>Nom</u> (*m*)	*nOH*
first name	prénom (*m*)	*prayn-OH*
surname, family name	nom (*m*) de famille	*nOHd fam-ee*
signature	signature (*f*)	*seen-ya-tewr*
<u>**Address**</u>	<u>Adresse</u> (*f*)	*ad-rehss*
street	rue (*f*)	*rew*
number	numéro (*m*)	*new-may-roh*
city	ville (*f*)	*veel*
postal code	code postal (*m*)	*kud pus-tal*
<u>**Telephone number**</u>	<u>Numéro de téléphone</u> (*m*)	*new-may-rohd tay-lay-fun*
area code	code régional (*m*)	*kud ray-zh-yun-al*
<u>**Date & place of birth**</u>	<u>Date et lieu de naissance</u>	*dat ay ly-uhd nehs-AH-ss*
date	date (*f*)	*dat*
place	lieu (*m*)	*ly-uh*

Age	Âge (*m*)	*ah-zh*
Sex	Sexe (*m*)	*sehks*
male	mâle (*m*)	*mahl*
female	femelle (*f*)	*fem-ehl*
Marital Status	État (*m*) civil	*ay-ta see-veel*
divorced	divorcé(e) (*adj, m, f*)	*dee-vor-say*
married	marié(e) (*adj, m, f*)	*mar-yay*
single	célibataire (*m, f*)	*say-lee-ba-tehr*
widow	veuve (*f*)	*vuv*
widower	veuf (*m*)	*vuhf*
Nationality	Nationalité (*f*)	*nas-yun-al-ee-tay*

See also Section 30d—Nationalities and Languages.

Education	Éducation (*f*)	*ay-dew-kas-yOH*
elementary school	école (*f*) primaire élémentaire	*ay-kul pree-mehr ay-laymAH-tehr*
junior high school	école (*f*) d'enseignement de cours moyen	*ay-kul dAHseh-ny-mAh de koor mwa-y-EH*
high school	lycée (*m*)	*lee-say*
university	université (*f*)	*ew-nee-vehr-see-tay*
Profession	Profession (*f*)	*pruf-ehss-yOH*
Résumé	Résumé (*m*)	*ray-zewm-ay*

c. THE OFFICE

adhesive tape	ruban (*m*) adhésif	*rewbAH ad-ay-zeef*
appointment book	agenda (*m*) de bureau	*azh-EH-da de bew-roh*
briefcase	serviette (*f*)	*sehrv-yeht*
calendar	calendrier (*m*)	*kal-AH-dr-yay*
chair	siège (*m*) de bureau	*sy-eh-zh de bew-roh*
	chaise (*f*) tournante	*sh-ehz toorn-AHt*
fax	télécopie (*f*)	*tay-lay-cup-ee*
file	classeur (*m*)	*klahs-ur*
	dossier-classeur (*m*)	*duss-yay-klahs-ur*
filing card	fiche (*f*)	*feesh*
intercom	interphone (*m*)	*EH-tehr-fun*
paper shredder	déchiqueteur (*m*)	*day-sheek-tur*
pen	stylo (*m*)	*stee-lo*
pencil	crayon (*m*)	*kreh-yOH*
photocopier	photocopieur (*m*)	*fu-tu-cup-y-ur*
ruler	règle (*f*)	*reh-gle*
scissors	ciseaux (*m, pl*)	*see-zo*

sorting	triage (*m*)	*tree-ah-zh*
staple	agrafe (*f*)	*ag-raf*
stapler	agrafeuse (*f*)	*ag-ra-fuhz*
tack	punaise (*f*)	*pew-nehz*
telephone	téléphone (*m*)	*tay-lay-fun*
typewriter	machine (*f*) à écrire	*mash-een a ay-kreer*
video conference	visioconférence (*f*)	*veezee-o-kOH-fay-rAH-ss*
wastebasket	corbeille (*f*) à papier (*m*)	*kor-beh-y a pap-yay*

d. ADDITIONAL WORK VOCABULARY

advertising	publicité (*f*)	*pewb-lee-see-tay*
boss (*in an office*)	chef (*m*) de bureau	*sh-ehf de bew-roh*
career	carrière (*f*)	*kar-yehr*
classified ad	petite annonce (*f*)	*pteet anOHs*
commerce	commerce (*m*)	*kum-ehrs*
company	société (*f*) commerciale	*suss-yay-tay kum-ehrs-yal*
contract	contrat (*m*)	*kOH-tra*
earn	gagner (*v*)	*gan-yay*
employ	employer (*v*)	*AH-plwa-yay*
employee	employé(e) (*m, f*)	*AH-plwa-yay*
employer	employeur (*m*)	*AH-plwa-yur*
	employeuse (*f*)	*AH-plwa-yuhz*
employment agency	agence (*f*) d'emploi	*a-zh-AHs dAH-plwa*
factory	usine (*f*)	*ew-zeen*
fire (*dismiss*)	renvoyer (*v*)	*rAH-vwa-yay*
hire	employer (*v*)	*AH-plwa-yay*
manager	directeur (*m*)	*dee-rehk-tur*
	directrice (*f*)	*dee-rehk-treess*
market	marché (*m*)	*marsh-ay*
office	bureau (*m*)	*bew-roh*
retirement, pension	retraite (*f*)	*re-treht*
	pension (*f*)	*pAH-syOH*
• **retire**	se retirer (*v*)	*se-re-tee-ray*
	être (*v*) en retraite	*eh-tre AH re-treht*
unemployment	chômage (*m*)	*sh-oh-mazh*
wage, salary	gages (*m, pl*)	*ga-zh*
	salaire (*m*)	*sal-ehr*
work	travail (*m*)	*tra-va-y*
• **work**	travailler (*v*)	*tra-va-yay*
• **work associate**	collègue (*m, f*)	*kul-ehg*

EMERGENCIES

39. REPORTING AN EMERGENCY

a. FIRE

alarm	alarme (*f*)	*al-arm*
ambulance	ambulance (*f*)	*AH-bewlAHs*
building	bâtiment (*m*)	*bah-teemAH*
	édifice (*m*)	*ay-dee-feess*
burn	brûlure (*f*)	*brew-lewr*
• **burn**	brûler (*v*)	*brew-lay*
call the fire department	appeler (*v*) les pompiers	*ap-lay lay pOHp-yay*
	appeler (*v*) les sapeurs-pompiers	*ap-lay lay sap-ur pOHp-yay*
catch fire	prendre (*v*) feu	*prAH-dre fuh*
	s'enflammer (*v*)	*sAH-flam-ay*
danger	danger (*m*)	*dAH-zh-ay*
destroy	détruire (*v*)	*day-trew-eer*
emergencies	urgences	*ewr-zh-AH-ss*
emergency exit	sortie (*f*) de secours	*sorteed sekoor*
escape, get out	fuir (*v*)	*few-eer*
	échapper (*v*)	*ay-sha-pay*
extinguish, put out	éteindre (*v*)	*aytEH-dre*
fire	feu (*m*)	*fuh*
	incendie (*m*)	*EH-sAH-dee*
• **be on fire**	être (*v*) en feu	*eh-tre AH fuh*
• **Fire!**	Feu!	*fuh*
• **fire alarm**	sirène (*f*) d'alerte au feu	*seer-ehn dal-ehrt oh fuh*
• **fire extinguisher**	extincteur (*m*)	*ehks-tEHkt-ur*
• **firefighter**	pompier (*m*)	*pOHp-yay*
	sapeur-pompier (*m*)	*sap-ur pOHp-yay*
• **fire hose**	tuyau (*m*) de pompe	*tew-ee-yo de pOHp*
• **fire hydrant**	borne (*f*) d'incendie	*born dEH-sAH-dee*
• **fire truck**	fourgon-pompe (*m*)	*foor-gOH-pOHp*
fireproof	incombustible (*adj*)	*EH-kOH-bews-teebl*
	ignifuge (*adj*)	*eeg-nee-few-zh*
first aid	soins (*m, pl*) d'urgence	*swEH dewr-zh-AH-s*
flame	flamme (*f*)	*flahm*
help	aider (*v*)	*ay-day*
• **Help!**	Au secours!	*oh-skoor*
• **give help**	donner (*v*) de l'aide	*dun-ay de l-ehd*
ladder	échelle (*f*)	*ay-shell*

out	dehors (*adv*)	*de-or*
• **Everybody out!**	Dehors! Tous!	*de-or toos*
protect	protéger (*v*)	*prut-ay-zh-ay*
rescue	sauver (*v*)	*soh-vay*
shout	cri (*m*)	*kree*
• **shout**	crier (*v*)	*kree-ay*
siren	sirène (*f*)	*seer-ehn*
smoke	fumée (*f*)	*few-may*
spark	étincelle (*f*)	*ayt-EH-sehl*
victim	victime (*f*)	*veek-teem*

b. ROBBERY AND ASSAULT

argue	se disputer (*v*)	*se-dees-pew-tay*
	se quereller (*v*)	*se ke-ray-lay*
arrest	arrêter (*v*)	*ar-ay-tay*
assault	agression (*f*)	*ag-rehss-yOH*
Come quickly!	Venez vite!	*vnay veet*
crime	crime (*m*)	*kreem*
• **crime wave**	masse (*f*) de crimes	*mas de kreem*
• **criminal**	criminel(le) (*m, f*)	*kree-meen-ehl*
description	description (*f*)	*dehs-kreeps-yOH*
fight	se battre (*v*)	*se-bat-re*
firearm	arme (*f*) à feu	*arm-a-fuh*
gun	revolver (*m*)	*re-vul-vehr*
	pistolet (*m*)	*pees-tul-eh*
handcuffs	menottes (*f, pl*)	*me-nut*
hurry	se dépêcher (*v*)	*se-day-pay-shay*
injure, wound	blesser (*v*)	*bleh-say*
• **injury, wound**	blessure (*f*)	*blay-sewr*
	plaie (*f*)	*pleh*
kill	tuer (*v*)	*tew-ay*
	assassiner (*v*)	*a-sa-see-nay*
• **killer**	tueur (*m*)	*tew-ur*
	assassin (*m*)	*a-sas-EH*
knife	couteau (*m*)	*koo-toh*
• **pocket knife**	couteau (*m*) pliant	*koo-toh plee-yAH*
	couteau (*m*) de poche	*koo-toh de pu-sh*
murder	meurtre (*m*)	*mur-tre*
	homicide (*m*)	*um-ee-seed*
• **to murder**	assassiner (*v*)	*a-sa-see-nay*
pickpocket	pickpocket (*m*)	*peek-puk-eht*
	voleur (*m*) à la tire	*vul-ur a la teer*
	voleuse (*f*) à la tire	*vul-uhz a la teer*

police	police (*f*)	*pul-eess*
• **policeman**	agent (*m*) de police	*azh-AHd pul-eess*
	policier (*m*)	*pul-eess-yay*
• **policewoman**	femme (*f*) policier	*fahm-pul-eess-yay*
• **call the police**	appeler (*v*) la police	*ap-lay la pul-eess*
rape	viol (*m*)	*vee-yul*
	violer (*v*)	*vee-yul-ay*
rifle	fusil (*m*)	*few-zee*
rob	voler (*v*)	*vul-ay*
• **robber, thief**	voleur (*m*)	*vul-ur*
	voleuse (*f*)	*vul-uhz*
• **armed robbery**	vol (*m*) à main armée	*vul-a-mEH arm-ay*
• **robbery**	vol (*m*)	*vul*
• **Stop thief!**	Au voleur!	*oh vul-ur*
shoplifting	vol (*m*) à l'étalage	*vul-al-ay-tal-azh*
steal	dérober (*v*)	*day-rub-ay*
	voler (*v*)	*vul-ay*
victim	victime (*f*)	*veek-teem*
violence	violence (*f*)	*vee-yul-AHs*
weapon	arme (*f*)	*arm*
• **shoot**	tirer (*v*)	*tee-ray*

> **Run for your life!** Sauve qui peut! *soh-v kee puh*
> **Someone assaulted me!** On m'a assailli(e)! *OH ma a-sa-yee*
> **Someone robbed me!** On m'a volé(e)! *OH ma vul-ay*

c. TRAFFIC ACCIDENTS

accident	accident (*m*)	*aks-eed-AH*
• **serious accident**	accident (*m*) grave	*aks-eed-AH grav*
• **traffic accident**	accident (*m*) de voiture	*aks-eed-AH de vwa-tewr*
ambulance		
• **call an ambulance**	appeler (*v*) une ambulance	*ap-lay ewn AH-bewlAHs*
be run over	être (*v*) renversé(e)	*eh-tre rAH-vehr-say*
bleed	saigner (*v*)	*sayn-yay*
• **blood**	sang (*m*)	*sAH*
broken bone	os (*m*) cassé	*us kah-say*
	os (*m*) fracturé	*us frak-tew-ray*
bump	heurter (*v*)	*ur-tay*
collision, smash	collision (*f*)	*kul-eez-yOH*
• **collide**	entrer (*v*) en collision	*AH-tray AH kul-eez-yOH*
	se heurter (*v*)	*se-ur-tay*

doctor	médecin (m)	mayd-sEH
	femme (f) médecin	fahm mayd-sEH
• get a doctor	chercher (v) un médecin	sh-ehr-shay UH mayd-sEH
first aid	soins (m, pl) d'urgence	swEH dewr-zh-AH-s
• antiseptic	antiseptique (m)	AH-tee-sehp-teek
• bandage	pansement (m)	pAHs-mAH
• gauze	gaze (f)	gahz
• scissors	ciseaux (m, pl)	see-zo
• splint	éclisse (f)	ay-kleess
• tincture of iodine	teinture (f) d'iode	tEH-tewr dee-yud
Help!	Au secours!	oh-skoor
hospital	hôpital (m)	oh-pee-tal
• emergency (ward)	service (m) des urgences	sehr-veess day-zewr-zh-AHs
• X-ray	radiographie (f)	rad-yo-grafee
	passer (v) une radiographie (f)	pah-say ewn rad-yo-grafee
police	police (f)	pul-eess
• call the police	appeler (v) la police	ap-lay la pul-eess
shock	choc (m)	shuk
wound, injury	plaie (f)	pleh
	blessure (f)	blay-sewr

40. MEDICAL CARE

a. THE DOCTOR

> See also Section 12—The Body.

acne	acné (f)	ak-nay
AIDS	le SIDA	see-da
AIDS patient	sidéen (m)	see-day-AH
	sidéenne (f)	see-day-ehn
AIDS researcher	sidologue (m, f)	see-du-lug
allergy	allergie (f)	al-ehrzh-ee
appendicitis	appendicite (f)	ap-AH-dee-seet
• appendix	appendice (m)	ap-AH-deess
appointment	rendez-vous (m)	rAH-day-voo
artery	artère (f)	ar-tehr
arthritis	arthrite (f)	ar-treet
aspirin	aspirine (f)	as-pee-reen
bandage	pansement (m)	pAHs-mAH
• bandage	panser (v)	pAH-say

blood	sang (*m*)	*sAH*
• **blood pressure**	tension (*f*) artérielle (veineuse)	*tAHs-yOH ar-tayr-yehl (vehn-uhz)*
• **blood test**	examen (*m*) hématologique	*ehg-zam-EH ay-ma-tu-luzh-eek*
	examen du sang	*ehg-zam-EH dew sAH*
	examen sérologique	*ehg-zam-EH say-ru-luzh-eek*
bone	os (*m, sing*)	*us*
	(*pl*) les os	*lay-zo*
brain	cervelle (*f*)	*sehr-vehl*
bronchitis	bronchite (*f*)	*brOH-sheet*
cold	rhume (*m*)	*rewm*
convalescence	convalescence (*f*)	*kOH-val-ay-sAHs*
cough	toux (*f*)	*too*
• **cough**	tousser (*v*)	*too-say*
cure	guérison (*f*)	*gay-reez-OH*
• **cure, look after**	guérir (*v*)	*gay-reer*
	soigner (*v*)	*swEHn-ay*
• **get cured, convalesce**	se guérir (*v*)	*se-gay-reer*
	être (*v*) en convalescence	*eh-tre AH kOH-val-ay-sAHs*
dandruff	pellicules (*f, pl*)	*pay-leek-ewl*
digestive system	système (*m*) digestif	*see-stehm dee-zh-ehs-teef*
• **anus**	anus (*m*)	*an-ewss*
• **defecate**	déféquer (*v*)	*day-fay-kay*
• **rectum**	rectum (*m*)	*rehk-tum*
• **stomach**	estomac (*m*)	*ehs-tum-a*
• **have a stomach ache**	avoir (*v*) mal à l'estomac	*av-war mal al ehs-tum-a*
DNA	ADN (*m*)	*ah-day-ehn*
doctor	médecin (*m*)	*mayd-sEH*
	femme (*f*) médecin	*fahm mayd-sEH*
• **at the doctor's**	chez le médecin	*shayl-mayd-sEH*
doctor's instruments	instruments (*m, pl*) du médecin	*EH-strewmAH dew mayd-sEH*
• **electro-cardiograph**	électrocardiographe (*m*)	*ay-lehk-tru-kard-yu-graf*
• **stethoscope**	stéthoscope (*m*)	*stay-tus-kup*
• **syringe**	seringue (*f*)	*se-rEHg*
• **thermometer**	thermomètre (*m*)	*tehr-mum-eht-re*
doctor's visit	visite (*f*) du médecin	*vee-zeet dew mayd-sEH*
examine (*medically*)	examiner (*v*)	*ehg-zam-ee-nay*
• **to get examined**	se faire (*v*) examiner	*se-fehr-ehg-zam-ee-nay*

eye doctor	ophtalmologiste (*m, f*)	*uf-tal-mul-uzh-eest*
	oculiste (*m, f*)	*uk-ew-leest*
• **contact lenses**	lentilles (*f, pl*) de contact	*lAH-tee-y de kOH-takt*
	verres (*m, pl*) de contact	*vehr de kOH-takt*
• **eyeglasses**	lunettes (*f, pl*)	*lew-neht*
• **sight**	vue (*f*)	*vew*
feel	se sentir (*v*)	*se-sAH-teer*
• **feel bad**	se sentir (*v*) mal	*se-sAH-teer mal*
• **feel well**	se sentir (*v*) bien	*se-sAH-teer byEH*
• **strong**	fort (*adj, m*)	*for*
	forte (*f*)	*fort*
• **weak**	faible (*adj, m, f*)	*feh-bl*
• **How do you feel?**	Comment vous sentez-vous?	*kum-AH voo sAH-tay voo*
• **I feel . . .**	Je me sens . . .	*zhem-sAH*
fever	fièvre (*f*)	*fy-ehvre*
flu	influenza (*f*)	*EH-flew-ehn-za*
	grippe (*f*)	*greep*
foot-and-mouth disease	fièvre (*f*) aphteuse	*fyeh-vr af-tuhz*
headache	mal (*m*) de tête	*mal de teht*
• **have a headache**	avoir (*m*) mal à la tête	*avwar mal a la teht*
heal	guérir (*v*)	*gay-reer*
health	santé (*f*)	*sAH-tay*
• **healthy**	sain (*adj, m*)	*sEH*
	saine (*adj, f*)	*sehn*
• **be healthy**	être (*v*) en bonne santé	*eht-re AH bun sAH-tay*
heart	cœur (*m*)	*kur*
• **heart attack**	crise (*f*) cardiaque	*kreez kard-yak*
HIV	VIH (*m*)	*vay-ee-ah-sh*
hurt	avoir (*m*) mal	*avwar mal*
	faire (*v*) mal à	*fehr mal a*
in vitro fertilization	fécondation (*f*) in vitro	*fay-kOH-das-yOH een veetro*
infection	infection (*f*)	*EH-fehks-yOH*
injection	piqûre (*f*)	*peek-ewr*
itch	démangeaison (*f*)	*daym-AH-zh-ehz-OH*
lymphatic system	système (*m*) lymphatique	*see-stehm lEH-fa-teek*
measles	rougeole (*f*)	*roozh-ul*
medicine (you take)	médicament (*m*)	*may-deek-am-AH*
muscle	muscle (*m*)	*mew-sk-le*

nerves	nerfs (*m, pl*)	*nehr*
• **nervous system**	réseau (*m*) de nerfs	*ray-zoh de nehr*
	système (*m*) nerveux	*see-stehm nehr-vuh*
nurse	infirmier (*m*)	*EH-feerm-yay*
	infirmière (*f*)	*EH-feerm-yehr*
operation	intervention (*f*) chirurgicale	*EH-tehrv-AHs-yOH sheer-ewr-zh-ee-kal*
• **operating room**	salle (*f*) de chirurgie	*sal de sheer-ewr-zh-ee*
optician	opticien (*m*)	*up-teess-yEH*
	opticienne (*f*)	*up-teess-yehn*
pain	douleur (*f*)	*dool-ur*
• **painful**	douleureux (*adj, m*)	*dool-ur-uh*
	douleureuse (*f*)	*dool-ur-uhz*
patient	patient (*m*)	*pas-yAH*
pill	pilule (*f*)	*peel-ewl*
pimple	bouton (*m*)	*boot-OH*
pneumonia	pneumonie (*f*)	*pnuh-mun-ee*
pregnant	enceinte (*adj, f*)	*AH-sEHt*
prescription	ordonnance (*f*)	*or-dun-AHs*
pulse	pouls (*m*)	*poo*
respiratory system	système (*m*) respiratoire	*see-stehm rehs-pee-rat-war*
• **breath**	haleine (*f*)	*al-ehn*
• **breathe**	respirer (*v*)	*rehs-pee-ray*
• **bad breath**	mauvaise haleine (*f*)	*muv-ehz al-ehn*
• **be out of breath**	être hors d'haleine (*f*)	*eh-tre or dal-ehn*
• **lung**	poumon (*m*)	*poo-mOH*
• **nostril**	narine (*f*)	*na-reen*
rheumatism	rhumatisme (*m*)	*rew-ma-teesme*
secretary	secrétaire (*m, f*)	*se-kray-tehr*
sedative	sédatif (*m*)	*say-da-teef*
shot	piqûre (*f*)	*pee-kewr*
sick	malade (*adj*)	*mal-ad*
• **get sick**	tomber (*v*) malade	*tOH-bay mal-ad*
• **sickness, disease**	maladie (*f*)	*mal-ad-ee*
sneeze	eternuement (*m*)	*ay-tehr-new-mAH*
• **sneeze**	éternuer (*v*)	*ay-tehr-new-ay*
sore back, have a	avoir (*v*) mal au dos	*avwar mal oh doh*
sore/twisted neck, have a	avoir (*v*) mal au cou	*avwar mal oh koo*
	avoir (*v*) un torticolis	*avwar UH tor-tee-kul-ee*
specialist	spécialiste (*m, f*)	*spay-sy-al-eest*
suffer	souffrir (*v*)	*soof-reer*
suppository	suppositoire (*m*)	*sew-po-zeet-war*

surgeon	chirurgien (*m*)	*sheer-ewr-zh-y-EH*
	femme (*f*) chirurgien	*fahm sheer-ewr-zh-y-EH*
• surgery	chirurgie (*f*)	*sheer-ewr-zh-ee*
swollen	enflé(e) (*m, f*)	*AH-flay*
tablet	comprimé (*m*)	*kOH-pree-may*
temperature (fever)	fièvre (*f*)	*fee-yehvre*
• take one's temperature	mesurer (*v*) la fièvre	*me-zew-ray la fee-yehvre*
throat	gorge (*f*)	*gor-zh*
• sore throat	mal (*m*) de gorge	*mal-de-gor-zh*
• have a sore throat	avoir (*v*) mal à la gorge	*avwar mal a la gor-zh*
throw up	rendre (*v*)	*rAH-dr*
• vomit	vomir (*v*)	*vum-eer*
tonsillitis	amygdalite (*f*)	*ameeg-da-leet*
tonsils	amygdales (*f, pl*)	*a-meeg-dal*
urinary system	système urinaire	*see-stehm ew-ree-nehr*
• kidney	rein (*m*)	*rEH*
• urinate	uriner (*v*)	*ew-ree-nay*
vein	veine (*f*)	*vehn*
wheelchair	fauteuil (*m*) roulant	*fo-tu-y rool-AH*

b. THE DENTIST

anesthetic	anesthésique (*m*)	*a-nehs-tay-zeek*
appointment	rendez-vous (*m*)	*rAH-day-voo*
cavity, tooth decay	carie (*f*) dentaire	*ka-ree dAH-tehr*
brush (teeth)	se brosser (*v*) les dents	*se-bruss-ay lay dAH*
crown	couronne (*f*)	*koor-un*
dentist	dentiste (*m, f*)	*dAH-teest*
• at the dentist's	chez le (la) dentiste	*shayl (la) dAH-teest*
• dentist's chair	fauteuil (*m*)	*fo-tu-y*
• dentist's office	cabinet (*m*) du (de la) dentiste	*kab-ee-neh dew (de la) dAH-teest*
denture, false teeth	dentier (*m*)	*dAHt-yay*
drill	fraise (*f*)	*frehz*
examine	examiner (*v*)	*ehg-zam-ee-nay*
extract, pull (a tooth)	extraire (*v*) une dent	*ehks-trehr ewn dAH*
• extraction	extraction (*f*)	*ehks-traks-yOH*
filling	obturation (*f*)	*up-tew-rahss-yOH*
mouth	bouche (*f*)	*boosh*
• gums	gencives (*f, pl*)	*zh-AH-seev*
• jaw	mâchoire (*f*)	*mah-sh-war*
• lip	lèvre (*f*)	*lehv-re*
• Open your mouth!	Ouvrez la bouche!	*oov-ray la boosh*
• palate	palais (*m*)	*pal-eh*
• tongue	langue (*f*)	*lAHg*

needle	aiguille (*f*)	*ehg-ew-ee-y*
office hours	heures de bureau (*m*)	*ur de bew-ro*
rinse	(se) rinser (*v*)	*(se) rEH-say*
tooth	dent (*f*)	*dAH*
• **canine**	la dent canine	*la dAH kan-een*
• **incisor**	la dent incisive	*la dAH EH-see-seev*
• **molar**	la dent molaire	*la dAH mul-ehr*
• **root**	racine (*f*)	*ra-seen*
• **wisdom tooth**	dent (*f*) de sagesse	*dAH de sazh-ehss*
toothache	mal (*m*) aux dents	*mal oh dAH*
• **have a toothache**	avoir (*v*) mal aux dents	*avwar mal oh dAH*
• **My tooth hurts!**	Une dent me fait mal!	*ewn dAH me feh mal*
toothbrush	brosse (*f*) à dents	*bruss a dAH*
toothpaste	dentifrice (*m*)	*dAH-tee-freess*
X-ray	radiographie (*f*)	*rad-yo-grafee*
	passer (*v*) une radiographie (*f*)	*pah-say ewn rad-yo-grafee*

41. LEGAL MATTERS

accusation	accusation (*f*)	*ak-ew-zas-yOH*
• **accuse**	accuser (*v*)	*ak-ew-zay*
• **accused (person)**	accusé(e) (*m, f*)	*ak-ew-zay*
address oneself to	s'adresser (*v*) à	*sad-rehs-ay a*
admit	admettre (*v*)	*ad-meht-re*
agree	être (*v*) d'accord	*eh-tre dak-or*
capital punishment	peine (*f*) capitale	*pehn ka-pee-tal*
chief of police	préfet (*m*) de police	*pray-feh de pul-eess*
controversy	controverse (*f*)	*kOH-truv-ehrss*
convince	convaincre (*v*)	*kOH-vEH-kre*
court	tribunal (*m*)	*tree-bewn-al*
• **court of appeal**	cour (*f*) d'appel	*koor dap-ehl*
courtroom	salle (*f*) du tribunal	*sal dew tree-bewn-al*
curfew	couvre-feu (*m*)	*koovr-fuh*
debate	débat (*m*)	*day-ba*
• **debate**	débattre (*v*)	*day-ba-tre*
defend oneself	se défendre (*v*)	*se-dayf-AH-dre*
disagree	se disputer (*v*)	*se-deess-pew-tay*
discuss	discuter (*v*)	*deess-kew-tay*
DNA	ADN (*m*)	*ah-day-ehn*
guilt	culpabilité (*f*)	*kewl-pa-bee-lee-tay*
• **guilty**	coupable (*adj, m, f*)	*koop-abl*
innocence	innocence (*f*)	*een-us-AH-s*
• **innocent**	innocent(e) (*adj, m, f*)	*een-us-AH(t)*
judge	juge (*m*)	*zh-ew-zh*
• **judge**	juger (*v*)	*zh-ew-zhay*
jury	jury (*m*)	*zh-ew-ree*

justice	justice (f)	zh-ew-steess
law	loi (f)	lwa
• lawful, legal	légal(e) (adj, m, f)	lay-gal
• unlawful, illegal	illégal(e) (adj, m, f)	ee-lay-gal
• civil law	loi (f) civile	lwa see-veel
	droit (m) civil	drwa see-veel
• criminal law	loi (f) pénale	lwa pay-nal
	droit (m) pénal	drwa pay-nal
lawsuit, charge	cause (f) civile	kohz see-veel
lawyer	avocat (m)	a-vuk-a
	femme (f) avocat	fahm a-vuk-a
• trial lawyer	avoué (m)	av-way
	femme (f) avoué	fahm av-way
litigation	litige (m)	lee-tee-zh
• litigate	faire (v) litige	fehr lee-tee-zh
	faire (v) cause	fehr koh-z
magistrate	magistrat (m)	mazh-ees-tra
persuade	persuader (v)	pehr-sew-ad-ay
plea	plaidoirie (f)	plehd-war-ee
• plea for mercy	supplication (f) pour clémence	sewp-lee-kas-yOH poor klaym-AH-s
• (to) plead	plaider (v)	play-day
police station	commissariat (m) de police	kum-ee-sar-ya de pul-eess
prison, jail	prison (f)	preez-OH
• imprison	emprisonner (v)	AH-pree-zun-ay
• life imprisonment	emprisonnement (m) à perpétuité	AH-pree-zun-mAH a pehr-pay-tew-ee-tay
public prosecutor	procureur (m) de la République	pruk-ewr-ur de la ray-pew-bleek
right, privilege	droit (m)	drwa
sentence	jugement (m)	zh-ew-zh-mAH
• life sentence	à la prison à vie (f)	a la preez-OH a vee
• prison sentence	à prison (f)	a preez-OH
• pass a sentence	prononcer (v) un jugement	prun-OH-say UH zh-ew-zh-mAH
• serve a sentence	subir (v) une condamnation	sew-beer ewn kOH-dah-nahs-yOH
sue	citer (v) dans un procès-verbal	see-tay dAHz-UH pruss-eh vehr-bal
summons	citation (f)	see-tahs-yOH
trial	procès (m)	pruss-eh
• be on trial	être (v) en procès	eh-tre AH pruss-eh
• put someone on trial	mettre (v) quelqu'un en procès	meht-re kehlk-UH AH pruss-eh
verdict	verdict (m)	vehr-deekt
• guilty	coupable (adj)	koop-abl
• not guilty	non coupable (adj)	nOH koop-abl

witness	témoin (*m*)	*taym-wEH*
• **eyewitness**	témoin (*m*) oculaire	*taym-wEH uk-ew-lehr*
• **for the defense**	témoin (*m*) à décharge	*taym-wEH a day-shar-zh*
• **for the prosecution**	témoin (*m*) à charge	*taym-wEH a shar-zh*

THE CONTEMPORARY WORLD

42. SCIENCE AND TECHNOLOGY

a. **THE CHANGING WORLD**

> For more vocabulary on basic matter, see Section 13.

antenna	antenne (*f*)	*AH-tehn*
• **dish antenna**	antenne (*f*) parabolique	*AH-tehn pa-ra-bul-eek*
astronaut	astronaute (*m, f*)	*as-tru-noht*
	cosmonaute (*m, f*)	*kus-mu-noht*
atom	atome (*m*)	*at-ohm*
• **electron**	électron (*m*)	*ay-lehk-trOH*
• **neutron**	neutron (*m*)	*nuh-trOH*
• **proton**	proton (*m*)	*prut-OH*
clone	cloner (*v*)	*kloh-nay*
compact disk	disque compact (*m*)	*deesk-kOH-pakt*
fax machine	télécopieur (*m*)	*tay-lay-kup-yur*
	émetteur-récepteur (*m*) de fac-similé	*ay-meht-ur-ray-sehp-tur-de-fak-see-mee-lay*
	fax (*m*)	*fahks*
laser	laser (*m*)	*la-zehr*
• **light beam**	rayon (*m*) de lumière	*reh-yOH d lewm-yehr*
microwave	micro-onde (*f*)	*meek-ru-OHd*
missile	missile (*m*)	*mee-seel*
• **launch pad**	rampe (*f*) de lancement	*rAHp de lAHs-mAH*
molecule	molécule (*f*)	*mul-ay-kewl*
monorail vehicle	monorail (*m*)	*mu-nu-rah-y*
nuclear industry	industrie (*f*) nucléaire	*EH-dews-tree new-klay-ehr*
• **fission reactor**	réacteur (*m*) à fission	*ray-akt-ur a feess-yOH*
• **fusion reactor**	réacteur (*m*) à fusion	*ray-akt-ur a fewz-yOH*
• **nuclear energy**	énergie (*f*) nucléaire	*ay-nehr-zh-ee new-klay-ehr*
• **nuclear fuel**	combustible (*m*) nucléaire	*kOH-bews-teebl new-klay-her*
• **nuclear reactor**	réacteur (*m*) nucléaire	*ray-akt-ur new-klay-ehr*

robot	robot (m)	*rub-oh*
satellite	satellite (m)	*sa-tay-leet*
• **artificial satellite**	satellite (m) artificiel	*sa-tay-leet ar-tee-fee-syehl*
scientific research	recherche (f) scientifique	*re-sh-ehrsh sy-AH-tee-feek*
spacecraft	vaisseau (m) spatial	*veh-so spas-yal*
• **lunar module**	module (m) lunaire	*mud-ewl lew-nehr*
• **space shuttle**	navette (f) spatiale	*na-veht spas-yal*
technology	technologie (f)	*tehk-nu-lu-zhee*
telecommunications	télécommunications (f, pl)	*tay-lay-kum-ewn-ee-kahs-yOH*
• **teleconferencing**	télé-audio-conférence (f)	*tay-lay-ohd-yu-kOH-fay-rAHs*
• **telex machine**	télex (m)	*tay-lehks*
	ordinateur-télex (m)	*or-dee-na-tur tay-lehks*
theory of relativity	théorie (f) de la relativité	*tay-or-ee de la re-la-tee-vee-tay*
• **quantum theory**	théorie (f) des quanta	*tay-or-ee day kwAH-ta*
video conference	visioconférence (f)	*veezee-o-kOH-fay-rAH-ss*

b. COMPUTERS

artificial intelligence	intelligence (f) artificielle	*EH-tehl-ee-zh-AHs ar-tee-fee-syehl*
byte	multiplet (m)	*mewl-teep-leh*
compatible	compatible (adj)	*kOH-pa-tee-bl*
computer	ordinateur (m)	*or-dee-na-tur*
• **computer-assisted instruction**	instructions (f, pl) automatisées	*EH-strewk-syOH ut-um-a-teez-ay*
• **computer language**	langage-machine (m)	*lAHg-azh-ma-sheen*
	langage (m) de programmation	*lAHg-azh de prug-ram-ahs-yOH*
• **computer science**	informatique (f)	*EH-form-at-eek*
crash	tomber (v) en panne (f)	*tOH-bay AH pahn*
data	données (f, pl)	*dun-ay*
	information (f)	*EH-form-ass-yOH*
• **data processing**	traitement (m) de l'information	*trehtmAH de lEH-form-ass-yOH*
disk	disque (m)	*deesk*
• **floppy disk**	disquette (f)	*deesk-eht*
	disque (m) souple	*deesk-soop-le*
download	télécharger (v)	*tay-lay-shar-zh-ay*
e-mail	courrier (m) électronique	*koo-ree-yay-aylehk-trun-eek*

e-mail address	adresse (*f*) électronique	*ad-rehss aylehk-trun-eek*
file, menu	archives (*f, pl*)	*arsh-eev*
flow chart	schéma (*m*) fonctionnel	*shay-ma fOH-ks-yun-ehl*
function	fonction (*f*)	*fOH-ks-yOH*
hard drive	disque (*m*) dur	*deesk dewr*
hardware	matériel (*m*)	*ma-tayr-yehl*
	hardware (*m*)	*ard-wehr*
integrated circuit	circuit (*m*) intégré	*seer-kew-ee EH-tay-gray*
interface	interface (*f*)	*EH-tehr-fahss*
keyboard	clavier (*m*)	*klav-yay*
• **keyboard operator**	claviste (*m, f*)	*klav-eest*
laptop (computer)	portable (*m*)	*por-ta-ble*
	portatif (*m*)	*por-ta-teef*
link	lien (*m*)	*lyEH*
memory	mémoire (*f*)	*may-mwar*
• **random access memory**	mémoire (*f*) à accès sélectif	*may-mwar a aks-eh say-lehk-teef*
microcomputer	micro-ordinateur (*m*)	*meek-ro-or-dee-na-tur*
microprocessor	microprocesseur (*m*)	*meek-ro-pru-say-sur*
modem	modem (*m*)	*mud-ehm*
mouse	souris (*f*)	*soo-ree*
office automation	automatisation (*f*) de bureau	*ut-um-a-teez-ah-syOH de bew-roh*
optical reader	lecteur optique (*m*)	*lehk-tur up-teek*
peripherals	périphériques (*m, pl*)	*pay-reef-ay-reek*
personal computer	ordinateur (*m*) personnel	*or-dee-na-tur pehr-sun-ehl*
printer	imprimante (*f*) d'ordinateur	*EHpreem-AHt dor-dee-na-tur*
program	programme (*m*) d'un ordinateur	*prug-ram dUH nor-dee-na-tur*
• **programmer (*person*)**	programmeur (*m*)	*prug-ram-ur*
	programmeuse (*f*)	*prug-ram-uhz*
• **programmer (*machine*)**	programmateur (*m*)	*prug-ram-at-ur*
• **programming**	programmation (*f*)	*prug-ram-ahs-yOH*
screen	écran (*m*) de visualisation	*ay-krAH d veez-ew-al-eez-as-yOH*
• **software**	logiciel (*m*)	*luzh-ee-syehl*
	software (*m*)	*suf-wehr*
terminal	terminal (*m*)	*tehr-mee-nal*
user-friendly	ordinateur (*m*) d'usage facile	*or-dee-na-tur dewz-azh fa-seel*
	ordinateur (*m*) "user friendly"	*or-dee-na-tur ew-zehr frehn-lee*

virus	virus (m)	vee-rews
window	fenêtre (f)	fneh-tre
word processing	traitement (m) de texte	treht-mAH de tekst
word processor	machine (f) de traitement de texte	ma-sheen de treht-mAH de tekst
World Wide Web	web (m)	wehb

43. POLITICS

See also Sections 16, 17, 21, and 22.

arms race	course (f) aux armements	koors oh zar-me-mAH
arms reduction	réduction (f) des armements	ray-dewks-yOH day-zar-me-mAH
assembly	assemblée (f)	as-AH-blay
association	association (f)	as-us-yah-syOH
communism	communisme (m)	kum-ew-neesme
• communist	communiste (m, f)	kum-ew-neest
conservative party	parti (m) conservateur	par-tee kOH-sehr-va-tur
council	conseil (m)	kOH-seh-y
democracy	démocratie (f)	day-muk-ra-see
• democrat	démocrate (m, f)	day-muk-rat
• democratic	démocratique (adj)	day-muk-ra-teek
demonstration	manifestation (f)	ma-nee-fehs-tas-yOH
	manif (f)	man-eef
disarmament	désarmement (m)	day-zar-me-mAH
economy	économie (f)	ay-kun-um-ee
elect	élire (v)	ay-leer
• elections	élections (f, pl)	ay-lehk-syOH
globalization	mondialisation (f)	mOHd-yal-ee-zas-yOH
govern	gouverner (v)	goo-vehr-nay
• government	gouvernement (m)	goo-vehrn-mAH
ideology	idéologie (f)	ee-day-ul-uzh-ee
inflation	inflation (f)	EH-flah-syOH
labor/trade union	syndicat (m)	sEH-dee-ka
legislation	législation (f)	lay-zhee-slah-syOH
liberal party	parti (m) libéral	par-tee lee-bay-ral
minister	ministre (m)	mee-nee-stre
monarchy	monarchie (f)	mun-ar-shee
• king	roi (m)	rwa

• queen	reine (f)	rehn
• prince	prince (m)	prEHs
• princess	princesse (f)	prEHs-ehs
parliament	parlement (m)	parl-emAH
• elected politician, representative	député (m) femme (f) député représentant(e) (m, f)	day-pew-tay fahm day-pew-tay re-prayz-AH-tAH(t)
• house/chamber of representatives	la Chambre des Députés (Assemblée Nationale)	la sh-AH-bre day day-pew-tay assAH-blay nas-yun-al
• President of the French Republic	Président(e) (m, f) de la République Française	pray-zeedAH(t) de la ray-pew-bleek frAH-sehz
• Senate	Sénat (m)	say-na
• senator	sénateur (m) femme (f) sénateur	say-na-tur fahm say-na-tur
• universal suffrage/right to vote	suffrage (m) universel	sewf-razh ew-nee-vehr-sehl
peace	paix (f)	peh
policy	politique (f)	pul-ee-teek
politician	homme (m) politique	um pul-ee-teek
	femme (f) politique	fahm pul-ee-teek
• left wing	gauche (f)	go-sh
• right wing	droite (f)	drwat
politics	politique (f, sing)	pul-ee-teek
• political party	parti (m) politique	par-tee pul-ee-teek
• political power	pouvoir (m) politique	poov-war pul-ee-teek
prime minister	premier ministre (m)	prem-yay mee-nee-str
protest	protestation (f)	prut-ehs-tah-syOH
reform	réforme (f)	ray-form
republic	république (f)	ray-pew-bleek
revolt	révolte (f)	ray-vult
• revolution	révolution (f)	ray-vul-ew-syOH
riot	émeute (f)	ay-muht
socialism	socialisme (m)	suss-yal-eesme
• socialist	socialiste (m, f)	suss-yal-eest
state	état (m)	ay-ta
• head of state	chef (m) d'état	sh-ehf day-ta
strike	grève (f)	grehv
• go on strike	être (v) en grève faire (v) grève	eh-tre AH grehv fehr grehv
Third World	Tiers Monde (m)	tyehr mOHd

underdeveloped countries	pays (*m, pl*) sous-développés	*peh-ee soo-day-vlup-ay*
unilateral	unilatéral(e) (*adj*)	*ew-nee-la-tehr-al*
vote	vote (*m*)	*vut*
• vote	voter (*v*)	*vut-ay*
war	guerre (*f*)	*gehr*
welfare	assistance (*f*) sociale	*a-seest-AHs sus-yal*

44. CONTROVERSIAL ISSUES

a. THE ENVIRONMENT

For more vocabulary, see Sections 13 and 42.

air pollution	pollution (*f*) atmosphérique	*pul-ew-syOH at-mus-fay-reek*
conservation	conservation (*f*)	*kOH-sehr-va-syOH*
consumption	consommation (*f*)	*kOH-sum-ass-yOH*
ecology	écologie (*f*)	*ay-kul-uzh-ee*
ecosystem	écosystème (*m*)	*ay-ku-see-stehm*
energy	énergie (*f*)	*ay-nehr-zhee*
• energy crisis	crise (*f*) d'énergie	*kreez day-nehr-zhee*
• energy needs	besoins (*m, pl*) d'énergie	*be-zwEH day-nehr-zhee*
• energy source	source (*f*) d'énergie	*soors day-nehr-zhee*
environment	environnement (*m*)	*AH-veer-un-mAH*
fossil fuels	combustibles (*m, pl*) fossiles	*kOH-bews-teebl fuss-eel*
geothermal energy	énergie (*f*) géothermique	*ay-nehr-zhee zh-ay-u-tehrm-eek*
greenhouse effect	effet (*m*) de serre	*ay-feh de sehr*
natural resources	ressources (*f, pl*) naturelles	*re-soors na-tewr-ehl*
petroleum	pétrole (*m*)	*pay-trul*
pollution	pollution (*f*)	*pul-ew-syOH*
radiation	radiation (*f*)	*rad-yah-syOH*
• radioactive waste	déchets (*m, pl*) radioactifs	*day-sh-eh rad-yo-akteef*
solar cell	cellule (*f*) solaire	*sehl-ewl sul-ehr*
solar energy	énergie (*f*) solaire	*ay-nehr-zhee sul-ehr*
thermal energy	énergie (*f*) thermique	*ay-nehr-zhee tehr-meek*
water pollution	pollution (*f*) des eaux	*pul-ew-syOH day-zoh*

| **wind energy** | énergie (*f*) éolienne | *ay-nehr-zhee ay-ul-yehn* |

b. SOCIETY

abortion	avortement (*m*)	*av-ort-mAH*
• **fetus**	fœtus (*m*)	*fay-tewss*
AIDS	SIDA (*m*)	*see-da*
AIDS patient	sidéen (*m*)	*see-day-AH*
	sidéenne (*f*)	*see-day-ehn*
AIDS researcher	sidologue (*m, f*)	*see-du-lug*
capital punishment	peine (*f*) capitale	*pehn ka-pee-tal*
censorship	censure (*f*)	*sAH-sewr*
drugs	drogue (*f*)	*drug*
• **drug addiction**	toxicomanie (*f*)	*tuks-ee-kum-an-ee*
• **drug pusher**	trafiquant(e) (*m, f*) des stupéfiants	*tra-feek-AH(t) day stew-pay-fyAH*
• **take drugs**	prendre (*v*) de la drogue	*prAH-dre de la drug*
	se droguer (*v*)	*se-drug-ay*
• **drug trafficking**	trafic (*m*) des stupéfiants	*tra-feek day stew-pay-fyAH*
feminism	féminisme (*m*)	*fay-meen-eesme*
• **feminist**	féministe (*m, f*)	*fay-meen-eest*
HIV	VIH (*m*)	*vay-ee-ah-sh*
homosexual	homosexuel(le) (*m, f*)	*um-u-sehks-ew-ehl*
• **homosexuality**	homosexualité (*f*)	*um-u-sehks-ew-al-ee-tay*
• **gay**	gai(e) (*adj, m, f*)	*gay*
• **lesbian**	lesbienne (*f*)	*lehs-by-ehn*
• **lesbianism**	lesb(ian)isme (*m*)	*lehs-b(y-an) ee-sme*
morality	moralité (*f*)	*mu-ra-lee-tay*
nuclear war	guerre (*f*) nucléaire	*gehr new-klay-ehr*
nuclear weapon	arme (*f*) nucléaire	*arm new-klay-ehr*
• **antinuclear potest**	protestation (*f*) anti-nucléaire	*prut-ehs-tah-syOH AH-tee-new-klay-ehr*
• **atomic bomb**	bombe (*f*) atomique	*bOHb a-tum-eek*
biological weapon	arme (*f*) bactériologique	*arm bak-tay-ree-yul-uzh-eek*
• **chemical weapon**	arme (*f*) chimique	*arm shee-meek*
pornography	pornographie (*f*)	*por-nug-ra-fee*
prostitution	prostitution (*f*)	*prus-tee-tew-syOH*
racism	racisme (*m*)	*ra-see-sme*

c. EXPRESSING YOUR OPINION

| **according to me** | selon moi | *slOH mwa* |
| **as a matter of fact** | à vrai dire | *a vreh deer* |

by the way	à propos	a pro-po
for example	par exemple	par-ehg-zAH-ple
from my point of view	de mon point de vue	de mOH pwEH de vew
I believe that . . .	Je crois que . . .	zhe krwa ke
I don't know if . . .	Je ne sais pas si . . .	zhen seh pah see
I doubt that . . .	Je doute que . . .	zhe doot ke
I think that . . .	Je pense que . . .	zhe pAHs ke
I'd like to say . . .	Je voudrais dire . . .	zhe vood-reh deer
I'm not sure that . . .	Je ne suis pas sûr(e) que . . .	zhen swee pah sewr ke
I'm sure that . . .	Je suis sûr(e) que . . .	zhe swee sewr ke
in conclusion	en conclusion	AH kOH-klew-zyOH
in my opinion	à mon avis (opinion)	a-mun-avee (up-ee-nyOH)
in my view	à mon point de vue	a-mOH pwEHd vew
It seems that . . .	Il semble que . . .	eel sAHble ke
It's clear that . . .	Il est clair que . . .	eel eh klehr ke
	Il est évident que . . .	eel eh tay-veed-AH ke
that is to say	c'est-à-dire	seh-ta-deer
There's no doubt that . . .	Il n'y a pas de doute que . . .	eel ny-a-pah de doot ke
therefore	donc (*conj*)	dOHk

ENGLISH-FRENCH WORDFINDER

This alphabetical listing of all the English words in *French Vocabulary* will enable you to find the information you need quickly and efficiently. If all you want is the French equivalent of an entry word, you will find it here. If you also want pronunciation and usage aids, or closely associated words and phrases, use the reference number(s) and letter(s) to locate the section(s) in which the entry appears. This is especially important for words that have more than one meaning.

Remember that numbers refer to sections, not page numbers, in this book.

A

a   un *(m, s)*; une *(f, s)*   8c
abbreviation   l'abréviation *(f)* 19c
able to   pouvoir *(v)*   21a
abortion   l'avortement *(m)* 44b
above   au-dessus *(adv)*   3d; en haut   3d
abroad   à l'étranger   19e, 30a
absent   absent(e) *(adj, m, f)* 37f
accelerator pedal   la pédale d'accélérateur   33e
accent   l'accent *(m)*   8a, 19c
accept   accepter *(v)*   21b
acceptable   acceptable *(adj)* 21b
accident   l'accident *(m)* 33c, 39c
according to me   selon moi 44c
accordion   l'accordéon *(m)* 28c
account   le compte   26; *(bill)* le compte   35b
accountant   le (la) comptable 38a
accounting   la comptabilité   37e
accusation   l'accusation *(f)* 41
accuse   accuser *(v)*   41
accused   accusé(e) *(adj, m, f)* 41

ace   l'as *(m)*   27a; **ace of spades** *(cards)* l'as de pique 27a
acid   l'acide *(m)*   13c
acne   l'acné *(f)*   40a
acquaintance   la connaissance 10b, 16b
across   à travers *(prep)*   3d, 36c
act   l'acte *(m)*   28e; **to act** jouer *(v)* dans une pièce   28e
active   actif *(adj, m)*, active *(adj, f)*   8a, 11e
activity   l'activité *(f)*   11e
actor   l'acteur *(m)*   28a, 38a
actress   l'actrice *(f)*   28a, 38a
actually   effectivement *(adv)* 17b
acute   aigu, aiguë (adj)   2b
adapt   adapter *(v)*   11e
adaptable   adaptable *(adj)* 11e
add (on)   ajouter *(v)* 1e
addition   l'addition *(f)*   1e
address   l'adresse *(f)*   11f, 19e, 38b
address oneself to   s'adresser *(v)* à   41
addressee   le destinataire   19e
adhesive strip   le sparadrap 25h
adhesive tape   le ruban adhésif transparent   19d, 25c, 38c

adjacent *(angle)*   adjacent *(adj)*
2b
adjective   l'adjectif *(m)*   8a,
8e, 8f
admit   admettre *(v)*   41
adolescence   l'adolescence *(f)*
11b
adolescent   adolescent(e) *(n,*
adj)   11b
adult   l'adulte *(m/f)*   11b
adventure novel   le roman
d'aventure *(f)*   20a
adverb   l'adverbe *(m)*   8a
advertising   la publicité   20a,
38d
advice   le conseil   17a
advise   conseiller *(v)*   17a
affection   l'affection *(f)*
11e
affectionate   affectueux,
affectueuse *(adj, m, f)*   11e,
21a
affectionately   affectueusement
(adv)   19b
Africa   l'Afrique *(f)*   30b
after   après *(adv)*   4e
afternoon   l'après-midi *(m)*
4a
again   de nouveau *(adv)*,
encore une fois   4e
age   l'âge *(m)*   11b, 38b
aggressive   agressif, agressive
(adj, m, f)   11e
aggressiveness   l'agressivité *(f)*
11e
agnostic   agnostique *(adj, m, f)*
11d
ago   il y a *(adv)*   4e
agree   être *(v)* d'accord *(m)*
21a, 22b, 41
agriculture   l'agriculture *(f)*
14a
ahead   avant *(adv)*   3d, 36c
AIDS   le SIDA   40a, 44b
AIDS patient   le sidéen, la
sidéenne   40a, 44b
AIDS researcher   le, la
sidologue   40a, 44b

aikido   l'aïkido *(m)*   27b
air   l'air *(m)*   6a, 13c
air bag   le sac gonflable   33e
air conditioner   le climatiseur
23e, 33e
air conditioning   la climatisation
23e
air pollution   la pollution
atmosphérique   44a
airline   la ligne aérienne   32a
airmail   par avion   19e
airplane   l'avion *(m)*   32c
airport   l'aéroport *(m)*   32a
aisle   l'allée *(f)*, le passage
28a, 32c
aisle seat   la place côté passage
32c
alarm   l'alarme *(f)*   39a
alarm clock   le réveil, le réveille-
matin   4d, 25i
albatross   l'albatros *(m)*
15b
alcoholic beverage   la boisson
alcoolique   24k
algebra   l'algèbre *(f)*   1f
algebraic   algébrique *(adj)*
1f
Algeria   l'Algérie *(f)*   30b
Algiers   Alger   30c
all   tout *(adj)*, toute chose
3c
All aboard!   En voiture!   34
all day   toute *(adj)* la journée
4a
allegory   l'allégorie   17a
allergy   l'allergie *(f)*   40a
allude   faire *(v)* allusion
17a
almost   presque *(adv)*   3c
almost never   presque *(adv)*
jamais *(adv)*   4e
alphabet   l'alphabet *(m)*
8a
already   déjà *(adv)*   4e
although   bien que *(conj)*,
quoique *(conj)*   8p
altruism   l'altruisme *(m)*
11e

altruist l'altruiste *(m, f)*
11e
altruistic altruiste *(adj, m, f)*
11e
always toujours *(adv)* 4e
amateur l'amateur *(m)*, le (la)
dilettante 27b
ambition l'ambition *(f)*
11e
ambitious ambitieux, ambitieuse
(adj, m, f) 11e
ambulance l'ambulance *(f)*
33a, 39a, 39c
America l'Amérique *(f)*
30b
American *(nationality)*
Américain *(m)*, Américaine *(f)*
30d; *(language)* américain
(m), anglais *(m)* 30d
ammonia l'ammoniaque *(f)*
13c
among parmi *(prep)* 3d,
8g
amphitheater l'amphithéâtre
(m) 36a
an un *(m, s)*, une *(f, s)* 8c
analogy l'analogie *(f)*
17a
anatomy l'anatomie *(f)*
37e
anchovy l'anchois *(m)* 24d
and et *(conj)* 8p
anesthetic l'anesthésique *(m)*
40b
anger la colère 11e, 21a
angle l'angle *(m)* 2b
angry en colère 11e;
fâché(e) *(adj, m, f)* 21a
animal l'animal *(m)* 15a
ankle la cheville 12a
anniversary l'anniversaire *(m)*
11c, 29a
announce annoncer *(v)*
17a
announcement l'annonce *(f)*
17a
annually annuel, annuelle
(adj), annuellement *(adv)* 4c

answer la réponse 9, 17a,
37f; répondre *(v)* 9, 17a,
18b, 37f
answering machine le
répondeur téléphonique, le
téléphone-répondeur 18a
ant la fourmi 15d
Antarctic Antarctique *(adj, m,
f)* 13b
Antarctic Circle le Cercle
antarctique 13e
antenna l'antenne *(f)* 20b,
42a
anterior antérieur(e) *(adj)*
4e
anthropology l'anthropologie
(f) 37e
antibiotic l'antibiotique *(m)*
25h
antidepressant l'antidépresseur
(m) 25h
antinuclear protest la
protestation antinucléaire 44b
antiseptic l'antiseptique *(m)*
39c
anus l'anus *(m)* 40a
anxiety l'anxiété *(f)* 21a
anxious anxieux, anxieuse
(adj, m, f) 11e, 21a
anxiousness l'anxiété *(f)*
11e, 21a
any *(partitive)* see **Partitive**
8d
apartment l'appartement *(m)*
23g
apartment building l'immeuble
(m) 23g
aperitif l'apéritif *(m)* 24g
apostrophe l'apostrophe *(f)*
19c
appeal court la cour d'appel
41
appendicitis l'appendicite *(f)*
40a
appendix l'appendice *(m)*
20a, 28d, 40a
appetizer les hors-d'oeuvre
variés *(m, pl)* 24g

appetizing appétissant(e) *(adj, m, f)* 24p
applaud applaudir *(v)* 28e
applause l'applaudissement *(m)* 28e
apple la pomme 14d, 24f
apple pie la tarte aux pommes 24g
apple tree le pommier 14c
appointment le rendez-vous 40a, 40b
appointment book l'agenda de bureau 38c
approval l'approbation *(f)* 21b
approve approuver *(v)* 21b
approximately à peu près *(adv)* 3c; environ *(adv)* 3c
apricot l'abricot *(m)* 14d, 24f
April l'avril *(m)* 5b
Aquarius le Verseau 5d
Arab *(nationality)* Arabe *(m/f)* 30d; *(language)* l'arabe *(m)* 30d
Arabic arabe *(adj, m, f)* 1d
archbishop l'archevêque *(m, f)* 11d
archeology l'archéologie *(f)* 37e
archipelago l'archipel *(m)* 13b
architect l'architecte *(m, f)* 38a
architecture l'architecture *(f)* 28b, 37e
Arctic Arctique *(adj, m, f)* 13b
Arctic Circle le Cercle arctique 13e
area la superficie 3a, 13e; la surface 3a, 13e
area code le code régional 18b, 38b
argue disputer *(v)*, arguer (de) 17a; se disputer *(v)*, se quereller *(v)* 39b

argument l'argument *(m)*, la dispute 17a
Aries le Bélier 5d
arithmetic l'arithmétique *(f)* 1f
arithmetical arithmétique *(adj)* 1f
arithmetical operations les opérations fondamentales 1e
arm le bras 12a
armchair le fauteuil 23c, 35c
armed robbery le vol à main armée 39b
arms race *(politics)* la course aux armements 43
arms reduction la réduction des armements 43
around autour de 3d
arrest arrêter *(v)* 39b
arrival l'arrivée *(f)* 32a
arrive arriver *(v)* 3e
arrogant arrogant(e) *(adj, m, f)* 11e
art l'art *(m)* 11e, 28b, 37e
art gallery la galerie d'art 36a
artery l'artère *(f)* 40a
arthritis l'arthrite *(f)* 40a
artichoke l'artichaut *(m)* 14e, 24e
article l'article *(m)* 8a, 8b, 8c, 20a
articulate articuler *(v)* 17a
artificial artificiel(le) *(adj, m, f)* 13d, 25i
artificial intelligence l'intelligence *(f)* artificielle 42b
artificial satellite le satellite artificiel 42a
artist l'artiste *(m, f)* 28b
artistic artistique *(adj)* 11e
arts *(humanities)* les lettres *(f, pl)* 37e
as *(since)* comme *(conj)* 8p

as a matter of fact   en fait
17b; à vrai dire   44c
as if   comme si   *(conj)*   8p
as much as   tant que   3c;
autant que   3c
as soon as   aussitôt que   *(conj)*,
dès que   *(conj)*   4e, 8p
Asia   l'Asie   *(f)*   30b
ask *(for)*   demander   *(v)*   9,
17a
ask a question   poser   *(v)* une
question   37f
ask for the bill   demander   *(v)*
le compte   35b
asparagus   l'asperge   *(f)*
14e, 24e
aspirin   l'aspirine   *(f)*   25h,
40a
assassin   l'assassin   *(m)*   39b
assault   l'agression   *(f)*   39b
assembly   l'assemblée   *(f)*
43
assignment book   le calepin, le
carnet   37f
assignments   les devoirs   *(m, pl)*
37f
assistant   l'assistant(e)   *(m, f)*
37d
association   l'association   *(f)*
43
Assumption (*August 15, National
French Holiday***)**
l'Assomption   *(f)*   5f, 29a
assure   assurer   *(v)*   21a
asterisk   l'astérisque   *(m)*
19c
asteroid   l'astéroïde   *(m)*
13a
astronaut   l'astronaute   *(m, f)*,
le (la) cosmonaute   42a
astronomy   l'astronomie   *(f)*
13a, 37e
astute   astucieux, astucieuse
(adj, m, f)   11e
astuteness   l'astuce   *(f)*   11e
at   à   *(prep)*   3d, 8g
at home   à la maison, chez soi
23f

at midnight   à minuit   *(m)*   4a
at night   dans la nuit   4a; de
nuit   4a
at noon   à midi   *(m)*   4a
at one o'clock   à une heure
4b
at someone's place   chez
quelqu'un   3d
at the beach   à la plage   36b
at the bottom   au fond, en bas
3d
at the dentist's   chez le (la)
dentiste   40b
at the doctor's   chez le docteur
40a
at the edge of   au bord de   3d
at the end of   au bout de, à la fin
de   36c
at the present time   à l'heure
actuelle   4a
at the same time   en même
temps, à la fois   4e
at the tip of one's tongue   au
bout de la langue   12a
at the top of   au sommet de
36c
at three o'clock   à trois heures
4b
at two o'clock   à deux heures
4b
At what time?   A quelle heure?
4b
atheism   l'athéisme   *(m)*
11d
atheist   l'athée   *(m, f)*   11d
athlete   l'athlète   *(m, f)*   27b
Atlantic   Atlantique   *(adj, m, f)*
13b
atlas   l'atlas   *(m)*   20a, 37b
ATM   le guichet automatique
26
atmosphere   l'atmosphère   *(f)*
13b
atmospheric   atmosphérique
(adj)   13b
atmospheric conditions   les
conditions   *(f, pl)* atmosphériques
6a

atom   l'atome *(m)*   13c, 42a

atomic bomb   la bombe
atomique   44b

attend school   assister *(v)* à
l'école *(f)*   37f

attic   le grenier   23a

attitude   l'attitude *(f)*   21a

attractive   attrayant, beau, bel
(adj, m); attrayante, belle *(f)*
11a, 11e

attractiveness   la fascination
11e

audience   les spectateurs *(m,
pl)*   28e

audio-visual equipment   les
appareils audio-visuels *(m, pl)*
20b

August   l'août *(m)*   5b

aunt   la tante   10a

Australia   l'Australie *(f)*
30b

Australian *(nationality)*
Australien *(m)*, Australienne
(f)   30d

Austria   l'Autriche *(f)*   30b

Austrian *(nationality)*
Autrichien *(m)*, Autrichienne
(f)   30d

authentic   authentique *(adj)*
13d

author   l'écrivain, une femme
écrivain, l'auteur, la femme auteur
20a

autobiography   l'autobiographie
(f)   28d

automobile   l'auto(mobile) *(f)*
33a

automobile fuel   l'essence *(f)*
13c

autumn   l'automne *(m)*   5c

avarice   l'avarice *(f)*   11e

avaricious   avare *(adj)*   11e

avenue   l'avenue *(f)*   11f,
36a

average   moyen(ne) *(adj, m, f)*
1f

average height   la taille
moyenne   11a

away   au loin *(adv)*   3d

awful   mauvais(e) *(adj, m, f)*
6a

awful weather   un temps
mauvais   6a

axis   l'axe *(m)*   2b

B

baby   le bébé   11b

bachelor   célibataire *(n/adj, m,
f)*   11c

back *(backward)*   en arrière
(adv)   3d; arrière *(adv)*
36c

back up   reculer *(v)*   33c

bacon   le bacon   24c

bad *(mean, nasty)*   méchant(e)
(adj, m, f)   11e

bad *(quality)*   mauvais(e) *(adj,
m, f)*   24p

Bad(ly)!   Mal! *(adv)*   16a

bad breath   la mauvaise haleine
40a

bad mood   la mauvaise humeur
21a

bag   le sac   23d; **shopping
bag** le sac à provisions   25a

baggage   les bagages *(m, pl)*
31

baggage claim   la délivrance des
bagages   32a

bagpipes   la cornemuse
28c

baked   au four   24p

baker   le boulanger, la
boulangère   38a

bakery   la boulangerie   24n

balcony   le balcon   35c

ball   la balle   27b; *(in
basketball, football, volleyball)* le
ballon   27b

ballet   le ballet   28c

ballpoint pen   le stylo à bille
19d, 25c, 37b

banana   la banane   14d, 24f

bandage   le pansement   25h;
39c, 40a; panser *(v)*   40a

bank   la banque   26

bank book   le carnet de banque   26

bank rate   le taux bancaire   26

banknote *(bill, currency)*   le billet de banque   26

baptism   le baptême   11d

barber   le coiffeur   12d, 38a

barber shop   le salon de coiffure *(f)* pour hommes   12d

Barcelona   Barcelone   30c

bark *(cry of a dog)*   aboyer *(v)*   15a

barley   l'orge *(f)*   24i

barn   la grange   15a

barometer   le baromètre   6c

barometric pressure   la pression barométrique   6c

bartender   le barman   24m

base *(sports)*   la base   27b

baseball   le base-ball   27b

basement   le sous-sol   23a

basil   le basilic   14e, 24j

basilica   la basilique   36a

basin   le bassin   13b

basket   la corbeille   23d; le panier   23d

basket *(in basketball)*   le panier   27b

basketball   le basket(ball)   27b

bass drum   la grosse caisse   28c

bassoon   le basson   28c

Bastille Day *(July 14)*   La Prise de la Bastille   29a

bat *(animal)*   la chauve-souris, la pipistrelle   15a

bat *(sports)*   la batte   27b

bath oil   l'huile *(f)* de bain   25f

bathing suit   le maillot de bain *(m)*   25k

bathroom   la salle de bains *(m, pl)*   23b, 35c

bathtub   la baignoire   23a, 35c

batter *(sports)*   le batteur   27b

battery   la pile   25b; *(of car)* la batterie, les accumulateurs, les accus *(m, pl)*   33e

bay   la baie   13b

be able   pouvoir *(v)*   21a

be about to   être *(v)* sur le point de   4e

be absent   être *(v)* absent(e) *(adj, m, f)*   37f

be absent-minded   être *(v)* dans la lune   13a

be afraid   avoir *(v)* peur *(f)*   21a

be against   être *(v)* contre *(prep)*   21a

be ashamed   avoir *(v)* honte *(f)*   21a

be at the tip of one's tongue   être *(v)* sur le bout de la langue   12a

be awful *(weather)*   faire *(v)* un temps mauvais   6a

be beautiful *(weather)*   faire *(v)* beau temps   6a

be born   naître *(v)*   11c

be called   s'appeler *(v)*   11f

Be careful!   Attention!   21c

be cold *(persons)*   avoir *(v)* froid *(m)*   6b, 12b

be cold *(weather)*   faire *(v)* froid   6a

be cool *(weather)*   faire *(v)* frais   6a

be damp *(weather)*   faire *(v)* humide   6a

be down *(mood)*   avoir *(v)* le cafard   21a

be early   être *(v)* de bonne heure   4e; être *(v)* tôt   4e

be enough   suffire *(v)*, être *(v)* assez   3c

be fond of   avoir *(v)* une passion pour   21b

be from . . .   être *(v)* de . . .   11f

be healthy être *(v)* en bonne
santé 40a

be hot *(persons)* avoir *(v)*
chaud *(m)* 6b, 12b

be humid *(weather)* faire *(v)*
humide 6a

be hungry avoir *(v)* faim *(f)*
12b, 24o

be in a bad mood être *(v)* de
mauvaise humeur 11e

be in a good mood être *(v)* de
bonne humeur 11e

be in the clouds *(distracted)* être
(v) dans les nuages *(m, pl)*
6a

be interested in s'intéresser
(v) à 22b

be late être *(v)* tard (en retard)
4e

be located se trouver *(v)*
13e

be mild *(weather)* faire *(v)*
doux 6a

be muggy *(weather)* faire *(v)*
un temps lourd 6a

be on a familiar *(first-name)* **basis**
tutoyer *(v)* 16b

be on a formal basis vouvoyer
(v) 16b

be on fire être *(v)* en feu
39a

be on strike être *(v)* en grève
43

be on the point/verge of être
(v) sur le point de 4e

be on time être *(v)* à l'heure
(f) 4a, 4e

be on trial être *(v)* en procès
41

be out of breath être *(v)* hors
d'haleine 40a

be pregnant être *(v)* enceinte
(adj, f) 11c

be present être *(v)* présent(e)
(adj, m, f) 37f

be promoted être *(v)* reçu(e)
(adj, m, f) 37f

be right *(persons)* avoir *(v)*
raison *(f)* 22b

be run over être *(v)*
renversé(e) 39c

be seated s'asseoir *(v)* 16b

Be seated, please. Asseyez-
vous, s'il vous plaît 16b;
Assieds-toi, s'il te plaît 16b

be sleepy avoir *(v)* sommeil
(m) 12b

be the fool in an affair être
(v) le pigeon dans une affaire
15b

be thirsty avoir *(v)* soif *(f)*
12b, 24o

be tired être *(v)* fatigué(e)
(adj) 12b

be up *(good mood)* être *(v)*
remonté(e) *(adj, m, f)* 21a

be white with fear être *(v)*
vert de peur 7a

be windy faire *(v)* du vent
(m) 6a

be wrong *(persons)* avoir *(v)*
tort *(m)* 22b

beach la plage 13b, 36b

beak le bec 15b

beam of light le rayon de
lumière 42a

bean le haricot, les fèves *(f,
pl)* de haricot 14e, 24e

bear l'ours *(m)* 15a

beard la barbe 12a

beast la bête 15a

beautician l'esthéticien,
l'esthéticienne 12d

beautiful beau, bel, beaux, belle,
belles *(adj)* 11a, 25l

beautiful weather beau temps
6a

beauty la beauté 11a

because parce que *(conj)*
8p

become devenir *(v)* 4e,
25a

become angry se fâcher *(v)*
11e

become big   grandir *(v)*   3c,
11a; agrandir *(v)*   3c; grossir
(v)   3c
become bored   s'ennuyer *(v)*
21a
become engaged   se fiancer *(v)*
11c
become fat   grossir *(v)*   11a
become friends   devenir *(v)*
amis *(m, pl);* faire *(v)* l'amitié
(f)   10b
become old   vieillir *(v)*   11b
become red with anger   devenir
(v) rouge de colère   7a
become sick   tomber *(v)*
malade *(adj)*   11a
become small   rendre *(v)* plus
petit   3c; rapetisser *(v)*   3c
become thin   maigrir *(v)*
11a
become weak   s'affaiblir *(v)*
11a
bed   le lit   23c, 35c
bed sheet   le drap   23d
bedbug   la punaise   15d
bedroom   la chambre à coucher
(v)   23b
bedside table   la table de nuit
(f), la table de chevet   23c, 35c
bedspread   le couvre-lit   23d
bee   l'abeille *(f)*   15d
beech tree   le hêtre   14c
beef   le boeuf   24c
beer   la bière   24k
beet   la betterave   14e, 24e
before   avant *(adv),* auparavant
(adv)   4e
beg to do *(something)*   prier *(v)*
de faire (quelque chose)   17a
begin   commencer *(v)*   4e
beginning   le commencement
4e; le début   3e
behind   derrière *(adv)*   36c
Beijing/Peking   Béjing/Pékin
30c
Belgian *(nationality)*   Belge
(m/f)   30d

Belgium   la Belgique   30b
belief   la crédence, la croyance
11d
believe   croire *(v)*   11d, 22b
believe in   croire en   11d
believer   le (la) croyant(e)
11d
bell tower   le campanile, le
clocher   36a
bellhop   le porteur   35b
below zero   dessous zéro   6c
belt   la ceinture   25k
Berlin   Berlin   30c
beside *(next to)*   à côté (de)
3d
best-seller   le best-seller   20a,
25o
Best wishes!   Meilleurs voeux!
16c, 29c
Better late than never!   Mieux
vaut tard que jamais!   4e
between   entre   3d, 8g
between friends   entre amis
10b
beverage   la boisson   24k
beyond   au-delà (de)   3d
bicycle   la bicyclette   33a
Bicycle Path   Piste Cycliste
33d
bicycle racing   les courses
cyclistes   27b
big   grand(e) *(adj)*   3c, 11a,
25l; gros *(adj, m),* grosse *(f)*
3c
bigness   la grandeur   11a
bike   le vélo   33a
bill *(banknote, currency)*   le
billet de banque   26
bill *(cash register tape)*   la fiche
de caisse   25a; le compte
35b
bill *(invoice)*   la facture   25a;
check *(to pay in a restaurant)*
l'addition *(f)*   24m
billiard ball   la bille   27a
billiard table   la table de billard
(m)   27a

billiards, to play   jouer (v) au
   billard (m)   27a
billionth   milliardième   1b
binary   binaire (adj)   1d
bingo   le bingo   27a
bingo card   la fiche   27a
biography   la biographie   28d
biological weapon   l'arme (f)
   bactériologique   44b
biology   la biologie   37e
bird   l'oiseau (m)   15b
birth   la naissance   11c
birthday   l'anniversaire (m) de
   naissance (f)   11c, 29a
bisector   la bissectrice   2b
bishop   l'évêque   11d; (in
   chess) le fou   27a
bitter   amer (adj, m), amère
   (adj, f)   24p
black   le noir   7a; **black
   coffee** le café noir   24k
blackbird   le merle   15b
blackboard   le tableau   37b
blackboard eraser   l'éponge
   (f) mouillée; le vieux chiffon
   37b
blade   la lame   23d, 25f
blank cassette   la cassette vierge
   20b
blanket   la couverture   23d,
   35c
bleat   bêler (v)   15a
bleed   saigner (v)   39c
Bless you! (after a sneeze)   A
   vos (tes) souhaits! Dieu vous (te)
   bénisse!   16c
blind   aveugle (n/adj, m, f)
   12c
blindness   la cécité   12c
blond   blond(e) (adj)   11a
blonde   blonde (f)   11a
blood   le sang   12a, 39c, 40a
blood pressure   la tension
   artérielle (veineuse)   40a
blood test   l'examen (m)
   hématologique, l'examen du sang,
   l'examen sérologique   40a

bloom   fleurir (v)   14a
blouse   le chemisier   25k
blue   le bleu   7a
blueberry   la myrtille   24f
blueprint   la copie cyanotype
   28b
boarding (travel)
   l'embarquement (m)   32a
boarding house   la pension
   35a
boarding pass   la carte
   d'embarquement (m)   32a
boat   le bateau   36b
bodily physique   le physique
   11a
body   le corps   11a, 12a; (of a
   letter) le contenu, le corps   19c
body building   le culturisme
   27b
boiling point   le point
   d'ébullition (f)   6c
bold (brash)   effronté(e) (adj)
   11e
bolt of lightning   un coup
   d'éclair   6a
bond (banking, commerce)
   l'obligation (f)   26
bone   l'os (m)   12a, 40a
book   le livre   20a, 25o, 37b
book of adventure   le livre
   d'aventure (f)   25o
bookcase   l'étagère (f) à livres
   (m, pl), la bibliothèque   23c,
   37b
bookstore   la librairie   25o
boot   la botte   25n
border   la frontière   13e, 31;
   borner (v)   13e; toucher (v)
   13e
bore   ennuyer (v)   21a
bored   see **become bored, feel
   bored**
boredom   l'ennui (m)   21a
boss in an office   le chef de
   bureau   38d
botanical   botanique (adj)
   14a

botany la botanique 14a, 37e

both les deux, tous les deux, toutes les deux 3c

bottle la bouteille 23d; 24l

bottom le fond 3d; au fond 3d

bouquet of flowers la botte de fleurs *(f)* 14b

bow *(of a stringed instrument)* l'archet *(m)* de violon 28c

bowl le bol, l'assiette *(f)* creuse 24l; **to bowl** jouer *(v)* au bowling 27b

bowling le bowling 27b

bowling alley la piste 27b

bowling ball la boule 27b

bowling pin la quille 27b

box la boîte 23d

box office le guichet 28a

boxing la boxe 27b

boxing glove le gant de boxe 27b

boxing ring *(sport)* le ring 27b

boy le garçon 11a, 11b

boyfriend l'ami, le petit ami 10b

bra le soutien-gorge 25k

bracelet le bracelet 25i

bracket le crochet 19c

brain le cerveau 12a; la cervelle 40a

brake le frein 33a, 33e; freiner *(v)* 33c

branch la branche 14a

brash effronté(e) *(adj)* 11e

brass instruments les cuivres *(m, pl)* 28c

Brazil le Brésil 30b

Brazilian *(nationality)* Brésilien *(m)*, Brésilienne *(f)* 30d

bread le pain 24i

break down *(vehicle)* tomber *(v)* en panne 33c

break off a friendship rompre *(v)* une amitié 10b

breakdown *(machine, vehicle)* la panne 33c

breakfast le petit déjeuner 24a, 35b

breakfast included le petit déjeuner compris 35b

breath l'haleine 40a

breathe respirer *(v)* 12b, 40a

bricklayer le maçon 38a

bridal suite la chambre matrimoniale 35b

bride la mariée 11c

bridegroom le marié 11c

bridge le pont 33c, 36a

brief bref, brève *(adj, m, f)* 4e, 37f

briefcase la serviette 25c, 38c

briefly brièvement *(adv)*, en bref 4e, 17b

bright éclatant(e) *(adj)* 7b

brilliant brillant(e) *(adj)* 11e

bring apporter *(v)* 25a

brioche la brioche 24i

broccoli le brocoli 14e, 24e

brochure la brochure, le dépliant 20a, 30a

broiled grillé(e) *(adj, m, f)* 24b

broken bone l'os cassé (fracturé) 39c

broken line la ligne brisée 2b

bronchitis la bronchite 40a

bronze le bronze 13c

brooch la broche 25i

brook le ruisseau 36b

broom le balai 23d

broth le bouillon 24g

brother le frère 10a

brother-in-law le beau-frère 10a

brown le brun, le marron 7a

brush la brosse 12d, 25f; *(artist's)* le pinceau 28b

brush oneself se brosser *(v)*
12d
brush teeth se brosser *(v)* les
dents 40b
buckle *(fasten)* **seat belt** boucler
(v) la ceinture de sécurité 32c
bud bourgeonner *(v)* 14a;
le bourgeon 14a
Buddhism le Bouddhisme
11d
Buddhist Bouddhiste *(m/f)*
11d
budget le budget 26
buffalo le buffle 15a
build construire *(v)* 23f
building l'édifice *(m)*; le
bâtiment 23g, 39a
bulb *(plant)* le bulbe 14a
bull le taureau 15a
bump heurter *(v)* 39c
bumper *(car)* le pare-chocs
33e
burn brûler *(v)* 39a; la
brûlure 39a
bus l'autobus *(m)* 33a;
(long-distance travel) l'autocar
(m), le car de voyage 34
bus driver le chauffeur, la
femme chauffeur 34, 38a
bus station la gare, la station
34
business letter la lettre
commerciale *(adj)* 19e
businessman l'homme d'affaires
38a
businesswoman la femme
d'affaires 38a
busy occupé(e) *(adj)* 18b
but mais *(conj)* 8p
butcher le boucher, la bouchère
38a
butcher shop la boucherie
24n
butter le beurre 24h
butterfly le papillon 15d
buttermilk le babeurre, le lait de
beurre 24h
button le bouton 25g

buy acheter *(v)* 23f, 25a
buy a ticket acheter *(v)* un
billet 30a, 34; procurer *(v)*
un billet 34
by boat en bateau *(m)* 30a
by plane en avion *(m)* 30a
by the way à propos 17b,
44c
by train par le train 30a
byte le multiplet 42b

C

cabbage le chou 14e, 24e
cabin *(travel)* la cabine 32c
cable le câble (téléphonique)
18a; *(hardware)* le câble 25b
cable television la télévision par
câble 20b
cafeteria le restaurant
self-service 24m
cake le gâteau 24g
calculate calculer *(v)* 1f
calculation le calcul 1f
calculus le calcul 37e
calendar le calendrier 5b,
38c
call appeler *(v)* 17a
call a taxi appeler *(v)* un taxi
35b
call an ambulance appeler *(v)*
une ambulance 39c
call the fire department appeler
(v) les pompiers, appeler *(v)* les
sapeurs-pompiers 39a
call the police appeler *(v)* la
police 39b, 39c
caller ID l'afficheur *(m)*
18a
calling/business card la carte de
visite 16b
calm calme *(adj)* 11e
calmness le calme 11e
camel le chameau 15a
camera l'appareil *(m)* photo
(l'appareil photographique)
25d
camera shop le magasin de
photo 25d

camomile   la camomille   24k

camping area   le camping   36b

campus   le campus   37c

Can you tell me . . . ?   Pourriez-vous me dire . . . ? *(pol)*; Peux-tu me dire . . . ? *(fam)*   9

Canada   le Canada   30b

Canadian *(nationality)*   Canadien *(m)*, Canadienne *(f)*   30d

canceled flight   le vol annulé   32b

Cancer *(sign of the zodiac)*   le Cancer   5d

canine *(tooth)*   la dent canine   40b

canoe   le canoë   36b

cap   la casquette   36b

capacity   la capacité   3c

capital *(finance)*   le capital

capital city   la capitale   13e, 30a

capital letter   la lettre majuscule   19c

capital punishment   la peine capitale   41, 44b

Capricorn *(sign of the zodiac)*   le Capricorne   5d

car   l'auto *(f)*, la voiture   33a

car body   la carrosserie   33e

car gas   l'essence *(f)*   13c

car racing   les courses *(f, pl)* de voitures   27b

car radio   l'autoradio *(m)*   20b

car window   la vitre   33e

caramel pudding   la crème au caramel   24h

carat   le carat   25i

carbon *(element)*   le carbone   13c; le charbon   13c

carburetor   le carburateur   33e

card   la carte   25e

cardigan   le chandail   25k

cardinal   cardinal(e)   *(adj, m, f)*   1a, 1d

career   la carrière   11f, 38d

carnation   l'oeillet *(m)*   14b

carpenter   le menuisier   38a

carpet   le tapis   23c; **wall-to-wall carpeting**   la moquette   23c

carriage *(of a typewriter)*   le chariot   19d

carrot   la carotte   14e, 24e

carry   porter *(v)*   31

carry on *(luggage)*   le sac de voyage   31

case *(container)*   le bac, la douille   23d

cash *(money in currency and coins)*   **to pay in cash**   payer   *(v)* en espèces   25a, 26, 35b

cash a check   toucher *(v)* un chèque   26

cash desk   la caisse   26

cash register   la caisse   25a, 26

cash register tape receipt   la fiche de caisse   25a

cashier   le caissier, la caissière   25a, 26

cassette   la cassette   20b, 25j; **cassette tape** la bande magnétique   20b

castle   le château   36a

cat   le chat, la chatte   15a

catch   attraper *(v)*   27b; **catch** *(the train, etc.)* prendre   *(v)* 34

catch fire   prendre *(v)* feu, s'enflammer *(v)*   39a

catcher's mask   le masque du receveur   27b

catechism   le catéchisme   11d

caterpillar   la chenille   15d

catfish   le poisson-chat   15c

cathedral   la cathédrale   36a

Catholic   Catholique *(m, f)*   11d

Catholicism le Catholicisme 11d

cauliflower le chou-fleur, les choux-fleurs *(m, pl)* 14e, 24e

cavity la carie dentaire 40b

ceiling le plafond 23a

celebrate one's birthday fêter *(v)* l'anniversaire *(m)* de naissance *(f)* 11c

celery le céleri 14e, 24e

cell la cellule 14a

cello le violoncelle 28c

cellular phone le téléphone cellulaire 18a

Celsius Celsius 6c

censorship la censure 44b

center le centre 2a

centigrade centigrade *(n/adj, m)* 6c

centimeter le centimètre 3a

Central America l'Amérique centrale *(f)* 30b

century le siècle 4c

chain la chaîne 25i

chain guard *(bicycle)* le couvre-chaîne 33a

chair la chaise 23c; la chaise tournante, le siège de bureau 38c

chalet le chalet 35a

chalk la craie 37b

Chamber of Representatives *(deputies)* la Chambre des Députés 43

change changer *(v)* 4e, 25a

change *(money return in a transaction)* la monnaie, le rendu 25a

change gears changer *(v)* de vitesse 33c

change subject changer *(v)* de sujet *(m)* 17a

channel *(television)* la chaîne, le canal 20b

channel *(water)* le canal 13b

chapter le chapitre 28d

character le caractère 11e; *(in literature)* le personnage 28d

characteristic caractéristique *(n/adj, f)* 11e

characterize caractériser *(v)* 11e

charge *(law)* la cause 41

charge *(atom)* la charge 13c

Charge it to my bill. Mettez-le sur mon compte. 35b

charter flight l'avion charter *(m)* 30a

chat causer *(v)* 17a

cheap (à) bon marché, économe *(adj, m, f)* 24p

check *(in a restaurant)* l'addition *(f)* 24m

check *(to pay with a)* payer *(v)* par chèque 25a, 26, 35b

check the oil vérifier *(v)* l'huile 33c

checkbook le carnet de chèques 26

checkerboard le damier 27a

checker piece le pion 27a

checkers, to play jouer *(v)* aux dames 27a

cheek la joue 12a

Cheers! A votre santé! A la vôtre! 16c, 24l

cheese le fromage 24h; **grated** au gratin; **melted** fondu; **puffed** soufflé 24h

cheesecake le gâteau au fromage 24i

chemical chimique *(adj)* 13c

chemical formula la formule chimique 13c

chemical weapon l'arme *(f)* chimique 44b

chemistry la chimie 13c, 37e

cherry la cerise 14d, 24f

cherry pie la tarte aux cerises 24g

cherry tree le cerisier 14c
chess, to play jouer *(v)* aux
  échecs 27a
chessboard l'échiquier *(m)*
  27a
chest la poitrine 12a
chest of drawers la commode
  23c, 35c
chestnut la châtaigne, le marron
  14d
chestnut tree le châtaignier
  14c
chick le poussin 15b
chicken le poulet 15b,
  24c
chief of police le préfet de
  police 41
child l'enfant *(m, f)* 11b
children les enfants 11b
chimney la cheminée 23a
chin le menton 12a
China la Chine 30b
Chinese *(nationality)* Chinois
  (m), Chinoise *(f)* 30d;
  (language) le chinois 30d
chlorine le chlore 13c
chlorophyll la chlorophylle
  14a
chocolate le chocolat 24g
chocolate ice cream la glace au
  chocolat 24h
chocolate pie la tarte au
  chocolat 24g
Christian Chrétien, Chrétienne
  (m, f) 11d
Christianity le Christianisme
  11d
Christmas le Noël 5f, 29a
chum le copain, la copine
  10b
church l'église *(f)* 11d,
  36a
cigar le cigare 25e
cigarette la cigarette 25e
cinema le cinéma, le ciné
  28a
circle le cercle 2a

circumference la circonférence
  2a
citric citrique *(adj)* 14d
citrus les agrumes *(m, pl)*
  14d
city la ville 11f, 13e, 30a,
  36a, 38b
city map le plan de la ville
  36a
civil law le droit civil, la loi
  civile 41
clam la palourde 24d
clamp *(hardware)* l'étau *(m)*
  25b
clap of thunder le tonnerre, le
  coup de tonnerre 6a
clarinet la clarinette 28c
class la classe 30a, 37f
class of students la classe
  d'étudiants (d'élèves) 37d
classical music la musique
  classique 25j, 28c
classified ad la petite annonce
  38d
classroom la salle de classe
  37c
clause la proposition 8a
clean propre *(adj)* 11a,
  12d, 25g; nettoyer *(v)* 23f
clean oneself se débarbouiller
  (v) 12d
clear clair(e) *(adj)* 6a;
  clear picture la photo nette
  25d
clear sky le ciel clair 6a
clear the table desservir *(v)* la
  table 23f, 24o
clerk l'employé(e) *(m, f)*, le
  commis 19e
clerk's window le guichet
  19e
clever ingénieux, ingénieuse
  (adj, m, f) 11e
cleverness l'ingénuité *(f)*
  11e
climate le climat 6a
climb monter *(v)* 3e

clip *(paper)* le trombone 19d

clock l'horloge *(f)* 4d, 25i

clone cloner *(v)* 42a

close an account arrêter *(v)* un compte, clore *(v)* un compte 26

close friend l'ami(e) intime 10b

closed fermé(e) *(adj, m, f)* 25a

closed circuit le circuit fermé 20b

closet l'armoire *(f)*, le placard 23b, 35c

closing *(of a letter)* la formule (la salutation) finale 19c

closing hours *(store)* les heures de fermeture 25a

clothes les vêtements *(m, pl)* 25g

clothes basket le panier à linge 25g

clothes hanger le cintre 23d, 35c

clothespin la pince à linge 25g

clothing les vêtements *(m, pl)*, l'habillement *(m)* 25k

clothing store le magasin d'habillement 25k

cloud le nuage 6a, 13b; la nuée 13b

cloudy nuageux *(adj, m)*, nuageuse *(adj, f)*, couvert *(adj, m)* 6a

clown le clown 11e

clubs *(cards)* le trèfle 27a

clutch pedal *(car)* la pédale d'embrayage 33e

coach *(sports)* l'entraîneur *(m/f)* 27b; *(of a train)* la voiture, le wagon 34

coal le charbon 13c

coal mine la mine de houille 13c

coal mining la houille 13c

coast la côte 13b

coat le manteau 25k; **fur**

coat le manteau de fourrure 25k

coat *(suit)* la veste, le veston 25k

cockroach la blatte, le cafard 15d

coconut macaroon le macaron 24i

codfish la morue 15c, 24d

coed school l'école *(f)* mixte 37a

coffee le café 24k; **black coffee** le café noir 24k; **coffee pudding** la crème au café 24k; **coffee with cream** un café-crème 24k; **light coffee** (half-and-half) le café au lait 24k

coffee machine la cafetière électrique, le percolateur 23d

coffee pot la cafetière 23d

coin la pièce de monnaie *(f)* 27a; **coin token** le jeton 18a

coin collecting la numismatique 27a

cold le froid, froid(e) *(adj, m, f)* 6a, 6b, 24p; *(illness)* le rhume 40a

cold cuts la charcuterie 24c

cold water l'eau *(f)* froide 35c

colleague le (la) collègue 10b

collect telephone call téléphoner en P.C.V. 18b

collide entrer *(v)* en collision, se heurter *(v)* 39c

collision la collision 39c

cologne l'eau *(f)* de cologne 25f

colon deux points *(m, pl)* 19c

color la couleur 7a–7c; colorer *(v)* 7c

color photo la photo en couleur 25d

colored coloré(e) *(adj, m, f)* 7c

coloring le colorant 7c

comb   le peigne   12d, 25f
comb *(one's hair)*   se peigner *(v)*   12d
come   venir *(v)*   3e
Come here!   Venez *(pol)* ici! Viens *(fam)* ici!   17b
come in   entrer *(v)* (dans) 16b; **Come in!** Entrez! *(pol)*; Entre! *(fam)*   16b
Come on!   Allons! Allons donc! 20b
Come quickly!   Venez (Viens) vite!   39b
come to light   mettre *(v)* en lumière *(f)*   13a
comedian   l'acteur (l'actrice) comique   28e
comedy   la comédie   20a, 28e
comet   la comète   13a
comics   la bande dessinée 20a, 25o
comma   la virgule   19c
commerce   le commerce 37e, 38d
commercial *(advertising)*   la publicité   20b
communicate   communiquer *(v)*   17a
communication   la communication   17a
communism   le communisme 43
communist   le (la) communiste 43
compact car   la voiture compacte   33a
compact disk   le disque compact 20b, 25j, 42a
company *(business)*   la société commerciale   38d
compare   comparer *(v)*   17a
comparison   la comparaison 8a, 17a
compartment *(of a train)*   le compartiment   34
compass   le compas   2b, 37b; la boussole   3d

compatible   compatible *(adj, m, f)*   42b
competition   le concours   27b
complain   se plaindre *(v)* 21a, 35b
complaint   la plainte   21a, 35b
complementary   complémentaire *(adj, m, f)*   2b
complex   complexe *(adj)* 1d
complicated   compliqué(e) *(adj, m, f)*   22a
Compliments!   Mes compliments! *(m, pl)*   29c
composer   le compositeur, la femme compositeur, la compositrice   25j, 28c
composition   la composition 28c; le thème   37f
compound   le composé   13c
computer   l'ordinateur *(m)* 42b
computer-assisted instruction les instructions *(f, pl)* automatisées   42b
computer language   le langage-machine, le langage de programmation   42b
computer printer   l'imprimante *(f)* d'ordinateur   42b
computer science   l'informatique *(f)*   42b
concave   concave *(adj)*   2b
concept   le concept   22a
concert   le concert   28c
conclude   conclure *(v)*   17a
conclusion   la conclusion 17a
conditional   conditionnel(le) *(adj, m, f)*   8a
condominium   l'immeuble *(m)* en copropriété *(f)*   23g
conductor *(of a public vehicle)* le conducteur, la conductrice 34
cone *(geometry)*   le cône   2a; **ice cream cone** le cornet   24h

confirmation la confirmation
11d

conformist le (la) conformiste
11e

congratulate féliciter *(v)*
17a

Congratulations! Félicitations!
(f, pl) 16c, 29c

conjugation la conjugaison
8a

conjunction la conjonction
8a, 8p

connection *(travel)* la
correspondance 32a, 34

conscience la conscience
11e, 22a

conscientious consciencieux
(adj, m), consciencieuse *(f)*
11e, 22a

consecutive consécutif,
consécutive *(adj)* 2b

consequently donc *(conj)*
8p

conservation la conservation
44a

conservative conservateur,
conservatrice *(adj, m, f)* 11e

conservative party *(politics)* le
parti conservateur 43

conservatory le conservatoire
37a

consonant la consonne 8a

constant constant(e) *(adj, m, f)*
1f

consumption la consommation
44a

contact lenses les lentilles *(f,
pl)* de contact, les verres *(m, pl)*
de contact 40a

contents le contenu 19c

continent le continent 13e,
30a

continental continental(e) *(adj,
m, f)* 6a, 13e

continually continuellement
(adv) 4e

continue continuer *(v)* 4e

contract le contrat 38d

controversy la controverse
41

convalesce être *(v)* en
convalescence 40a

convalescence la convalescence
40a

conversation la conversation
17a

convex convexe *(adj, m, f)*
2b

convince convaincre *(v)*
22b, 41

cook le cuisinier, la cuisinière
38a; cuire *(v)*, faire *(v)* la
cuisine, cuisiner *(v)* 24o

cookbook le livre de cuisine
25o

cookie le sablé, le petit-beurre,
le gâteau sec 24i

cooking la cuisine 24b

cool frais *(adj, m)*, fraîche
(adj, f) 6a

cool weather faire *(v)* frais
6a

coordinate la coordonnée
2b

co-pilot le (la) copilote 32c

copper le cuivre 13c

copy la copie 37f

cordless phone le téléphone
sans fil 18a

corn le maïs 14e, 24i

corner le coin 36a

corner *(street)* le coin de la rue
33c

correspondence la
correspondance 19e

corridor le couloir 23a

cortisone la cortisone 25h

cosecant la cosécante 2b

cosine le cosinus 2b

cosmetics/perfume shop la
parfumerie 25f

cosmos le cosmos 13a

cost coûter *(v)* 24o, 25a;
price le prix, le coût 25a

cost of living le coût de la vie
26

cotangent la cotangente 2b
cotton le coton 13c, 251
cough la toux; tousser *(v)*
40a
Could you tell me . . . ?
Pourriez-vous me dire . . . ?
36c
council le conseil 43
count compter *(v)* 1f
countable comptable *(adj)*
1f
counter le comptoir 25a
country le pays 11f, 13e,
30a
courage le courage 11e
courageous courageux,
courageuse *(adj)* 11e
course le cours 37f
court *(of law)* le tribunal 41
court of appeal la cour d'appel
41
courtesy la courtoisie 11e
courteous courtois(e) *(adj)*
11e
courtroom la salle du tribunal
41
cousin le cousin, la cousine
10a
cover la couverture 20a
cover charge *(dining out)* le
couvert 24m
cow la vache 15a
crash tomber *(v)* en panne
(f) 42b
crayon le crayon de couleur
7c
crazy fou, fol, folle *(adj)*
11e
cream la crème 24h, 25f
cream cake *(pie)* le gâteau à la
crème 24i
cream puff le chou à la crème
24i
creamed horn le cornet feuilleté
à la crème 24i
creative créatif *(adj, m)*,
créative *(adj, f)* 11e
credit le crédit 26

credit card *(to pay with a credit
card)* payer *(v)* avec carte
(f) de crédit 25a; la carte de
crédit 26, 35b
crime le crime 39b
crime wave la masse de crimes
39b
criminal le criminel, la
criminelle 39b
crew *(travel)* l'équipage *(m)*
32c
criminal law le droit pénal, la
loi pénale 41
critical critique *(adj)*
11e
criticism la critique 20a,
28d
crocodile le crocodile 15c
cross-country skiing le ski de
fond 27b
cross over traverser *(v)*
36c
cross the street traverser *(v)* la
rue 36c
crouton le croûton 24i
crow le corbeau 15b
crown la couronne 40b
cruise la croisière 36b
crumb la miette 24i
crust la croûte 24i
cry *(weep)* pleurer *(v)* 11e,
21a
crying en larmes *(f, pl)*
11e
cube le cube 2a
cube root la racine cubique
1e
cubed au cube 1e
cubic centimeter le centimètre
cubique 3a
cubic kilometer le kilomètre
cubique 3a
cubic meter le mètre cubique
3a
cubic millimeter le millimètre
cubique 3a
cucumber le concombre
14e, 24e

cue *(billiards)*   la queue de
  billard *(m)*   27a
cultivate   cultiver *(v)*   14a
cultivation   la culture   14a
cultured   cultivé(e) *(adj)*
  11e
cup   la tasse   23d, 241
cure   la guérison; guérir *(v)*
  40a
curfew   le couvre-feu   41
curiosity   la curiosité   11e
curious   curieux, curieuse *(adj)*
  11e
curler   le bigoudi   12d, 25f
curls   les boucles *(f)* de
  cheveux   12d; les cheveux
  (m, pl) frisés   12d
curly-haired   les cheveux *(m,
  pl)* bouclés, les cheveux frisés
  11a
currency *(bill, banknote)*   le
  billet de banque   26
current   le courant   35c
current account   le compte
  courant   26
curtains   les rideaux *(m, pl)*
  23c, 28e, 35c
curve   la courbe   2b, 33c
curved line   la ligne courbe
  2b
cushion *(billiard table)*   le rebord
  élastique   27a
custard   le flan   24h
customer   le client, la cliente
  25a, 26
customs   la douane   31
customs officer   le douanier, la
  douanière   31
cut   couper *(v)*   24o
Cut it out!   Arrêtez! Arrêtez
  donc!   20b
cut one's hair   se faire *(v)*
  couper *(v)* les cheveux *(m, pl)*
  12d
cutlet   la côtelette   24g
cyclamen   le cyclamen   14b
cylinder   le cylindre   2a

cymbals   les cymbales *(f, pl)*
  28c
cypress tree   le cyprès   14c

D
dad   le papa   10a
dahlia   le dahlia   14b
daily   quotidien, quotidienne
  (adj), quotidiennement *(adv)*
  4c, 20a
daily newspaper   le journal
  quotidien   20a
dairy product   le produit laitier
  24h
dairy shop   la laiterie   24n
daisy   la marguerite   14b
Damn it!   Zut! Zut alors!
  20b
damp   humide *(adj)*   6a
dance   danser *(v)*   28c, 29b;
  le bal   28c, 29b
dance music   la musique de
  danse   25j
dancer   le danseur, la danseuse
  28c
dandruff   les pellicules *(f, pl)*
  40a
danger   le danger   39a
Danish *(nationality)*   Danois
  (m), Danoise *(f)*   30d;
  (language) le danois   30d
dark *(color)*   sombre, foncé
  (adj)   7b
dark *(weather)*   faire *(v)*
  sombre *(adj)*   6a
dark blue   le bleu foncé
  7a
dark-haired   les cheveux *(m,
  pl)* bruns   11a
dashboard   le tableau de bord
  33e
data   les données *(f, pl)*,
  l'information *(f)*   42b
data processing   le traitement de
  l'information   42b
date   la date   5e, 11f, 19c;
  (fruit) la datte   14d, 24f

date of birth   la date de naissance *(f)*   11f, 38b

daughter   la fille   10a

daughter-in-law   la belle-fille   10a; la bru   10a

dawn   l'aube *(f)*   4a

day   le jour   4a, 4c

day after tomorrow   le lendemain   4a

day before yesterday   avant-hier *(adv)*   4a

day care   l'école maternelle   37a

day of the week   le jour de la semaine   5a

deaf   sourd, sourde *(adj, m, f)*   12c

deafness   la surdité   12c

Dear . . .   Cher, Chère, Chers, Chères . . .   19b

dear friend   cher ami, chère amie   10b

Dear Madam . . .   Madame, Chère Madame . . .   19a

Dear Sir . . .   Monsieur, Cher Monsieur . . .   19a

death   la mort   11c

debate   le débat; débattre *(v)*   17a, 41

debit   le débit   26

debit card   la carte de retrait   26

debt   la dette   26

decade   la décennie   4c

decagon   le décagone   2a

December   le décembre   5b

decimal   décimal(e) *(adj, m, f)*   1f

declarative   déclaratif *(adj, m)*, déclarative *(adj, f)*   8a, 8n

declare   déclarer *(v)*   17a, 31

decorating   la décoration   23c

decrease   diminuer *(v)*, la diminution   3c

deer   le cerf   15a

defecate   déféquer *(v)*   40a

defend oneself   se défendre *(v)*   41

definite   défini(e) *(adj, m, f)*   8a, 8b

definition   la définition   20a

degree   le degré   2b, 6c

degree *(university)*   la licence   11f, 37f; le doctorat   11f, 37f; le diplôme universitaire   37f

delicate   délicat(e) *(adj)*   11e

delicatessen   la charcuterie   24n

Delighted!   Heureux! Heureuse!   16b

democracy   la démocratie   43

democrat   le (la) démocrate   43

democratic   démocratique *(adj, m, f)*   43

demonstrate   démontrer *(v)*   22b

demonstration *(politics)*   1a   manifestation, la manif   43

demonstrative   démonstratif *(adj, m)*, démonstrative *(adj, f)*   8a, 8e, 8m

Denmark   le Danemark   30b

dense   dense *(adj)*   3b

density   la densité   3b, 13d

dentist   le (la) dentiste   38a, 40b

dentist's chair   le fauteuil   40b

dentist's office   le cabinet du (de la) dentiste   40b

denture   le dentier   40b

deny   nier *(v)*   17a

deodorant   le déodorant   25f

depart   partir *(v)*   3e, 34

department *(of a store)*   le rayon   25a

department store   le grand magasin   25a

departure   le départ   32a

deposit le versement 26;
  verser *(v)* 26
deposit slip la fiche de
  versement 26
depot *(station)* la gare, la station
  34
depressed déprimé(e) *(adj, m,
  f)* 21a
depression la dépression
  21a
descend descendre *(v)* 3e
describe décrire *(v)* 17a
description la description 17a,
  39b
descriptive descriptif *(adj, m)*,
  descriptive *(adj, f)* 8a
desert le désert 13b
desk *(pupil's)* le pupitre;
  (teacher's) le bureau, la chaire
  37b; le bureau 38c
desperate désespéré(e) *(adj,
  m, f)* 21a
desperation le désespoir
  21a
dessert le dessert 24g
destroy détruire *(v)* 39a
detest détester *(v)* 21b
dial *(of a timepiece)* le cadran
  4d, 25i
dial a telephone number
  composer le numéro 18b
diameter le diamètre 2a
diamond le diamant 25i;
  (cards) le carreau 27a
diamond anniversary les noces
  (f) de diamant 11c
dice *(to play)* jouer *(v)* aux dés
  (m, pl) 27a
dictate dicter *(v)* 17a
dictation la dictée 37f
dictionary le dictionnaire
  20a, 25o, 37b
die mourir *(v)* 11c
diesel le gazole 13c
difference la différence 1f
difficult difficile *(adj, m, f)*
  22a
dig creuser *(v)* 14a

digestive system le système
  digestif 40a
digit le chiffre 1d
digress faire *(v)* une digression
  17a
diligence la diligence 11e
diligent diligent(e) *(adj)*
  11e
dimension la dimension 3b
dining room la salle à manger
  (v) 23b
dinner le dîner 24a
diploma le diplôme 11f, 37f
diplomatic diplomatique *(adj)*
  11e
direct direct(e) *(adj, m, f)*
  8a, 8i
direct dialing téléphoner *(v)*
  en direct 18b
direct train le train direct
  34
direction la direction 3d
dirty sale *(adj)* 11a, 12d,
  25g
dirty word le mot grossier
  20b
disagree être *(v)* en désaccord
  (m) 21a; se disputer *(v)*
  41
disagreement le désaccord
  21a
disappoint décevoir *(v)*
  21a
disappointed déçu(e) *(adj, m,
  f)* 21a
disappointment la déception
  21a
disarmament le désarmement
  43
disco la discothèque 29b
discount le rabais, la remise
  25a
discourse le discours 8a
discourteous discourtois(e)
  (adj) 11e
discuss discuter *(v)* 17a,
  41
discussion la discussion 17a

disease   la maladie   40a
disgust   le dégoût   21b
disgusted   dégoûté(e)   *(adj, m, f)*   21b
dish antenna   l'antenne   *(f)* parabolique   42a
dishonest   malhonnête   *(adj)* 11e
dishonesty   la malhonnêteté 11e
dishwasher   le lave-vaisselle 23d
disk   le disque   42b; **floppy disk** la disquette, le disque souple 42b
dislike (not to like)   ne pas aimer *(v)*   21b
disorganized   désorganisé(e) *(adj, m, f)*   11e
dissatisfaction   l'insatisfaction *(f)*   21a
dissatisfied   insatisfait(e)   *(adj, m, f)*   21a
distance   la distance   3d, 33c
divide   diviser   *(v)*   le
divided by   divisé par   1e
division   la division   1e
divorce   le divorce; divorcer   *(v)* 11c
divorced   divorcé(e)   *(adj)* 11c, 38b
DNA   ADN   *(m)*   40a, 41
do   faire   *(v)*   18b; **do the dishes** faire   *(v)* la vaisselle 23f
Do you have a vacant room? Avez-vous une chambre libre? 35b
doctor   le médecin, la femme médecin, le docteur, la femme docteur   38a, 39c, 40a
doctorate degree   le doctorat 37f
doctor's instruments   les instruments   *(m, pl)* du médecin 40a
doctor's visit   la visite du médecin   40a

documentary   documentaire *(adj, m, f)*   20b
documents   les documents   *(m, pl)*   31
dodecahedron   le dodécaèdre 2a
does not equal   n'est pas égal à 1f
dog   le chien, la chienne   15a
dollar   le dollar   26
dolphin   le dauphin   15c
donkey   l'âne *(m)*   15a
Don't mention it!   Il n'y a pas de quoi! De rien!   16c
door   la porte 23a; *(of car)* la portière   33e
doorbell   le bouton de sonnette *(f)*   23a
doorman   le portier   35b
double   double *(n/adj, m, f)* 3c
double bass   la contrebasse   28c
double bed   le grand lit   35c
double roll *(of bread)*   le petit pain double   24i
double room   une chambre double   35b
doubt   le doute   22a; douter *(v)*   22b
dove   la colombe   15b
down   bas *(adv)* 3d, 36c; en bas 3d
downhill skiing   le ski alpin 27b
download   télécharger   *(v)* 42b
downtown   en ville   *(f)*, le centre de la ville   30a, 36a
Dr. *(M.D. degree)*   Dr., le docteur, la femme docteur, le docteur femme 11f, 16b; *(Ph.D. degree)* Dr., le docteur, la doctoresse   16b
draft *(promissory note)*   le billet à ordre   26
draft *(rough copy)*   la copie brute, la copie en état brut, le brouillon   37f

drama le drame 20a, 28e

draw dessiner *(v)* 2b, 37f

draw *(score in sports)* le match nul 27b; terminer *(v)* à match nul (à égalité) 27b

drawer le tiroir 23c

drawing le dessin 37f

drawing instruments les instruments *(m)* de dessin *(m)* 2b

dress la robe 25k

dresser la commode 23c, 35c

dressing room la cabine 25k

dried cod la merluche 24d

drill *(dentist's)* la fraise 40b

drill *(hardware)* la foreuse 25b

drink boire *(v)* 12b, 24o; la boisson 24k

drive conduire *(v)* 3e, 33b, 33c

driver *(of a car)* le chauffeur, l'automobiliste *(m/f)* 33b

driver's license le permis de conduire 33b

drop *(e.g., of rain)* la goutte 6a

drug addiction la toxicomanie 44b

drug pusher le (la) trafiquant(e) des stupéfiants 44b

drug trafficking le trafic des stupéfiants 44b

drugs la drogue 44b

drugstore la pharmacie 25h

drum *(music)* le tambour 28c

dry sec *(adj, m)*, sèche *(adj, f)* 6a

dry cleaning le nettoyage à sec 25g

dry oneself se sécher *(v)* 12d

dryer *(clothes)* la sécheuse, le sèche-linge 23d

duck le canard 15b, 24c

dull *(color)* terne *(adj)* 7b

dumpling la boulette 24g

dump truck le camion à triple mouvement 33a

during pendant *(prep)* 4e

Dutch *(nationality)* Hollandais *(m)*, Hollandaise *(f)* 30d; *(language)* le hollandais 30d

duty tax le tarif douanier 31

DVD D.V.D. *(m)* 20b

dynamic dynamique *(adj)* 11e

E

each chaque *(adj)* 3c

eagle l'aigle *(m)* 15b

ear l'oreille *(f)* 12a

early de bonne heure *(adv)*, tôt *(adv)* 4e, 32b, 34; *(arrival/departure time)* en avance 32b, 34

earn gagner *(v)* 38d

earphone l'écouteur *(m)* 18a

earring la boucle d'oreille 25i

Earth la Terre 13a

earthquake le tremblement de terre 13b

easel le chevalet 28b

east l'est *(m)* 3d; **to the east** à l'est 3d

Easter les Pâques *(f)* 5f, 29a

eastern oriental(e) *(adj)* 3d

easy facile *(adj, m, f)* 22a

eat manger *(v)* 12b, 24o

eccentric excentrique *(adj)* 11e

eclair l'éclair *(m)* 24i

eclipse l'éclipse *(f)* 13a

ecology l'écologie *(f)* 44a

economics l'économie *(f)* 37e

economy l'économie *(f)* 43

economy class *(travel)*   la classe
   touriste   30a, 32a, 34
ecosystem   l'écosystème   *(m)*
   44a
edge   le bord   3d
editor   le rédacteur, la rédactrice
   20a, 38a
editor (correcting)   correcteur
   (m)   20a
editor (writing)   rédacteur   *(m)*
   20a
editorial   éditorial(e)   *(adj, m, f)*
   20a
education   l'éducation   *(f)*
   11f, 37f, 38b
eel   l'anguille   *(f)*   15f, 24d
egg   l'oeuf   *(m)*   24h
eggplant   l'aubergine   *(f)*
   14e, 24e
egoism   l'égoïsme   *(m)*   11e
egoist   l'égoïste   *(m, f)*   11e
egoistic   égoïste   *(adj)*   11e
Egypt   l'Egypte   *(f)*   30b
eight   huit   1a
eighteen   dix-huit   1a
eighth   huitième   1b
eighty   quatre-vingts   1a
eighty-one   quatre-vingt-un   la
elastic   élastique   *(n, m/adj)*
   13d
elbow   le coude   12a
elderly person   une personne
   âgée   11b
elect   élire   *(v)*   43
elected politician   le député, la
   femme député   43
elections   les élections   *(f, pl)*
   43
electric razor   le rasoir
   électrique   12d, 25f
electric stove   la cuisinière
   électrique   23d
electrical   électrique   *(adj, m, f)*
   13c, 25b
electrician   l'électricien   *(m)*
   38a
electricity   l'électricité   *(f)*
   13c, 23e

electrocardiograph
   l'électrocardiographe   *(m)*   40a
electron   l'électron   *(m)*
   13c, 42a
elegance   l'élégance   *(f)*
   11a
elegant   élégant(e)   *(adj)*
   11a, 251
elegantly   élégamment   *(adv)*
   11a
element   l'élément   *(m)*   13c
elementary school   l'école   *(f)*
   primaire élémentaire   37a, 38b
elementary school teacher   le
   maître, la maîtresse   37d
elephant   l'éléphant   *(m)*
   15a
elevator   l'ascenseur   *(m)*
   23g, 35b
eleven   onze   1a
eleventh   onzième   1b
eloquence   l'éloquence   *(f)*
   11e
eloquent   éloquent(e)   *(adj)*
   11e
e-mail   le courrier électronique
   42a
e-mail address   l'adresse   *(f)*
   électronique   42b
emerald   l'émeraude   *(f)*
   25i
emergencies   les urgences   *(f,*
   pl)   39
emergency exit   la sortie de
   secours   32c, 39a
emergency lane   la piste
   d'urgence   *(f)*   33d
emergency ward   le service des
   urgences   39c
emphasis   l'emphase   *(f)*
   17a
emphasize   accentuer   *(v)*
   17a
employ   employer   *(v)*   38d
employee   l'employé(e)   *(m, f)*
   11f, 26, 38d
employer   l'employeur,
   l'employeuse   11f, 38d

employment l'emploi *(m)*
11f

employment agency l'agence
(f) d'emploi *(m)* 38d

empty vide *(adj)*, vider *(v)*
3c

encourage encourager *(v)*
21a

encouragement
l'encouragement *(m)* 21a

encyclopedia l'encyclopédie
(f) 20a, 25o, 37b

end la fin 4e; finir *(v)* 4e

endorse endosser *(v)* 26

endorsement l'endossement
(m), l'endos *(m)* 26

enemy l'ennemi(e) 10b

energetic énergique *(adj)* 11e

energy l'énergie *(f)* 11e,
13c, 44a

energy crisis la crise d'énergie
(f) 44a

energy needs les besoins *(m)*
d'énergie *(f)* 44a

energy source la source
d'énergie *(f)* 44a

engaged fiancé(e) *(adj)*
11c

engagement les fiançailles *(f,
pl)* 11c, 29a

engineer l'ingénieur, la femme
ingénieur 38a

engineering les études *(f, pl)*
polytechniques 37e

England l'Angleterre *(f)*
30b

English *(nationality)* Anglais
(m), Anglaise *(f)* 30d;
(language) l'anglais *(m)*
30d

enjoy oneself s'amuser *(v)*
21a

Enjoy your meal! Bon appétit!
16c, 241

enjoyment l'amusement *(m)*
21a

enlarge *(clothing)* faire *(v)*
élargir 25m

enough assez *(adv)* 3c;
suffisant(e) *(adj)* 3c

Enough! Assez! 21c

enter entrer *(v)* (dans) 3e,
16b, 36c

entire entier, entière *(adj)*
3c

entrance l'entrée *(f)* 23a,
25a, 35b

entrance exam l'examen *(m)*
d'entrée 37f

envelope l'enveloppe *(f)*
19d, 19e, 25c

envious envieux, envieuse
(adj) 11e

environment l'environnement
(m) 13b, 44a

envy l'envie *(f)* 11e

equality l'égalité *(f)* 1f

equals est égal à 1f

equation l'équation *(f)* 1f

equator l'équateur 13e

equilateral équilatéral *(adj)*
2a

equinox l'équinoxe *(m)*
5c

eraser *(for pencil)* la gomme
2b, 19d; la gomme à effacer 37b

error l'erreur *(f)*, la faute
37f

eruption l'éruption *(f)* 13b

escape, get out fuir *(v)*,
échapper *(v)* 39a

essay l'essai *(m)* 20a

Europe l'Europe *(f)* 30b

even pair *(adj, m)* 1d

even though même si *(conj)*
8p

evening le soir 4a

evening school l'école *(f)*
d'adultes, l'école du soir 37a

every tout, toute, tous, toutes
(adj) 3c; chaque *(adj, m/f)*
3c

everbody, everyone tout le
monde 3c, 8o

Everybody out! Dehors! Tous!
39a

everything tout, toute, toute chose, toutes les choses   3c, 80
everywhere partout *(adv)* 36c
exam l'examen *(m)* 37f
examine examiner *(v)* 40a, 40b
exchange échanger *(v)* 25a; le change, changer *(v)* 26
exchange rates le cours du change   26
exclamation point le point d'exclamation *(f)* 19c
excursion l'excursion *(f)* 30a
excuse l'excuse *(f)* 17a
Excuse me! Excusez-moi! *(pol),* Excuse-moi! *(fam),* Pardonnez-moi! *(pol),* Pardonne-moi! *(fam)* 16c
excuse oneself s'excuser *(v)* 17a
exercise l'exercice *(m)* 37f
exhibition l'exposition *(f)* 28b
existence l'existence *(f)* 22a
exit sortir *(v)* 3e, 25a, 36c; la sortie   35b
expensive cher *(adj, m, s),* chère *(adj, f, s)* chers *(adj, m, pl)* chères *(adj, f, pl)* 24p; coûteux *(adj, m),* coûteuse *(adj, f)* 24p, 25a
expiration *(date)* l'échéance *(f)* 26
explain expliquer *(v)* 17a, 37f
explanation l'explication *(f)* 17a, 37f
express exprimer *(v)* 17a
express bus l'autocar express 34
express oneself s'exprimer *(v)* 17a
express train le train express 34

expression l'expression *(f)* 17a
extension l'extension *(f)* 3b
extinguish éteindre *(v)* 39a
extract extraire *(v)* 40b
extract a root *(numbers)* extraire *(v)* la racine   1e
extraction l'extraction *(f)* 40b
eye l'oeil *(m)* 12a; les yeux *(m, pl)* 12a
eye doctor l'ophtalmologiste *(m/f),* l'oculiste *(m/f)* 38a, 40a
eyebrow le sourcil   12a
eyeglasses les lunettes *(f)* 37b, 40a
eyelash le cil   12a
eyelid la paupière   12a
eyewitness le témoin oculaire 41

F
fable la fable   28d
fabric le tissu   251
face le visage, la figure   12a
face powder la poudre   25f
factor le facteur   1f; mettre *(v)* en facteurs *(m, pl)* 1f
factorization la factorielle 1f
factory l'usine *(f)* 38d
factory worker l'ouvrier, l'ouvrière   38a
Fahrenheit Fahrenheit   6c
fail an exam échouer *(v)* à un examen, être collé(e) à un examen 37f
fairy tale le conte de fées *(f)* 28d
faith la foi   11d; la confiance 21a
faithful fidèle *(adj)* 11d, 11e
fake faux, fausse *(adj)* 13d, 25i
falcon le faucon   15b

fall tomber *(v)* 3e
fall *(season)* l'automne 5c
fall asleep s'endormir *(v)* 12b
fall in love tomber *(v)* amoureux 11c
false faux *(adj, m)*, fausse *(adj, f)* 25i
false teeth le dentier 40b
family la famille 10a
family friend l'ami(e) de famille *(f)* 10b
family name le nom de famille *(f)* 11f, 38b
family relationship la parenté 10a
fan *(of a vehicle)* le ventilateur d'aération 33e
far loin *(adv)* 3d; **far from** loin de 36c; lointain(e) *(adj)* 3d
Farewell! Adieu! 16a
farm la ferme 15a
farmer le fermier, la fermière 15a, 38a
farmland le terrain agricole 13b
fascinate fasciner *(v)* 11e
fascinating fascinant(e) *(adj)* 11e
fascination la fascination 11e
fashion la mode 25k, 25l
fast vite *(adj/adv)* 3d; rapide 3d
fast food le fast-food 24m
fasten *(buckle)* **seat belt** boucler *(v)* la ceinture de sécurité 32c
fat gros, grosse *(adj)* 11a
father le père 10a
father-in-law le beau-père 10a
faucet le robinet 23a, 35c
fax la télécopie 18a, 18b, 38c
fax machine le télécopieur, l'émetteur-récepteur de fac-similé, le fax 18a, 42a

fear la peur; avoir *(v)* peur 21a
Feast of the Assumption *(National French Holiday)* l'Assomption *(f)* 5f, 29a
feather la plume 15b
February le février 5b
feel sentir *(v)* 12c, 21a; se sentir *(v)* 40a
feel bad avoir *(v)* mal *(m)* 12b; se sentir *(v)* mal *(m)* 12b, 40a
feel bored crever *(v)* d'ennui *(m)* 21a
feel like avoir *(v)* envie de 21a
feel well aller *(v)* bien *(adv)* 12b; se sentir *(v)* bien *(adv)* 12b, 40a
feeling *see* **mood**
felt-tip pen le stylo-feutre 7c, 19d
female la femelle 11a, 38b
feminine féminin(e) *(adj, m, f)* 8a, 11a
feminism le féminisme 44b
feminist le (la) féministe 44b
fence la barrière, la clôture 15a
fencing *(sport)* l'escrime *(f)* 27b; **to fence** faire *(v)* de l'escrime 27b
fender *(of vehicle)* le pare-chocs intégré 33e
fennel le fenouil 14e
fetus le foetus 44b
fever la fièvre 40a
fiance le fiancé 10b, 11c
fiancee la fiancée 10b, 11c
fiber la fibre 13c
fiction l'ouvrage *(m)* de fiction 20a; le livre de fiction *(f)* 28d
field le champ 13b, 27b
field of study la matière d'études 37f

fifteen   quinze   1a; **about fifteen**   une quinzaine   1c
fifth   cinquième   1b
fifty   cinquante   1a; **about fifty**   une cinquantaine   1c
fifty-one   cinquante et un   1a
fifty-two   cinquante-deux   1a
fig   la figue   14d, 24f
fig tree   le figuier   14c
fight   se battre *(v)*   39b
figure of speech   la figure de rhétorique   17a
file, menu *(computers)*   les archives   *(f, pl)*   42b
file *(hardware)*   la lime   25b
file *(office)*   le classeur, le dossier-classeur   38c
filet   le filet   24g
filing card   la fiche   38c
fill   remplir *(v)*   3c
fill up *(gasoline, petrol tank)*   faire   *(v)* le plein   33c
filling *(tooth)*   l'obturation   *(f)*   40b
film   le film   25d, 28a
film projector   le projecteur de film   37b
filter *(of vehicle)*   le filtre   33e
fin   la nageoire   15c
fine *(traffic ticket)*   1a   contravention   33c
Fine!   Bien!   *(adv)*   16a
fine arts   les beaux-arts   *(m, pl)*   37e
finger   le doigt   12a
fingernail   l'ongle   *(m)*   12a
finish   finir   *(v)*   4e
finish school   finir   *(v)* l'école *(f)*   11f; finir la dernière année d'école   37f
fir tree   le sapin   14c
fire   le feu, l'incendie   *(m)*   13c, 39a
Fire!   Feu!   39a
fire *(to discharge an employee)*   renvoyer   *(v)*   38d

fire alarm   la sirène d'alerte   39a
fire extinguisher   l'extincteur   *(m)*   39a
fire hose   le tuyau de pompe   39a
fire hydrant   la borne d'incendie   39a
fire truck   le fourgon-pompe   33a, 39a
firearm   l'arme   *(f)* à feu   39b
firefighter   le pompier, le sapeur-pompier   39a
fireman   le pompier   38a
fireplace   la cheminée   23a
fireproof   ignifuge   *(adj)*, incombustible   *(adj)*   39a
first   premier   *(adj, m)*, première   *(adj, f)*   1b, 8a
first aid   les soins   *(m, pl)* d'urgence   39a, 39c
first class *(travel)*   la première classe   *(f)*   30a, 32a, 34
first name   le prénom   11f, 38b
first showing *(entertainment)*   la première représentation   28a
fish   le poisson   15c, 24d; pêcher   *(v)*, aller   *(v)* à la pêche   15c
fish stew   la bouillabaisse   24g
fish store   la poissonnerie   24n
fishbone   l'arête   *(f)*   15c
fisherman   le pêcheur, la pêcheuse   15c
fishing   la pêche   15c, 36b
fishing rod   la canne à pêche   15c
fission reactor   le réacteur à fission   42a
fit *(size)*   la mesure, la taille   3b, 25k
five   cinq   la
fix   ajuster   *(v)*, réparer   *(v)*   25i, 33c

fixed bank rate   le taux fixe
26

fixed price   le prix fixe   24m,
25a

flame   la flamme   39a

flash   le flash   25d

flash of lightning   le coup
d'éclair, faire *(v)* des éclairs
6a

flashlight   la lampe de poche
25b

flatter   flatter *(v)*   21a

flattery   la flatterie   21a

flavor   la saveur   12c

flea   la puce   15d

Flemish *(language)*   le flamand
30d

flight   le vol   32a; **canceled
flight** le vol annulé   32b

flight attendant   le steward,
l'hôtesse de l'air   32c

floor   le plancher, le parquet
23a

floor *(level, story of a building)*
l'étage *(m)*   23a, 35b

floppy disk   la disquette, le
disque souple   42b

Florence   Florence   30c

flour   la farine   24i

flow   couler *(v)*   13b

flow chart   le schéma
fonctionnel   42b

flower   fleurir *(v)*   14a; la
fleur   14b

flower bed   le parterre de fleurs
14b

flu   l'influenza   *(f)*, la grippe
40a

fluorescent   fluorescent(e)   *(adj,
m, f)*   25b

flute   la flûte   28c

fly *(insect)*   la mouche   15d

focus   mettre *(v)* en mise au
point   25d

fog   le brouillard   6a

foggy   brumeux *(adj, m)*,
brumeuse *(adj, f)*   6a

foil *(fencing)*   le fleuret français
27b

foliage   le feuillage   14a

folk music   la musique
folklorique   28c

follow   suivre *(v)*   3e, 36c

food   la nourriture   24a

food coloring   le colorant
alimentaire   7c

fool   le bouffon   11e

foolish   bête   *(adj, m, f)*   11e

foot   le pied   12a

foot-and-mouth disease   la
fièvre aphteuse   40a

football   le football américain
27b

footnote   la note en bas de page
20a

for   pour   8g

for example   par exemple
44c

for now   pour le moment   4e

for sale   à vendre   *(v)*   25a

for *(since)* three days   depuis
trois jours   4e

for the first time   pour la
première fois   16b

force an uneasy smile   sourire
(v) jaune   7a

forehead   le front   12a

foreign currency   la monnaie
étrangère   31

foreign languages   les langues
(f, pl) étrangères   37e

foreigner   l'étranger   *(m)*,
l'étrangère   *(f)*   31

forest   la forêt   13b

forget   oublier   *(v)*   22b

fork   la fourchette   23d, 241

form *(to fill out)*   la formule
31

Fortunately!   Heureusement!
(adv)   21c

forty   quarante   1c; **about forty**
une quarantaine   1c

forty-one   quarante et un   1a

forty-two   quarante-deux   1a

forward avant *(adv)* 3d

fossil le fossile 13c

fossil fuels les combustibles *(m)* fossiles 13c, 44a

foul line *(sports)* la ligne de pénalité 27b

four quatre 1a

four-sided figures les figures *(f)* à quatre côtés 2a

four thousand quatre mille 1a

fourteen quatorze 1a

fourth quatrième 1b

fox le renard 15a

fraction la fraction 1d

fractional fractionnel(le) *(adj, m, f)* 1d

France la France 30b

Frankfurt Francfort 30c

free *(not occupied)* libre *(adj, m, f)* 18b

freeze geler *(v)* 6a

freezer le congélateur 23d

French *(nationality)* Français *(m)*, Française *(f)* 30d; *(language)* le français 30d

French foil *(fencing)* le fleuret français 27b

French franc le franc français 26

French fries les frites *(f, pl)* 24g

French National Holiday la Fête Nationale (le 14 juillet) 29a

frequent fréquent(e) *(adj, m, f)* 4e

frequently fréquemment *(adv)* 4e

fresco painting la fresque 28b

Friday le vendredi 5a

fried frit(e) *(adj, m, f)* 24p

fried egg (sunny side up) l'oeuf *(m)* sur le plat 24h

friend l'ami(e) 10b

friendly amical(e) *(adj)* 11e

friendship l'amitié *(f)* 10b

frog la grenouille 15c

from de *(prep)* 3d, 8g

from my point of view de mon point de vue 44c

from now on dès maintenant 4e

From what country are you? De quel pays êtes-vous? 13e

front page *(of newspaper)* la une, la première page 20a

frozen gelé(e) *(adj, m, f)* 6a

fruit le fruit 14d, 24f

fruit flan le flan aux fruits 24i

fruit tartlet la tartelette aux fruits 24g

fruit tree le fruitier 14c

fuel le carburant 13c

fuel, automobile l'essence *(f)* 13c

fuel pump la pompe à essence 33e

full plein *(adj/m)*, pleine *(f)* 3c

full moon la pleine lune 13a

fun l'amusement *(m); to have fun* s'amuser *(v)* 21a

function la fonction 1f, 42b

funny comique *(adj)* 11e; drôle *(adj)* 11e; marrant(e) *(adj, m, f)* 11e

fur coat le manteau de fourrure 25k

furnace la chaudière 23e

furniture le meuble 23c

fuse *(hardware)* le fusible, le plomb fusible 25b

fusion reactor le réacteur à fusion 42a

fussy méticuleux, méticuleuse *(adj, m, f)* 11e

future le futur, l'avenir *(m)* 4e, 8a

G

Gaelic *(language)* le gaélique
30d
gain weight prendre *(v)* du
poids 11a
galaxy la galaxie 13a
game le jeu, le match, la partie
27a, 27b
garage le garage 23a, 35b
garbage bin la poubelle 36a
garbage truck le camion de
collecte 33a
garden le jardin 14e, 23a
garlic l'ail *(m)* 24g, 24j
gas le gaz 13c, 23e
gas stove la cuisinière à gaz
23d
gasoline l'essence *(f)* 13c,
33c
gasoline pedal la pédale
d'accélérateur 33e
gasoline pump la pompe à
essence 33e
gasoline service station la
station-service 33c
gasoline tank le réservoir
d'essence 33e
gate *(travel)* la porte 32a
gather récolter *(v)*, cueillir
(v) 14a
gauze la gaze 39c
gay *(homosexual)* gai(e) *(adj,
m, f)* 44b
gearshift le levier de
changement de vitesse 33e
Gemini les Gémeaux *(m, pl)*
5d
gender le genre 8a
general delivery *(post office)* la
poste restante 19e
generator la génératrice 33e
generosity la générosité 11e
generous généreux, généreuse
(adj) 11e
genre le genre 28d
gentle doux *(adj, m)*, douce
(adj, f) 11e
gentleman le monsieur 11a

geographical géographique
(adj) 13e
geography la géographie
13e, 37e
geometrical géométrique *(adj)*
2b
geometry la géométrie 2b,
37e
geothermal energy l'énergie
(f) géothermique 44a
geranium le géranium 14b
German *(nationality)* Allemand
(m), Allemande *(f)* 30d;
(language) l'allemand *(m)*
30d
Germany l'Allemagne *(f)*
30b
gerund le gérondif 8a
get a degree obtenir *(v)* un
diplôme universitaire 37f
get a diploma obtenir *(v)* un
diplôme 37f
get a doctor chercher *(v)* un
médecin 39c
get a loan obtenir *(v)* un prêt
26
get a suntan se bronzer *(v)*
36b
get an education recevoir *(v)*
une éducation; recevoir *(v)* une
solide formation 37f
get cured se guérir *(v)* 40a
get dressed s'habiller *(v)*
25m
get examined se faire *(v)*
examiner 40a
Get lost! Allez-vous en! Va-t'en!
20b
get out *(to escape a danger)* fuir
(v), échapper *(v)* 39a
get sick tomber *(v)* malade
40a
get some sun prendre *(v)* un
peu de soleil *(m)* 36b
get up se lever *(v)* 3e, 12b
get used to s'habituer *(v)*
11c
gift le cadeau 11c, 25a

gingerbread   le pain d'épices
24i

giraffe   la girafe   15a

girl   la jeune fille   11a, 11b

girlfriend   l'amie, la petite amie
10b

give a gift   donner *(v)* un
cadeau   11c

give a tip *(gratuity)*   donner *(v)*
un pourboire   24m

give back   rendre *(v)*   37f

give back the key . . .   rendre
(v) la clef . . .   35b

give birth   accoucher *(v)*
11c

give help   donner *(v)* de l'aide
39a

give me a kiss   donne-moi un
bisou   11c

Give my regards to . . .   Un bon
souvenir à . . .   19b

give the porter a tip   donner
(v) un pourboire au porteur
35b

gladiolus   le glaïeul   14b

glass *(drinking)*   le verre
23d, 241

glazed, iced, icing   glacé(e)
(adj, m, f)   24i

globalization   la mondialisation
43

globe   le globe   13e

glove   le gant   25k, 27b

glove compartment *(of a car)*   la
boîte à gants, le vide-poches
33e

glue   la colle   19d

go   aller *(v)*   3e, 36c

Go ahead!   Allez-y! *(pol)*, Vas-y!
(fam)   17b

go away   s'en aller *(v)*   3e

go down   descendre *(v)*   3e,
36c

go forward   avancer *(v)*
33c

go on a trip *see* take a trip

go on board   monter *(v)* à bord
32a

go on foot   aller *(v)* à pied
(m)   3e

go on strike   faire *(v)* la grève,
être *(v)* en grève   43

go out   sortir *(v)*   3e, 29b,
36c

go to bed   se coucher *(v)*
12b

go to school   aller *(v)* à l'école
(f)   11c, 11f; assister *(v)* à
l'école   37f

go up   monter *(v)*   3e, 36c

goal   le but   27b

goalie   le gardien (la gardienne)
de but   27b

goat   la chèvre   15a

God   le Dieu   11d

gold   l'or *(m)*   13c, 25i

gold *(color)*   or de couleur   7a

golden anniversary   les noces
(f) d'or   11c

goldfish   le poisson rouge
15c

golf, to play   jouer *(v)* au golf
(m)   27b

good   bon *(adj, m),* bonne
(adj, f)   11e, 24p

good *(at something)*   habile
(adj)   11e

Good afternoon!   Bonjour!
16a

Good evening!   Bonsoir!   16a

good, final copy   la bonne copie
37f

Good heavens!   Oh! là! là!
21c

Good luck!   Bonne chance!
16c

good mood   la bonne humeur
21a

Good morning!   Bonjour!
16a

Good night!   Bonsoir! Bonne
nuit!   *(when going to bed)*
16a

Good-bye!   Au revoir!   16a

goodness   la bonté   11e

goose   l'oie *(f)*   15b

gossip le potin, potiner 17a
govern gouverner *(v)* 43
government le gouvernement 43
graceful gracieux, gracieuse *(adj, m, f)* 11e
grade la classe 37a
grade *(mark)* la note 37f
grade one en première classe 37a
grade two en deuxième classe 37a
graduate obtenir *(v)* un diplôme 11f
graduate *(from a university)* obtenir *(v)* sa licence (son doctorat) 11f
grain le froment, le blé 14a
gram le gramme 3a
grammar la grammaire 8a, 37f
grand piano le piano à queue *(f)* 28c
grandchildren les petits-enfants *(m)* 10a
grandfather le grand-père 10a
grandfather clock l'horloge *(f)* à pendule *(f)*, l'horloge *(f)* normande 4d
grandmother la grand-mère 10a
grapefruit le (la) pamplemousse 14d, 24f
grapes le raisin 14d, 24f
grass l'herbe *(f)* 13b, 14e
grated cheese le fromage râpé 24h
gratuity *(tip)* le pourboire 24m
gravitation la gravitation 13a
gravity la gravité 13a
gravy au jus 24b
gray le gris 7a
Greece la Grèce 30b
greed l'avarice *(f)* 11e

greedy avare *(adj)* 11e
Greek *(nationality)* Grec *(m)*, Grecque *(f)* 30d; *(language)* le grec 30d
green le vert 7a
green bean le haricot vert 14e
green pepper le poivron vert 14e
greenhouse la serre 14a
greenhouse effect l'effet *(m)* de serre 44a
greet saluer *(v)* 16a
greeting le salut, la salutation 16a
Greetings! Sincères salutations! 19b
grilled grillé(e) *(adj, m, f)* 24b
grocery store l'épicerie *(f)* 24n
groom (bridegroom) le marié 11c
grooming la toilette 12d
ground floor (main floor) le rez-de-chaussée 23a, 23g
grow croître *(v)* 3c
grow up grandir *(v)* 11b
growth la croissance 3c
guide le (la) guide 36a
guidebook le guide 25o
guilt la culpabilité 41
guilty coupable *(adj, m, f)* 41
guitar la guitare 28c
guitarist le (la) guitariste 28c
gulf le golfe 13b
gums *(mouth)* les gencives *(f, pl)* 40b
gun le revolver, le pistolet 39b
gymnasium le gymnase 27b; la salle de gymnastique 37c
gymnastics la gymnastique 27b

H

habit *(custom)* l'habitude *(f)* 11e

hail *(weather)* la grêle 6a; grêler *(v)* 6a

hair *(on head)* les cheveux *(m, pl)* 12a

hair dryer le séchoir à cheveux 25f

hairdresser le coiffeur, la coiffeuse 12d, 38a

hair spray la laque (le spray) pour les cheveux 12d

Haiti le Haïti 30b

half demi *(m)*, demie *(f)* 1c, 3c

hallway le couloir 37c

ham le jambon 24c

hammer le marteau 25b

hand la main 12a

hand *(of a timepiece)* l'aiguille *(f)* 4d, 25i

hand back rendre *(v)* 37f

hand luggage les bagages *(m, pl)* à main 31

handcloth la serviette de toilette *(f)* 12d

handcuffs les menottes *(f, pl)* 39b

handkerchief le mouchoir 25k

handle le manche 23d; *(car door)* la poignée 33e

handlebar *(bicycle)* le guidon 33a

handshake la poignée de main 16a

handsome beau, bel, beaux 11a

hang up *(telephone)* raccrocher *(v)* 18b

happen arriver *(v)*, se produire *(v)* 4e

happiness le bonheur 11e, 21a; le contentement 11e; la félicité 11e

happy content(e) *(adj)* 11e, 21a; fortuné(e) *(adj)* 11e; heureux, heureuse *(adj)* 11e, 21a

Happy birthday! Bon anniversaire! *(m)* 11c, 29c

Happy Easter! Bonnes Pâques! Joyeuses Pâques! *(f, pl)* 29c

Happy New Year! Bonne et heureuse année! *(f)* 16c, 29c

Happy to make your acquaintance! Heureux (Heureuse) de faire votre (ta) connaissance! 16b

hard dur(e) *(adj, m, f)* 13d

hard-boiled egg l'oeuf *(m)* dur 24h

hard drive le disque dur 42b

hardware la quincaillerie 25b

hardware *(computers)* le matériel, le hardware 42b

hardware store la quincaillerie 25b

hard-working diligent(e) *(adj)* 11e

hare le lièvre 15a

harmony l'harmonie *(f)* 28c

harp la harpe 28c

harpsichord le clavecin 28c

hat le chapeau 25k

hate la haine 11e, 21b; haïr *(v)* 11e, 21b

hateful détestable *(adj)* 11e

hatred la haine 11e, 21b

have a baby avoir *(v)* un enfant 11c

have a class avoir *(v)* une leçon 37f

Have a good holiday! Bonnes vacances! *(f, pl)* 16c, 29c

Have a good time! Amusez-vous bien! *(pol)*, Amuse-toi bien! *(fam)* 16c

Have a good trip! Bon voyage! *(m)* 16c

Have a happy birthday! Bon anniversaire! *(m)* 11c, 16c, 29c

have a headache avoir *(v)* mal à la tête 40a

Have a nice day! Bonne journée *(f)* 29c

Have a nice trip! Bon voyage! *(m)* 30a

have a snack prendre *(v)* un goûter 24o

have a sore back avoir *(v)* mal au dos 40a

have a sore neck avoir *(v)* mal au cou 40a

have a sore throat avoir *(v)* mal a la gorge 40a

have a stomach ache avoir *(v)* mal à l'estomac 40a

have a toothache avoir *(v)* mal aux dents 40b

have a twisted neck avoir *(v)* mal au cou (un torticolis) 40a

have baggage taken to one's room faire *(v)* porter les bagages dans la chambre 35b

have chills être *(v)* frileux *(adj, m)*, frileuse *(adj, f)* 6b

have dinner dîner *(v)* 24o

have fun s'amuser *(v)* 29b; **Have fun!** Amusez-vous! *(pol)*, Amuse-toi! *(fam)* 29c

have lunch déjeuner *(v)* 24o

have one's head in the clouds être *(v)* dans les nuages *(m, pl)* 6a

have patience avoir *(v)* de la patience 21a

have reason to be worried avoir de quoi s'inquiéter 21a

have to (must) devoir *(v)* 21a

have white hair avoir *(v)* les cheveux blancs *(m, pl)* 11b

hazard flash (of a vehicle) les feux *(m, pl)* de détresse 33e

he il 8h; lui 8l

He/She is a pain in the neck! C'est un casse-pieds! 12a

head la tête 12a

head of state le chef d'état 43

head office le siège central 26

headache le mal de tête 40a

heading (newspaper) la rubrique 20a

heading (of a letter) l'en-tête *(f)* 19c

headline la manchette 20a

headlights (of a vehicle) les phares *(m, pl)*, les projecteurs *(m, pl)* 33e

headphones le casque à écouteurs 20b; **(on a plane)** le casque d'écoute 32c

heal guérir *(v)* 40a

health la santé 11a, 40a

healthy sain(e) *(adj)* 11a, 40a; en bonne santé *(f)* 11a, 40a

hear entendre *(v)* 12c

hearing l'ouïe *(f)* 12c

heart le coeur 12a, 27a, 40a

heart attack la crise cardiaque 40a

heat la chaleur 13c

heater (of a vehicle) le système de chauffage 33e

heating le chauffage central 23e

heavy lourd(e) *(adj, m, f)* 3b, 11a, 13d, 31

Hebrew (language) le hébreu 30d

hectare l'hectare *(m)* 3a

hectogram l'hectogramme *(m)* 3a

hedge la haie 14a

height la taille, la stature 11a

Hello! Bonjour! *(during daytime)*; Bonsoir! *(during evening hours)* 16a, 17b *(answering a telephone call)* Allô! 18b

helmet le casque 27b

help aider *(v)* 39a

Help!   Au secours!   39a,
39c

hemisphere   l'hémisphère *(m)*
13e

hemispheric   hémisphérique
13e

hen   la poule   15b

heptagon   l'heptagone *(m)*
2a

her *(possessive)*   son *(m, s)*, sa
(f, s), ses   *(m/f, pl)*   8f; la
8i; elle   8l

herb   l'herbe *(f)*   24j

here   ici *(adv)*   3d, 36c

heredity   l'hérédité *(f)*   11c

hero   le héros   28e

heroine   l'héroïne *(f)*   28e

herring   le hareng   24d

herself *(reflexive)*   se   8k

hesitate   hésiter *(v)*   17a

hesitation   l'hésitation   17a

hexagon   l'hexagone *(m)*
2a

Hi!   Salut!   16a, 17b

high school   l'école *(f)*
d'enseignement secondaire, le
lycée   37a, 38b

high school diploma   le
baccalauréat   37f

high school teacher/professor
le professeur, la femme professeur
37d

high temperature   la
température élevée   6c

highway   l'autoroute *(f)*
33c

highway police   l'agent *(m)* de
police routier   33b

hill   la colline   13b

him   le   8i; lui   8l

himself *(reflexive)*   se   8k

Hindu   Hindou(e) *(n/adj, m, f)*
11d

hip   la hanche   12a

hippopotamus   l'hippopotame
(m)   15a

hire *(to employ)*   employer *(v)*
38d

his   son *(m, s)*, sa *(f, s)*, ses
(m/f, pl)   8f

history   l'histoire *(f)*   37e

hit *(ball)*   battre *(v)*   27b

HIV   VIH *(m)*   40a, 44b

hobby   le passe-temps   27a

hockey   le hockey   27b; **ice
hockey**   le hockey sur glace
27b

hockey player   le joueur (la
joueuse) de hockey   27b

hockey stick   la crosse, le stick
27b

hole   le trou   25g

holiday *(official)*   le jour férié
5a, 29a

holidays   les jours *(m, pl)* de
fête *(f)*   29a

Holland   La Hollande   30b

home base *(sports)*   la base du
batteur   27b

homework   les devoirs *(m, pl)*
37f

homosexual   homosexuel(le)
(m, f)   44b

homosexuality   l'homosexualité
(f)   44b

honest   honnête *(adj)*   11e

honesty   l'honnêteté *(f)*
11e

honey   le miel   24j

honeymoon   la lune de miel
(m)   11c, 13a

hood *(of a vehicle)*   le capot
33e

hoof-and-mouth disease   is
another term for **foot-and-mouth
disease.**   See 40a.

hook *(fishing)*   l'hameçon *(m)*
15c

hope   l'espoir   21a; espérer
(v)   21a

horizontal   horizontal(e) *(adj)*
3d

horn *(musical instrument)*   le
cor   28c

horn *(of a vehicle)*   le klaxon,
l'avertisseur *(m)* sonore   33e

horoscope l'horoscope *(m)* 5d

horse le cheval 15a

horsepower le cheval-vapeur 33e

horse racing les courses *(f)* de chevaux, la course au galop 27b

horseradish sauce la sauce au raifort 24j

horticulture l'horticulture *(f)* 14a

hospital l'hôpital *(m)* 39c

hot chaud(e) *(adj, m, f)* 6a, 6b, 24p

hot water l'eau *(f)* chaude 35c

hotel l'hôtel *(m)* 35a; **luxury hotel** l'hôtel de luxe 35a

hotel clerk l'employé *(m)*, l'employée *(f)* 35b

hour l'heure *(f)* 4c

hourly à l'heure 4c

house la maison 23a

House/Chamber of Representatives (Deputies) la Chambre des Députés 43

house number le numéro de la maison 11f

how comment *(adv)* 9

How are you? Comment allez-vous? *(pol)* 16a; Comment vas-tu? *(fam)* 16a

How come? Mais comment? 9

How do you feel? Comment vous sentez-vous? 40a

How do you get to . . .? Comment va-t-on à . . . ? 36c

How do you say . . . in French? Comment dit-on . . . en français? 17b

How do you spell your name? Comment s'écrit votre (ton) nom? 11f

How far away . . . ? À quelle distance . . . ? 36c

how much/many combien *(adv)* 3c, 9

How much do you weigh? Combien pesez-vous? 11a

How much does it come to? Ça fait combien? 25a

How much does it cost? Ça coûte combien? 25a

How much is it? C'est combien? 25a

How old are you? Quel âge avez-vous (as-tu)? 11b

How tall are you? Quelle taille avez-vous? 11a

How's it going? Comment ça va? Ça va? 16a

How's the weather? Quel temps fait-il? 6a

however pourtant *(conj)* 8p

howl hurler *(v)* 15a

hug l'embrassement *(m)*, l'étreinte *(f)* 19b

human humain(e) *(adj, m, f)* 11d, 15a

human being l'être *(m)*, l'être *(m)* humain 11d, 15a

humanitarian humanitaire *(adj)* 11e

humanities (arts) les lettres *(f, pl)* 37e

humanity l'humanité *(f)* 11d

humble humble *(adj)* 11e

humid humide *(adj)* 6a

humidity l'humidité *(f)* 6a

humility l'humilité *(f)* 11e

humor l'humour *(m)* 11e

hundredth centième 1b

hunger la faim 12b

hunter le chasseur, la chasseuse 15a

hunting la chasse 15a

hurricane l'ouragan *(m)* 6a

hurry se dépêcher *(v)* 39b

hurt avoir *(v)* mal, faire *(v)* mal à 40a

husband   le mari   10a, 11c;
l'époux   11c

hydrogen   l'hydrogène   *(m)*
13c

hyena   l'hyène   *(f)*   15a

hygiene   l'hygiène   *(f)*   12d

hygienic   hygiénique   *(adj, m, f)*
12d

hyphen   le tiret, le trait d'union
19c

hypothesis   l'hypothèse   *(f)*
22a

I

I   je   8h

I am . . . (+ name)   Je suis . . .
16b

I am looking for . . .   Je cherche
. . .   36c

I am . . . old   J'ai . . . ans   11b

I am . . . tall   J'ai la taille . . .
11a

I believe that . . .   Je crois que
. . .   44c

I can't stand him (her)!   Je ne
peux pas le (la) supporter!   21b

I can't stand the cold!   Je ne
supporte pas le froid!   6b

I can't stand the heat!   Je ne
supporte pas la chaleur!   6b

I don't believe it!   Je ne le crois
pas!   21c

I don't feel like . . .   Je n'ai pas
envie de . . .   21c

I don't know if . . .   Je ne sais
pas si . . .   44c

I don't understand.   Je ne
comprends pas.   9, 17b

I doubt that . . .   Je doute que
. . .   44c

I feel . . .   Je me sens . . .
40a

I have some of it (them).   J'en
ai.   3c

I live on . . . Street   Je demeure
rue . . .   11f

I love the cold!   J'aime le froid!
6b

I love the heat!   J'aime la
chaleur!   6b

I think that . . .   Je pense que . . .
44c

I was born in . . . (year)   Je suis
né(e)   *(m, f)* en . . .   5e

I was born on . . .   Je suis né(e)
le . . .   11c

I weigh . . .   Je pèse . . .   11a

I wish! (If only . . . !)   Si
seulement . . . !   21c

I would like to say that . . .   Je
voudrais dire que . . .   44c

ice   la glace   6a, 13b; **ice
chips** les glaçons   *(m, pl)*   24p

ice cream   la glace, la crème
glacée   24h; **cone**   le cornet
24h

ice hockey   le hockey sur glace
27b

ice skate   patiner   *(v)* sur glace
(f)   27b

iced bun   le gâteau américain
24i

icing, iced, glazed   glacé(e)
(adj, m, f)   24i

icosahedron   l'icosaèdre   *(m)*
2a

idea   l'idée   *(f)*   22a

idealism   l'idéalisme   *(m)*
11e

idealist, idealistic   idéaliste
(m, f)   11e

identification   l'identification
(f)   11f

identification card (papers)   la
carte d'identité   31, 35b

identify   identifier   *(v)*   17a

ideology   l'idéologie   *(f)*   43

if   si   *(conj)*   8p

ignorant   ignorant(e)   *(adj, m, f)*
22a

illegal   illégal(e)   *(adj, m, f)*
41

illustration   l'illustration   *(f)*
20a

I'm not sure that . . .   Je ne suis
pas sûr(e) que . . .   44c

I'm serious! Je suis sérieux *(adj, m)*, sérieuse *(adj, f)*! 21c

I'm sorry! Je regrette! 21c

I'm sure that . . . Je suis sûr(e) que . . . 17b, 44c

imaginary imaginaire *(adj, m, f)* 1d

imagination l'imagination *(f)* 11e, 22a

imaginative imaginatif, imaginative *(adj, m, f)* 11e

imagine imaginer *(v)* 22b

impatient impatient(e) *(adj, m, f)* 11e

imperative impératif *(adj, m)*, impérative *(adj, f)* 8a, 8n

imperfect imparfait(e) *(adj, m, f)* 8a

import importer *(v)* 31

Impossible! Pas possible! 21c

imprison emprisonner *(v)* 41

impudence l'impudence *(f)* 11e

impudent impudent(e) *(adj, m, f)* 11e

impulse l'impulsion *(f)* 11e

impulsive impulsif, impulsive *(adj, m, f)* 11e

in dans *(prep)* 3d, 8g

in an hour's time dans une heure 4e

in black and white en noir et blanc 25d

in conclusion en conclusion 44c

in front of devant *(adv/prep)* 3d, 36b

in love amoureux *(adj)* 11c

in my opinion à mon avis 22a, 44c

in my view à mon point de vue 44c

in order that afin que *(conj)*, pour que *(conj)* 8p

in the afternoon dans *(de)* l'après-midi *(m)* 4a

in the country(side) à la campagne 36b

in the evening dans le soir, du soir 4a

in the latest style/fashion à la mode, au dernier cri 25l

in the meantime entre-temps 4e

in the middle au centre, au milieu 3d

in the morning dans le matin 4a; du matin 4a

in the mountains dans les montagnes 36b

in time à temps *(m)* 4e

in two minutes' time dans deux minutes 4e

in vitro fertilization la fécondation in vitro 40a

incisor *(tooth)* la dent incisive 40b

income le revenu 26

increase l'augmentation *(f)* augmenter *(v)* 3c

indecisive indécis(e) *(adj, m, f)* 11e

indefinite indéfini(e) *(adj, m, f)* 8a, 8c

independent indépendant(e) *(adj, m, f)* 11e

index l'index *(m)* 20a

index finger l'index *(m)* 12a

India l'Inde *(f)* 30b

indicate indiquer *(v)* 17a

indication l'indication *(f)* 17a

indicative indicatif *(adj, m)*, indicative *(adj, f)* 8a

indifference l'indifférence *(f)* 21a

indifferent indifférent(e) *(adj, m, f)* 21a

indirect indirect(e) *(adj, m, f)* 8a, 8j

individualist individualiste
(adj) 11e
industrial industriel(le) *(adj, m, f)* 13c
industry l'industrie *(f)* 13c
inelegant inélégant(e) *(adj)* 11a
inexpensive à bon marché, économe *(adj, m, f)* 25a
infection l'infection *(f)* 40a
infinitive l'infinitif *(m)* 8a
inflation l'inflation *(f)* 43
inform informer *(v)*, faire savoir *(v)* 17a
informal restaurant le bistro (bistrot) 24m
information le renseignement 18b
information desk le bureau de renseignements 32a
infrared light la lumière infrarouge 13a
ingenious ingénieux, ingénieuse *(adj, m, f)* 11e
ingenuity l'ingénuité *(f)* 11e
ingenuous ingénu(e) *(adj, m, f)* 11e
inherit hériter *(v)* 11c
injection l'injection *(f)*, la piqûre 25h, 40a
injure blesser *(v)* 39b
injury la blessure, la plaie 39b, 39c
ink l'encre *(f)* 19d, 37b
innocence l'innocence *(f)* 11e, 41
innocent innocent(e) *(adj, m, f)* 11e, 41
inorganic inorganique *(adj, m, f)* 13c
insect l'insecte *(m)* 15d
inside dedans *(prep/adv)* 3d, 36c
insolence l'insolence *(f)* 11e

insolent insolent(e) *(adj, m, f)* 11e
instant l'instant *(m)* 4c
instrument l'instrument *(m)* 28c; **to play an instrument** jouer *(v)* de (du, de l', de la) 28c
insulation l'isolant *(m)* 25b
insulin l'insuline *(f)* 25h
insurance l'assurance *(f)* 26, 30a
insurance card la carte d'assurance 33b
integer le nombre entier 1d
integrated circuit le circuit intégré 42b
intelligence l'intelligence *(f)* 11e
intelligent intelligent(e) *(adj, m, f)* 11e
intercom l'interphone *(m)* 18a, 38c
interest l'intérêt *(m)* 26
interest rate le taux d'intérêt 26
interesting intéressant(e) *(adj, m, f)* 22a
interface *(computers)* l'interface *(f)* 42b
intermission l'entracte *(m)* 28e
interrogative interrogatif *(adj, m)*, interrogative *(f)* 8a
interrupt interrompre *(v)* 17a
interruption l'interruption *(f)* 17a
intersection le carrefour, le croisement 33c, 33d, 36a
interview l'interview *(f)* 20a, 20b; l'entrevue *(f)* 38b
intransitive intransitif *(adj, m)*, intransitive *(adj, f)* 8a
introduce someone présenter *(v)* quelqu'un 16b
introduction la présentation 16b

invertebrate invertébré(e) *(adj, m, f)* 15a

invest investir *(v)* 26

investment l'investissement *(m)* 26

invitation l'invitation *(f)*, le faire-part 19e

invite inviter *(v)* 17a

iodine l'iode *(m)* 13c

irascible irascible *(adj)* 11e

Ireland l'Irlande *(f)* 30b

Irish (*nationality*) Irlandais *(m)*, Irlandaise *(f)* 30d

iron (*metal*) le fer 13c; *(for ironing, pressing)* le fer à repasser 25g; repasser *(v)* 25g

ironical ironique *(adj)* 11e

irony l'ironie *(f)* 11e

irrational irrationnel(le) *(adj, m, f)* 1d

irregular irrégulier *(adj, m)*, irrégulière *(adj, f)* 8a

irritable irritable *(adj)* 11e

Is . . . (*name of person*) in? Est-ce que . . . est là? 18b

is equivalent to est équivalent à 1f

is greater than est supérieur à 1f

is less than est inférieur à 1f

is similar to est pareil à 1f

Islamic Islamique *(adj)* 11d

island l'île *(f)* 13b

Isn't it so? N'est-ce pas? 17b

isosceles isocèle *(adj)* 2a

Israel l'Israël *(m)* 30b

Israeli (*nationality*) Israélite *(m, f)* 30d

it (*subject pro*) il *(m, s)*, elle *(f, s)* 8h; *(direct obj pro)* le *(m)*, la *(f)* 8i

It costs an arm and a leg! Cela coûte les yeux de la téte! (*lit.*, It costs both eyes of your head!) 25a

It doesn't matter! Peu importe! 21c

It seems that . . . Il semble que . . . 17b, 44c

It's . . . C'est . . . 7a

It's a bit cold (*weather*). Il fait un peu froid. 6a

It's a bit hot (*weather*). Il fait un peu chaud. 6a

It's a quarter to three. Il est trois heures moins le quart. 4b; Il est deux heures quarante-cinq. 4b

It's awful (*weather*)! Il fait un temps affreux! 6a

It's beautiful (*weather*). Il fait beau temps. 6a

It's clear that . . . Il est clair que . . . , Il est évident que . . . 44c

It's cloudy. Il fait un temps couvert. 6a

It's cold (*weather*). Il fait froid. 6a

It's cool (*weather*). Il fait frais. 6a

It's dark (*weather*) today. Il fait sombre aujourd'hui. 6a

It's exactly three o'clock. Il est trois heures précises. 4b

It's five o'clock (AM). Il est cinq heures. 4b

It's five o'clock (PM). Il est dix-sept heures. 4b

It's foul weather. Il fait un temps pourri. 6a

It's four twenty-five. Il est quatre heures vingt-cinq. 4b

It's hot (*weather*). Il fait chaud. 6a

It's humid (*weather*). Il fait humide. 6a

It's January second. C'est le deux janvier. 5e

It's mild (*weather*). Il fait doux. 6a

It's Monday. C'est lundi *or* Nous sommes lundi. 5a

It's muggy *(weather).*   Il fait un temps lourd.   6a
It's my pleasure!   C'est mon plaisir!   16b
It's necessary that . . .   Il est nécessaire que . . . ; Il faut que . . .   17b
It's 2002.   C'est 2002   5e
It's not true.   Ce n'est pas vrai.   17b
It's obvious that . . .   Il est évident que . . .   17b
It's October first.   C'est le premier octobre.   5e
It's one o'clock.   Il est une heure.   4b
It's one ten.   Il est une heure dix.   4b
It's pleasant *(weather).*   Il fait un temps agréable.   6a
It's raining.   Il pleut.   6a
It's raining buckets.   Il pleut à seaux.   6a
It's rainy.   Il fait un temps pluvieux.   6a
It's snowing.   Il neige.   6a
It's sunny   Il fait (du) soleil.   6a
It's ten minutes to six.   Il est six heures moins dix.   4b
It's ten o'clock (AM).   Il est dix heures.   4b
It's ten o'clock (PM).   Il est vingt-deux heures.   4b
It's three fifteen.   Il est trois heures et quart.   4b
It's three o'clock.   Il est trois heures.   4b
It's three o'clock on the dot.   Il est trois heures juste (pile).   4b
It's three thirty.   Il est trois heures et demie.   4b
It's thundering!   Il tonne!   6a
It's true!   C'est vrai!   17b
It's two o'clock.   Il est deux heures.   4b

It's very cold *(weather).*   Il fait très froid.   6a
It's very good!   C'est très bon!   17b
It's very hot *(weather).*   Il fait très chaud.   6a
It's windy!   Il fait du vent!   6a
Italian *(nationality)*   Italien *(m)*, Italienne *(f)*   30d; *(language)* l'italien *(m)*   30d
italics   en italique *(m)*   19c
Italy   l'Italie *(f)*   30b
itch   la démangeaison   40a

J
jacket   la veste, le veston   25k
jail   la prison   4l
jam (preserves)   la confiture   24j
janitor   le nettoyeur, la nettoyeuse   37d
January   le janvier   5b
Japan   le Japon   30b
Japanese *(nationality)*   Japonais *(m)*, Japonaise *(f)*   30d; *(language)* le japonais   30d
jaw   la mâchoire   12a, 40b
jazz   le jazz   25j, 28c
jealous   jaloux, jalouse *(adj, m, f)*   11e
jelly   la gelée   24j
jelly roll   le roulé   24i
jest   plaisanter *(v)*   17a
jewel   le bijou   25i
jewelry store   la bijouterie, la joaillerie   25i
Jewish   Juif, Juive   11d
job   le travail   11f; le métier, l'occupation *(f)*   38a
jog   faire *(v)* du jogging *(m)*   27b
jogging   le jogging   27b
joke   la plaisanterie   17a
joker *(cards)*   le joker   27a
journalist   le (la) journaliste   20a, 38a

journey le voyage 30a
joy la joie 21a
judge le juge; juger *(v)* 41
judgment le jugement 22a
judo le judo 27b
juice le jus 24k
July le juillet 5b
June le juin 5b
junior high school l'école *(f)* d'enseignement de cours moyen 37a, 38b
Jupiter Jupiter *(m)* 13a
jury le jury 41
just now à l'instant *(m)* 4e
justice la justice 22a, 41

K

karate le karaté 27b
Keep quiet! Taisez-vous!/ Tais-toi! 21c
kettle la bouilloire 23d
key la clef 23d, 35b
keyboard le clavier 19d, 42b
keyboard instruments les instruments *(m/pl)* à clavier *(m)* 28c
keyboard operator le (la) claviste 42b
kick donner *(v)* un coup de pied 27b
kidney le rein 40a
kill tuer *(v)*, assassiner *(v)* 39b
killer le tueur, l'assassin *(m)* 39b
kilogram le kilogramme 3a
kilometer le kilomètre 3a
kind (person) gentil *(adj, m)*, gentille *(adj, f)* 11e
kindergarten le jardin d'enfants 37a
kindness la bonté 11e
king le roi 27a, 43
kiosk le kiosque à journaux 36a
kiss le baiser, la bise 11c, 19b; embrasser *(v)* 11c, 21b

kitchen la cuisine 23b
knapsack le sac à dos *(m)* 27b, 31, 36b
knee le genou 12a
knife le couteau 23d, 24l, 39b; **blade** la lame 23d; **handle** le manche 23d
knight (in chess) le cavalier 27a
know (a fact) savoir *(v)* 22b
know (be acquainted with) connaître 22b
know someone connaître quelqu'un 16b, 22b
knowledge la connaissance 22a
knowledgeable connaisseur *(adj, m)*, connaisseuse *(f)* 22a
Knucklehead! Tête de noeud! 12a
knuckles les jointures *(f)* des doigts *(m, pl)* 12a

L

label l'étiquette *(f)* 25a
labor/trade union le syndicat 43
laboratory le laboratoire 13c, 37c
lack manquer (à) *(v)* 25a
ladder l'échelle *(f)* 25b, 39a
ladle la louche 23d
lady la dame 11a
laity la laïcité 11d
lake le lac 13b, 36b
lamb l'agneau *(m)* 15a, 24c
lamp la lampe 23c, 35c
land la terre 13b; le terrain 13b; *(airplane)* atterrir *(v)* 32c
landing (airplane) l'atterrissage *(m)* 32c
landing gear (airplane) le train d'atterrissage 32c

landlord   le (la) propriétaire   23g

landscape   le paysage   13b

lane *(traffic)*   la piste   33c

language laboratory   le laboratoire de langues   37c

languages *(foreign)*   les langues *(f, pl)* étrangères   37e

laptop *(computer)*   le portable, le portatif   42b

large   grand(e) *(adj)*   3c, 11a; gros *(adj, m)*, grosse *(f)*   3c

large bill *(banknote, currency)*   le gros billet   26

laser   le laser   42a

last *(previous)*   dernier *(adj, m)*, dernière *(f)*, passé(e) *(adj)*   4e

last   durer *(v)*   4e

last a long time   durer *(v)* longtemps *(adv)*   4e

last a short time   durer *(v)* peu de temps   4e

last month   le mois dernier (passé)   4e

last night   cette nuit (actual night), hier soir (actual evening)   4a

last year   l'an *(m)* dernier *(m)*, l'année *(f)* dernière *(f)*   4e

late   tard *(adv)*, en retard *(adv)*   4e, 34; *(arrival/departure)* en retard   32b, 34

Latin America   l'Amérique *(f)* Latine   30b

latitude   la latitude   13e

laugh   rire *(v)*   11e, 21a

laugh halfheartedly, reluctantly   rire *(v)* jaune, rire *(v)* à contrecoeur   21a

laughter   le rire   11e, 21a

launch pad   la rampe de lancement   42a

laundry   la lessive, le linge   25g

lava   la lave   13b

law   les études *(f, pl)* de droit   37e; la loi   41

lawful   légal(e) *(adj, m, f)*   41

lawn   la pelouse   13b

lawnmower   la tondeuse   25b

lawsuit   la cause civile   41

lawyer   l'avocat *(m)*, l'avocate *(f)*   38a, 41; **trial lawyer** l'avoué *(m)*, la femme avoué   41

layer   la couche   13b

layperson   laïc, laïque *(adj, m, f)*   11d

laziness   la paresse   11e

lazy   paresseux, paresseuse *(adj, m, f)*   11e

lead   le plomb   13c

leaded gasoline   l'essence *(f)* plombée   33c

leaf   la feuille   14a

leaf through *(a book, magazine, etc.)*   feuilleter *(v)*   20a

leap year   l'année *(f)* bissextile   5b

learn   apprendre *(v)*   22b, 37f

learn by memory   apprendre *(v)* par coeur   37f

leather   le cuir   13c, 25l

leave   partir *(v)*, quitter *(v)*   3e, 34

lecture   la conférence; donner *(v)* une conférence   17a; faire une conférence   37f

left *(location)*   gauche *(adj)*   3d; **to the left** à gauche   3d, 33c

left wing *(politics)*   la gauche   43

leg   la jambe   12a

legal   légal(e) *(adj, m, f)*   41

legislation   la législation   43

lemon   le citron   14d, 24f

lemon tree   le citronnier   14c

length   la longueur   3a

lengthen *(clothing)* faire *(v)* allonger *(v)* 25m
lens *(camera)* l'objectif *(m)* 25d
lentil la lentille 14e
Leo *(sign of the zodiac)* le Lion 5d
leopard le léopard 15a
lesbian la lesbienne 44b
lesbianism le lesbianisme, le lesbisme 44b
less moins *(adv)* 3c
letter la lettre 8a, 19c, 19d
letter carrier le facteur (de lettres) 19e
letterhead le papier à en-tête 19d
lettuce la laitue 14e, 24e
level le niveau 3d; *(story, floor of a building)* l'étage *(m)* 35b
Level Crossing le Passage à niveau 33d
liar le menteur, la menteuse 17a
liberal libéral(e) *(adj)* 11e
liberal party *(politics)* le parti libéral 43
Libra la Balance 5d
librarian le (la) bibliothécaire 37d
library la bibliothèque 37c
license plate la plaque 33e
lid le couvercle 23d
lie *(falsehood)* le mensonge 17a; *(to tell a lie)* mentir *(v)* 17a
lie down se coucher *(v)* 3e
life la vie 11c
life imprisonment l'emprisonnement *(m)* à perpétuité 41
life sentence à la prison à vie 41
lifejacket le gilet de sauvetage 32c
lift lever *(v)* 3e

lift *(elevator)* l'ascenseur 23g
light *(color)* clair *(adj)* 7b
light *(weight)* léger, légère *(adj, m, f)* 3b, 11a, 13d, 31; la lumière 6a, 13a; *(power)* l'éclairage *(m)* 23e
light beam le rayon de lumière 42a
light blue le bleu clair 7a
light bulb l'ampoule *(f)* 25b, 25d
light music la musique légère 28c
light saber *(fencing)* le sabre d'escrime *(f)* 27b
light year l'année *(f)* lumière 13a
lighter *(cigar, cigarette)* le briquet 25e
lightning l'éclair *(m)* 6a
lights *(electric)* les lumières 35c
lights *(headlights of a vehicle)* les phares *(m, pl)*, les projecteurs *(m, pl)* 33e
like aimer *(v)* bien 11e, 21b
likeable *(person)* aimable *(adj, m, f)*, sympathique *(adj, m, f)* 11e
liking *(taste for)* le penchant 21b
lily le lis (lys) 14b
lima bean la fève 14e
line la ligne 2b, 19c; la queue 26
line of work le genre de travail *(m)* 11f
line up faire *(v)* la queue 15a, 26
link *(computer)* le lien 42b
lion le lion 15a
lip la lèvre 12a, 40b
lipstick le rouge (le fard) à lèvres 25f
liqueur la liqueur 24k

liquid   le liquide   13c
listen (to)   écouter *(v)*   12c, 17a, 20b, 37f
Listen!   Ecoutez! *(pol)*, Ecoute! *(fam)*   17b
liter   le litre   3a
literal   litéral(e) *(adj, m, f)*   17a
literary work   l'ouvrage *(m)*   28d
literature   la littérature   28d, 37e
litigate   faire *(v)* litige, faire cause   41
litigation   le litige   41
little *(size)*   petit(e) *(adj)*   3c, 11a; *(quantity)* peu *(adv)*   3c
little finger   le petit doigt   12a
live   vivre *(v)*   11c
live somewhere   demeurer *(v)*   11f; habiter *(v)*   23f
lively   vif, vive *(adj, m, f)*   7b, 11e
liver   le foie   24c
living room   le salon, la salle de séjour *(m)*   23b
loan   le prêt   26; **get a loan** obtenir *(v)* un prêt   26
lobby   le foyer   28a, 35b
lobster   le homard, la langouste   24d
local train   le train omnibus   34
locate   localiser *(v)*   13e; situer *(v)*   13e
located   se trouver *(v)*   13e
location   la localité   13e
logarithm   le logarithme   1f
logarithmic   logarithmique *(adj)*   1f
London   Londres   30c
long   long *(adj, m)*, longue *(f)*   3b, 37f
long-distance telephone call   l'appel *(m)* à l'extérieur *(m)*   18b

long loaf of bread   le pain long   24i
long stick of bread   la baguette, la flûte   24i
long-term   à long terme   4e
longitude   la longitude   13e
look (at)   regarder   12c, 20b
look for something (or someone)   chercher *(v)*   25a
look forward to   s'attendre à *(v)*   4e
loose *(clothing)*   ample *(adj, m, f)*, non-ajusté(e) *(adj, m, f)*, vague *(adj, m, f)*   25l
loose change   la monnaie   26
lose   perdre *(v)*   27b
lose weight   perdre *(v)* du poids   11a
loss   la perte   27b
lost and found   les objets *(m, pl)* perdus   32a
lotion   la lotion   25f
lots of   beaucoup (de) *(adv)*   3c
loudspeaker   le haut-parleur   20b
louse   le pou, les poux   15d
lovable   adorable *(adj, m, f)*   11e
love   l'amour *(m)*   11c, 11e, 21b; aimer *(v)*   11c, 11e, 21b
love affair   l'affaire *(f)* d'amour *(m)*, une liaison   10b
love and kisses   grosses bises *(f, pl)*   19b
lover   l'amant(e) *(m, f)*   10b
low season *(tourism)*   la basse saison   35b
low temperature   la température basse   6c
luggage   les bagages *(m, pl)*   31, 35b
lunar eclipse   l'éclipse *(f)* lunaire   13a
lunar module   le module lunaire   42a
lunch   le déjeuner   24a

lung le poumon 12a, 40a
Luxembourg le Luxembourg 30b
luxury hotel l'hôtel *(m)* de luxe 35a
lymphatic system le système lymphatique 40a

M

macaroon le macaron 24i
mackintosh (raincoat) l'imperméable *(m)* 25k
mad (crazy) fou, fol, folle *(adj)* 11e
madness la folie 11e
magazine le magazine, la revue 20a, 25o, 37f
maggot l'asticot *(m)* 15d
magistrate le magistrat 41
maid la bonne, la domestique 35b
mail le courrier, la poste 19e; mettre *(v)* une lettre à la poste 19e
mail delivery la distribution du courrier *(m)* 19e
mailbox la boîte à lettres *(f, pl)* 19e, 23a
mailman *see* **letter carrier**
main principal(e) *(adj, m, f)* 8a
main door la porte principale 35b
main floor le rez-de-chaussée 35b
main office la direction 37c
make faire *(v)* 18b, 23f
make a movie tourner *(v)* un film 28a
make a request faire *(v)* une demande 9
make a telephone call faire *(v)* un appel téléphonique 18b
make mistakes faire *(v)* des fautes 37f
make the bed faire *(v)* le lit 23f

make-up le fard 12d; le maquillage 12d, 25f
male le mâle 11a, 38b
malicious malicieux, malicieuse *(adj, m, f)* 11e
malign diffamer *(v)* 17a
malleable malléable *(adj, m, f)* 13d
mammal le mammifère 15a
man l'homme *(m)* 11a
management la gestion 37e
manager le directeur, la directrice 26, 35b, 38d; le gérant, la gérante 35b
mandarin orange la mandarine 14d, 24f
mandolin la mandoline 28c
manicure les soins *(m, pl)* esthétiques des mains *(f, pl)* 12d
Many thanks! Merci mille fois! Merci infiniment! 16c
map la carte 13e; **map of France** la carte de France 13e; la carte géographique 37b
maple tree l'érable *(m)* 14c
March le mars 5b
margin la marge 19c
marinated mariné(e) *(adj, m, f)* 24b
marital status l'état *(m)* civil 11c, 38b
mark (grade) la note 37f
marker (for writing) le marqueur, le crayon-feutre 19d, 25c
market le marché 24n, 38d
marmalade la confiture d'oranges 24j
marriage le mariage 11c
married marié(e) *(n/adj, m, f)* 11c, 38b
marry (someone) épouser *(v)*, se marier *(v)* avec 11c
Mars Mars *(m)* 13a
Marseilles Marseille 30c

mascara le mascara 12d; le fard pour les yeux 25f

masculine masculin(e) *(adj, m, f)* 8a, 11a

mask le masque 27b

masking tape le papier cache 25b

Mass la Messe 11d

mass la masse 3b

massage le massage 12d

masterpiece *(art)* le chef d'oeuvre 28b

master's degree la licence 37f

match *(sports)* le jeu, le match, la partie 27b

matches les allumettes *(f)* 25e

material le matériel 13c

mathematics les mathématiques *(f, pl)* 37e

matter la matière 13c; **to matter (be of importance)** importer *(v)* 21a

matrimony le mariage 11c

maximum le maximum 3b, 31; **maximum temperature** la température maximum 6c

May *(month)* le mai 5b

May I . . . ? Puis-je . . . ? 16c

May I come in? Puis-je entrer? 16c

May I help you? Vous désirez? Puis-je vous aider? 16c

me me 8i; moi 8l

meal le repas 24a

mean (nasty) méchant(e) *(adj, m, f)* 11e

mean (signify, have in mind) signifier *(v)*, vouloir dire *(v)* 17a

meaning la signification, le sens 17a

meanness la méchanceté 11e

measles la rougeole 40a

measure mesurer *(v)* 3b

measuring tape le mètre à ruban 3b

meat la viande 24c

mechanic le mécanicien, la mécanicienne 33c, 38a

mechanical mécanique *(adj, m, f)* 25b

medicine *(field of study)* la médecine 37e

medicine (medication) le médicament 25h, 40a

mediocre médiocre *(adj, m, f)* 21b

Mediterranean méditerranéen *(adj, m)*, méditerranéenne *(f)* 6a

medium moyen *(adj)* 3b

medium (average) height la taille moyenne 11a

medium *(cooked food)* à point 24b

meet rencontrer *(v)* 16b

Melba toast la biscotte 24i

melon le melon 14d

melted cheese le fromage fondu 24h

melting point le point de fusion *(f)* 6c

membrane la membrane 14a

memory la mémoire 42b

mend raccommoder *(v)* 25g

men's shop/clothing le magasin d'habillement masculin 25k

mention mentionner *(v)* 17a

menu la carte, le menu 24g

meow miauler *(v)* 15a

mercury le mercure 6c, 13c

Mercury Mercure *(m)* 13a

Merge Confluence 33d

meridian le méridien 13e

meringue la meringue 24i

Merry Christmas! Joyeux Noël! *(m)* 16c, 29c

message le message 18b, 35b

metal le métal   13c
metamorphosis la métamorphose   15d
metaphor la métaphore   17a
meteor le météore   13a
meteorite la météorite   13a
meter le mètre   3a
meter postage la vignette   19e
methane le méthane   13c
Mexico le Mexique   30b
microcomputer le micro-ordinateur   42b
microphone le microphone   20b
microprocessor (*computer*) le microprocesseur   42b
microscope le microscope   13c
microwave la micro-onde   42a
microwave oven le four à micro-ondes   (*f, pl*)   23d
middle finger le médius   12a
midnight le minuit   4a
Milan Milan   30c
mild (*weather*) doux   (*adj, m*), douce   (*adj, f*)   6a
mild (*temperature of liquid*) tiède   (*adj, m, f*)   24p
milk le lait   24h
millennium le millénaire   4c
millimeter le millimètre   3a
millionth millionième   1b
mime le (la) mime   28e
mind l'esprit   (*m*)   22a
mineral le minéral   13c
mineral water l'eau   (*f*) minérale   24k
minimum le minimum   3b;
  minimum temperature la température minimum   6c
miniskirt la minijupe   25k
minister le ministre, la femme ministre   11d, 43
mini-van la fourgonnette   33b
mint la menthe   14e, 24j

minus moins   (*adv*)   1e, 6c
minute la minute   4c
mirror le miroir   23c, 35c; la glace   35c
mischievous capricieux, capricieuse   (*adj, m, f*)   11e
miser avare   (*adj, m/f*)   11e
Miss Mademoiselle   11f, 16b
miss (*the train, etc.*) manquer   (*v*), rater   (*v*)   34
missile le missile   42a
mistake la faute   37f; **to make mistakes** faire   (*v*) des fautes   37f
modal modal(e)   (*adj, m, f*)   8a
model (*molecule*) le modèle   13c
modem (*computers*) le modem   42b
molar (*tooth*) la dent molaire   40b
mole la taupe   15a
molecular formula la formule moléculaire   13c
molecule la molécule   42a
mom la maman   10a
moment le moment   4c
monarchy la monarchie   43
Monday le lundi   5a
money l'argent   (*m*)   26
money order le mandat de paiement   (*m*)   19e, 26
monk le moine   11d
monkey le singe   15a
monorail vehicle le monorail   42a
month le mois   4c
month of the year le mois de l'année   5b
monthly mensuel   (*adj*), mensuellement   (*adv*)   4c, 5b
Montreal Montréal   30c
monument le monument   36a
mood (*grammar*) le mode   8a
mood (*feeling*) l'humeur   (*f*)   11e, 21a

moon la lune 5c, 6a, 13a

moonray/moonbeam le rayon de lune *(f)* 13a

morality la moralité 44b

more plus *(adv)* 3c

morning le matin 4a

mortgage l'hypothèque *(f)* 26

Moscow Moscou 30c

mosque la mosquée 11d

mosquito le moustique 15d

motel le motel 35a

moth la phalène 15d

mother la mère 10a

mother-in-law la belle-mère 10a

motion la motion 3e

motor le moteur 33e

motorcycle la motocyclette, la moto 33a

motorcycle driver le (la) motocycliste 33a

mountain la montagne 13b

mountain boot la chaussure d'escalade *(f)* 27b; la chaussure de montagne 36b

mountain chain la chaîne de montagnes *(f, pl)* 13b

mountain climbing l'alpinisme *(m)* 27b, 36b

mountainous montagneux, montagneuse *(adj, m, f)* 13b

mouse *(animal)* la souris 15a; *(computer)* la souris 42b

moustache la moustache 12a

mouth la bouche 12a, 40b

move bouger *(v)*, remuer *(v)* 3e

move oneself bouger *(v)*, se déplacer *(v)* 3e

move *(out of a house)* déménager *(v)* 23f

movement le mouvement 3e

movie *(film, motion picture)* le film 28a

movie camera la caméra, l'appareil *(m)* cinématographique 25d

movie director le réalisateur, la réalisatrice, le metteur en scène, la femme metteur en scène 28a, 38a

movies *(cinema)* le cinéma, le ciné 28a

Mr. M., Monsieur 11f, 16b

Mrs. Mme, Madame 11f, 16b

Ms. Mlle, Mademoiselle 11f, 16b

much beaucoup *(adv)* 3c

muffler *(of a vehicle)* le pot d'échappement 33e

mugginess *(weather)* la lourdeur 6a

muggy *(weather)* lourd *(adj, m)*, lourde *(adj, f)* 6a

mule le mulet 15a

multiple le multiple 1f

multiplication la multiplication 1e

multiplication table la table de multiplication *(f)* 1e

multiplied by multiplié par 1e

multiply multiplier *(v)* 1e

mumble grommeler *(v)* 17a

murder le meurtre, l'homicide 39b; assassiner *(v)* 39b

murmur murmurer *(v)* 17a

muscle le muscle 12a, 40a

museum le musée 36a

mushroom le champignon 14e, 24e

music la musique 25j, 28c, 37e

musician le musicien, la musicienne 28c, 38a

Muslim Musulman(e) *(m, f)* 11d

mussels les moules *(f, pl)* 24d

mute *(person)*   muet, muette
   (adj, m, f)   12c
my   mon *(m, s)*, ma *(f, s)*,
   mes *(m/f, pl)*   8f
My God!   Mon Dieu!   21c
My name is . . .   Mon nom est
   . . .   11f; Je m'appelle . . .
   16b; **I am . . .**   Je suis . . .
   16b
My tooth hurts!   Une dent me
   fait mal!   40b
myself *(reflexive)*   me   8k
mystery novel   le roman policier
   20a, 25o
myth   le mythe   11d, 28d
mythology   la mythologie   28d

N

nag (torment, pester)   grogner
   (v)   17a
nail *(hardware)*   le clou   25b
nail polish   le vernis à ongles
   (m, f)   12d, 25f
naive   naïf, naïve *(adj, m, f)*
   11e
name   le nom   11f, 38b
napkin   la serviette   23d, 24l
Naples   Naples   30c
napoleon *(pastry)*   le millefeuille
   24i
narrow   étroit *(adj, m)*, étroite
   (f)   3b
nation   la nation   13e, 30a
national   national(e) *(adj, m, f)*
   13e
National Assembly   l'Assemblée
   (f) Nationale   43
nationality   la nationalité
   11f, 38b
natural   naturel(le) *(adj, m, f)*
   1d, 13b
natural gas   le gaz naturel
   13c
natural resources   les ressources
   (f) naturelles   13c, 44a
natural sciences   les sciences
   (f, pl) naturelles   37e

nature   la nature   13b
near   près (de) *(adv)*   3d,
   36c
nearly   presque *(adv)*   3c
neat   ordonné(e) *(adj, m, f)*
   11e
neck   le cou   12a; **stiff
   (twisted) neck**   le torticolis
   40a; **sore neck**   le mal au cou
   40a
necklace   le collier   25i
necktie   la cravate   25k
need   le besoin; avoir *(v)*
   besoin de   21a
needle   l'aiguille *(f)*   40b
negative   négatif; négative *(adj,
   m, f)*   1d, 8n
neigh   hennir *(v)*   15a
neon   au néon   25b
nephew   le neveu   10a
Neptune   Neptune *(m)*   13a
nerves   les nerfs *(m, pl)*
   40a
nervous system   le réseau de
   nerfs, le système nerveux   40a
net *(sports)*   le but   27b
network   le réseau   20b
neutron   le neutron   13c,
   42a
never   jamais *(adv)*   4e
nevertheless   néanmoins   9p
new moon   la nouvelle lune
   13a
New Year   le Nouvel An   5f
New Year's Day   le Jour de l'An
   5f, 29a
New Year's Eve   la Nuit de la
   Saint-Sylvestre   5f, 29a
New Zealand   la Nouvelle-
   Zélande   30b
newlyweds   les nouveaux-mariés
   (m, pl)   11c
news   les actualités   20a
news report   les nouvelles, les
   actualités   20b
newscast *(on radio)*   le journal
   parlé   20b; *(on television)* le
   journal télévisé   20b

newspaper le journal 20a, 25o

newsstand le kiosque à journaux 34

next to à côté (de) *(prep)* 3d

nice *(person)* sympathique *(adj, m, f)* 11e

niece la nièce 10a

night la nuit 4a

nightingale le rossignol 15b

nine neuf 1a

nineteen dix-neuf 1a

ninety quatre-vingt-dix 1a

ninety-one quatre-vingt-onze 1a

ninth neuvième 1b

nitrogen l'azote *(m)*, le nitrogène 13c

No! Non! 16c

No Entry Défense d'entrer 33d

No Left Turn Virage à gauche interdit 33d

no one personne 3c, 8o

No Parking Stationnement interdit 33d

No Passing Interdiction de dépasser 33d

No Problem! Pas de problème! 22a

No Right Turn Virage à droite interdit 33d

No Smoking Défense de fumer 32a

No Stopping Arrêt interdit 33d

No Thoroughfare Circulation interdite 33d

No U-Turn Demi-tour interdit 33d

No way! Pas de moyen! Pas possible! Pas question! 17b, 20b

noise le bruit 12c

noisy bruyant(e) *(adj, m, f)* 12c

nonconformist le (la) non-conformiste 11e

nonfiction l'ouvrage *(m)* de réalité 20a

nonsmoking compartment non-fumeurs 34

noon le midi 4a

north le nord 3d; **to the north** au nord 3d

North America l'Amérique *(f)* du Nord 30b

North Pole le Pôle Nord 13e

northern septentrional(e) *(adj)* 3d

Norway la Norvège 30b

Norwegian *(nationality)* Norvégien *(m)*, Norvégienne *(f)* 30d; *(language)* le norvégien 30d

nose le nez 12a

nostril la narine 12a, 40a

Not bad! Pas mal! *(adv)* 16a

not guilty non coupable 41

not nice antipathique *(adj, m, f)* 11e

note la note 37f; **to take notes** prendre *(v)* des notes 37f

note *(communication)* le billet 19e, 20a; *(music)* la note 28c

note pad le bloc-notes 25c

notebook le cahier 37b

nothing rien *(adv/pro)*, nul *(adj/pro, m)*, nulle *(f)* 3c

nothing to declare rien à déclarer 31

noun le nom 8a

novel le roman 20a, 25o, 28d

November le novembre 5b

now maintenant *(adv)* 4e, 17b; à présent 4e

nowadays de nos jours 4e

nowhere nulle part *(adv)* 3d

n-sided figures   les figures *(f)* à côtés n   2a
nth root   à la racine n   1e
nuclear energy   l'énergie *(f)* nucléaire   13c, 42a
nuclear fuel   le combustible nucléaire   42a
nuclear industry   l'industrie *(f)* nucléaire   42a
nuclear reactor   le réacteur nucléaire   42a
nuclear war   la guerre nucléaire   44b
nuclear weapon   l'arme *(f)* nucléaire   44b
nucleus   le noyau   13c, 14a
number   le nombre   1d, 8a; le numéro   1d, 38b; numéroter *(v)*   1d
numeral   le numéral   1d
numerical   numérique *(adj)*   1d
nun   la religieuse   11d
nurse   l'infirmier *(m)*, l'infirmière *(f)*   38a, 40a
nursery school   l'école *(f)* maternelle   37a
nylon   le nylon   251

O

oak tree   le chêne   14c
oat   l'avoine *(f)*   24i
obesity   l'obésité *(f)*   11a
obituary   la notice nécrologique, la nécrologie   20a
object *(grammar)*   le complément d'objet *(m)*   8a, 8i, 8j, 8l
oboe   le hautbois   28c
obstinate   obstiné(e) *(adj, m, f)*   11e
obtuse   obtus *(adj)*   2b
obtuse-angled   obtusangle *(adj)*   2a
occasionally   de temps en temps *(adv)*   4e
occupation   l'occupation *(f)*   38a

occur   arriver *(v)*, se produire *(v)*   4e
ocean   l'océan *(m)*   13b
octagon   l'octogone *(m)*   2a
octahedron   l'octaèdre *(m)*   2a
October   l'octobre *(m)*   5b
octopus   la pieuvre, le poulpe   15c
odd   impair *(adj, m)*   1d
odious   antipathique *(adj, m, f)*   11e
of   de   8g
of it   en *(pron)*   3c, 8o
of the day   du jour   24g
of them   en *(pron)*   8o
offend   offenser *(v)*   17a
office   le bureau   38d
office automation   l'automatisation *(f)* de bureau   42b
office hours   les heures *(f, pl)* de bureau   40b
often   souvent *(adv)*   4e
Oh, my!   Oh! là! là!   21c
oil   l'huile *(f)*   13c, 24j, 33e
oil filter   le filtre à huile   33e
ointment   la pommade   25h
OK!   D'accord! Entendu!   16c
old   vieux *(m)*, vieille *(f)*   11b
old age   la vieillesse   11b
older brother   le frère aîné   11b
older sister   la soeur aînée   11b
olive   l'olive *(f)*   14d, 24e
olive tree   l'olivier *(m)*   14c
omelette   l'omelette *(f)*   24h; **with cheese**   au fromage; **with ham**   au jambon; **with whipped cream**   mousseline   24h
on   sur *(prep)*   3d, 8g
On guard! *(fencing)*   En garde! *(f)*   27b
on Mondays   le lundi   5a

on sale   en vente   *(f)*   25a
on Saturdays   le samedi   5a
on Sundays   le dimanche
5a
on the air *(radio and television)*
en émission   20b
on the dot *(telling time)*   juste
(pile)   4b
on time   à l'heure   32b, 34
on vacation   en vacances   *(f, pl)*
36b
once   une fois   4e
once in a while   de temps à autre
4e
once upon a time   il était une
fois   4a, 4e
one   un   *(m)*, une   *(f)* la; on
8h, 8o
one billion   un milliard   1a
one-fifth   un cinquième   1c
one-fourth   un quart   1c
one-half   un demi   1c
one hundred   cent la;   **about
one hundred**   une centaine
1c
one hundred and one   cent un
1a
one hundred million   cent
millions   1a
one hundred thousand   cent
mille   1a
one million   un million   1a
one million and one   un million
un   1a
one-third   un tiers   1c
one thousand   mille la;   **about a
thousand**   un millier   1c
one thousand and one   mille un
1a
one turn (360°)   le tour   2b
oneself   (reflexive pron) se
8k; soi   8l
One-Way Street   Sens Unique
33d
one-way ticket   le billet simple
30a
onion   l'oignon   *(m)*   14e,
24e

onion soup   la soupe à l'oignon
24g
only   seulement   *(adv)*   4e
opal   l'opale   *(f)*   25i
opaque   opaque   7b, 13d
open   ouvert(e)   *(adj, m, f)*
25a
open an account   ouvrir   *(v)* un
compte   26
Open your mouth!   Ouvrez la
bouche!   40b
opening hours *(store)*   les heures
d'ouverture   25a
opera   l'opéra   *(m)*   28c
operating room   la salle de
chirurgie   40a
operation *(surgery)*
l'intervention   *(f)* chirurgicale
40a
operator *(telephone)*   le (la)
téléphoniste   18b
opinion   l'opinion   *(f)*   22a;
in my opinion   à mon opinion
22a
opposite   opposé(e)   *(adj, m, f)*
2b
optic fiber   la fibre optique   18a
optical reader   le lecteur optique
42b
optician   l'opticien, l'opticienne
40a
optimism   l'optimisme   *(m)*
11e
optimist   l'optimiste   *(m, f)*
11e
optimistic   optimiste   *(adj, m, f)*
11e
or   ou   *(conj)*   8p
oral   oral(e)   *(adj, m, f)*   17a
oral exam   l'examen   *(m)* oral
37f
orally   oralement   *(adv)*   17a
orange   l'orange   *(f)*   14d,
24f
orange *(color)*   l'orangé   *(m)*
7a
orange tree   l'oranger   *(m)*
14c

orbit l'orbite *(f)* 13a; être *(v)* en orbite, mettre *(v)* en orbite, placer *(v)* sur orbite 13a

orchestra l'orchestre *(m)* 28c

orchestra conductor le chef d'orchestre *(m)* 28c

orchid l'orchidée *(f)* 14b

order l'ordre *(m)*, ordonner *(v)* 17a; *(food)* commander *(v)* 17a, 24o

ordinal ordinal(e) *(adj, m, f)* 1b, 1d

organ *(music)* l'orgue *(m)* 28c

organic organique *(adj, m, f)* 13c

organism l'organisme *(m)* 14a, 15d

oriental oriental(e) *(m, f)* 11d

original original(e) *(adj, m, f)* 11e

Orthodox Orthodoxe *(m, f)* 11d

ostrich l'autruche *(f)* 15b

others autrui *(indef pron)*, les autres 8o

our notre *(m/f, s)*, nos *(m/f, pl)* 8f

ourselves *(reflexive pron)* nous 8k

out dehors *(adv)* 39a

out of focus *(photo)* la photo floue 25d

outlet la prise 18a, 25b

outside dehors *(adv)* 3d, 36c

outskirts *(suburbs)* la banlieue, les environs *(m, pl)* 30a

outspokenly carrément *(adv)*, franchement *(adv)* 17a

oven le four 23d; microwave oven le four à micro-ondes *(f, pl)* 23d

overhead projector le rétroprojecteur 37b

owl la chouette, le hibou 15b

ownership papers les documents *(m)* de propriété 33c

ox le boeuf, les boeufs 15a

oxygen l'oxygène *(m)* 13c

oyster l'huître *(f)* 24d

P

Pacific Pacifique *(adj, m, f)* 13b

pack (one's bags/luggage) faire *(v)* les bagages 31

package le colis, le paquet 19e, 25a

pad le bloc-notes 19d

pagan païen, païenne *(n/adj, m, f)* 11d

page la page 19d, 20a

pager le pager 18a

pail le seau 23d

pain la douleur 40a

painful douloureux *(adj, m)*, douloureuse *(adj, f)* 40a

paint peindre *(v)* 7c, 23f, 28b

painter le peintre, la femme peintre 7c, 38a; l'artiste-peintre *(m/f)* 28b, 38a

painting (picture) le tableau 23c; la peinture 28b

pair la paire 3c, 25n

pajamas le pyjama 25k

palate le palais 40b

pale pâle *(adj)* 7b

palette la palette 28b

palm tree le palmier 14c

pamphlet le dépliant, la brochure 20a

pan la casserole, la sauteuse 23d

pancake la crêpe 24g

pantomime la pantomime 28e

pants (slacks) le pantalon 25k

paper le papier 19d, 25c, 37b

paper clip le trombone 19d
paper shredder le déchiqueteur 38c
paragraph le paragraphe 19c
parakeet la perruche 15b
parallel line la ligne parallèle 2b
parallelogram le parallélogramme 2a
parenthesis la parenthèse 19c
parents les parents *(m)* 10a
Paris Paris 30c
park *(a vehicle)* stationner *(v)* 33c
park le parc 36a; **park bench** le banc 36a
parking le stationnement 33c
parking meter le parcmètre 36a
Parliament le Parlement 43
parrot le perroquet 15b
parsley le persil 14e, 24j
part la part, la partie 3c
participle le participe 8a
particle la particule 13c
partitive le partitif 8a, 8d
party la fête 29b
pass passer *(v)* 27b
pass a sentence (judgment) prononcer *(v)* un jugement 41
pass a vehicle dépasser *(v)* 33c
pass an exam être *(v)* reçu(e) à un examen 37f
pass by passer *(v)* 3e
passenger le passager, la passagère 32c, 33b
passenger van le fourgon automobile 33a
Passing Lane Piste pour dépasser 33d
passive passif *(adj, m)*, passive *(adj, f)* 8a

Passover la Pâque 5f, 29a
passport le passeport 31, 35b
passport control le contrôle de passeports 31
past le passé 4e; passé(e) *(adj, m, f)* 8a
past *(grammar)* le passé composé 8a, 8n
past definite *(grammar)* le passé simple 8a
past participle le participe passé 8a
pasta les pâtes *(f, pl)* 24g
pastel le pastel 28b
pastries les pâtisseries *(f, pl)* 24i
pastry shop la pâtisserie 24n
patience la patience 11e, 21a; **to have patience** avoir *(v)* de la patience 21a
patient patient(e) *(adj, m, f)* 11e
paw la patte 15a
pawn *(in chess)* le pion 27a
pay payer *(v)* 25a, 26, 35b
pay customs/duty payer *(v)* les droits de douane 31
pay off acquitter *(v)* 26
pay phone le téléphone public 18a
pay through the nose payer *(v)* un oeil 12a
payment le paiement 26
peace la paix 43
peach la pêche 14d, 24f
peach pie la tarte aux pêches 24g
peach tree le pêcher 14c
peak le sommet 13b
peak season *(tourism)* la haute saison 35b
peanut l'arachide *(f)*, la cacahouète 24f
pear la poire 14d
pear tree le poirier 14c
pearl la perle 25i

peas   les (petits) pois *(m)*
14e, 24e

pedal   la pédale 33a

pedestrian   le piéton, la piétonne
33b

pedestrian crossing   le passage
pour piétons, le passage piétonnier,
le passage clouté 33c, 36a

peel   éplucher *(v)* 24o

Peking/Beijing   Pékin/Béjing
30c

pelican   le pélican 15b

pen   le stylo 2b, 7c, 19d,
25c, 37b, 38c

penalty *(sports)*   la pénalité
27f

pencil   le crayon 2b, 19d,
25c, 37b, 38c

penguin   le pingouin 15b

penicillin   la pénicilline 25h

peninsula   la péninsule, la
presqu'île 13b

penis   le pénis 12a

pension (retirement)   la retraite,
la pension 38d

pentagon   le pentagone 2a

people   les gens *(m & f, pl)*
11d; *(of a nation)* le peuple
43

pepper   le poivre 24j

per hour   à l'heure *(f)* 3a

per minute   à la minute 3a

per second   à la seconde 3a

perceive   percevoir *(v)*,
apercevoir *(v)* 12c

percent   pour cent 1f

percentage   le pourcentage
1f

perception   la perception 12c

percussion instruments   les
instruments *(m, pl)* à percussion
(f) 28c

perfect   parfait(e) *(adj, m, f)*
8a

perfection   la perfection 11e

perfectionist   perfectionniste
(m, f) 11e

perfume   le parfum 12d, 25f

perfume/cosmetics shop   1a
parfumerie 25f

period *(punctuation)*   le point
19c

periodical *(weekly)*
hebdomadaire *(adj/n, m, f)*
20a

peripherals   les périphériques
(m, pl) 42b

permanent (wave)   la
permanente 12d

perpendicular line   la ligne
perpendiculaire 2b

person   la personne 8a, 11d

personal   personnel(le) *(adj, m,
f)* 8a

personal computer   l'ordinatuer
(m) personnel 42b

personality   la personnalité
11e

perspire   transpirer *(v)* 6b

persuade   persuader *(v)*
22b, 41

pessimism   le pessimisme
11e

pessimist   le (la) pessimiste
11e

pessimistic   pessimiste *(adj, m,
f)* 11e

pet   l'animal *(m)* favori
(domestiqué) 15a

petal   le pétale 14b

petrol *see* **gasoline**

petroleum   le pétrole 13c,
44a

petunia   le pétunia 14b

pharmaceutical drug   1e
remède, le médicament 25h

pharmacist   le pharmacien, la
pharmacienne 25h, 38a

pharmacy   la pharmacie 25h

Ph.D. Dr.,   le docteur, la
doctoresse 16b

philosophy   la philosophie
37e

phone (to telephone)   téléphoner
(v) 18b

phone bill   la facture 18b

phone book l'annuaire (m) du téléphone, le bottin 18a

phone booth la cabine téléphonique 18a

phone call l'appel (m) téléphonique 18b

phone line la ligne téléphonique 18b

phone number le numéro de téléphone 11f, 18b

phone *see also* **telephone**

phonetics la phonétique 8a

photo la photo(graphie) 20a, 25d

photocopier le photocopieur 38c

photosynthesis la photosynthèse 14a

phrase la phrase 19c

physical physique (adj, m, f) 13c

physics la physique 13c, 37e

physiology la physiologie 37e

physique (*appearance*) l'aspect (m) physique 11a

pianist le (la) pianiste 28c

piano le piano 28c

pick (*hardware*) le pic, la pioche 25b

pick flowers cueillir (v) des fleurs 14b

pick up the phone décrocher (v) 18b

pickup truck la camionnette 33a

pickpocket le pickpocket, le voleur (la voleuse) à la tire 39b

picky (*person*) tatillon, tatillonne (adj, m, f), difficile (adj, m, f) 11e

picnic le pique-nique 29a

picture (*photo*) la photo(graphie) 20a, 25d

pie la tarte 24g

piece la pièce 3c

piece of furniture le meuble 23c

piece of luggage la valise 31

pig le cochon 15a

pigeon le pigeon 15b

pill la pilule 25h, 40a

pillow l'oreiller 23d, 35c

pillowcase la taie d'oreiller 23d

pilot le (la) pilote 38a

pimple le bouton 40a

pine tree le pin 14c

pineapple l'ananas (m) 14d, 24f

pink la rose 7a; **to see life through rose-colored glasses** voir (v) la vie en rose 7a

pipe (*smoking*) la pipe 25e

Pisces les Poissons (m) 5d

piston le piston 33e

pitcher (*sports*) le lanceur 27b

pizza parlor la pizzeria 24m

place l'endroit (m) 3d; le lieu 3d, 19c

place of birth le lieu de naissance (f) 11f, 38b

place of employment le lieu d'emploi (m) 11f

plain (*terrain*) la plaine 13b

plane (*hardware*) le rabot 25b

plane figures les figures (f) planes 2a

planet la planète 13a

plant la plante, planter (v) 14a

plastic le plastique (adj, m, f) 13c

plate (dish) l'assiette (f) 23d, 241

platinum le platine 13c

play jouer (v) 27a; le jeu 27b

play (*theater*) la pièce de théâtre 20a, 28e

play a musical instrument jouer (v) de (du, de l', de la) 28c

play a record   passer *(v)* un disque   20b

play cards   jouer *(v)* aux cartes *(f, pl)*   27a

play hooky   faire *(v)* l'école buissonnière   37f

player   le joueur, la joueuse   27b, 28c

playwright   le (la) dramaturge, l'auteur *(m)* dramatique, la femme auteur dramatique   28e

plea   la plaidoirie   41

plea for mercy   la supplication pour clémence   41

plead   plaider *(v)*   41

pleasant (*person*)   aimable *(adj, m, f)*   11e; sympathique *(adj, m, f)*   11e; agréable *(adj, m, f)*   21b

Please!   S'il vous plaît! *(pol)*, S'il te plaît! *(fam)*   16c

Please accept . . . (*in a business letter*)   Veuillez accepter, Veuillez agréer . . .   19a

Please give my regards/greetings to . . .   Mon bon souvenir à . . .   16a

pleasure   plaisir *(m)*   16b; **The pleasure is mine!**   C'est mon plaisir!   16b

pliers   les pinces *(f, pl)*, les tenailles *(f, pl)*   25b

plot (*of a novel*)   l'intrigue *(f)*   20a, 28d, 28e

plug (*hardware*)   la fiche de prise de courant   25b

plug (*telephone*)   la fiche téléphonique   18a

plum   la prune   14d, 24f

plumber   le plombier   38a

plumbing   la plomberie   25b

pluperfect (*grammar*)   le plus-que-parfait   8a

plural   le pluriel, pluriel(le) *(adj, m, f)*   8a

plus   plus *(adv)* le, 6c; et *(conj)*   1e

Pluto   Pluton *(m)*   13a

pneumonia   la pneumonie   40a

poached egg   l'oeuf *(m)* poché   24h

pocket   la poche   25g; **billiard table pocket**   le trou   27a

pocket book/paperback   le livre de poche   20a

pocket knife   le couteau pliant, le couteau de poche   39b

poem   le poème   20a

poet   le poète, la femme poète   28d

poetry   la poésie   20a, 25o, 28d

point   le point   2b; *(sports)* la marque   27b

point out   indiquer *(v)*   17a

Poland   la Pologne   30b

pole   le pôle   13e; **North Pole**   le Pôle Nord; **South Pole**   le Pôle Sud   13e

police   la police   33b, 39b, 39c

police station   le commissariat de police   41

policeman   l'agent *(m)* de police, le policier   33b, 38a, 39b

policewoman   la femme policier   33b, 38a, 39b

policy (*politics*)   la politique   43

Polish (*nationality*)   Polonais *(m)*, Polonaise *(f)*   30d; *(language)* le polonais   30d

political party   le parti politique   43

political power   le pouvoir politique   43

political science   la science politique, la science po   37e

politician   l'homme *(m)* politique, la femme politique   43

politics   la politique   43

pollen   le pollen   14a

pollution la pollution 13c, 44a

polyester le polyester 251

polyhedron le polyèdre 2a

pony le poney 15a

pool *(swimming)* la piscine 27b, 35b

poor pauvre *(adj, m, f)* 11e

Poor man! Pauvre homme! 21c

Poor woman! Pauvre femme! 21c

poplar tree le peuplier 14c

poppy le pavot, le coquelicot 14b

porch le porche, la véranda 23a

pork le porc 24c

pornography la pornographie 44b

portable phone le téléphone portatif 18a

portable radio la radio portative 20b

porter le porteur 32a, 34, 35b

portion le morceau, la portion 3c

portrait le portrait 28b

Portugal le Portugal 30b

Portuguese *(nationality)* Portugais *(m)*, Portugaise *(f)* 30d; *(language)* le portugais 30d

position la position 3d

positive positif, positive *(adj, m, f)* 1d

possessive possessif, possessive *(adj, m, f)* 8a, 8f, 8n, 11e

post office le bureau de poste 19e

post office box la case postale, la boîte postale 19e

postage l'affranchissement *(m)* 19e; **meter postage** la vignette 19e

postage stamp le timbre-poste 19e

postal code le code postal 19e, 38b

postal rate le tarif 19e

postcard la carte postale 19e

postdate postdater *(v)* 26

posterior postérieur(e) *(adj)* 4e

postman *see* **letter carrier**

pot *(cooking)* le faitout, la marmite 23d

potato la pomme de terre 14e, 24e

potato salad la salade de pommes de terre 24e

poultry la volaille 24c

pour verser *(v)* 24o

powder la poudre 25f, 25h

power brake le servofrein 33e

power steering la servodirection 33e

power window la vitre à commande automatique 33e

practice a sport faire *(v)* du sport *(m)* 27b

praise louer *(v)* 17a

prawn la langoustine 24d

pray prier *(v)* 11d, 17a

prayer la prière 11d, 17a

preach prêcher *(v)* 17a

precious précieux *(adj, m)*, précieuse *(adj, f)* 25i

predicate le prédicat *(m)* 8a

predicate adjective l'attribut *(m)* 8a

preface la préface 28d

prefer préférer *(v)* 21b

pregnancy la grossesse 11c

pregnant enceinte *(adj, f)* 11c, 40a

premier showing la première représentation 28a

preposition la préposition 8a, 8g, 8l

prescription l'ordonnance *(f)* 25h, 40a

present le présent 4e; présent(e) *(adj, m, f)* 4e, 8a, 8n, 37f; actuel(le) *(adj, m, f)* 4e

present participle le participe présent 8a

presently actuellement *(adv)* 4e

president of a university le recteur, la femme recteur 37d

President of the French Republic le (la) Président(e) de la République Française 43

presumptuous présomptueux, présomptueuse *(adj, m, f)* 11e

pretentious prétentieux, prétentieuse *(adj, m, f)* 11e

pretzel le bretzel 24i

previous précédent(e) *(adj, m, f)* 4e

previously précédemment *(adv)* auparavant *(adv)* 4e

price le prix 24m, 25a; **rate** le tarif 35b

price tag l'étiquette *(f)* 25a

priest le prêtre 11d

primate le primate 15a

prime le nombre premier 1d

prime meridian le méridien origine 13e

prime minister le premier ministre 43

prime number le nombre premier 1d

prince le prince 43

princess la princesse 43

principal le directeur, la directrice 37d

print imprimer *(v)* 20a

Print your name Ecrivez votre nom (Ecris ton nom) en caractères d'imprimerie 11f

printed matter les imprimés *(m, pl)* 19e

printer *(computer)* l'imprimante *(f)* d'ordinateur 42b

printing la typographie 20a

printing edition (in publishing) le tirage 20a

prism le prisme 2a

prison la prison 41

prison sentence à prison 41

private school l'école *(f)* privée 37a

privilege le droit 41

problem le problème 1f, 22a, 37f

problem to solve le problème à résoudre *(v)* 1f, 37f

produce market le marché aux légumes et fruits 24n

product le produit 1f

production *(theater)* la mise en scène 28e

Prof. le Prof., le professeur, la femme professeur 11f

profession la profession 11f, 27b, 38a, 38b

professional professionnel(le) *(adj, m, f)* 11f, 38a

professor le professeur, la femme professeur 11f, 37d, 38a

professor's office le cabinet du professeur 37c

program le programme, l'émission *(f)* 20b, 28e

program *(computer)* le programme d'un ordinateur 42b

programmer *(person)* le programmeur, la programmeuse 38a, 42b; *(machine)* le programmateur 42b

programming *(computer)* la programmation 42b

projector le projecteur 20b

promise la promesse, promettre *(v)* 17a

promissory note le billet à ordre 26

promoted reçu(e) *(adj, m, f)* 37f

pronoun   le pronom   8a, 8h–8o
pronounce   prononcer   *(v)*   17a
pronunciation   la prononciation   8a, 17a
proofreader   correcteur   *(m)*   20a
propose   proposer   *(v)*   17a
prostitution   la prostitution   44b
protect   protéger   *(v)*   39a
protest   la protestation   43
Protestant   Protestant(e)   *(m, f)*   11d
Protestantism   le Protestantisme   11d
proton   le proton   13c, 42a
protractor   le goniomètre   2b
proud   fier, fière   *(adj, m, f)*   11e
provided that   pourvu que   *(conj)*   8p
province   la province   13e
prudent   prudent(e)   *(adj, m, f)*   11e
prune   le pruneau   14d, 24f
P. S.   P.-S., le post-scriptum   19c
psychiatrist   le (la) psychiatre   38a
psychologist   le (la) psychologue   38a
psychology   la psychologie   37e
public garden   le jardin public   36a
public notices   les affiches   *(f, pl)* publiques   36a
public parking   le stationnement public   33c
public phone   le téléphone public   36a
public prosecutor   le procureur de la République   41
public washrooms   les toilettes   *(f, pl)* publiques   36a
publish   publier   *(v)*   20a

publisher   l'éditeur   *(m)*   20a
puck   le palet, le puck   27b
pudding   la crème   24h
puffed cheese   le fromage soufflé   24h
pull   tirer   *(v)*   3e
pull out a tooth   extraire   *(v)* une dent   40b
pulse   le pouls   40a
pumpernickel bread   le pain noir   24i
pumpkin   la citrouille   14e
punch *(hardware)*   le poinçon   25b
punctuation   la ponctuation   19c
pupil   l'élève   *(m/f)*   37d
purchase   l'achat   *(m)*, acheter   *(v)*   25a
pure   pur(e)   *(adj)*   7b, 13d
purple   le pourpre, le violet   7a
put   mettre   *(v)*, placer   *(v)*   3e
put a room in order   mettre   *(v)* une pièce en ordre   23f
put down   poser   *(v)*   3e
put on   (se) mettre   *(v)*   25m
put on make-up   se farder   *(v)*, se maquiller   *(v)*   12d
put on perfume   se parfumer   *(v)*   12d
put out (extinguish)   éteindre   *(v)*   39a
put someone on trial   mettre   *(v)* quelqu'un en procès   41
pyramid   la pyramide   2a

Q
quantity   la quantité   3c
quantum theory   la théorie des quanta   42a
quart   le quart de gallon   *(m)*   3a
queen   la reine   27a, 43; *(in chess)* la dame   27a

question la question 37f; **to ask a question** poser *(v)* une question 37f

question mark le point d'interrogation *(f)* 19c

queue up faire *(v)* la queue 15a

quiche la quiche 24g; **with cheese** au fromage; **with ham** au jambon 24g

quickly vite *(adv)* 3e

Quiet! Silence! 21c

Quite well! Très bien! *(adv)* 16a

quotation mark le guillemet 19c

quotient le quotient 1f

R

rabbi le rabbin 11d

rabbit le lapin 15a

race (*population*) la race 11d; *(sports)* la course 27b

racism le racisme 44b

radiation la radiation 44a

radiator le radiateur 33e

radio la radio 20b, 23d, 35c

radioactive waste les déchets *(m)* radioactifs 13c, 44a

radish le radis 14e

radius le rayon 2a

railroad le chemin de fer 34; **station** la gare 34

railway crossing le passage à niveau 34

rain la pluie; pleuvoir *(v)* 6a

raincoat l'imperméable *(m)* 25k

rainforest la forêt pluviale 13b

rainy weather un temps pluvieux 6a

raise (*someone*) élever *(v)* 11c

raise to a power élever *(v)* à une puissance 1e

raisin le raisin sec 14d, 24f

rake le râteau 25b

Ramadan le ramadan 5f, 29a

ramp la rampe 33c

random access memory (*computers*) la mémoire à accès sélectif 42b

rap le rap 28c

rape le viol; violer 39b

rare rare *(adj)* 4e

rare (*cooked food*) saignant(e) *(adj, m, f)* 24b

rarely rarement *(adv)* 4e

raspberry la framboise 14d, 24f

rat le rat 15a

rate le tarif 35b

ratio la proportion 1e

rational rationnel(le) *(adj, m, f)* 1d

razor le rasoir 12d, 25f; le rasoir électrique 12d, 25f

razor blade la lame 12d

read lire *(v)* 20a, 37f

reader (*person*) le lecteur, la lectrice 20a

reading (*passage, selection*) la lecture 37f

real réel(le) *(adj, m, f)* 1d

Really? Vraiment? 21c

reap récolter *(v)*, cueillir *(v)* 14a

rear window (*vehicle*) la lunette arrière 33e

rear-view mirror (*vehicle*) le rétroviseur intérieur 33e

reason la raison 22a; raisonner *(v)* 22b

rebellious rebelle *(adj, m, f)* 11e

receipt l'acquit *(m)*, le récépissé, le reçu 25a, 26, 35b

receive recevoir *(v)* 19e

receiver (telephone handset) le combiné 18a

recent récent(e) *(adj)* 4e

recently   récemment   *(adv)*
4e
reception   la réception   11c
reciprocal   réciproque   *(adj)*
1d
recommend   recommander   *(v)*
17a
record (recording)   le disque
20b, 25j;   **to record**   enregistrer
(v)   20b;   **to play a record**
passer   *(v)* un disque   20b
record player   le tourne-disque
20b
rectangle   le rectangle   2a
rectum   le rectum   40a
red   le rouge   7a;   **to become
red with anger**   devenir   *(v)*
rouge de colère   7a
red-haired   roux, rousse   *(adj,
m, f)*   11a
reduced price   le prix réduit
25a
referee   l'arbitre   *(m/f)*   27b
reference book   l'ouvrage   *(m)*
de référence   20a, 25o
refined   raffiné(e)   *(adj, m, f)*
11e
reflect (think)   réfléchir   *(v)*
22b
reflexive pronoun   le pronom
personnel réfléchi   8a, 8k
reflexive verb   le verbe
pronominal   8a
reform   la réforme   43
refrigerator   le réfrigérateur, le
frigo   23d
region   la région   13e
registered letter   la lettre
recommandée   19e
registration   l'inscription   *(f)*
37f;   **fee**   les droits   *(m, pl)*
d'inscription   37f
registration papers *(vehicle)*   la
carte grise   33b
regular   régulier   *(adj, m)*,
régulière   *(adj, f)*   4e, 8a
regularly   régulièrement   *(adv)*
4e

rehearsal   la répétition   28e
relate   raconter   *(v)*   17a
relative   relatif   *(adj, m)*,
relative   *(adj, f)*   8a
relatives   les proches parents
(m)   10a
relax   se relaxer   *(v)*   12b
relief   le soulagement   21a;
sigh of relief   le soupir de
soulagement   21a
religion   la religion   11d
religious   pieux, pieuse   *(adj, m,
f)*   11d
remain   rester   *(v)*   29b
remember   se rappeler   *(v)*, se
souvenir   *(v)* de   22b
remote control *(television)*   la
télécommande   20b
rent   le loyer; louer   *(v)*   23g
rented car   l'auto   *(f)* en
location   33a
repair   réparer   *(v)*   25i
repeat   répéter   *(v)*   17a, 37f
repetition   la répétition   17a
reply   la réponse, répondre   *(v)*
19e
report   le compte rendu, faire
(v) un compte rendu, faire   *(v)* un
rapport sur   17a
reporter   le (la) journaliste
(reporter)   20a
representative   le (la)
représentant(e)   43
reproach   reprocher   *(v)*
17a
reproduce   reproduire   *(v)*
14a
reproduction   la reproduction
14a
reptile   le reptile   15c
republic   la république   43
request   la demande, demander
(v)   17a
rescue   sauver   *(v)*   39a
researcher   le chercheur, la
chercheuse   38a
reservation   la réservation
24m, 32a, 35b

reserve réserver *(v)* 35b
reserved réservé(e) *(adj, m, f)* 11e, 24m
residence le domicile 11f
resistant résistant(e) *(adj, m, f)* 13d
respiratory system le système respiratoire 40a
rest se reposer *(v)* 12b
restaurant le restaurant 24m; **informal restaurant** le bistro (bistrot) 24m
restless agité(e) *(adj, m, f)* 11e
restore restaurer *(v)* 23f
résumé le résumé 38b
retire se retirer *(v)*, être en retraite 38d
retirement (pension) la retraite, la pension 38d
return retourner *(v)* 3e, 29b; revenir *(v)* 29b
return an item rendre *(v)* 25a
return address l'adresse *(f)* de l'expéditeur 19e
review la révision; faire *(v)* une révision 37f
review (on media) la critique 20a
revolt la révolte 43
revolution la révolution 43
rhetoric la rhétorique 17a, 28d
rhetorical rhétorique *(adj, m, f)* 17a
rhetorical question la question rhétorique 17a
rheumatism le rhumatisme 40a
rhinoceros le rhinocéros 15a
rhombus le rhombe 2a
rhythm le rythme 28c
ribbon le ruban 19d
rice le riz 24i
rice pudding la crème de riz 24h

rice with vegetables le riz aux légumes *(m, f, pl)* 24g
rich riche *(adj, m, f)* 11e
rifle le fusil 39b
right (*privilege*) le droit 41
right (*location*) droit(e) *(adj, m, f)* 3d; **to the right** à droite 3d, 33c
right (*angle*) droit(e) *(adj, m, f)* 2b
right (*accurate*) correct(e) *(adj, m, f)* 37f
right away tout de suite *(adv)* 4e
right prism le prisme droit 2a
right wing (*politics*) la droite 43
right-angled rectangle *(adj)* 2a
right to vote le suffrage universel 43
right (*jewelry*) la bague, l'anneau *(m)* 25i
ring (*telephone*) sonner *(v)* 18b
ring finger l'annulaire *(m)* 12a
rinse (se) rinser *(v)* 40b
riot l'émeute *(f)* 43
ripe mûr(e) *(adj, m, f)* 14a
rise se lever *(v)* 3e
rite le rite 11d
river le fleuve 13b, 36b; (small) la rivière 13b
road le chemin 33c
road map la carte routière 33b
roar rugir *(v)* 15a
roast rôti(e) *(adj, m, f)* 24b
roast beef le rosbif 24g
rob voler *(v)* 39b
robber le voleur, la voleuse 39b
robbery le vol 39b
robin le rouge-gorge 15b
robot le robot 42a

robust   robuste   *(adj)*   13d

rock   la roche, le rocher   13b

rock music   la musique rock   25j

roll *(of bread)*   le petit pain   chapelet   24i

roll *(of film)*   le rouleau de film   (pellicule), la pellicule   25d

roll *(sweet)*   la brioche   24i

roller skate   patiner *(v)* à roulettes *(f, pl)*   27b

Roman   romain(e) *(adj, m, f)*   1d

romance novel   le roman d'amour   20a, 25o

romantic   romantique *(adj, m, f)*   11e

Rome   Rome   30c

roof   le toit   23a, 33e

rook *(chess)*   la tour   27a

room   la pièce   23b; la chambre   35b

room with bath   la chambre avec bain   35b

room with two beds   la chambre à deux lits   35b

rooster   le coq   15b

root   la racine   14a, 40b

rope   la corde   27b, 36b;   **ropes** (boxing) les cordes *(f, pl)*   27b

rose   la rose   14b

rosemary   le romarin   14e, 24j

rotten   pourri(e) *(adj, m, f)*   14a

rough   brut, brute *(adj, m, f)*   11e; rude *(adj)*   13d

rough copy, draft   la copie brute, la copie en état brut, le brouillon   37f

round bread   le pain rond   24i

round-trip ticket   le billet aller-retour   30a

row   le rang   28a

ruby   le rubis   25i

rude   rude *(adj, m, f)*, grossier, grossière *(adj, m, f)*   11e

rug   le tapis   23c; **wall-to-wall carpeting** la moquette   23c

ruler   la règle   2b, 19d, 37b, 38c

rumor   le bruit   17a

run   courir *(v)*   3e, 12b, 27b

Run for your life!   Sauve qui peut!   39b

run into someone   rencontrer *(v)* quelqu'un   16b

runway *(airplane)*   la piste   32c

rush hour   les heures *(f, pl)* d'affluence, les heures de pointe   33c

rusk *(Melba toast)*   la biscotte   24i

Russia   la Russie   30b

Russian *(nationality)*   Russe *(m/f)*   30d; *(language)* le russe   30d

rye and wheat bread   le pain de campagne   24i

rye bread   le pain au seigle   24i

S

saber *(fencing)*   le sabre d'escrime *(f)*   27b

sad   triste *(adj, m, f)*   11e, 21a

sadness   la tristesse   11e, 21a

safe *(for valuables)*   le coffre-fort   26

safety deposit box   le coffre de sécurité   26

Sagittarius   le Sagittaire   5d

salad   la salade   24g

salamander   la salamandre   15c

salami   le salami   24c

salary   le salaire   26, 38d

sale   la vente   25a; **for sale** à
   vendre   *(v)*   25a; **on sale** en
   vente   *(f)*   25a
salmon   le saumon   24d
salt   le sel   13c, 24j
salty   salé(e)   *(adj, m, f)*   24p
salutation *(of a letter)*   la
   formule (la salutation) initiale
   19c
sand   le sable   13b
sandwich   le sandwich   24g;
   with cheese au fromage; **with
   ham** au jambon   24g
sap *(plants)*   la sève   14a
sapphire   le saphir   25i
sarcasm   le sarcasme   11e
sarcastic   sarcastique   *(adj, m,
   f)*   11e
sardine   la sardine   15c, 24d
satellite   le satellite   13a, 42a
satellite television   la télévision
   par satellite   20b
satisfaction   la satisfaction
   21a
satisfied   satisfait(e)   *(adj, m, f)*
   21a
Saturday   le samedi   5a
Saturn   Saturne   *(m)*   13a
saucer   la soucoupe   23d, 24l
sausage   la saucisse   24c
save   économiser   *(v)*, épargner
   (v)   26
savings   l'épargne   *(f)*   26
saw *(hardware)*   la scie   25b
saxophone   le saxophone
   28c
say   dire   *(v)*   17a
scalene   scalène   *(adj)*   2a
scarf   l'écharpe   *(f)*   25k
scene   la scène   28e
scenery *(theater)*   le décor
   28e
schedule   l'horaire   *(m)*   4e,
   34
school   l'école   *(f)*   37f
school yard   la cour   37c
school year   l'année   *(f)*
   scolaire   5b

schoolbag   le sac d'écolier
   37b
schoolmate   le (la) camarade
   d'école   37d
science fiction   la science-fiction
   20a, 25o
sciences   les sciences   *(f, pl)*
   37e
scientific research   la recherche
   scientifique   42a
scientist   le (la) scientifique
   38a
scissors   les ciseaux   *(m, pl)*
   12d, 19d, 38c, 39c
scooter   le scooter   33a
score *(sports)*   la marque
   27b
Scorpio   le Scorpion   5d
scorpion   le scorpion   15d
screen   l'écran   *(m)*   25d,
   28a
screen *(computer)*   l'écran de
   visualisation   42b
screw   la vis   25b
screwdriver   le tournevis
   25b
sculpt   sculpter   *(v)*   28b
sculptor   le sculpteur   28b
sculptress   la femme sculpteur
   28b
sculpture   la sculpture   28b
sea   la mer   6a, 13b, 36b
seafood   les fruits de mer
   24d
seagull   la mouette   15b
seal *(animal)*   le phoque   15c
season   la saison   5c
Season's Greetings   Meilleurs
   vœux   16c
seat   la place   28a, 32c, 34; le
   siège   28a, 33e
seat *(bicycle)*   la selle   33a
seat belt   la ceinture de sécurité
   32c, 33e
secant   la sécante   2b
second   deuxième, second(e)
   (adj, m, f)   1b, 8a; *(time)* la
   seconde   3a, 4c

secretary le (la) secrétaire 37d, 38a, 40a

secularism la laïcité 11d

sedative le sédatif 40a

seduction la séduction 11e

seductive séduisant(e) *(adj, m, f)* 11e

see voir *(v)* 12c, 30a

see life through rose-colored glasses voir la vie en rose 7a

See you! Salut! 16a

See you later! A tout à l'heure! 16a

See you soon! A bientôt! 16a

See you Sunday! A dimanche! 16a

seed la semence; semer *(v)* 14a

segment *(line)* la ligne segmentée 2b

self-service le self-service 33c

self-sufficient indépendant(e) *(adj, m, f)* 11e

sell vendre *(v)* 23f, 25a

semicolon le point virgule 19c

Senate le Sénat 43

senator le sénateur, la femme sénateur 43

send envoyer *(v)* expédier *(v)* 3e, 19e

sender le destinateur, l'expéditeur 19d, 19e

sense le sens; sentir *(v)* 12c

sense of humor le sens de l'humour 11e

sensitive sensible *(adj, m, f)* 11e

sentence *(grammar)* la phrase 8a, 8n, 19c

sentence *(law)* le jugement 41

sentimental sentimental(e) *(adj, m, f)* 11e

separate (se) séparer *(v)* 11c

separated séparé(e) *(adj, m, f)* 11c

separation la séparation 11c

September le septembre 5b

series *(television)* la série d'émissions 20b

serious sérieux *(adj, m)*, sérieuse *(f)* 11e

serious accident l'accident *(m)* grave 39c

sermon le sermon 17a

serve servir *(v)* 24o

serve a prison sentence subir *(v)* une condamnation 41

service le service 24m; **services** les services 35b

set *(numbers)* l'ensemble *(m)* 1f

set of drums *(music)* la batterie 28c

set the table mettre *(v)* le couvert 23f; mettre la table 24o

seven sept 1a

seventeen dix-sept 1a

seventh septième 1b

seventy soixante-dix 1a

several plusieurs *(adj/adv)* 3c

sew coudre *(v)* 25g

sewing machine la machine à coudre 23d

sex le sexe 11a, 38b

shade l'ombre *(f)* 6a

shadow l'ombre *(f)* 6a

shaft *(of motor)* l'arbre-moteur *(m)*, l'arbre de couche 33c

shake hands serrer *(v)* la main à quelqu'un, donner *(v)* la main à quelqu'un 16a

shame la honte 21a

shampoo le shampooing 12d, 25f, 35c

shave *(oneself)* (se) raser *(v)* 12d

shaving cream   la crème à raser
    25f
she   elle   8h
shed light on   tirer *(v)* quelque
    chose au clair   13a
sheep   le mouton   15a
sheet *(bed)*   le drap   23d; les
    draps   35c
sheet *(of paper)*   la feuille de
    papier   5c
shelf   l'étagère *(f)*   23a
shellfish   les crustacés *(m, pl)*
    24d
sherbet   le sorbet   24g
shirt   la chemise   25k
shock   le choc   39c
shoe   la chaussure   25n
shoe horn   le chausse-pied
    25n
shoe repair store   la cordonnerie
    25n
shoe store   le magasin de
    chaussures   25n
shoelace   le lacet   25n
shoot   tirer *(v)*   39b
shop   la boutique   25a; **to
    shop**   faire *(v)* des achats, faire
    des emplettes, faire du shopping
    25a
shop for food   acheter *(v)* des
    provisions   24o
shop window   la vitrine   25a
shoplifting   le vol à l'étalage
    39b
shopping bag   le sac à provisions
    23d
shopping mall   le centre
    commercial, la grande surface
    25a
short *(height)*   petit(e) *(adj, m,
    f)*   3c, 11a, 25l
short *(thing)*   court(e) *(adj, m,
    f)*   3b, 37f
short story   le conte, la nouvelle
    20a, 28a
shorten *(clothing)*   raccourcir
    (v)   25m
short-term   à court terme   4e

shot *(injection)*   la piqûre,
    l'injection *(f)*   25h, 40a
shoulder   l'épaule *(f)*   12a
shout   le cri; crier *(v)*   17a,
    39a
shovel   la pelle   25b
show *(entertainment)*   le
    spectacle   20b, 28c
shower   la douche   23a, 35c
shredder, paper   le déchiqueteur
    38c
shrewd   rusé(e) *(adj, m, f)*
    11e
shrewdness   la ruse   11e
shrimp   la crevette   24d
shrink   rétrécir *(v)*   25m
Shut up!   Ferme-la!   17a, 21
shy   timide *(adj, m, f)*   11e
sick   malade *(adj)*   11a, 40a
sickness   la maladie   11a, 40a
side *(angle)*   côté *(adj)*   2b
sideburns   les pattes *(f, pl)*
    12a
side-view mirror *(vehicle)*   le
    rétroviseur extérieur   33e
sidewalk   le trottoir   36a
sigh of relief   le soupir de
    soulagement *(m)*   21a
sight   la vision   12c, 40a; la
    vue   12c, 40a
sign *(one's name)*   signer *(v)*
    11f, 19c, 26
signal   le signal   33c
signature   la signature   11f,
    19c, 26, 38b
signs of the zodiac   les signes
    (m) du zodiaque   5d
silence   le silence   17a
silent   silencieux *(adj, m)*,
    silencieuse *(adj, f)*   17a; **to
    be silent** se taire *(v)*   17a
silk   la soie, en soie   13c, 25l
silkworm   le ver à soie   15d
silly   bête *(adj, m, f)*   11e
silver   l'argent *(m)*   13c,
    25i
silver *(color)*   argenté *(m)*
    7a

silver anniversary les noces (*f*) d'argent 11c

simple simple (*adj, m, f*) 11e, 22a

simultaneous simultané(e) (*adj*) 4e

simultaneously simultanément (*adv*) 4e

since depuis (*prep*) 4e; comme (*conj*) 8p; depuis que (*conj*) 8p

since Monday depuis lundi 4e

since yesterday depuis hier 4e

sincere sincère (*adj, m, f*) 11e

sincerity la sincérité 11e

sine le sinus 2b

sing chanter (*v*) 28c

singer le chanteur, la chanteuse 25j, 28c

single *(unmarried)* célibataire 38b

single room une chambre à un lit 35b

singular le singulier (*adj, m*), singulière (*adj, f*) 8a

sink *(kitchen)* l'évier (*m*) 23a; *(bathroom)* le lavabo 23a, 35c

siren la sirène 39a

sister la soeur 10a

sister-in-law la belle-soeur 10a

sit down s'asseoir (*v*) 3e, 32c

six six 1a

sixteen seize 1a

sixth sixième 1b

sixty soixante 1a; **about sixty** une soixantaine 1c

size la mesure, la taille 3b, 25k; *(of shoe)* la pointure 25n

skate patiner (*v*) 27b; **(ice skate)** le patin à glace 27b

ski faire (*v*) du ski, skier (*v*) 27b

ski resort la station de ski 36b

skier le skieur, la skieuse 27b

skiing le ski 27b, 36b

skimmed milk le lait écrémé 24h

skin la peau 12a

skinny maigre (*adj*) 11a

skip a class sécher (*v*) un cours 37f

skip school faire (*v*) l'école buissonnière 37f

skirt la jupe 25k

sky le ciel 6a, 13b

sleep dormir (*v*) 12b

sleeping bag le sac de couchage 36b

sleeve la manche 25g

slice la tranche 24i; trancher (*v*) 24o

slice of cream cake la tranche de gâteau à la crème 24i

slide la diapositive 20b, 25d

slide projector le projecteur pour diapositives (*f, pl*) 20b, 37b

sliding door la porte coulissante 35c

slim maigre (*adj*) 11a

slip *(undergarment)* la combinaison, le fond de robe, le jupon 25k

slipper le chausson, la pantoufle 25n

Slippery When Wet Chaussée glissante 33d

sloppy désorganisé(e) (*adj, m, f*) 11e

slot *(for tokens)* la fente 18a

slow lent(e) (*adj*) 3e, 4e

slow down ralentir (*v*) 33c

slowly lentement (*adv*) 3e, 4e

small *(size)* petit(e) (*adj, m, f*) 3c, 11a, 25l

small bill *(banknote, currency)* le petit billet 26

small letter *(lower case letter)*   la
lettre minuscule   19c
small round loaf of bread   la
petite boule   24i
smart   intelligent(e) *(adj, m, f)*
11e
smash *(auto collision)*   la
collision   39c
smell   l'odeur *(f)*   12c; la
senteur   12c; sentir *(v)*
12c
smile   le sourire; sourire *(v)*
11e, 21a; **to force an uneasy
smile** sourire *(v)* jaune   7a
smock   la blouse   25k
smoke   la fumée   13c, 39a
smoke shop   le bureau de tabac
25e
smoking compartment   fumeurs
34
smooth   lisse *(adj)*   13d
snack   le casse-croûte, le goûter
24a
snack bar   le buffet   24m
snails   les escargots *(m, pl)*
24g
snake   le serpent   15c
sneeze   l'éternuement; éternuer
(v)   40a
snob   snob *(n/adj, m, f)*   11e
snobbish   hautain(e) *(adj, m, f)*
11e
snow   la neige; neiger *(v)*
6a
snow goggles   les lunettes *(f,
pl)* de glacier *(m)*   27b
So?   Et alors?   9
So, so!   Comme-ci, comme-ça!
(adv)   16a
so that   afin que *(conj)*, pour
que *(conj)*   8p
soap   le savon   12d, 25f, 35c
soap opera *(radio and television)*
le mélo   20b
soap powder   le savon en poudre
25g
soccer   le foot   27b; **to play
soccer** jouer *(v)* au foot   27b

soccer ball   le ballon   27b
Social Welfare   l'Assistance
(f) sociale   43
socialism   le socialisme   43
socialist   le (la) socialiste   43
sociology   la sociologie   37e
sock (clothing)   la chaussette
25n
sodium   le sodium   13c
sodium bicarbonate   le
bicarbonate de soude   25h
sodium citrate   le citrate de
soude   25h
sofa   le canapé   23c
soft   mou *(adj, m)*, doux *(adj,
m)*   13d
soft-boiled egg   l'oeuf *(m)* à la
coque   24h
soft drink   la gazeuse   24k
software *(computers)*   le logiciel,
le software   42b
solar cell   la cellule solaire
44a
solar eclipse   l'éclipse *(f)*
solaire   13a
solar energy   l'énergie *(f)*
solaire   13c, 44a
solar system   le système solaire
13a
sole *(fish)*   la sole   15c, 24d
solid   le solide   13c
solid figures   les figures *(f)*
solides   2a
solstice   le solstice   5c
soluble   soluble *(adj)*   13d
solution   la solution   1f
solve   résoudre *(v)*   1f
solve a problem   résoudre *(v)*
un problème   1f, 37f
some   quelque(s) *(adj)*   3c;
see also **partitive**   8d
some of it (them)   en *(pron)*
3c, 8o
some (people)   des gens   8o
someone   quelqu'un *(m)*,
quelqu'une *(f) (pron)*   8o
Someone assaulted me!   On m'a
assailli(e)!   39b

Someone robbed me!   On m'a volé(e)!   39b
something   quelque chose *(pron)*   8o
something to declare   quelque chose à déclarer   31
somewhere   quelque part *(adv)*   3d
son   le fils   10a
son-in-law   le gendre   10a
song   la chanson   25j, 28c
soon   bientôt *(adv)*   4e
sooner or later   tôt ou tard   4e
sore back   le mal au dos   40a
sore throat   le mal de gorge   40a
sore/twisted neck   le mal au cou, un torticolis   40a
sorrow   le chagrin   21a
sorting   le triage   38c
soul   l'âme *(f)*   11d
sound   le son   12c
soundtrack   la bande sonore   28a
soup   la soupe, le potage   24g; **of the day** du jour   24g
sour   aigre *(adj, m, f)*   24p
south   le sud   3d; **to the south** au sud   3d
South America   l'Amérique *(f)* du Sud   30b
South Pole   le Pôle Sud   13e
southern   méridional(e) *(adj)*   3d
space   l'espace *(m)*   2b, 13a
space bar *(of a typewriter)*   la barre d'espacement   19d
space shuttle   la navette spatiale   42a
spacecraft   le vaisseau spatial   42a
spades *(cards)*   la pique   27a
Spain   l'Espagne *(f)*   30b
Spanish *(nationality)*   Espagnol *(m),* Espagnole *(f)*   30d; *(language)* l'espagnol *(m)*   30d

spark   l'étincelle *(f)*   39a
spark plug *(vehicle)*   la bougie   33e
sparrow   le moineau   15b
speak   parler *(v)*   17a
speak badly of someone   diffamer *(v)* quelqu'un   17a
speaker *(audio apparatus)*   la caisse acoustique   20b
special delivery   l'expédition express   19e
specialist   le (la) spécialiste   40a
species   l'espèce *(f)*   14a
speech   le discours   17a
speed   la vitesse   3a, 33c
Speed Limit   Vitesse maximum   33d
speed up   accélérer *(v)*   33c
speedometer   le compteur de vitesse   33e
spelling   l'orthographe *(f)*   19c
spend *(money)*   dépenser *(v)*   4e, 25a
spend *(time)*   passer *(v)*   4e
sphere   la sphère   2a
spice   l'épice *(f)*   24j
spicy   épicé(e) *(adj, m, f)*   24p
spider   l'araignée *(f)*   15d
spinach   les épinards *(m, pl)*   14e, 24e
spirit   l'esprit *(m)*   11d
spiritual   spirituel(le) *(adj, m, f)*   11d
splint   l'éclisse *(f)*   39c
spoke *(bicycle)*   le rayon   33a
spoon   la cuiller (la cuillère)   23d, 24l
sporadic   sporadique *(adj)*   4e
sporadically   sporadiquement *(adv)*   4e
sport   le sport   27b
sport utility vehicle   le véhicule sport utilitaire   33a

sports car   la voiture de sport
33a

sports fan   l'enthousiaste *(m/f)*
du sport, le fan, le (la) fanatique
du sport   27b

spot *(stain)*   la tache   25g

spouse   l'époux, l'épouse   11c

spring *(metal coil)*   le ressort
25i

spring *(season)*   le printemps
5c

square   la place   11f, 36a;
le carré   2a

square bracket   le crochet
19c

square centimeter   le centimètre
carré   3a

square kilometer   le kilomètre
carré   3a

square meter   le mètre carré
3a

square millimeter   le millimètre
carré   3a

square root   la racine au carré
1e

squared   au carré   1e

squid   le calmar   24d

stable   stable *(adj, m, f)*
13d

stadium   le stade   27b

stage *(theater)*   la scène
28e

stain   la tache   25g

stainless steel   l'acier *(m)*
inoxydable   13c

stairs   l'escalier   23a, 35b

stamp *(postage)*   le timbre-poste
19e, 27a

stamp collecting   la collection de
timbres   27a

stand in line   faire *(v)* la queue
15a

staple   l'agrafe *(f)*   19d,
25c, 38c

stapler   l'agrafeuse *(f)*
19d, 25c, 38c

star   l'étoile *(f)*   6a, 13a

starch   l'amidon *(m)*   25g

start *(car)*   mettre *(v)* en
marche, démarrer *(v)*   33c

state   l'état *(m)*   13e, 43

state (to make a statement)
affirmer *(v)*   17a

statement   l'affirmation *(f)*
17a

station *(radio)*   la station de
radio   20b

station *(train, bus, subway)*   la
gare, la station   34

station wagon   le break   33b

stationery store   la papeterie
25c

statistical   statistique *(adj)*
1f

statistics   la statistique   1f, 37e

steak   le bifteck   24g

steal   dérober *(v)*, voler *(v)*
39b

steel   l'acier *(m)*   13c

steering wheel   le volant   33e

stem   la tige   14a

stereo   la chaîne-stéréo,
stéréo(phonique) *(adj)*   20b

stethoscope   le stéthoscope
40a

stiff (twisted) neck   le torticolis
40a

still (as yet)   encore *(adv)*,
toujours *(adv)*   4e

stingy   radin *(m)*, radine *(f)*
11e

stitch   le point   25g

stock (share)   l'action *(f)*
26

stock market / exchange   la
Bourse   26

stocking   le bas   25n

stomach   l'estomac *(m)*
12a, 40a

stone   la pierre   13b

stool *(furniture)*   le tabouret
23c

stop   arrêter *(v)*   3e

Stop   Arrêt   33d, 34

stop oneself   s'arrêter *(v)*
3e

Stop thief!   Au voleur!   39b
store   le magasin   25a
store clerk   l'employé(e)   (m/f)
25a
store hours   les heures   (f, pl)
25a
store window   la vitrine   25a
stork   la cigogne   15b
storm   la tempête   6a
story *(literature)*   le conte,
l'histoire   (f)   17a
stove   la cuisinière électrique
(à gaz)   23d
straight *(angle)*   droit   (adj)
2b
straight ahead   tout droit   (adv)
36c
straight line   la ligne droite
2b
strawberry   la fraise   14d,
24f
strawberry ice cream   la glace
aux fraises   24h
street   la rue   11f, 36a, 38b
street corner   le coin de la rue
33c
street sign   la plaque de nom de
rue   36a
streetcar   le tram, le tramway
33a
strength   la force   11a
strike *(labor)*   la grève   43
string   la ficelle   19d, 25c;
(of a musical instrument) la corde
28c
string bean   le haricot vert
14e, 24e
stringed instruments   les
instruments   (m, pl) à cordes   (f)
28c
striped   rayé(e)   (adj, m, f)
25l
strong   fort(e)   (adj)   11a,
11e, 13d, 40a
structure   la structure   13c
stubborn   têtu(e)   (adj, m, f)
11e; entêté(e)   (adj, m, f)
11e

student   l'étudiant(e)   (m/f)
37d
study   étudier   (v)   22b, 37f
stuff   l'étoffe   (f), le tissu
13c
stuffed egg   l'oeuf   (m) dur farci
24h
stupid   bête, stupide   (adj, m, f)
11e
style *(fashion)*   la mode, à la
mode, au dernier cri   25k, 25l;
(writing) le style   28d
subject   le sujet   8a, 8h
subject *(learning matter)*   la
matière   37e
subjunctive   subjonctif   (adj,
m), subjonctive   (adj, f)   8a
subordinate   subordonné(e)
(adj, m, f)   8a
substance   la substance   13c
subtract   soustraire   (v)   1e
subtraction   la soustraction
1e
suburbs   la banlieue, les environs
(m, pl)   30a
subway   le métro(politain)
34
subway station   la station de
métro   34
sue   citer   (v) dans un procès-
verbal   41
suffer   souffrir   (v)   40a
suffice   suffire   (v)   3c
sufficient   suffisant(e)   (adj)
3c
sugar   le sucre   24j
suggest   suggérer   (v)   17a
suit *(clothing)*   le complet, le
costume   25k
suitcase   la valise   31
sulphur   le soufre, le sulfure
13c
sulphuric acid   l'acide   (m)
sulfurique   13c
sum   la somme   1f
sum up   sommer   (v)   1f
summarize   résumer   (v), faire
un résumé   17a

tack   la punaise   37b, 38c

tail   la queue   15a

tailor   le tailleur, la couturière   38a

tailored suit (*woman's*)   le costume tailleur   25k

take   prendre *(v)*   25a, 34

take a holiday   avoir *(v)* congé *(m)*   36b

take a picture (photo)   prendre *(v)* une photo   25d

take a subject/course   suivre *(v)* un cours   37f

take a trip   faire *(v)* un voyage   30a

take a walk   faire *(v)* une promenade   3e

take an exam   passer *(v)* un examen   37f

take an excursion   faire *(v)* une excursion   36a

take attendance   faire *(v)* l'appel   37f

take back (*return an item*)   rendre *(v)*   25a

take drugs   prendre *(v)* de la drogue, se droguer *(v)*   44b

take notes   prendre *(v)* des notes   37f

take off (*remove*)   enlever (v) 25m; *(airplane)* le décollage 32c; décoller *(v)*   32c

take one's temperature   mesurer *(v)* la fièvre   40a

take-out (*food*)   à emporter *(v)* 24m, 24o

take place   avoir lieu   4e

talcum powder   le talc   25f

talented   artistique *(adj)*   11e

talk   parler *(v)*   17a; le discours   17a

tall   grand(e) *(adj)*   3b, 11a; haut(e) *(adj)*   3b

tangent   la tangente   2a, 2b

tanker (*truck*)   le camion-citerne   33a

tape (*magnetic*)   la bande magnétique   20b, 25j

tape recorder   le magnétophone   20b, 37b

tapioca pudding   le tapioca au lait   24h

tariff   le tarif   31

tarot   le tarot   27a

tartlet   la tartelette   24i

taste   goûter *(v)*   12c

tasty   savoureux *(adj, m)*, savoureuse *(f)*   24p

Taurus   le Taureau   5d

taxi   le taxi   33a

tea   le thé   24k

teach   enseigner *(v)*   37f

teacher   l'enseignant(e) *(m/f)* 37d; le professeur, la femme professeur   38a

teacher's desk   le bureau, la chaire   37b

team   l'équipe *(f)*   27b

teapot   la théière   23d

tears (*weeping*)   les larmes *(f, pl)*   21a

teaspoon   la cuiller à café   23d, 24l

technical book   le livre de technologie   25o

technical school   l'institut *(m)* d'enseignement technique   37a

technician   le technicien, la technicienne   37d

technology   la technologie   42a

teenager   adolescent(e) *(n, adj)*   11b

telecommunication   la télécommunication   18a, 42a

telecommunications satellite   le satellite de télécommunications   18a

teleconferencing   la télé-audio-conférence   42a

telephone   le téléphone, téléphoner *(v)*   18a, 18b, 23e, 35c, 38c

telephone credit card   la télécarte   18a

telephone number   le numéro de téléphone *(m)*   11f, 18b, 38b

telephone operator   le (la) téléphoniste   18b

telephone set   l'appareil *(m)* téléphonique   18a

telephone switchboard operator   le (la) standardiste   18b

telephone see also phone

television   la télévision   20b

television set   le téléviseur   20b, 23d, 35c

telex   le télex   18b, 42a

tell   dire *(v)*   17a

tell a joke   dire (raconter) *(v)* une plaisanterie, une blague   17a

tell a story   raconter *(v)* une histoire, conter   17a

teller (cashier)   le caissier, la caissière   26

teller's window   le guichet   26

telly (TV)   la télé   20b

temperature   la température   6c; *(fever)* la fièvre   40a

template   le gabarit   2b

temple   le temple   11d, 36a

temporarily   temporairement *(adv)*   4e

temporary   temporaire *(adj)*   4e

ten   dix la; **about ten** une dizaine   1c

tenant   le (la) locataire   23g

tennis (to play)   jouer *(v)* au tennis   27b; *(the sport)* le tennis   27b

tennis racket   la raquette   27b

tense (verb)   le temps   8a, 8n

tent   la tente de camping   36b

tenth   dixième   1b

terminal   le terminal   32a, 42b

termite   le termite   15d

terrace   la terrasse   23a

territory   le territoire   13e

tetrahedron   le tétraèdre   2a

test   l'épreuve *(f)*   37f

text   le texte   19c, 20a

textbook   le livre de classe *(f)*, le livre d'étude *(f)*,   25o, le livre de cours   37b

textile   le textile   13c

Thailand   la Thaïlande   30b

thank   remercier *(v)*   17a, 21a

Thank goodness!   Grâce à Dieu!   21c

Thank you!   Merci!   16c

thankful   reconnaissant(e) *(adj, m, f)*   21a

thankfulness   la gratitude, la reconnaissance   21a

that   ce *(m, s)*, cet *(m, s)*, cette *(f, s)*   8e

that is to say . . .   c'est-à-dire . . .   44c

the   le *(m, s)*, la *(f, s)*, l' *(m/f, s)*, les *(m/f, pl)*   8b

the one   celui *(m)*, celle *(f)*   8m

the ones   ceux *(m)*, celles *(f)*   8m

theater   le théâtre   28e

their   leur *(m/f, s)*, leurs *(m/f, pl)*   8f

them   les   8i; eux *(m)*, elles *(f)*   8l

theme   le thème   28d

themselves   se   8k

then   alors *(adv)*, lors *(adv)*   4e; ensuite *(adv)*   4e

theory of relativity   la théorie de la relativité   42a

there   là *(adv)*   3d, 36c

There's lightning!   Il fait des éclairs!   6a

therefore   donc *(conj)*   8p, 44c

thermal energy   l'énergie *(f)* thermique   44a

thermometer   le thermomètre
6c, 25h, 40a

thermostat   le thermostat   6c,
35c

these   ces   *(m/f, pl)*   8e

thesis   la thèse   37f

they   ils   *(m)*, elles   *(f)*   8h;
eux   *(m)*, elles   *(f)*   8l

thick   épais   *(adj, m)*, épaisse
(f)   3b

thick soup   le potage   24g

thief   le voleur, la voleuse
39b

thigh   la cuisse   12a

thin   maigre   *(adj)*   3b, 11a;
mince   *(adj)*   3b

think   penser   *(v)*   22b

third   troisième   *(adj, m, f)*
1b, 8a

Third World   le Tiers Monde
43

thirst   la soif   12b

thirteen   treize   1a

thirteenth   treizième   1b

thirty   trente   1a; **about thirty** une
trentaine   1c

thirty-one   trente et un   1a

thirty-two   trente-deux   1a

this   ce   *(m, s)*, cet   *(m, s)*, cette
(f, s)   8e

this afternoon   cet   *(adj, m)*
après-midi   *(m)*   4a

this evening   ce   *(adj, m)* soir
(m)   4a

**This is . . . (+ *name in telephone
call*)**   Ici . . .   18b

This looks bad on me.   Ceci ne
me va pas bien.   25l

This looks nice on me.   Ceci me
va bien.   25l

this morning   ce   *(adj, m)* matin
(m)   4a

this night   cette nuit   4a

thorn   l'épine   *(f)*   14b

those   ces   *(m/f, pl)*   8e

thought   la pensée   22a

thousandth   millième   1b

threat   la menace   17a

threaten   menacer   *(v)*   17a

three   trois   1a

three-dimensional space
l'espace   *(m)* tridimensionnel
13a

three hundred   trois cents
1a

three million   trois millions
1a

three thousand   trois mille
1a

three-year-old   de trois ans
11b

throat   la gorge   12a, 40a

through   à travers, par   *(prep)*
3d, 36c

throw   lancer   *(v)*   27b

throw up (vomit)   rendre   *(v)*
40a

thumb   le pouce   12a

thunder   le tonnerre, le coup de
tonnerre   6a; faire   *(v)* un
bruit de tonnerre, tonner   *(v)*
6a

Thursday   le jeudi   5a

tick (*insect*)   la tique   15d

ticket   le billet, le ticket   27b,
30a, 32a, 34

ticket (*traffic fine*)   la
contravention   33c

ticket cancelling machine   le
composteur de billets   34

ticket counter   la délivrance des
billets   34

ticket window   le guichet
32a

tide   la marée   13b

tide, high   la marée haute
13b

tide, low   la marée basse   13b

tie (*necktie*)   la cravate   25k

tie (*score in sports*)   le match nul
27b

tiger   le tigre   15a

tight   serré(e)   *(adj, m, f)*
25l

tighten   faire   *(v)* serrer   *(v)*
25m

time *(hour)* l'heure *(f)*; **every time** la fois; *(in general)* le temps 4a

Time flies! Le temps fuit! 4a

timetable *(schedule)* l'horaire *(m)* 4e, 34

timpani la timbale 28c

tincture of iodine la teinture d'iode 25h, 39c

tint teindre *(v)*, la teinte 7c

tip le pourboire 24m; donner *(v)* un pourboire 24m

tire *(of wheel)* le pneu(matique) 33a, 33e

tissue le mouchoir de papier 25h

title le titre 11f, 16b, 20a

to *(prep)* 3d, 8g

to clone cloner *(v)* 42a

to go + à + city; to go to Paris aller *(v)* à Paris 30c

to go + prep. + country; to go to France aller *(v)* en France 30c

to have reason to be worried avoir de quoi s'inquiéter 21a

to her lui (à elle) 8j

to him lui (à lui) 8j

to laugh halfheartedly, reluctantly rire *(v)* jaune, rire *(v)* à contrecoeur 21a

to me me (à moi) 8j

to someone's place chez quelqu'un 3d

to sum up en somme 17b

to the east à l'est 36c

to the fourth power à la quatrième puissance 1e

to the left à gauche 3d, 33c, 36c

to the north au nord 36c

to the nth power à la puissance n 1e

to the power of à la puissance de 1e

to the right à droite 3d, 33c, 36c

to the south au sud 36c

to the west à l'ouest 36c

to them leur 8j

to this day jusqu'à ce jour *(adv)* 4e

to us nous 8j

To whom it may concern A qui de droit 19a

to you te *(s, fam)*, vous *(pl)* 8j

toad le crapaud 15c

toast *(in honor of someone)* porter *(v)* un toast 17a

toast griller *(v)* 24o; **Melba toast** la biscotte 24i

toaster le grille-pain 23d

tobacco le tabac 25e

tobacconist le buraliste 25e

today aujourd'hui *(adv)* 4a

toe l'orteil *(m)* 12a

toilet les toilettes *(f. pl)* 32c, 35c; W. C. *(m, pl)* 35c, 37c

toilet paper le papier hygiénique 35c

token *(coin)* le jeton 18a; **slot for tokens** la fente 18a

tolerance la tolérance 21a

tolerate tolérer *(v)* 21a

Toll Péage 33d

toll booth le poste de péage 33c

tomato la tomate 14d, 24f

tomorrow demain *(adv)* 4a

tomorrow afternoon demain après-midi *(m)* 4a

tomorrow evening demain soir *(m)* 4a

tomorrow morning demain matin *(m)* 4a

tomorrow night demain pendant la nuit 4a; demain soir *(m)* 4a

tongue la langue 12a, 40b

tonight ce soir *(evening)*, cette nuit *(actual night)* 4a

tonsillitis l'amygdalite *(f)* 40a

tonsils les amygdales *(f, pl)* 40a

Too bad! Dommage! 21b

too much trop *(adv)* 3c

tool l'outil *(m)* 25b

tools les outils *(m, pl)* 23d, 33c

tooth la dent 12a, 40b

tooth decay la carie dentaire 40b

toothache le mal aux dents 40b

toothbrush la brosse à dents *(f, pl)* 12d, 25h, 40b

toothpaste la pâte dentifrice 12d, 25h; le dentifrice 40b

toothpick le cure-dent 24l

top le sommet 3d; **at (to) the top** au sommet 3d

topaz la topaze 25i

tornado la tornade 6a

touch le toucher 12c; toucher *(v)* 12c

tour *(travel)* le voyage organisé 30a

tour bus l'autocar *(m)* de tourisme (d'excursion) 30a

tour guide le (la) guide 30a

tourist le (la) touriste 30a, 36c

Tow-Away Zone Zone de remorquage 33d

tow truck la dépanneuse 33a

toward vers *(prep)* 3d

towel la serviette de toilette 12d; la serviette de bain 35c

tower la tour 36a

town la ville 11f

track la piste 27b; *(of a train)* la voie 34

tractor truck le camion-tracteur 33a

trade/labor union le syndicat 43

traditional traditionnel(le) *(adj, m, f)* 11e

traffic la circulation 33c

traffic accident l'accident *(m)* de voiture 39c

traffic jam l'embouteillage *(m)*, l'encombrement *(m)* 33c

traffic lane la piste 33c

traffic lights les feux *(m, pl)* 33c, 36a

traffic police l'agent *(m)* de patrouille 33c

tragedy la tragédie 20a, 28e

trailer la remorque 33a

train le train 34; **direct train** le train direct 34; **express train** le train express 34

train station la gare 34

transformer *(hardware)* le transformateur 25b

transitive transitif *(adj, m)*, transitive *(adj, f)* 8a

translate traduire *(v)* 17a

translation la traduction 17a

transmission *(radio, television)* l'émission 20b

transparent transparent(e) *(adj, m, f)* 7b, 13d

transplant la transplantation, transplanter *(v)* 14a

transport truck le camion des marchandises 33a

trapezoid le trapèze 2a

travel voyager *(v)* 30a

travel agency l'agence *(f)* de voyages *(m, pl)* 30a

traveler's check le chèque de voyage *(m)* 26, 35b

tray le plateau à servir 23d, 24l, 32c

tree l'arbre *(m)* 14c

trial le procès 41; **trial lawyer** l'avoué *(m)*, la femme avoué 41; **to be on trial** être *(v)* en procès 41

triangle le triangle 2a

trigonometric trigonométrique
(adj) 2b

trigonometry la trigonométrie
2b, 37e

trip le voyage 30a, 36b

triple triple (n/adj, m, f)
3c

tripod (easel) le chevalet
28b

trolley le trolley 33a

trombone le trombone 28c

tropic le tropique 13e

Tropic of Cancer le Tropique du
Cancer 13e

Tropic of Capricorn le
Tropique du Capricorne 13e

tropical tropique (adj)
13e; tropical(e) (adj, m, f)
6a

troublemaker provocateur,
provocatrice (adj, m, f) 11e

trout la truite 15c, 24d

truck le camion 33a

truck, pickup la camionnette
33a

trumpet la trompette 28c

trunk (of tree) le tronc 14a;
(of a vehicle) le coffre 33e

trust la confiance 21a; avoir
(v) confiance en 21a

try on (clothing) essayer (v)
25m

tuba le tuba 28c

Tuesday le mardi 5a

tulip la tulipe 14b

tuna fish le thon 15c, 24d

tunnel le tunnel 33c

turbulence la turbulence
32c

turkey la dinde 15b, 24c

turn tourner (v) 3e, 36c;
(vehicle) virer (v) 33c

turn left tournez à gauche
36c

turn off éteindre (v) 20b,
35c

turn on allumer (v) 20b,
35c

turn pages, leaf through
tourner (v) les pages, feuilleter
(v) 20a

turn right tournez à droite
36c

turn signal (vehicle) le
clignotant (m) 33e

turned out badly (photo, picture)
la photo mal réussie 25d

turned out well (photo, picture)
la photo bien réussie 25d

turtle la tortue 15c

TV la télé 20b

TV movie le téléfilm 20b

twelfth douzième 1b

twelve douze 1a

twenty vingt la; **about twenty**
une vingtaine 1c

twenty-one vingt et un 1a

twenty-two vingt-deux 1a

twin le jumeau, la jumelle
10a

twist bun (pastry) la tresse
24i

twisted neck le torticolis
40a

two deux 1a

two billion deux milliards
1a

two hundred deux cents 1a

two hundred and one deux cent
un 1a

two hundred thousand deux
cent mille 1a

two million deux millions
1a

two thousand deux mille
1a

two thousand and one deux
mille un 1a

two-year-old de deux ans
11b

type taper (v) à la machine
19d, 37f

typewriter la machine à écrire
(v) 19d, 37f, 38c

typist le dactylographe, la
dactylographe 38a

typography   la typographie
20a

U

Ugh!   Pouah!   21c
ugliness   la laideur   11a
ugly   laid(e)   *(adj, m, f)*
11a, 25l
ultraviolet light   la lumière
ultraviolette   13a
unacceptable   inacceptable
(adj)   21b
Unbelievable!   Incroyable!
21c
uncle   l'oncle   10a
under   sous   *(prep)*   3d
underdeveloped countries   les
pays   *(m, pl)* sous-développés
43
underlining   le soulignement
19c
understand   comprendre   *(v)*
22b, 37f
underwear   les sous-vêtements
(m, pl)   25k
undress   se déshabiller   *(v)*
25m
unemployment   le chômage
38d
Unfortunately!
Malheureusement!   21c
unilateral   unilatéral(e)   *(adj, m,
f)*   43
United States of America   les
Etats-Unis   *(m, pl)* d'Amérique
30b
universal suffrage   le suffrage
universel   43
universe   l'univers   *(m)*
13a
university   l'université   *(f)*
37a, 38b
university degree   la licence
11f; le doctorat   11f
unlawful   illégal(e)   *(adj, m, f)*
41
unleaded gasoline   l'essence
(f) non-plombée   33c

unless   à moins que   *(conj)*
8p
unmarried   célibataire   *(adj)*
11c
unpleasant   désagréable   *(adj,
m, f)*   21b
until   jusque(s)   *(prep)*   4e;
jusqu'à ce que   *(conj)*   8p
up   haut   *(adv)*, en haut   3d
upright piano   le piano droit
28c
Uranus   Uranus   *(m)*   13a
urinary system   le système
urinaire   40a
urinate   uriner   *(v)*   40a
us   nous   8i, 8l
user-friendly *(computers)*
l'ordinateur   *(m)* d'usage facile,
l'ordinateur "user-friendly"
42b
usually   d'habitude   *(adv)*
4e

V

vacation   les vacances   *(f, pl)*
29a, 36b
vacuum cleaner   l'aspirateur
23d
vagina   le vagin   12a
vain   vaniteux, vaniteuse   *(adj,
m, f)*   11e
valley   le val, la vallée   13b
valve *(a vehicle)*   la soupape, le
clapet   33e
van   le fourgon   33a
vanilla   la vanille   24h
vanilla ice cream   la glace à la
vanille   24h
vapor   la vapeur   13c
variable *(numbers)*   la variable
1f
variable bank rate   le taux
variable   26
VCR   le VCR, le magnétoscope,
le système d'enregistrement   *(m)*
à vidéocassettes   20b
veal   le veau   24c
vector   le vecteur   2b

vegetable   le (la) légume
14e, 24e

vegetable garden   le potager
14e

vegetation   la végétation   13b

vehicle   le véhicule   33a

vein   la veine   40a

velocity   la vélocité   3a

Venice   Venise   30c

vent *(vehicle)*   le trou d'aération
(f)   33e

Venus   Vénus *(f)*   13a

verb   le verbe   8a, 8n

verdict   le verdict   41

versatile   versatile *(adj, m, f)*
11e

vertebrate   vertébré(e) *(adj, m, f)*   15a

vertex (angle)   le sommet   2b

vertical   vertical(e) *(adj)*
3d

vest   le gilet   25k

Very well!   Très bien! *(adv)*
16a

VHS/SECAM/TV   le
VHS/SECAM/TV, le système
séquentiel à mémoire   20b

vibrant   vibrant(e) *(adj)*   7b

victim   la victime   39a, 39b

video camera   la caméra vidéo
25d

video conference   la
visioconférence   38c, 42a

video game   le jeu-vidéo   20b

videocassette recorder   la
vidéocassette   20b

videorock   le vidéorock   20b

videotape   la bande magnétique
20b

view   la vue   35b

village   le village   11f

vinegar   le vinaigre   24j

viola   la viole   28c

violence   la violence   39b

violet   la violette   14b

violin   le violon   28c

violinist   le (la) violoniste
28c

Virgo   la Vierge   5d

virile   viril(e) *(adj)*   11a

virus   le virus   42b

visa   le visa   31

visit *(a person)*   rendre *(v)*
visite à   29b

visit *(a place)*   visiter *(v)*
30a

vitamin   la vitamine   25h

vocabulary   le vocabulaire
17a

vocational school   l'institut *(m)*
d'enseignement technique   37a

volcano   le volcan   13b

volleyball   le volley-ball   27b

volume   le volume   3a

volume control   le réglage de
volume   20b

vomit   vomir *(v)*   40a

vote   le vote; voter *(v)*   43

vowel   la voyelle   8a

vulnerable   vulnérable *(adj, m, f)*   11e

W

wafer   la gaufrette   24i

waffle   la gaufre   24i

wages   les gages *(m, pl)*
38d

waist   la taille   12, 12a

wait *(for)*   attendre *(v)*   4e,
19e, 34

waiter   le serveur   24m

waiting room   la salle d'attente
(f)   32a

waitress   la serveuse   24m

wake up   se réveiller *(v)*
12b

wake-up call   le réveil par
téléphone   35b

walk   marcher *(v)*   3e, 12b;
aller *(v)* à pied *(m)*   3e; la
promenade   3e

walkie-talkie   le talkie-walkie
20b

wall   le mur   23a

wall map   la carte murale
37b

wall-to-wall carpeting   la moquette   23c
walnut   la noix   14d, 24f
walnut tree   le noyer   14c
want to   désirer *(v)*, vouloir *(v)*   21a
war   la guerre   43
warm up   se chauffer *(v)*   6b
warn   avertir *(v)*, prévenir *(v)*   17a
warning   l'avis *(m)*, la prévenance   17a
wash   laver *(v)*   23f, 25g
wash basin *(sink)*   le lavabo   23a, 35c
wash one's hair   se laver *(v)* les cheveux *(m, pl)*   12d
wash oneself   se laver *(v)*   12d
wash the clothes   laver *(v)* le linge   23f
wash the dishes   faire *(v)* la vaisselle   23f
washable   lavable *(adj, m, f)*   25g
washcloth   le gant de bain, le gant de toilette   12d
washing machine   le lave-linge, la machine à laver *(v)*   23d
wasp   la guêpe   15d
wastebasket   la corbeille à papier   38c
watch   regarder *(v)*   20b
watch *(timepiece)*   la montre   4d, 25i; **The watch is fast.** La montre avance.   4d; **The watch is slow.** La montre retarde.   4d
watchband   le bracelet d'une montre   4d, 25i
watch battery   la pile d'une montre   4d
water   l'eau *(f)*   13c, 23e, 24k; arroser *(v)*   14a
water fountain   la fontaine   36a
water pollution   la pollution des eaux   44a

water polo   le water-polo   27b
water skiing   le ski nautique   27b
watercolor   l'aquarelle *(f)*   28b
watermelon   la pastèque   14d, 24f
wave   l'onde *(f)*, le flot, la vague   13b
we   nous   8h, 8l
weak   faible *(adj, m, f)*   11a, 11e, 13d, 40a
weakness   la faiblesse   11a
weapon   l'arme *(f)*   39b
wear   porter *(v)*   25m
weather   le temps   6a; **The weather is beautiful.** Il fait beau temps.   6a **The weather is rotten.** Il fait un temps pourri.   6a
weather forecast   la prévision scientifique du temps, la météo   6c
weather report   le bulletin météorologique   6c
wedding   le mariage   11c, 29a; la noce   11c; les noces *(f, pl)*   29a
wedding invitation   le faire-part de mariage   11c
wedding ring   l'anneau *(m)* d'alliance, l'anneau *(m)* de mariage, l'alliance *(f)*   11c
Wednesday   le mercredi   5a
week   la semaine   4c
weekend   le week-end, la fin de semaine   5a
weekly   hebdomadaire *(adj)*, hebdomadairement *(adv)*   4c; *(periodical)* hebdomadaire *(adj, n, m, f)*   20a
weigh   peser *(v)*   3b, 24o
weigh oneself   se peser *(v)*   11a
weight   le poids   3a, 11a, 31
weight (due to gravity)   la pesanteur   3a

weight lifting l'haltérophilie *(f)* 27b

Welfare l'Assistance *(f)* sociale 43

well-done (*cooked food*) bien cuit(e) *(adj, m, f)* 24b

well-mannered bien élevé(e) *(adj, m, f)* 11e

west l'ouest *(m)* 3d; **to the west** à l'ouest 3d

western occidental(e) *(adj, m, f)* 3d, 11d

whale la baleine 15c

What? Comment? Pardon? Quoi? 9

What a bore! (*person*) Quel raseur! *(m);* Quelle raseuse! *(f)* 21c

What color is it? De quelle couleur est-ce? 7a

What day is it? Quel jour est-ce? 5a

What do you call this (that) in French? Comment appelle-t-on ceci (cela) en français? 9

What do you think of it? Qu'en pensez-vous? *(pol),* Qu'en penses-tu? *(fam)* 22b

What does it mean? Que veut dire cela? Que signifie cela? 9

What month are we in? Quel mois sommes-nous? 5b

What month is it? Quel mois est-ce? 5b

What time is it? Quelle heure est-il? 4b

What was I saying? Qu'est-ce que je disais? 17b

What year is it? Quelle année est-ce? 5e

What's the weather like? (How's the weather?) Quel temps fait-il? 6a

What's today's date? Quelle est la date aujourd'hui? 5e

What's your name? Quel est votre nom (ton nom)? 11f; Comment vous appelez-vous?

(pol), Comment t'appelles-tu? *(fam)* 16b

wheat le froment, le blé 14a, 24i

wheel la roue 33e

wheelchair le fauteuil roulant 40a

wheel, landing gear (*airplane*) le train d'atterrissage 32c

when quand *(adv)* 4e, 8p, 9

When were you born? Quand êtes-vous né(e)? *(m, f, pol)* 5e

where où *(adv)* 3d, 9

Where do you live? Où demeurez-vous (demeures-tu)? 11f

Where is . . .? Où est . . . ? 36c

whereas tandis que *(conj)* 8p

which (*one*) lequel *(m),* laquelle *(f)* 9

which (*ones*) lesquels *(m, pl),* lesquelles *(f, pl)* 9

while pendant que *(conj)* 4e; tandis que *(conj)* 8p

whipped cream la crème Chantilly 24h; **omelette with whipped cream** l'omelette *(f)* mousseline 24h

whisper chuchoter *(v)* 17a

white le blanc *(m);* la blanche *(f)* 7a; **to be white with fear** être *(v)* vert de peur 7a

who qui *(pron)* 9

Who knows? Qui sait? 17b

Who's speaking? Qui parle? 18b

whole wheat bread le pain complet 24i

why pourquoi *(adv, conj)* 9

wide large *(adj)* 3b

widow la veuve 11c, 38b

widower le veuf 11c, 38b

width la largeur 3b

wife   la femme, l'épouse   10a, 11c

wild animal   l'animal *(m)* sauvage   15a

wildflower   la fleur sauvage   14b

willingly   volontiers *(adv)*   11e

wilted flower   la fleur fanée   14b

win   gagner *(v)*, le gain   27b

wind *(a timepiece)*   remonter *(v)*   4d, 25i

wind *(weather)*   le vent   6a; **It's windy.**   Il fait du vent.   6a

wind energy   l'énergie *(f)* éolienne   44a

wind instruments   les instruments *(m, pl)* à vent   28c

windbreaker *(clothing)*   le blouson   25k

window   la fenêtre   23a; **store/shop window**   la vitrine   25a

window *(airplace)*   le hublot   32c

window *(computer)*   la fenêtre   42b

window seat   la place côté fenêtre   32c

window sill   le rebord de la fenêtre   23a

windshield *(vehicle)*   le pare-brise   33e

windshield wiper   l'essuie-glace *(m)*, l'essuie-vitre *(m)*   33e

windy weather   faire *(v)* du vent   6a

wine   le vin   24k

wine cellar   la cave à vin *(m)*   23b

wineglass   le verre à vin   24l

wing   l'aile *(f)*   15b, 32c

winter   l'hiver *(m)*   5c

wire   le fil métallique   25b

wisdom   la sagesse   11e, 22a

wisdom tooth   la dent de sagesse   40b

wise   sage *(adj, m, f)*   11e

with   avec   8g

With cordial greetings . . . *(in a letter)*   Sentiments cordiaux   19a

with ice chips   avec glaçons *(m, pl)*   24p

with sauce (gravy)   au jus   24b

withdraw *(banking)*   prélever *(v)*   26

withdrawal *(banking)*   le prélèvement   26

withdrawal slip   la fiche de prélèvement *(m)*   26

within *(a certain time)*   en *(prep)*   4e

witness   le témoin   41; **for the defense**   à décharge; **for the prosecution**   à charge   41

wolf   le loup   15a

woman   la femme   11a

women's shop/clothing   le magasin d'habillement féminin   25k

woods   le (les) bois *(m)*   13b

wool   la laine   13c; en laine   25l

word   le mot *(written)*, la parole *(spoken)*   17a, 19c

word processing *(computer)*   le traitement de texte   42b

word processor *(computer)*   la machine de traitement de texte   42b

work   travailler *(v)*   11f, 38d; le travail   11f, 38d; *(literary)* l'ouvrage *(m)*   28d

workday   le jour de travail   5a

Work in Progress   Travaux   33d

work out *(body exercises)*   pratiquer *(v)* les exercises du corps   27b

world le monde 13a, 30a
World Wide Web le web 42b
worm le ver 15d
wound la blessure, la plaie 39b, 39c; blesser *(v)* 39b
wrench *(hardware)* la pince universelle 25b
wrestling la lutte 27b
wrist le poignet 12a
wristwatch le bracelet-montre 4d, 25i; la montre-bracelet 25i
write écrire *(v)* 19e, 20a, 37f
writer l'écrivain *(m)*, la femme écrivain 28d, 38a
wrong incorrect(e) *(adj, m, f)* 37f
Wrong number! *(telephone)* Mauvais numéro! 18b

X, Y Z
X-ray la radiographie, passer *(v)* une radiographie 39c, 40b

yawn le bâillement, bâiller *(v)* 17a
year l'an *(m)*, l'année *(f)* 4c
year two thousand l'an *(m)* deux mille 4c
yell le cri; crier *(v)* 17a
yellow le jaune 7a
yellow pages les pages jaunes *(f, pl)* 18a
Yes! Oui! 16c
yesterday hier *(adv)* 4a
yesterday afternoon hier après-midi 4a
yesterday morning hier matin 4a
yet encore *(adv)* 4e
Yield Cédez 33d
yogurt le yaourt 24h
you tu *(s, fam)*, vous *(s, pl, pol)*, te *(s, fam)* 8h, 8i; toi 8l; vous 8l

young jeune *(adj)* 11b
young lady la demoiselle 11a
young man le jeune homme 11a
younger plus jeune 11b
younger brother le frère cadet 11b
younger sister la soeur cadette 11b
your *(pol)* votre *(m/f, s)*, vos *(m/f, pl)* 8f; *(fam)* ton *(m, s)*, ta *(f, s)*, tes *(m/f, pl)* 8f
You're welcome! Je vous en prie! *(pol)*, Je t'en prie! *(fam)* De rien! Il n'y a pas de quoi! 16c
Yours . . . *(closing of a letter)* Bien à toi *(fam)* 19b
Yours truly . . . *(in a business letter)* Salutations distinguées 19a
yourself *(reflexive)* te *(s, fam)*, vous *(s, pol)* 8k
yourselves *(reflexive)* vous 8k
youth la jeunesse 11b
youth hostel l'auberge *(f)* de la jeunesse 35a
youthful juvénile *(adj)*, jeune *(adj, m, f)* 11b
Yuch! Berk! 20b

zebra le zèbre 15a
zenith le zénith 13e
zero zéro 1a, 6c
zipper la fermeture à glissière, la fermeture éclair 25g
zodiac le zodiaque 5d
zone la zone 13e
zoo le zoo, le jardin zoologique 15a
zoology la zoologie 15a, 37e
zoom le zoom 25d
zucchini la courgette 14e

NOTES

NOTES

NOTES

NOTES

NOTES

NOTES

AT A GLANCE Series

Barron's new series gives travelers instant access to the most common idiomatic expressions used during a trip—the kind one needs to know instantly, like "Where can I find a taxi?" and "How much does this cost?"

Organized by situation (arrival, customs, hotel, health, etc.) and containing additional information about pronunciation, grammar, shopping plus special facts about the country, these convenient, pocket-size reference books will be the tourist's most helpful guides.

Special features include a bilingual dictionary section with over 2000 key words, maps of each country and major cities, and helpful phonetic spellings throughout.

Each book paperback, 256 pp., 3 3/4" x 6"

ARABIC AT A GLANCE, Wise (0-7641-1248-1) $8.95, Can. $12.50
CHINESE AT A GLANCE, Seligman & Chen (0-7641-1250-1) $8.95, Can. $12.50
FRENCH AT A GLANCE, 4th, Stein & Wald (0-7641-2512-5) $6.95, Can. $9.95
GERMAN AT A GLANCE, 4th, Strutz (0-7641-2516-8) $6.95, Can. $9.95
ITALIAN AT A GLANCE, 4th, Costantino (0-7641-2513-3) $6.95, Can. $9.95
JAPANESE AT A GLANCE, 3rd, Akiyama (0-7641-0320-2) $8.95, Can. $11.95
KOREAN AT A GLANCE, Holt (0-8120-3998-X) $8.95, Can. $11.95
RUSSIAN AT A GLANCE, Beyer (0-7641-1251-1) $8.95, Can. $12.50
SPANISH AT A GLANCE, 4th, Wald (0-7641-2514-1) $6.95, Can. $9.95

Barron's Educational Series, Inc.
250 Wireless Blvd., Hauppauge, NY 11788
Call toll-free: 1-800-645-3476
In Canada: Georgetown Book Warehouse, 34 Armstrong Ave.
Georgetown, Ont. L7G 4R9, Call toll-free: 1-800-247-7160
Visit our website at: www.barronseduc.com

Books may be purchased at your bookstore, or by mail from Barron's. Enclose check or money order for total amount plus sales tax where applicable and 18% for postage and handling (minimum charge $5.95). New York State and California residents add sales tax. Prices subject to change without notice. Can. $ = Canadian dollars

(#25) R 3/03

3 Foreign Language Series From Barron's!

The **VERB SERIES** offers more than 300 of the most frequently used verbs.
The **GRAMMAR SERIES** provides complete coverage of the elements of grammar. The **VOCABULARY SERIES** offers more than 3500 words and phrases with their foreign language translations. Each book: paperback.

FRENCH GRAMMAR
ISBN: 0-7641-1351-8
$5.95, Can. $8.50

GERMAN GRAMMAR
ISBN: 0-8120-4296-4
$6.95, Can. $8.95

ITALIAN GRAMMAR
ISBN: 0-7641-2060-3
$6.95, Can. $9.95

JAPANESE GRAMMAR
ISBN: 0-7641-2061-1
$6.95, Can. $9.95

RUSSIAN GRAMMAR
ISBN: 0-8120-4902-0
$6.95, Can. $8.95

SPANISH GRAMMAR
ISBN: 0-7641-1615-0
$5.95, Can. $8.50

FRENCH VERBS
ISBN: 0-7641-1356-9
$5.95, Can. $8.50

GERMAN VERBS
ISBN: 0-8120-4310-3
$7.95, Can. $11.50

ITALIAN VERBS
ISBN: 0-7641-2063-8
$5.95, Can. $8.50

SPANISH VERBS
ISBN: 0-7641-1357-7
$5.95, Can. $8.50

FRENCH VOCABULARY
ISBN: 0-7641-1999-0
$6.95, Can. $9.95

GERMAN VOCABULARY
ISBN: 0-8120-4497-5
$6.95, Can. $8.95

ITALIAN VOCABULARY
ISBN: 0-7641-2190-1
$6.95, Can. $9.95

JAPANESE VOCABULARY
ISBN: 0-8120-4743-5
$6.95, Can. $8.95

RUSSIAN VOCABULARY
ISBN: 0-8120-1554-1
$6.95, Can. $8.95

SPANISH VOCABULARY
ISBN: 0-7641-1985-3
$6.95, Can. $9.95

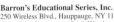

Barron's Educational Series, Inc.
250 Wireless Blvd., Hauppauge, NY 11788 • Call toll-free: 1-800-645-3476
In Canada: Georgetown Book Warehouse
34 Armstrong Ave., Georgetown, Ontario L7G 4R9 • Call toll-free: 1-800-247-7160
www.barronseduc.com

Can. $ = Canadian dollars

Books may be purchased at your bookstore or by mail from Barron's. Enclose check or money order for total amount plus sales tax where applicable and 18% for postage and handling (minimum charge $5.95 U.S. and Canada). Prices subject to change without notice. New York State and California residents, please add sales tax to total after postage and handling.   (#26) R 3/04